Hellenic Studies 87

Audible Punctuation

Recent Titles in the Hellenic Studies Series

Audible Punctuation

PERFORMATIVE PAUSE IN HOMERIC PROSODY

by
Ronald J. J. Blankenborg

CENTER FOR HELLENIC STUDIES
Trustees for Harvard University
Washington, DC
Distributed by Harvard University Press
Cambridge, Massachusetts, and London, England
2022

Library of Congress Cataloging-in-Publication Data

Names: Blankenborg, Ronald J. J., author.
Title: Audible punctuation : performative pause in homeric prosody / Ronald J.J. Blankenborg.
Other titles: Hellenic studies ; 87.
Description: Washington : Center for Hellenic Studies, Trustees for Harvard University, 2019. | Series: Hellenic studies ; 87 | Includes bibliographical references and index.
Identifiers: LCCN 2019021517 | ISBN 9780674237957
Subjects: LCSH: Homer—Language. | Homer. Iliad. | Homer. Odyssey. | Caesura in versification.
Classification: LCC PA4176 .B57 2019 | DDC 883/.01—dc23
LC record available at https://lccn.loc.gov/2019021517

Contents

Acknowledgments

"Please stop dithering!"

J.M. Coetzee, *Slow Man* (2005)

Audible Punctuation started out as *Rhythm Without Beat*, a study on metrics and enjambment in Homeric poetry, a topic in scholarship that has been discussed extensively over the past decades. I planned to start from the notion of "rhythm," but soon realized that the terminology was not without controversy. In due course it became clear that instead of meter and rhythm, syntactical issues moved to a place at the center; notably, the clause in Homeric discourse, and the emergence of grammar from the fortuitous collocation of formulas in the oral tradition. The work readily developed into a study of grammar and syntax in Homer, as both were motivated by the prosodic movement that enables the performer to construct larger-scale wholes out of the formulaic building blocks. Enjambment turned out to be merely one of the collateral phenomena of the composition and performance in larger-scale wholes. *Rhythm Without Beat* was submitted as a dissertation in 2011, but unfortunately did not meet with approval in time.

As a result, the study was reorganized and largely rewritten, this time with its focus on a postulate: the performative pause in Homeric prosody. Starting from the various already existing notions and concepts of compositional pause, I have discussed the issue of pause in performance. To that end I have identified the possibilities for pause based on evidence from phonology, mainly from metrical surface structure. Working from the assumption that Homeric phonology aptly reflects phonetics, and that ancient Greek is a language like any other, I was able to select from the ubiquitous compositional pauses those pauses that under specific circumstances double as rests of some duration in performance. It turns out that phonological phrases and grammatical clauses differ in the way they terminate. And enjambment is still a collateral phenomenon.

Acknowledgments

Many have helped me in the process of producing *Audible Punctuation*, some have truly been inspiring. First and foremost, I thank André Lardinois and Joel Lidov. Professor Lardinois appointed me as lecturer and gave me the opportunity to do research. He has supervised the entire process that led to *Rhythm Without Beat* and *Audible Punctuation* from its earliest beginnings. I benefitted greatly from his broad knowledge and stimulating discussion. Professor Lidov has shared with me his impressive overview of all matters metrical, rhythmical, and phonological. His acute understanding of the workings of Greek prosody do not cease to amaze me.

At several stages in the process, I benefitted greatly from the observations of Egbert J. Bakker. I thank all my colleagues at Radboud University Nijmegen, especially Ton Kessels, Willeon Slenders, Floris Overduin, Bé Breij, Claire Stocks, and Vincent Hunink. I am grateful for the comments by Marc van der Poel, Ineke Sluijter, Irene de Jong, and Mark Janse. The Dutch school for Classical Studies, OIKOS, has enabled me to participate in conferences abroad (APA Chicago 2008, APA 2009 Philadelphia, ICAGL 2009 Agrigento) where issues from *Audible Punctuation* were presented as papers. Colleagues at school have been very helpful, both at Gymnasium Apeldoorn and at Marianum, as have been friends and relatives; many of them must remain unnamed, but I wish to explicitly mention Lisette van Heeringen, Karin Visser, Nicky Konings, Hans Tanke, Elbert Jaap Schipper, Edwin Woerdman, Casper van Dijk, Gerard Bosman, and Marijke Schlebusch. I cannot even start to list all the students, both in the Gymnasia and at Radboud University, who have contributed to the content of *Audible Punctuation*, but I am nonetheless very grateful for all their opinions and criticism.

A special word of thanks to Gregory Nagy, who suggested the publication of *Audible Punctuation* in the Hellenic Studies Series, and the staff at the Harvard Center for Hellenic Studies, Washington DC: Leonard Muellner, Casey Dué, and Jill Curry Robbins. With their help, *Audible Punctuation* has been turned into a publication that will find its way to scholars interested in Homeric prosody and performance. Professor Nagy and his staff have also made possible the publication of *Rhythm Without Beat*, a reissue of the 2014 publication, in the same series.

Stimulating and valuable as the writing process itself has been, these years have also demanded sacrifice from my family. I thank Lysander, Bente, Revelin, and Liv for their patience, and for the indescribable joy and happiness they bring; may you keep reminding me that professional satisfaction will always come in second place, at best. It is difficult to find the words to thank you, Rachel, for what you are and what you do for me, or to express my admiration.

May it suffice to say here, in addition to your innumerable qualities, that you are still the only one capable of summarizing this entire study in one sentence.

RB April 2018

Audible Punctuation

Introduction
Pause in Homer

NO POET OR RHAPSODE COULD PERFORM THE *ILIAD* OR *ODYSSEY* without regularly stopping to breathe. Pause is a requirement, so where in the lines would he pause? This is the question this study seeks to answer. At first sight, there are numerous possibilities for pause: at verse end, at the main caesura, at syntactical breaks, indicated in modern editions by punctuation, such as the comma or the full stop. There are, in fact, so many possibilities that they cannot all have been realized as pauses in performance. The purpose of this study is to identify those places in the verse that a performer was most likely to have used to pause. The result will be a seemingly irregular and rather unpredictable distribution of pauses over Homer's hexameters.

Pause implies termination. Absence of pause implies coherence. Termination and coherence in Homer have been identified in a number of different ways, depending on the linguistic level of analysis: studies on Homeric meter, rhythm, and syntax identify termination on various grounds, with a variety of "pauses" as a result. Studies on the sound system (phonology) and sound act of speech (phonetics) of ancient Greek have their own way of identifying termination, each using yet another definition. What the different linguistic levels have in common is that their identification of termination implies the identification of phrases — between, and separated by, pauses. At different linguistic levels, in other words, different pauses are recognized. Not all these different pauses are relevant for the identification of the pause in Homeric performance, however, and insofar as they are relevant, the different pauses must be clearly distinguished and tied to the proper linguistic level. Before I start my attempt to identify the pause in Homeric performance, I list below the most important linguistic levels at which pauses have so far been identified.

0.1 Pause on the Level of Metrics

In metrical-rhythmical analysis, the verse and the metrical colon constitute the phrases in between metrical pauses. O'Neill 1942 provides a basic representation for the hexameter:

$$1 \ 1\tfrac{1}{2} \ 2 \quad 3 \ 3\tfrac{1}{2} \ 4 \quad 5 \ 5\tfrac{1}{2} \ 6 \quad 7 \ 7\tfrac{1}{2} \ 8 \quad 9 \ 9\tfrac{1}{2} \ 10 \ 11 \ 12$$

$$\cup \cup \quad \cup \cup \quad \cup \cup \quad \cup \cup \quad \cup \cup$$

$$- \ - \quad - \ - \quad - \ - \quad - \ - \quad - \ - \quad - \quad \times$$

(1) μῆνιν ἄειδε θεά Πηληιάδεω Ἀχιλῆος

　　Sing, Goddess, of the wrath of Achilles, son of Peleus[1]

The hexameter-verse, ending in a metrically indifferent element (indicated as x: the exact quantity of the verse-final syllable is not set), is the metrical phrase that makes metrical surface structure repetitive. Consequently, metrical pause is put on a par with the metrical boundary that is the verse end.

　　As the metrical colon equally counts as a metrical phrase, its boundaries qualify as metrical pauses. Identification of pause on the basis of cola multiplies the number of instances of metrical pause; the third-foot word end already at least doubles it. Word end in the third foot occurs in practically every Homeric verse, and varies between a masculine (indicated as :⁵ in example 2) and a feminine word end (indicated as :⁵¼ in example 3):

(2) μῆνιν ἄειδε θεά :⁵ Πηληιάδεω Ἀχιλῆος

Iliad I 1

　　Sing, Goddess, of the wrath of Achilles, son of Peleus

(3) στέμματ' ἔχων ἐν χερσὶν :⁵¼ ἑκηβόλου Ἀπόλλωνος

Iliad I 14

　　Holding the ribbons in his hands of far shooting Apollo

The number of metrical pauses increases with the acceptance of frequently occurring word end after positions 2, 3, 7, 8, and 9 as metrical pause. Fränkel 1926 applied the various positions of frequently occurring word end to advocate a division of the verse into four cola (examples 4 and 5; metrical pauses are

---

[1]　All quotations from the *Iliad* are taken from Monro and Allen 1920/Allen 1931, from the *Odyssey* Allen 1917/1919. Quotations from Greek are presented without any printed punctuation. Translations are freely based on Murray and Wyatt (*Iliad* Loeb 1999) and Murray and Dimock (*Odyssey* Loeb 1995).

indicated by the number of the metrical position they follow, in both the Greek example and its translation):

(4) εἶκε Διὸς ³ θύγατερ ⁵ πολέμου ⁷ καὶ δηιοτῆτος

Iliad V 348

>   Remove yourself, Zeus's ³ daughter ⁵ from the war ⁷ and the fighting

(5) ὣς ἔφαθ' ² ἡνίοχος ⁵ δ' ἵμασεν ⁷ καλλίτριχας ἵππους

Iliad XI 280

>   Thus he spoke ² and his charioteer ⁵ put the whip on ⁷ the horses with beautiful manes

Kirk 1966 introduces a tripartition of the verse as a distinct verse-type (example 6):

(6) διογενὲς ³ Λαερτιάδη ⁷ πολυμήχαν' Ὀδυσσεῦ

Iliad II 173

>   Descendant of Zeus ³ son of Laertes ⁷ resourceful Odysseus

In my opinion, the metrical pauses are too ubiquitous to make them equivalent to pauses in performance: realization of all metrical pauses as pauses in performance does not contribute to an understandable or enjoyable performance. To allow for verse end and third-foot word end to double as performance pauses is to distinguish between metrical pauses without proper motivation.

0.2 Pause on the Level of Rhythmics

Rhythm is the perceptible recurrence of some sort of regularity. As meter provides regularity, and scansion evidences recurrence of this regularity, meter and rhythm are at times used as synonyms. Meter is then the equivalent of scansion, rhythm of metrical recurrence: it has proven tempting to identify the audible phenomenon of rhythm as the visible regularity of meter. Studies that understand metrical phrases as rhythmical unities identify the rhythmical pause as the termination of the verse and, possibly, the colon (the third-foot word end is a well accepted rhythmical pause). The metrical indifference of the verse-final syllable is considered evidence of rhythmical indeterminacy, a sign of termination that concludes the rhythmical profile of the hexametric line. The hexametric line, in other words, is seen as the rhythmical unit, and the verse end as the rhythmical pause.

Within the rhythmical phrase, rhythm is created by the recurrence of the metrical feet, an alternation of strong and weak rhythmical elements. The regular alternation of syllables that may be labeled metrically "long" and "short" results in a recurrence of metrically "long" syllables that are considered the rhythmically "strong" elements. As mentioned, rhythmical indeterminacy concludes the rhythmical phrase. Not all studies on rhythmical pause agree on the possibility for pause *within* the hexametric line. Many allow for a rhythmical pause at third-foot word end, but most are reluctant to treat every metrical pause (that is, word end at a position at which word end frequently occurs) as a rhythmical pause. For that reason I have marked some of the possible rhythmical pauses in example (7) with a question mark. I have left out the question mark for the rhythmical pauses that existing studies generally agree upon:

(7) ἀλλὰ σὺ εἰ δύνασαί γε περίσχεο παιδὸς ἑῆος

Iliad I 393

Please, if you can, make a stand on behalf of your son

ἀλλὰ σὺ	εἰ δύνασαί γε	περίσχεο	παιδὸς ἑῆος

1st foot	2nd foot	3rd foot	4th foot	5th foot	6th foot
— ᴗ ᴗ	— ᴗ ᴗ	— ᴗ	ᴗ	— ᴗ ᴗ	— ᴗ	— ×

[colon]	*p?*	[colon]	*p*	[colon]	*p?*	[colon]	*p*

p = rhythmical pause

Iliad I 393 thus features at least two rhythmical pauses, and possibly up to four.

Dionysius of Halicarnassus considers the rhythmical profile of the verse to be enhanced when the line features many words that take the same rhythmical shape as the line as a whole (Ruijgh 1987): in the case of the hexameter, when the line contains many words (or only words) that are shaped as a dactyl (– ᴗ ᴗ). While such coincidence strengthens dactylic rhythm within the line, the occurrence of the verse final rhythmical indeterminacy (again indicated as ×) allegedly terminates the rhythmical phrase the more explicitly:

(8) ὕβριος εἵνεκα τῆσδε σὺ δ' ἴσχεο πείθεο δ' ἡμῖν

Iliad I 214

$$- \cup \cup, - \cup \cup, - \cup, \cup, - \cup \cup, - \cup \cup, - x,$$

dactyl	dactyl	dactyl	dactyl	dactyl	spondee (alternatively: trochee)

Because of this affront; control yourself, and do as we tell you

In the approach described in this section, rhythm implies a level of regularity with regard to the occurrence and recurrence of pause. In my view, the rhythmical pause is too closely tied to the metrical pause to automatically qualify as a pause in performance in all instances. When compared to the metrical pauses, the rhythmical pauses are not necessarily as ubiquitous. They are, however, selected rather arbitrarily from the abundance of metrical pauses.

0.3 Pause on the Level of Syntax

On the linguistic level of syntactical analysis, phrases coincide with the units of Homeric discourse and syntax. Pauses in discourse and syntax are sense-pauses. The units receive their internal coherence from grammatical structure and the fulfilment of syntactical requirements. Depending on the exact approach taken to the analysis of Homeric discourse, a sense-pause may indicate the termination of a word group, a constituent, a main or subordinate clause, or the continuation of the narrative via asyndeton or a sentence-initial connector. Within the line, sense-pauses do separate units of discourse, but they are the termination of word groups rather than the termination of sense. The latter is the result of the former. Chantraine 1953 allows for high levels of autonomy for the word groups, thus leaving much room for potential sense-pauses within the line (sense-pauses are indicated as *s-p* in examples 9–12; the question marks draw attention to syntactical pauses that hardly apply as true sense-pauses):

(9) ὣς εἰπὼν προτὶ ἄστυ μέγα φρονέων ἐβεβήκει

Iliad XXII 21

Having spoken thus he made his way to the city, full of
   confidence

ὣς εἰπὼν [*s-p?*] προτὶ ἄστυ [*s-p?*] μέγα φρονέων [*s-p?*] ἐβεβήκει [*s-p*]

Word groups often coincide with metrical cola. Bakker 1997b explains the coincidence as a correlate of *special speech*, the stylisation of speech in accordance with metrical cola. His discourse-units, which he labels *intonation units*, are equally colon-shaped. Some intonation units are shorter than the metrical colon (Bakker labels them *phrases*), allowing, potentially, for more sense-pauses (1997b:291–292):

(10)

a	μῆνιν ἄειδε θεά	s-p
b	Πηληιάδεω Ἀχιλῆος	s-p
c	οὐλομένην	s-p
d	ἣ μυρί᾽ Ἀχαιοῖς ἄλγε᾽ ἔθηκε	s-p
e	πολλὰς δ᾽ ἰφθίμους ψυχὰς	s-p?
f	Ἄιδι προιαψεν	s-p
g	ἡρώων	s-p
h	αὐτοὺς δὲ ἑλώρια τεῦχε κύνεσσιν	s-p
i	οἰωνοῖσί τε πᾶσι	s-p
j	Διὸς δ᾽ ἐτελείετο βουλή	s-p
k	ἐξ οὗ δὴ τὰ πρῶτα	s-p?
l	διαστήτην ἐρίσαντε	s-p
m	Ἀτρείδης τε ἄναξ ἀνδρῶν	s-p
n	καὶ δῖος Ἀχιλλεύς	s-p

Iliad I 1–7

a	Sing, Goddess, of the wrath
b	Of Achilles, son of Peleus
c	So destructive
d	It bestowed innumerable pains on the Greeks
e	Many excellent souls
f	It sent to the house of Hades
g	Of heroes
h	But their bodies it turned into loot for the dogs
i	And all birds
j	The will of Zeus gradually became fulfilled
k	From the very first moment
l	The two of them stood opposite one another in anger
m	Atreus's son, the lord of men
n	And godlike Achilles

It turns out that in the organization of word groups into larger syntactical wholes, the exact realization of the verse-internal sense-pause is of little relevance in existing studies. There is necessarily a sense-pause, as defined by Chantraine or Bakker, at verse end; however, this sense-pause is always treated, in the scholarly literature, as a performance pause too. As the verse end is understood as signaling a rhythmical pause, the sense-pause at verse end is endowed with special poetic effect, notably emphasis, when the verse end does not coincide with syntactical termination. In these instances, the verse end is allegedly *enjambed*, putting the sense-pause at verse end, and the continuation of syntax into the subsequent line, into extra relief (Parry 1929; Kirk 1966; Higbie 1990; Clark 1997). Composition over the verse end is considered a special poetic feature, that breaks, on purpose, the Homeric compositional principle of one-sentence-per-verse. The sense-pause at verse end supposedly "strengthens" the out-of-line composition at almost every occurrence in examples 11–12:

(11)   ἔβλαψάς μ᾿ ἑκάεργε θεῶν ὀλοώτατε πάντων (s-p)
       ἐνθάδε νῦν τρέψας ἀπὸ τείχεος ἦ κ᾿ ἔτι πολλοὶ (s-p)
       γαῖαν ὀδὰξ εἷλον πρὶν Ἴλιον εἰσαφικέσθαι (s-p: not enjambed)

Iliad XXII 15–17

You have done me wrong, far-shooter, most wrecked of all gods, | by turning me away from the wall now; definitely many more | would have bitten the dust before reaching the safety of Troy

(12)   Ἕκτορ μή μοι μίμνε φίλον τέκος ἀνέρα τοῦτον (s-p)
       οἶος ἄνευθ᾿ ἄλλων ἵνα μὴ τάχα πότμον ἐπίσπῃς (s-p)
       Πηλεΐωνι δαμείς, ἐπεὶ ἦ πολὺ φέρτερός ἐστι (s-p)
       σχέτλιος αἴθε θεοῖσι φίλος τοσσόνδε γένοιτο (s-p)
       ὅσσον ἐμοί τάχα κέν ἑ κύνες καὶ γῦπες ἔδοιεν (s-p)
       κείμενον ἦ κέ μοι αἰνὸν ἀπὸ πραπίδων ἄχος ἔλθοι (s-p: not
       enjambed)

Iliad XXII 38–43

Hector, my child, please do not wait for that man | all by yourself without others, lest you get yourself killed | overcome by the son of Peleus, as for sure he is by far the better | endurer; if only he were as dear to the gods | as he is to me; then the dogs and the vultures would quickly devour him | lying dead; a terrible sorrow would then finally fall from my heart.

A syntactical pause may be ignored as a true pause in sense, and no conclusions can be drawn with regard to its usage as pause in performance. I therefore consider the sense-pause within the line a compositional feature, not a performative consideration. Verse end is often defensible as a sense-pause, but the *automatic* identification of the verse end as a pause in performance—ill-judged in my view—has led to the attribution of special syntactical and compositional features, which should not be analyzed solely on this assumption.

0.4 Pause on the Level of Phonology

Pause is also an issue at the level of Homeric phonology. Phonology is the study of the sound system of a language. It focuses on the representation (or description) of individual sounds (segments), and on the role of the distinct sound in the acoustic environment (the phoneme). Individual segments are for example /η/, /ι/, and /v/ in *Iliad* 1.1 μῆνιν; as phonemes they represent /ē/, /ĭ/, and /n/. Segments may represent more than one sound, depending on the acoustic environment: for example, /γ/ is /g/ in γὰρ, but /ŋ/ (≈ /ng/) in -γγ- as in ἄγγελος. Syllables are treated as strings of distinct segments centered around a vowel, longer words as a string of syllables.

In Homeric poetry, phonology maintains metrical surface structure. The structure of syllables corresponds to metrical requirements: depending on metrical position, syllables have a structure that accounts for a *breve*, or they have one of the structures for a *longum*. Phonology's maintenance of metrical surface structure goes so far that the orthographic division into syllables seems to be rather irrelevant: as long as syllables' structures meet metrical requirements, segments may be part of the orthographic syllable, or of an adjacent syllable. This transposition of syllables is called resyllabification. Overall, word-initial syllable structures are such that the preceding word-final syllable meets the expectations (*longum*, *breve*, or *biceps*) of its metrical position (Devine and Stephens 1994:243–248). In examples 13 and 14, this phonological legato precludes pause at various locations (explained in "footnotes" A–G in 13 and 14) within the verse:

(13) ὦ πάτερ ἡμέτερε Κρονίδη ὕπατε κρειόντων

Iliad VIII 31

Our father, son of Kronos, highest of the mighty

ὦ πάτερ[A] ἡμέτερε[B] Κρονίδη ὕπατε[C] κρειόντων
[A]: resyllabification .τε.ρη. is required to keep -τερ a *breve* (˘)
[B]: resyllabification .ρεκ.ρο. is required to keep -ρε a *longum* (–)
[C]: resyllabification .τεκ.ρει. is required to keep -τε a *longum* (–)

(14) οἵ κεν δὴ κακὸν οἶτον ἀναπλήσαντες ὄλωνται

Iliad VIII 34

They will fulfil their unpleasant fate and perish

οἵ κεν^D δὴ κακὸν^E οἶτον^F ἀναπλήσαντες^G ὄλωνται
^D: κεν remains a *longum* (–) if resyllabification .κε.ν- is avoided
^E: resyllabification .κὸ.νοῖ. is required to keep -κὸν a *breve* (˘)
^F: resyllabification .το.να.να. is required to keep -τον a *breve* (˘)
^G: resyllabification .τε. σό.λων. is required to keep -τες a *breve* (˘)

Homeric phonology seems to be more about coherence than about pause so far. Phonological coherence is furthered through the "leaning" of words onto other words. Words that cannot stand on their own feet as constituents in a sentence, like prepositions, particles, negations, and adjectives, "lean" onto other words that can. Words are thus tied so closely together that the word boundary between them is too weak to allow for a phonological pause (Ruijgh 1987); Kirk 1966 introduced a similar restriction on phonological separation when he extended his tripartite verse to include the "syntactical rising threefolder":

(15) ἕζετ᾽ ἔπειτ᾽ ἀπάνευθε νεῶν μετὰ δ᾽ ἰὸν ἕηκε

Iliad I 48

Then he sat down at some distance from the ships and he let go an arrow

ἕζετ᾽ ἔπειτ᾽			ἀπάνευθε νεῶν			μετὰ δ᾽ ἰὸν ἕηκε		
[	colon	]	s-p	[	colon	]	s-p	[	colon	]	s-p
as a preposition ἀπάνευθε "leans" on νεῶν								

Phonological pause is the absence of phonological cohesion. That means that phonological pause is identified where there is no "leaning" of one word onto the other, and where segments do not jump over word boundaries to join adjacent words. Phonological pause, in other words, occurs whenever the metrical realization of word-final syllables is not influenced by subsequent syllables and words. Phonological pauses demarcate the phonological substance between them, the phonological phrases. These are internally organized through phonological "leaning" and segment shifts. Example (16) features two lines from the *Odyssey* divided into phonological phrases ([. . .]), demarcated by phonological pauses (*p*):

(16) αἰνῶς γὰρ τάδε εἵματ' ἔχω κακά μή με δαμάσσῃ
      στίβη ὑπηοίη ἔκαθεν δέ τε ἄστυ φάτ' εἶναι

Odyssey xvii 24–25

For to my shame I have these worthless clothes; I fear that I may be overcome | by morning dew, and the city is far from here he says

[αἰνῶς γὰρ] *p* [τάδε εἵματ' ἔχω κακά] *p* [μή με δαμάσσῃ] *p* [στίβη ὑπηοίη] *p* [ἔκαθεν δέ τε ἄστυ] *p* [φάτ' εἶναι] *p*

I consider elision (as in εἵματ' ἔχω and φάτ' εἶναι in example 16) an indicator of cohesion (usually it is not considered an indicator of cohesion when it coincides with a metrical boundary).

The phonological phrases presented above are rather limited in size. I do not agree with Devine and Stephens 1994:410 when they identify larger scale phonological phrases as the equivalent of utterances, based on syntactical considerations and, in verse, positions of frequently occuring word end (sometimes referred to as *commonsensical* grounds). In example 17, "utterances" are separated by pauses (*p*) that are metrical-syntactical, but not necessarily phonological:

(17) αἰνῶς γὰρ τάδε εἵματ' ἔχω κακά μή με δαμάσσῃ
      στίβη ὑπηοίη ἔκαθεν δέ τε ἄστυ φάτ' εἶναι

Odyssey xvii 24–25

For to my shame I have these worthless clothes; I fear that I may be overcome | by morning dew, and the city is far from here he says

[αἰνῶς γὰρ τάδε εἵματ' ἔχω κακά] *p* [μή με δαμάσσῃ στίβη ὑπηοίη] *p* [ἔκαθεν δέ τε ἄστυ φάτ' εἶναι] *p*

0.5 Pause on the Level of Phonetics

Finally, there is pause on the linguistic level of phonetics. Phonetics is the study of the production and perception of speech. It focuses on characteristics of sound that phonology cannot fully account for, like the hertz frequency of pitch, and the intensity of volume. In ancient Greek metrical texts, like Homer's *Iliad* and *Odyssey*, phonetics also studies the relative lengthening and shortening of metrical elements and syllables. In their realization, syllables are not merely *longum* or *breve*: depending on their position in the word and in the line, *brevia* may be slightly prolongated, and *longa* shortened in speech production and perception. It is a cross-linguistic feature of word-final syllables to be prolongated due to a slackening of the tempo of speech: the metrical bipartition *longum/breve* is insufficient to account for such realities in speech production. Phonetics focus on durational differences within the metrical categories *longum* and *breve*, depending on the metrical position of syllables and their location in the word and in the phrase: syllables that have the same phonological structure may thus be sligthly lengthened or shortened, like the word-final syllables featuring alpha's in example 18:

(18) ἄνδρα μοι ἔννεπε μοῦσα πολύτροπον ὃς μάλα πολλὰ
      πλάγχθη

Odyssey i 1–2a

Sing, Muse, of the man of many ways, who long and far | wandered

ἄνδρα μοι ἔννεπε μοῦσα πολύτροπον ὃς μάλα πολλὰ
– ᴜ ᴜ |– ᴜ ᴜ |– ᴜ   ᴜ |– ᴜ ᴜ | – ᴜ ᴜ | – x | |

→ word-final -δρα (ἄνδρα) is located on the first *breve* of the *biceps*; given its location at the start of the line (where rates of speech are high), the alpha has little duration

→ word-final -σα (μοῦσα) is also located on the first *breve* of the *biceps*, but immediately precedes the third-foot word end; -σα may thus be slighter longer than –δρα, also because of the gradual slackening of the tempo of speech

→ word-final -λα (μάλα) is located on the second *breve* of the *biceps*; the avoidance of a spondaic fifth foot, and hence the reduction of the duration of the fifth foot in general, suggests that word-final alpha was pronounced with short duration

→ word-final -λα (πολλὰ) is located on the verse-final element, allowing for phrase-final lengthening

In phonetics, pause equals termination of phonation: the production of sound stops. Phonetic pause may coincide with breathing. The rhythmical indeterminacy (– or ᴜ) of the verse-final element (x) is often treated as an indication of breathing, as if each verse ends in termination of phonation:

(19) βῆ ῥ' ἐς Φαιήκων ἀνδρῶν δῆμόν τε πόλιν τε

Odyssey vi 3

She went to the land and the city of the Phaeacians

[βῆ ῥ᾽ ἐς Φαιήκων ἀνδρῶν δῆμόν τε πόλιν τε]
[on a single breath   ] followed by breathing
[‒   ‒ | ‒‒|‒   ‒| ‒   ‒| ‒ ◡   ◡|‒ x] + breathing

I do not subscribe to that point of view: if the verse-final syllable is a *longum*, I see no reason to treat it in a way different from *longa* on the foot's second element *within* the line. The slackening of tempo of speech makes the indeterminacy of the verse-final syllable irrelevant: it is a *longum* in metrical analysis (Ruijgh 1987; Dee 2004):

(20)   οὔτε τοι ἡμιόνων φθονέω τέκος οὔτε τευ ἄλλου

Odyssey vi 68

I will not withhold you the mules, my child, nor anything else

[οὔτε τοι ἡμιόνων φθονέω τέκος οὔτε τευ ἄλλου]
‒   ◡◡ |‒◡◡ |‒   ◡◡ | ‒   ◡◡ | ‒   ◡◡ |‒‒ ||
[dactylic line   with spondaic ending]

(21)   ὣς εἰπὼν δμώεσσιν ἐκέκλετο τοὶ δ᾽ ἐπίθοντο

Odyssey vi 71

Having spoken thus he called out for for his servants, and they
came to his bidding

[ὣς εἰπὼν δμώεσσιν ἐκέκλετο τοὶ δ᾽ ἐπίθοντο]
‒   ‒ | ‒   ‒ | ‒◡◡ |‒ ◡◡|‒   ◡◡ |‒ ‒ ||
[dactylic line   ending in *brevis in longo*]

When looking for a pause in phonetics, I propose that we do not stick to fixed metrical positions, but start identifying where phonetics support the phonological indicators of pause: through the possibility of correlates of pause like word-final lengthening. Phonetic lengthening is most easily illustrated where it coincides with metrical lengthening (word-final –τος in example 22): here, the two types of lenghtening reinforce one another. In other instances of word-final lengthening (like ἀλκῆς and φόβοιο), the phonetic adjustment of syllable duration is limited by phonological circumstances:

(22)   οὐδ᾽ ἔτ᾽ ἀδήριτος ἥτ᾽ ἀλκῆς ἥτε φόβοιο

Iliad XVII 42

And no longer uncontested, (to prove) either our courage or our fear

οὐδ' ἔτ' ἀδήριτος ἥτ' ἀλκῆς ἥτε φόβοιο
$- \cup \cup | -- | -- | -- | - \cup \cup | - \mathrm{x} | |$

Pause in performance implies phonetic pause.

So far, five different systems of analysis presented five different "pauses." In metrical analysis, a pause is equal to a metrical boundary, a position of frequent word end. Rhythmical analysis considers the verse end a pause, and sometimes allows for verse-internal word end to double as a pause. In syntactical analysis, pause is identified commonsensically. There are numerous syntactical breaks; coincidence of the syntactical break with verse end attracts special attention in the analysis of out-of-line composition. The system of phonological analysis postulates pause as the opposite of the coherence, evidenced by segment shift and "leaning." Phonetic analysis of metrical text identifies the possibility or the likeliness of termination of phonation from phonological clues. Underlying the differences between these analyses is a difference of level in the analysis of the prosodic unit, the syllable: meter categorizes syllables as either *longum* or *breve*, rhythm classifies them as either *more prominent* or *less prominent*. Phonology looks at syllable structure and classifies syllables into binary categories, whereas phonetics differentiates, within those categories, between syllables that are prepausal, and others that are non-prepausal or avoid pause. I will argue that the pause in performance is a synergy of all these systems, but not of all of them at one and the same time and location.

0.5.1 Aim of the study: The reconstruction of performative pause

Audible Punctuation explores possibilities in performance: this study aims to *reconstruct* the performative pause in Homer. Given certain assumptions (summarized in 3.2 and 5.1 below), and applying a consistent method of analysis, *Audible Punctuation* makes an argument for the possibilities and limits of expressing phrases in performance. To that end, I will analyze the possibilities and limits of expressing metrical, rhythmical, syntactical, and phonological phrasing in performance, starting from the assumption that pause in performance is a phonetic pause, and that phonetic pause is evidenced by phonology: the text creates different options for performative pauses. Performative pause is defined as *a rest of some duration in performance due to the termination of phonation*. The definition implies that this study deals with pause in a very strict sense: as an audible phenomenon and a performative feature. My definition of pause as a performative feature is less generic than the widely, and rather loosely, applied terminology "pause" for the *compositional* pause: the termination of a metrical, phonological, or syntactic unit. All these compositional pauses appear in the Homeric epic to demarcate units of composition, but only few, I will argue, double to demarcate units, or rather phrases, in performance.

0.5.2 Organization of the study

The reconstruction of performative pause starts from the identification of all the various compositional pauses, but depends on the reconstruction of the phonetics of pause: performative pause is first and foremost a phonetic pause. I will argue that absence of phonological clues for coherence suggests performative pause, and against the identification of termination of phonological phrases on metrical or syntactical grounds.

Not all breaks in meter and syntax reflect a performative feature. From the ubiquitous and manifold compositional pauses, I will identify the ones that double as performative pause according to a set of criteria for the pause as audible phenomenon. In this study I will argue that, in order to maintain dactylic rhythm within the verse and between verses, only selected metrical positions in the line allow for a rest of some duration, a rest that is welcome, but not always possible, at word and phrase end. Word and phrase end are both marked by lengthening due to slackening of tempo of speech, but any lengthening may not disturb the regularity of rhythm; in metrical text this regularity is so strict that rests of considerable duration in performance are only allowed following the foot's first syllable. Selected positions share another characteristic, in addition to their being non-disturbing to rhythm: I will argue that syllables occupying these positions have to be free from any and all phonetic assimilation to the subsequent syllable. As I understand the metrical surface structure as the equivalent of phonology and as the reflection of phonetic realization, I reconstruct the phonetic pause on the basis of metrical evidence. Having argued for the phonetic pause, I will then turn back to the various and ubiquitous compositional pauses. The reconstruction of the phonetics of pause brings out when and where compositional pause may double as a rest in performance. For that reason I will summarize existing opinions on compositional pauses in the first three chapters, and acknowledge these pauses as compositional features. In Chapter 4, I will discuss pause as a requirement of performance: with the text creating options for pause, phonology determines the possibilities for rest in performance. Then, in Chapter 5, I will add a reconstruction of phonetic pause as the pause in performance.

I will compare the outcome of my reconstruction, the performative pause, with the distribution of compositional pauses, the termination of metrical, phonological, or syntactic units, in Chapters 6 and 7. Comparison of performative and compositional pauses will show (I) that only a selection of the compositional pauses may be exploited as a rest of some duration in performance, and (II) that the patterning of rests in performance results in a rhythmical mosaic of phrases and utterances of various and varying sizes. Comparison will also suggest (III) a different approach towards several widespread concepts of "termination-mismatch," notably enjambment.

0.5.3 Outcome of the study: Phrases in composition and performance terminate differently

Application of the term pause has been rather loose and arbitrary. As a boundary in composition the pause frames the verse, the metrical colon, the rhythmical phrase, and the syntactical units of discourse. Compositional pause tells us little about the rests, the audible pauses, in performance: surely not all compositional pauses are meant to incite the performer to take a rest and end phonation. Every line of Homeric poetry contains numerous compositional pauses. A line would not have contained as many rests in performance.

As compositional pauses have been treated as pauses in performance randomly and arbitrarily, mismatches of the various types of termination attract attention. What is going on when sense-pauses do not coincide with the strongest metrical boundaries? Why do sentences take different shapes when rhythmical phrases are, in principle, repetitive and similar in size? Is there a special ring in the audience's ears to the start of the hexameter when it is not the start of the sentence? Are specific metrical positions sensitive to extra emphasis?

All these issues are widely discussed in existing studies citing examples where the various compositional pauses seem to be used to special effect. The identification of such special effects does not postulate the likelihood of a rest of some duration in performance. Regularly, compositional pauses are granted status as pause in performance due to metrical, rhythmical, or syntactical considerations that exclude, stengthen, or replace one another without clear criteria for the relative importance of the various considerations. Phonetic effects of the identification of compositional pause as pause in performance have not been taken into account.

Pause in performance, however, is first and foremost about phonetic effect. For that reason I have explored the possibilities and limitations of phonetic pause within the framework of Homer's phonology and metrical surface structure. As I will show in this study, performative pause means that the performer has the *choice* to exploit options for pause in performance. Rate of speech determines whether or not options for pause may actually be used. These options will be explored in accordance with the phonetics of pause, not with the occurrence of compositional pauses or the common sense of syntactical composition. For that reason the conclusion reached in this study may appear counter-intuitive, or contrary to expectations: the phrases of performance, demarcated by performative pauses, do not always match the compositional units. Alignment of compositional phrases with phrases in performance may well occur, but is not automatically to be expected. Mapping the pattern of performative pauses onto those of the various compositional pauses will make clear to what extent verses and phrases terminate differently.

0.5.4 Evidence from text? — The status of a written *Iliad* and *Odyssey*

This study analyzes the possibilities of performative pauses in the texts of the Homeric epics, as we have them today. As the printed text of the *Iliad* and the *Odyssey* is the closest one can get to surface phonetic rhythmics in Homer, the status of the text has to be accounted for, with regard both to the value of these texts as a reflection of performance and to the reliability of them as evidence for conclusions concerning phonology and phrase formation.

The relation of text to performance has been much discussed over the past decades.[2] As the *Iliad* and the *Odyssey* are accepted as examples of poetry that had originally been composed and enjoyed orally, the focus has been on the detectable characteristics of such poetry in the transmitted text. Comparing the Homeric epic with orally composed and performed epics worldwide, scholars have been able to provide the structure, technique of composition, and aesthetics of the *Iliad* and *Odyssey* with a firm basis in orality. The relation of text to performance has, however, been studied from very different perspectives. Janko 1992:20–38 argues for an early date for the text as we have it: our text, he claims, does not differ substantially from the text, as it was written down some time before the Pisistratean recension. Following Lord 1960, Janko hypothesizes that our text dates back to the eight century BCE and resembles contemporary bardic performance. From a neoanalystic point of view, West 2011:72–74 argues that our text does not differ substantially from the original version in writing, which he dates between 680 and 640 BCE. Another approach to the relation of text and performance is found in Bird 2010, who has recently restated

---

[2] Nagy's "evolutionary model" (1996a:29–63) claims that transcripts of particularly successful performances served as the basis for re-composition, causing the *Iliad* and the *Odyssey* to expand continuously. "Dictation theory" (West 2001, 2011, Ready 2015) supposes that both epics kept changing with every performance until the moment of being written down, allegedly at the end of the eighth century BCE or a little later (Blankenborg 2017). Bakker (2013:157–169) shows how the composing performer created conscious allusions and motives to help structure the expanding narrative. González (2013) argues that rhapsodic delivery resembled that of tragic texts by actors: delivery relied on memorization, with little room for improvisation and hardly any for re-composition.

the theory of multitextuality, already confirmed in other oral traditions and compared to Greek by, amongst others, De Vet 1996, Nagy 1996b, and Thomas 2003. On the basis of textual variance in the Ptolemaic papyri, Bird defends the concept of a fluid "text"—oral performance and transmission—as an alternative view of Homeric transmission. He shows that the transmitted text of the *Iliad* may be enlarged by "plus verses" here and there and claims that these verses were optional for the performances of (passages from) the *Iliad* until Ptolemaic times. As "plus verses" and their context were still both the basis and the materialization of actual performance, so the whole *Iliad* remains a reflection of the content and compositional technique of the Homeric epic in performance, even if the written form is smoothed over in the course of time. Regardless of the exact approach chosen, we may safely conclude that our text of Homer's *Iliad* and *Odyssey* is close enough to contemporary bardic performance to serve as evidence for conclusions on phonology and phonetics at work in performance.

With regard to the reliability of text as evidence for conclusions concerning phonology and phrase formation, much seems to depend on the choice of editor. Allen 1917, 1919, and 1931, and Monro and Allen 1920 are prominent among text editions of the *Iliad* and *Odyssey*; they hold the middle between adopting the reading of the medieval manuscripts and that of the papyri. Other editions rely more on the readings of papyri, or strive towards a more consistent treatment of comparable phonological phenomena. West's *Iliad* edition 1998–2000 differs from Allen's at many points, most notably with regard to the persistent printing of movable *nu*, the accentuation of pronouns, and the possibility for two subsequent acute accents within the appositive group. The *Odyssey* editions by Van der Mühll 1962 and Van Thiel 1991 follow the medieval text. Leaf's *Iliad* 1900–1902 applies punctuation that later editors did not follow.

The position taken in this study is that the text of passages from the *Iliad* and the *Odyssey* should be in accordance with (i) the edition that is closest to the transmitted text, and (ii) the phonological requirements of higher-level rhythmics. In other words, orthography need not run counter to the maintenance of metrical surface structure. I do not consider any licenses or variants in the orthography of the *Iliad* and *Odyssey* as running counter to the phonological requirements of higher-level rhythmics. I realize that the exact reading of the manuscripts will have been smoothed over in the course of the centuries. In accordance with the Hellenistic and Roman practice of treating, more and more, the metrical unit of the hexameter as the syntactical unit, pausal mismatching may have been corrected here and there. The mismatching patterns that I will identify in our text, however, must always have been there. The rhythmical indeterminacy of the verse-final anceps, common in later hexametric development, may have obscured mismatches, especially at verse end, in Homer, but many instances of pausal mismatch remain, suggestive of many more that may once have characterized the performed text of the *Iliad* and the *Odyssey*. In my study, I have chosen the OCT text of (Monro and) Allen, as it stays closest to the transmitted text and deals most consistently with the rendering of phonological phenomena.

1

Pause in Metrics and Rhythmics

*Technical terms followed by * on their first occurrence in this chapter are in the glossary.*

1.0   Introduction

This chapter investigates the compositional pause* in meter and rhythm*. Metrical boundaries, positions of frequently recurring word end, are often considered metrical pauses. The metrical pause that is the verse end appears as the most important rhythmical pause. Metrical and rhythmical pause is generally treated as a compositional phenomenon without any claims concerning performance*. In the search for special effects due to the mismatch of pause and syntactical phrasing, however, metrical pause is understood as more than merely compositional; it is then implicitly taken as a performative feature. My main criticism concerning the common treatment of pause in meter and rhythm is that the special performative effects are granted at random and without a clear set of criteria to determine pause as an audible phenomenon.

Most important among the existing studies on meter and rhythm are Snell 1962, Korzeniewski 1968, and West 1982/1997. Their views, especially West's, have gained broad acceptance and are commonly presented as the standard approach to issues pertaining to meter and rhythm in Greek. I will present them accordingly, and name the work of others where their views are more explicit on the issue of pause.

My overview will show that the metrical pause as such can only be understood as a compositional feature. Some aspects of the metrical pause will be carried forward from this chapter as they may coincide with those of the performative pause that I will reconstruct in a later chapter, as may aspects of meter in general. For the reconstruction of performative pause, meter is a most helpful factor, as it provides evidence not only for phonetically important issues like syllable division*, duration*, and weight*, but also for the nature of the Greek accent. Meter provides evidence for the coherence and demarcation of phonological phrases* like the appositive group* (Chapter 3). I will start this overview with generally accepted theories on pause in prosody* (§1.1), then I will proceed to the issue of pause in rhythm (§1.2). At the end of the chapter, I will summarize the aspects of metrical pause that will reappear in my reconstruction of performative pause in subsequent chapters.

1.1   Pause in Prosody

Meter, the duration of syllables, is a feature of prosody. What is known as metrical pause depends, in fact, on pausal characteristics of all the features of prosody. The term prosody refers to three features of sound, individually or all three together: duration, frequency, and intensity. The main unit of analysis in the study of prosody is the syllable, the smallest scale sequence of vowel and consonant.[1] In the study of ancient Greek, a quantifying language, the three features of sound are labelled syllable length, pitch*, and stress*. Syllable length is studied in the field of meter; pitch is studied in relation with tone; and stress is linked to weight. Outside this study the term prosody is commonly used for the identification of duration, frequency, and intensity in larger sound waves (encompassing several syllables) as well. Section 1.1 focuses on the syllable, and aims to list its pausal qualities based on the study of meter, pitch, and stress.

1.1.1 Meter

Meter in Greek refers to three different phenomena: scansion*, the patterning of syllables onto feet (footing*), and colometry*.

1.1.1.1 Scansion

Scansion is the bipartition of syllables into two categories of syllable length: *longum* (–) and *breve* (◡). Both categories encompass syllables of various structures, that is, different ways to combine consonants (C) and vowels (V). The central element in the structure of the syllable, the nucleus*, is always a vowel so that .V. (the dots demarcate the syllable) is the smallest syllable structure. A consonant (or cluster of consonants) preceding the syllable's nucleus is known as the onset*. The consonantal closing of a syllable is called the coda*. Together, the nucleus and the coda are known as the syllable's rime*. In metrical text,

---

[1]   Duration, frequency, and intensity are suprasegmental* features of sound. The syllable is the smallest scale level apart from the single vocalic and consonantal segment.

the onset appears to be irrelevant for syllable length: only the structure of the rime is decisive for the categorization of syllables as long or short. To that end, rime structures are treated as a computation of morae. The mora* is the unit of measurement: it is an instrument to account for meter's surface structure. In scansion, the mora accounts for the way syllable length relates to syllable structure. A rime composed of two or more morae counts as *longum*, otherwise it is categorized as *breve* (and the syllable with it). Short vowels (α, ε, ι, ο, υ) have mora count 1 in scansion; long vowels (ᾱ, η, ῑ, ῡ, ω) and diphthongs (αι, αυ, ει, ευ, οι, ου, ᾳ, ῃ, ῳ, ηυ) have mora count 2. A consonantal coda contributes one mora to the total mora count of the syllable's rime. Therefore, in the scansion of Greek, syllables ending in a coda are always categorized as *longa*. Further distinction between *longa* and *brevia* thus stems from the variation in vowel length. *Brevia* can be built from .V. or .CV. if V is a naturally short vowel, with mora count 1; *longa* can be built from .V. or .CV. if V is a naturally long vowel or a diphthong, when they are not built from .CVC. (regardless of vowel length). If the vowel in .CVC. is a naturally long vowel or a diphthong, the syllable is labelled overlong*: the mora count of its rime is then at least 3. In the metrical surface structure, the mora forms the basis for the distinction of syllables into the categories *longum* and *breve*, but it is primarily a rhythmic measurement (see below §1.2).[2]

Scansion of Greek metrical text is based on the regard for syllable structures, especially the syllable's rime. There are, however, two important points to be added: (I) under specific circumstances, outlined in the sections below, syllable structures categorized as *longum* are treated as *breve*, and vice versa; (II) the syllabification* of Greek metrical text is not in accordance with orthographic syllabification as used in alphabetic inscriptions and formulated in the Greek grammatical tradition. In the latter, internal division of the word is achieved by clustering as many consonants into the syllable's onset as is allowed at the beginning of a word. Therefore, as Greek words may begin with κτ-, word internal division will also result in an onset .κτ- rather that -κ.τ-. This principle was apparently extended to clusters like -γδ-, -σγ-, -σδ-, -θμ-, and -φν-.[3] Metrical syllabification differs from

---

[2] Devine and Stephens 1994:47–48. Whereas the consonantal coda contributes to mora count for the purpose of scansion, it has no contribution to the mora count of the word's tonal pattern; see §1.1.2 below.

[3] Probably due to the irrelevance of the difference between voiced and voiceless consonants. Devine and Stephens 1994:36–39 further suggest that the difference between metrical and orthographic syllabification may pertain to rate of speech: orthographic syllabification represents not the syllables of normal speech but those of an artificially slow rate of speech associated with the teaching and probably also the practice of writing. Metrical syllabification is closer to the phonetic reality.

orthographic syllabification as it considers *every* syllable juncture, including word division, as *word internal* and divides words according to the principle that *a syllable's coda consists of one consonant at most, provided the subsequent syllable's onset consists of at least one consonant.*[4] Devine and Stephens 1994:38 speculate that metrical syllabification best represents the perception of syllables by a Greek audience. Metrical syllabification shows that pause in prosody does not prevent that the syllable length of word-final syllables depends on the onset of the subsequent word-initial syllable.

1.1.1.2 Footing

Apart from scansion, the term meter also refers to footing: the patterning of syllables onto metrical feet,[5] implying regularity and repetition. The foot* is the smallest scale unit of this regularity and repetition. In Homer, feet take the trisyllabic shape of dactyls, *longum-breve-breve* ($|- \cup \cup|$), or the disyllabic shape of spondees, *longum-longum* ($|- -|$). The larger scale phrase, the verse, contains six feet (hexameter) so that the typical Homeric line is a series of six dactylic or spondaic feet. The first four feet are either trisyllabic or disyllabic; the fifth foot is only rarely disyllabic;[6] the verse-final foot is always disyllabic. This way the hexameter contains a minimum of twelve syllables, and of seventeen syllables at the most.[7] Through the exchangeability of dactyls and spondees in the hexameter's first five feet the number of verse variants amounts to 32.[8]

The regular recurrence suggesting the repetition is the *longum* that comes first in every foot. The foot's first element is invariably a *longum*; the remainder of the foot varies between a single *longum* or two *brevia*. Lidov 1989 labels the first element of the hexametric foot *stable*, the remainder *changeable*. Devine and Stephens 1994 use *more* and *less energetic* (*stressed* and *unstressed*); West 1982, like many authors preceding him and many authors following him, uses *thesis* (T)* and *arsis* (A)* so that the dactylic foot takes the shape TA.[9] In the

---

[4] This principle's definition is the only contribution to this section that is entirely my own; to my knowledge, there has not been an attempt to define metrical syllabification before. In Chapter 3, I will show that my definition is in line with existing observations on phonological phenomena.

[5] The adjective *metrical* is necessary here as stress and intensity typology also use the term *feet*; see further below and the glossary.

[6] If a verse features a disyllabic fifth foot, it is called a spondaic verse. Spondaic verses occur every 1 in 21.8 lines in Homer. Holodactylic and holospondaic verses are relatively rare in Homer.

[7] Hypermetric verse* as found in Latin poetry (e.g., Vergil *Aeneid* I 46–47: *Iovisque* || *et soror et coniunx*), hypercatalexis*, and extrametrical syllables* do not occur in the *Iliad* and *Odyssey*.

[8] All variants in the repertory by Dee 2004.

[9] As scholars have, for centuries, used thesis and arsis in various ways (to indicate the lifting and lowering of the foot, or, alternatively [especially for Latin, see Hardie 1920], the rising and lowering of the voice [applied to Homer in Leaf 1900–1902]), it is necessary to choose between

case of the disyllabic foot, A is occupied by a single *longum*; if the foot is trisyllabic, A consists of two *brevia*. To account for the difference between dactylic and spondaic feet in the representation of scansion, the syllables in the feet are refered to as positions: a spondaic (disyllabic) foot has a position for T (1), and for A (2). The trisyllabic, dactylic foot has a position for T (1), and two positions for A (1½, 2). When dactylic/spondaic feet are in a sequence, the numbers simply continue: 3, (3½), 4, 5 (5½), 6, etc.[10]

The structural elements of the foot, the thesis and the arsis, are in some sort of foot-internal proportion* to one another. Terminology from antiquity (like γένος ἴσον "balanced type" for the foot-internal proportion of the hexameter[11]) suggests that this proportion is measurable and purely quantitative, but most modern scholars do not readily accept such analysis. Lidov 1989 rejects the assumption that the proportion T-A in Greek meter is quantifiable, as if the adding-up of T and A, two measurable durations, results in a fixed outcome for the foot as a whole. Devine and Stephens 1994 consider the quantifiability of syllable duration in Greek, but point out that cross-linguistic research does not provide evidence for a direct relation between syllable structure and quantifiable duration. In their view, there is in ancient Greek (as in many modern languages) a direct relation between syllable structure and intensity, not so much between syllable structure and duration. Scholars that do incline towards a quantifiable foot-internal proportion T-A must decide whether the proportion is indeed balanced ($T^{duration} = A^{duration}$, with T and A of equal duration), or tips the balance in either direction. West 1982:20 (and 1998/2000) and Wefelmeier 1994 accept that $A^{duration} > T^{duration}$ in the hexameter. Arguments in favour of $A^{duration} < T^{duration}$ are listed in Ruijgh 1987: in hexametric poetry, the thesis is the preferred location for the word-final *longum*, whereas the arsis may only accomodate *longa* when they are word internal.

In Homer, dactylic and spondaic feet team up to form larger scale phrases, the dactylic hexameters. With regard to feet, structural elements, positions and metrical realizations, the hexameter can be described in the following way:

---

the various uses. Throughout this study, I will use thesis (T) to indicate the first, invariable element of the hexametric foot, and arsis (A) to indicate the remainder of the foot.

[10] O'Neill 1942, see p. 2 above. Alternative notations, not always that different from O'Neill's, are presented in Porter 1951; Beekes 1972; Kirk 1966; Sicking/Van Raalte 1993. Hagel 1994–1995 presents a notation based on mora count (^{1}[*longum*]2[*breve*]3[*breve*]4 ^{2}[*longum*]6[*breve*]7[*breve*]8 etc.). Janse 1998:138 and 2003 offers a notation ^{1}[*longum*]1a[*breve*]1b[*breve*]1c ^{2}[*longum*]2a[*breve*]2b [*breve*]2c etc.

[11] Aristides Quintilianus 1.15.

Feet:

1st foot	2nd foot	3rd foot	4th foot	5th foot	6th foot

Structural elements:

T A	T A	T A	T A	T A	T A

Positions:

1 1½ 2	3 3½ 4	5 5½ 6	7 7½ 8	9 9½ 10	11 12

Metrical realizations:

‿ ‿	‿ ‿	‿ ‿	‿ ‿	‿ ‿	
— —	— —	— —	— —	— —	— ×

Iliad I 1 may serve as an example to illustrate this description of Homeric verses:

(23) μῆνιν ἄειδε θεά Πηληιάδεω Ἀχιλῆος

Sing, Goddess, of the wrath of Achilles, son of Peleus

1st foot	2nd foot	3rd foot	4th foot	5th foot	6th foot
T A	T A	T A	T A	T A	T A
1 1½ 2	3 3½ 4	5 6	7 7½ 8	9 9½ 10	11 12
— ‿ ‿	— ‿ ‿	— —	— ‿ ‿	— ‿ ‿	— ×
μῆνιν ἄ	ειδε θε	ά Πη	ληιά	δεω Ἀχι	λῆος

The *longum-breve* alternation is repetitive, with slight variation, and the end of the larger scale phrase, the verse, is signalled by some sort of variation or aberration that breaks up the repetitive pattern, such as word end in combination with distinctive syllable quantity*. Such larger scale phrases are labelled stichic verse*.[12] The dactylic hexameter terminates in an invariably disyllabic foot ending in an anceps* element. Despite the metrical variation that the verse-final

---

[12] Stichic verse is thus the result of a single type of metrical aberration in a sequence of similar, regularly repeating feet. Apart from the dactylic hexameter, repetitive *longum-breve* alternation is found in iambic trimeter, trochaic tetrameter, anapaestic dimeter, and various types of monometer. When feet, or clusters of feet, are repeated after the intervention of other, dissimilar (clusters of) feet, *longum-breve* alternation is *responsive*. In responsive alternation* it is often very hard to determine the size of any larger scale units: regularly, the tentatively identified larger scale units (also referred to as *verses*) are merely grouped together into strophes* or stanzas*.

foot offers between a trochee ($|$– ⏑$|$) and a spondee (as the arsis may be occupied by either a *breve* or a *longum*), many modern studies treat the sixth foot as a spondee. The verse-final arsis is then granted prosodic neutrality*: position 12 may be occupied by a *breve* or a *longum*, but it always counts as a *longum*. Such prosodic neutrality—actually a licence for verse end in a *longum*—is then in itself considered a sign of termination. If prosodic neutrality is not accepted as a licence for termination at verse end, the dactylic hexameter appears to be a catalectic verse*, that may still terminate in a *breve*:[13] the identification of the hexameter as catalectic verse does not automatically result in termination of the verse in a *longum*. A *longum*, however, is considered crucial for termination: analysis of the sixth foot as verse-final is based on the disruption of the repetitive pattern of feet due to word end in combination with distinctive syllable quantity. In the case of the hexametric verse end, the specific syllable quantity is a *longum* on the foot's arsis, a type of word end (spondaic: word end in a spondee) that is practically restricted to the verse end: the restriction is the reason for the identification of hexameters as stichic verse. Spondaic word end* at other positions (positions 4, 8, and 10) is only sparsely allowed, under very specific circumstances (see Glossary: bridges). The restriction on spondaic word end shows that the thesis, as mentioned before, is the preferred location for word end in a *longum* within the verse.[14]

1.1.1.3 Colometry

Just like the second aspect of meter, the patterning of syllables onto feet, meter's third aspect, colometry, deals with domains whose size well outgrows that of the domain of prosody proper, the syllable. Where the first two aspects of meter may also be referred to as outer metrics*, colometry is known as inner metrics*: it is the technical term for the cutting up of the verse into smaller scale metrical phrases.[15] Cutting up the verse naturally brings with it the issue of compositional pause demarcating the smaller scale phrases that are its result.

The hexameter is a relatively long verse, twelve to seventeen syllables. Ever since Aristotle, there has been the notion that the hexameter may be divided into smaller metrical phrases. In an attempt to shed light on the syllabic division

---

[13] West 1997:221. Van Raalte 1986:32 lists the arguments against identification of the dactylic hexameter as catalactic verse.

[14] In the reconstruction of performative pause this will be the most important restriction of the mapping of syllables, especially word-final syllable, onto feet. The two long syllables, on the thesis and on the arsis, are treated differently: therefore, in metrical notation, the dactylic/spondaic thesis is regularly accentuated with an ictus* (´). The term ictus may suggest a downbeat-like character for the thesis. Implicitly, such a downbeat-like character assigned to the foot's thesis is a statement on phonetics (see further Chapter 3).

[15] See Clark 2004; Edwards in Finkelberg 2011:517–519.

of specific hexametric verse variants (*Metaphysics* 1093a30), Aristotle subdivides the hexameter into two half-verses, eight and nine syllables respectively. His subdivision is related to musical phenomena concerning scale. Hermogenes (*De Ideis*, second century CE), possibly following Heliodorus (first century CE) uses the term τομή ("cut," "caesura*") for the position within the verse where a subdivision could be made in cola. These cola resemble the shape of smaller metrical phrases known from non-stichic lyric poetry.[16] Aristotle's division of the hexameter, for example, splits the verse into two halves, the first of which is a hemiepes (– ◡ ◡ – ◡ ◡ –). Despite a later, Byzantine development[17] of the caesura into a rhetorical sense-pause*, the main characteristic of the caesura is that it is a position of frequent word end *within* a metrical foot. If a position of frequent word end falls *between* feet, it is called a dieresis*.

Modern scholars name the caesura after the position in the verse (as does Korzeniewski 1968, following Aristides Quintilianus and Hephaestion) or designate it as A, B, or C caesura (West 1982, 1997; Clark 2004[18]). Following a lead from antiquity (found in Dionysius of Halicarnassus), they speak of a masculine caesura following a long syllable, and a feminine caesura following a short syllable. The main caesura in the verse's third foot divides the hexameter into two half-verses, the hemistichs. With only few exceptions, the main caesura occurs in every Homeric verse, and varies between a masculine (πενθημιμερής/-ές/ penthemimeres*; indicated as :5 in example 2) and a feminine caesura (trochaic caesura*, κατὰ τὸν τρίτον τροχαῖον; indicated as :5¼ in example 3):

(2) μῆνιν ἄειδε θεά :5 Πηληιάδεω Ἀχιλῆος

Iliad I 1

Sing, Goddess, of the wrath of Achilles, son of Peleus

(3) στέμματ᾽ ἔχων ἐν χερσὶν :5¼ ἑκηβόλου Ἀπόλλωνος

Iliad I 14

Holding the ribbons in his hands of far shooting Apollo

Very few verses do not allow for a main caesura in the third foot:

---

16 Hardie 1920:14–26; Basset 1938:145–149. Lidov 1989:83 warns against the assumption of a pre-existence of the cola in the I-E tradition.

17 Basset 1938:147.

18 Labeled A1 (following position 2), A2 (position 3), C1 (position 7), and C2 (position 8) in the overview of Clark 2004:120–121. The third-foot caesura is labeled B1 (following position 5) or B2 (position 5½). The caesura following position 9 is not mentioned in Clark's overview.

(24)   Ἥρη τ’ ἠδὲ Ποσειδάων καὶ Παλλὰς Ἀθήνη

Iliad I 400

Hera, Poseidon, and Pallas Athena

Together with the dieresis at verse end the main caesura is considered the strongest metrical pause of the hexameter, due to its persistent occurrence. Other, less frequently recurring positions of word end, both caesurae and diereses, are applied to further subdivide the hemistichs. The less frequently occurring positions of word end are known as auxiliary caesurae* (though the term is also used for diereses).[19] Well accepted auxiliary caesurae are the dieresis following the first foot after position 2, the caesura following the second foot’s thesis after position 3 (trithemimeres*), the caesura following the fourth foot’s thesis after position 7 (hephthemimeres*), the bucolic dieresis (“bucolic” because it is lavishly used by bucolic poets, such as Theocritus) following the fourth foot after position 8, and the caesura following the fifth foot’s thesis after position 9 (ennehemimeres*). The exact subdivision of hemistichs varies with the occurrence of the various auxiliary caesurae. Fränkel 1926 applied the various positions for word end to advocate a division of the verse into four cola. Some examples (25 below, and, from the Introduction, 4 and 5) to illustrate this principle (caesurae/diereses are indicated by the number of the metrical position they follow, in both the Greek example and its translation):

Division into two hemistichs:

(25)   εἶκε Διὸς θύγατερ ⁵ πολέμου καὶ δηιοτῆτος

Iliad V 348

Remove yourself, daughter of Zeus ⁵ from the war and the fighting

that can each be divided into two cola:

(4)   εἶκε Διὸς 3 θύγατερ ⁵ πολέμου ⁷ καὶ δηιοτῆτος

Iliad V 348

Remove yourself, Zeus’s ³ daughter ⁵ from the war ⁷ and the fighting

or directly into four cola:

---

[19]   Fränkel 1968; Kirk 1966; Ingalls 1970; Beekes 1972; Kirk 1985:18–24; Barnes 1986; Steinrück 1994; Wefelmeier 1994; Hagel 1994–1995; Barnes 1995; Clark 2004; David 2006.

(5) ὣς ἔφαθ᾿ ² ἡνίοχος ⁵ δ᾿ ἵμασεν ⁷ καλλίτριχας ἵππους

Iliad XI 280

Thus he spoke ² and his charioteer ⁵ put the whip on ⁷ the horses with beautiful manes

Kirk 1966 introduces an addition to Fränkel's system when he identifies the rising threefolder*, a tripartition of the verse into cola of increasing length. This can be seen in examples 6 (from the Introduction) and 26[20]:

(6) διογενὲς ³ Λαερτιάδη ⁷ πολυμήχαν᾿ Ὀδυσσεῦ

Iliad II 173

Descendant of Zeus ³ son of Laertes ⁷ resourceful Odysseus

(26) εἰ δὴ ὁμοῦ ³ πόλεμός τε δαμᾷ ⁷ καὶ λοιμὸς Ἀχαιούς

Iliad I 61

Since together war and pestilence ravish the Greeks

Recent overviews of Homeric meter, such as West 1997, Nünlist 2000, Clark 2004, and Edwards (in Finkelberg 2011), accept the tripartite verse, and consider the (trithemimeres in combination with the) hephthemimeres a replacement for the third-foot caesura, as indicated in examples 6 and 26 above. Other metrical pauses may step in to replace the third-foot caesura.

When metrical cola are considered units of composition and performance, the metrical boundary is treated as pause. To identify cola, considerations other than metrical are also commonly taken into account and, with them, other pauses. In antiquity no mention is made of the value of colometry nor of any necessity to divide the hexametric verse into smaller scale phrases. Fränkel 1926 defends his colometry with reference to its usefulness for internal articulation: the hexameter features three zones into which the positions of frequent word end can be found. He further points out that the metrical cola are regularly units of meaning, and that the word breaks that limit them are sense-pauses*.

---

[20] Initially, Kirk introduced the new colometry to account for lines that do not allow for a main caesura for orthographical reasons (like *Iliad* II 173 and *Iliad* I 400, example 24 above), but he extended his definition to encompass lines where the possibility for a main caesura was questioned for reasons other than statistics or orthography. In *Iliad* I 48, for example, ἕζετ᾿ ἔπειτ᾿ ³ ἀπάνευθε νεῶν ⁷ μετὰ δ᾿ ἰὸν ἕηκε ‘, "Then he sat down ³ *at some distance from the ships* ⁷ and he let go an arrow," Kirk does not allow for a main caesura because the words around it are too tightly bound together syntactically. As the genitive case νεῶν is understood as being strengthened by ἀπάνευθε, the word juncture in ἀπάνευθε νεῶν is considered word-group internal and not equal to the word end that terminates word groups. Sicking 1993:77 considers such verses as lines without a caesura at all.

Porter 1951 shows that this is not always the case. He argues that metrical cola are due to prosodic reasons ("an expected sequence of syllables produced by a brief rhythmical impulse"[21]), and that cola only tend to comprise "organic" word groups: the words tied together within the colon may form a semantic unit, but this is not necessary. His colon is a "rhythmical impulse" that is being kept together in performance, and it exercises a normative effect on the meaning. Ingalls 1970 rejects Porter's criticism of Frankel when he concludes that Porter works from *a priori* notions (Porter seems to reject the idea of an iamb-shaped colon between positions 5½ and 7). Kirk 1966 meets with similar criticism, as he identifies metrical boundaries as indicators of sense-structure or, alternatively, of cognitive structure (cf. Ingalls 1970; 1972): for Kirk syntax comes first, and metrical cola are identified in accordance with the syntactic structure. Ingalls 1972:122 allows for the coincidence of metrical cola and syntactic structure in the case of formulas:

> The formulae from Parry's analysis, then, continue the intimate connection between formular usage and the colometric structure of the hexameter. Just as the formulae are the linguistic building blocks of the verse, so the cola are the metrical blocks. In other words, the metrical shapes of the formulas tend to coincide with those of the cola with which the verse is composed.

This explanation for, at least, part of the metrical cola has been given new life by the study of Homeric discourse as spoken language[22] (see, further, Chapter 2). The metrical pauses that separate the cola have been explained as demarcative on different levels, the metrical and the syntactical. The various analyses and identifications of metrical pauses in colometry focus on compositional pauses. Additional clues are required to decide which of the ubiquitous compositional pauses double as performative pause.

1.1.2 Tone[23]

On the level of the syllable, tone is qualified as pitch, expressed on the Hertz scale (Hz) of frequency. For ancient Greek, the evidence for the reconstruction of syllable pitch derives mainly from the musical setting of what remains of vocal music, especially the Delphic hymns[24]. Short vowels (ᾰ, ε, ῐ, ο, ῠ) feature a single frequency; long vowels (ᾱ, η, ῑ, ῡ, ω) and diphthongs may be produced using two

---

[21] Porter 1951:17.
[22] Oesterreicher 1997; Bakker 1997b; 2005.
[23] = Pitch. For intonation as phrasing contour (Hagel 2004a/b, Nagy 2010) see 6.2.2.2.
[24] Devine and Stephens 1994:171–172.

different, subsequent frequencies, so that a tonal rise and fall is achieved within the syllable (in printed accentuation the perispomenon ~). To account for such dichotomy of the syllable, long vowels and diphthongs as the syllable's nucleus are analyzed as bimoraic; the mora is the single frequency. Bimoraic vocalic sounds may have a high tone on either mora: it is, therefore, better to speak of mora pitch than of syllable pitch. Short vowels have mora count 1. Therefore they cannot accommodate an accentual rise and fall within a single syllable. Mora pitch is evidenced in ancient Greek in printed accentuation. Mora count as the basis of accentuation differs from mora count in scansion in that it does not count any consonantal moraic sound[25] in the syllable's coda.

As Allen 1973:246 showed, in Greek the turning point between falling and rising tone coincides with the word boundary. West 1982 and Ruijgh 1987 speak of the phonetic word*, the combination of the word and its clitics, as the domain of accentual rise and fall. Every accented phonetic word shows a tonal pattern of initial rise, followed (in case of words ending in an unaccented final mora) by an accentual fall. If the accentual rise ends in a high tone on the word-final mora, with no room left for a fall, the word-final syllable carries grave accent: as the word-final mora now has to combine both the high tone and the word-final lower tone, the grave accent is considered a lower high tone. Word-final grave accent may also reflect the need for the following word to have some form of pre-accentual rise[26]. In addition to the musical evidence, Dionysius of Halicarnassus presents some evidence for the tonal patterns of the word. He states that (I) the interval between high and low tone in speech is limited to three tones and a semitone, and that (II) there is only one high-toned syllable per accented word. Syllables that are phonologically unaccented are phonetically low toned.[27]

In writing, the tonal pattern of mora pitch is indicated through the printed accentuation. The number of pre-accentual syllables determines the magnitude of the rise to the word's accentual peak (itself constant across various word lengths), but the number of post-accentual syllables determines the depth of the accentual fall (as it can be higher or lower).[28] Devine and Stephens 1994 explain from the musical evidence that accentual fall is strongest in the first post-accentual syllable and tends to flatten somewhat in subsequent syllables. They also show that in situations where word-final pitch would be more than three semitones lower that the initial pitch of the subsequent word, there is a

---

[25] With the possible exception of the resonants ν, μ, ρ as evidenced in notation; see below, end of this section.

[26] Devine and Stephens 1994:180–183.

[27] Dionysius of Halicarnassus *On literary composition* 11.40 (Usener-Radermacher).

[28] Devine and Stephens 1994:187.

rise in pitch following the accentual fall: so-called secondary rise*. Finally, they point to the possibility for resonants (ν, μ, ρ) to carry part of a melism in notation: apparently resonants may have mora count in accentuation as well.

Together, grave accent and secondary rise reflect the coherence between words at the expense of pause in prosody.

1.1.3 Weight

The final contribution of the mora to the issue of compositional pause lies in the prosodic category of intensity, the basis of rhythm. As mentioned in §1.1.1, the mora, a unit of computation for both scansion and pitch, is a rhythmic measurement: it determines the categorization of syllables into the rhythmic categories prominent and less prominent, as well as into the metrical categories *longum* and *breve*. Antiquity's use of the term mora (χρόνος) for metrical and rhythmical purposes indicates that rhythmic prominence is related to metrical syllable length or duration. The precise relation has been a subject of debate, as I will explain below. As rhythmic prominence constitutes regular patterns, the rhythmical pause can be computed in mora count.

1.1.3.1 Weight and duration

Like others, Devine and Stephens 1994 do not accept any absolute duration for Greek syllables. They note that the phonological bipartition of syllables into two categories of syllable length abstracts away from physically existing distinctions: the syllables of Greek must, in fact, so they claim, have had a very large number of different durations. The rhythmic characterization of the bipartition of syllables is hence best indicated using terminology other than duration or length. Devine and Stephens, like most modern metrists, indicate rhythmic prominence as weight, and syllables as either heavy or light. "Long" and "short" are merely the denominations for the syllable's vocalic nucleus, *longum* and *breve* for the syllable in metrical analysis. Devine and Stephens point out that the "purely metrical" approach rationalizes the timing of the audible segmentation of language:[29]

> [Phonological and morphophonological rules, especially rules governing the location of word and phrase accent] classify syllables into at most two, or rarely three, categories of syllable weight, according as they contain one, two or, less commonly, three units of rhythmic measurement called morae. If syllables having different structures are assigned to the same class by the phonology in rules relating to rhythm,

[29] Devine and Stephens 1994:47–48.

that must be because they share some intrinsic property relating to rhythm, namely their mora count. ... The status of the mora is not the same in all languages. In so-called syllable weight languages, light syllables have one mora and heavy syllables have two morae overall. In so-called mora timed languages, heavy syllables also have two morae, but there is a greater tendency for each mora to be timed independently, so that particularly in slow speech vocalic morae and consonantal morae tend to make roughly equal contributions to bimoraic weight. This difference is not grounds for dispensing with the mora in syllable weight languages.

For Devine and Stephens, mora count is a matter of looking at the phonological syllable structure. The count rationalizes differences in syllable weight, as it is determined by differences in the duration of syllables' rime structure. Devine and Stephens are keen, however, to stress the importance of the syllable's phonetic realization:[30]

Whereas there has been a tendency in the phonologically influenced tradition to assume that submoraic duration is uninteresting and definitionally irrelevant, in the philological tradition there has been a tendency to make just the opposite assumption, namely that submoraic duration is automatically relevant. In antiquity, the diversity of syllable durations within the categories of heavy and light syllables arising from differences in segmental structure (subcategorical syllable duration) was widely recognized. Dionysius of Halicarnassus has a full discussion in the fifteenth chapter of *De Compositione Verborum*. ...

Despite the ancient distinction between rhythmics and metrics, Devine and Stephens 1994:51 stress the modern metrist's position that assumes a categorization of quantities, rather than the direct, sensory perception of quantitative relationships, as in music:

The ancient distinction between rhythmics and metrics correlates to a certain extent with the modern distinction between phonetics and phonology. Modern metrists, by contrast, have increasingly come to claim that Greek metre is immediately sensitive to segmentally motivated infracategoric differences in syllable duration.

---

[30] Devine and Stephens 1994:50.

The phonetic realization of syllables reflects their submoraic duration: infracategoric differences in syllable duration, so that there may be different ("lengthened" and "shortened") heavy and light syllables. Such differences are not strictly phonologically motivated—let alone demonstrable; they are suggested by phonology but hardly relevant phonologically. The categorization of quantities serves a rhythmic bipartition. Devine and Stephens show that the phonetic realization of syllables in speech reflects their rhythmical intensity. Often, phonetic realization in speech, especially in other than slow speech, mirrors significant submoraic adjustment*: the computation of the mora count runs counter to the intensity or the prominence of syllables in speech. Regularly, the bipartition heavy-light of syllables in a metrical text seems to make submoraic differences rather irrelevant. Evident submoraic adjustment is found in case of the single *longum* on the arsis (phonetic shortening), word-final phonetic lengthening, and synecphonesis. Phonetic shortening and lengthening are indicators of the avoidance and the possibility of pause respectively.

Syllable weight is reflected in the rime structure. The correlation between syllable weight and pitch (§1.1.2) is not easily demonstrable for ancient Greek. In later development, the rise of dynamic accent led to the coincidence of syllable weight and pitch. In Homer, there is no sign of such coincidence.

Although it is common to use the terminology of stress to indicate rhythmical prominence or intensity due to syllabic weight, scholars have sought for specific terminology to explain the nature of rhythmic prominence in ancient Greek, in order to avoid confusion with regard to dynamic accent.[31] The motor theory of syllabic weight (Allen 1973) takes into account syllable duration (as short vowels have ostensibly roughly 50% the duration of long vowels), but considers syllabic arrest, the post-nuclear closure of the syllable, the decisive factor. In this theory, light syllables are unarrested (as they do not feature any

---

[31] Devine and Stephens 1994:215 underline the "dynamic" aspect of stress. They also point at the terminological confusion concerning "stress" in the typological literature: "As such, 'stress' is not a very suitable term for nonaccentual durational prominence. Nevertheless, there are signs that it is beginning to be used in this latter sense in the typological literature, and should this sense of the term become current, there would be little reason not to speak of 'stress' in Greek." If Greek prosody is in any way the key to the identification of word stress or sentence stress, it is then tempting to assume that word stress is in some way related to the pitch accent and to the *longum* or heavy syllable. Devine and Stephens note that, in general, pitch accented languages (like ancient Greek) have a tonal accent and not automatically a dynamic stress accent. Sentence stress, as expressed through energization of speech musculature, is therefore approached with equal care. Any reference to dynamic stress, both on the level of individual words and the sentence, must take into account that the development of the dynamic stress accent in Greek has been a matter of what Devine and Stephens describe as restructuring. According to this approach, the eventual stress accent in Greek is the result of the alignment of pitch with heavy, or phonetically lengthened, syllables. In Homer (and many metrical texts after Homer), however, there is no such alignment, or rather, not yet.

segment beyond the vocalic nucleus), closed syllables are arrested by the coda, and long open syllables by the movement of the chest (so-called thoracic arrest: the second mora of the vocalic nucleus represents the completion of the chest-pulse that is the single syllable). Allen's motor theory maintains the bipartition of syllables (now labeled *arrested–unarrested*), but notes that the distribution of syllable structures over metrical positions suggests that coda-arrested sylla-bles (CVC) are rhythmically more prominent than thoracically arrested sylla-bles (CV). Coda-arrested syllables featuring a long vowel or diphthong, so-called superheavy* syllables, are rhythmically treated as other heavy syllables. Allen's theory uses the syllabic arrest to account for the extra mora in bimoraic sylla-bles: the difference between coda arrest and thoracic arrest may explain the metrical difference between CVC and CV, though they appear to be of equal duration. The rhythmical weight of the mora differs from its metrical length. Allen's attempt to differentiate between syllables of equal length on the basis of their rhythmical weight explains the distribution of (heavy) syllable structures onto thesis and arsis position, and as such it throws light on the structure of prepausal heavy syllables.[32]

On the other hand, there are scholars (Snell 1962; Daitz 1991) who continue to explain rhythmic weight in terms of duration and syllable length, as if the rhythmic mora is equal to the metrical mora. In their view, syllable length can be determined by the metronome, analogous to music. Morae serve to calculate the duration of syllable structures, and, in accordance to a theory from antiq-uity, even the silence between words or phrases. A short syllable has 50% the duration of a long syllable; a resolvable long syllable equals two short syllables. In some systems, notably that of Snell 1962, there is a third durational category, between the short and the long syllable, for the anceps element. Cross-linguistic analysis of natural languages, however, has declared durational differences between syllables almost irrelevant.

1.1.3.2 Weight as equivalent of sonority

General linguistic theory uses the term sonority* to account for the perceptual correlate of intrinsic intensity or acoustic energy. In a strict sense, sonority refers to voiced phonation and higher intensity of the syllabic nucleus. In more general terms, it indicates the combination of some or all of the properties of acoustic prominence, including duration.[33] Theory attributes most sonority to the vocalic nucleus of the syllable and to the consonantal coda. The sonority of the onset is limited. Consonantal clusters in the onset and the coda mirror

---

[32] In my reconstruction of performative pause, I will combine the findings of Allen with other characteristics of prepausal syllables, one of them being weight as the equivalent of intensity.

[33] Devine and Stephens 1994:22–24.

each other: in the onset the mouth widens, in the coda it closes, so that certain clusters of consonants that are useful for the syllable's onset appear in reversed order in the coda. The sonority of consonants is the key to the metrical syllabification of Greek. My rule to determine metrical syllabification (quoted in §1.1.1 above: *a syllable's coda consists of one consonant at most, provided the subsequent syllable's onset consists of at least one consonant*) is the rationalization of sonority sequencing.[34] Sonority explains metrical irregularities like *muta cum liquida*.[35] The distribution of syllable structures underlines the usefulness of the terminology for the description of syllabic weight.

As do others, Devine and Stephens use the terminology stress to indicate rhythmical prominence or intensity due to syllabic weight, though they are well aware of the possible typological confusion: stress may easily be understood as dynamic accent, the extra energization of speech musculature. They use the terminology because it offers the possibility to analyze metrical rhythm in terms of stress feet, as rhythm is analyzed cross-linguistically. I follow in their footsteps: the analysis of rhythm in Greek metrical text as stress feet brings out more peculiarities of phonetics in Homer than do other approaches. In relation to performative pause, the approach of metrical rhythm as stress feet does away with the assumption of durational equilibrium between thesis and arsis: performative pause depends not on durational equilibrium, but on the permission for durational differences despite the regularity of rhythm.

1.2   Rhythm

Rhythm features a pause of its own, as rhythm is suggestive of coherence while describing perceptible recurrence in utterances. Unfortunately, rhythm's quality as providing coherence is commonly deduced from compositional pauses like metrical boundaries, and only rarely from the analysis of the distribution of syllabic weight. In my approach and reconstruction of performative pause, rhythm is not only the regularity that suggests the coherence of speech acts, it is also a feature of poetry in performance that cannot be disrupted, not even by compositional pauses.

In a broad, general sense, any regular recurrence implies rhythm. In a more narrow sense, and with a focus on auditory stimuli, rhythm implies a patterned temporal sequence of stimuli. Rhythm in speech regularizes intense and less intense auditory stimuli into a pattern that suggests coherence, stresses

---

[34] Devine and Stephens 1994:23–24.

[35] As their position in the hierarchy of decreasing sonority shows: open vowels > closed vowels > glides > central liquids > lateral liquids > nasals > voiced fricatives > voiced stops > voiceless fricatives > voiceless stops.

recurrence, and allows for small variations. As Aristotle remarks (*Rhetoric* III 8), both metrical and non-metrical utterances are rhythmical. The rhythm of both types of utterances has been the object of study in the past century of scholarship. Rhythm in Greek metrical texts, including the Homeric epic, has been understood in various ways: as (I) the recurrence of the thesis in subsequent metrical feet; as (II) the recurrence of subsequent metrical cola; as (III) a way to describe word types; and as (IV) the regularization of utterances into stress-feet, analogous to normal speech. Regularly, the alternation between dactyls and spondees is referred to as rhythmic variation, but in §1.1.1 such alternation has been labelled metrical variation. All four descriptions of rhythm imply pause, but their treatment of its compositional value differs. Consequences of pause in performance are left assumed in the first two types, but referred to in the third approach (rhythmical word type recurrence) and the fourth (timing mechanism of speech).

1.2.1 Thesis recurrence

West 1982 uses the term rhythm to describe the organization of metrical feet into cola: the recurrence of the thesis structural element in subsequent feet forms the basis of the repetitive pattern that is rhythm. A series of subsequent dactylic and/or spondaic feet, for example, creates dactylic rhythm, just as dactylic rhythm is resumed following the bucolic dieresis or the verse end. Rhythm is treated as an organizational aspect of metrical speech, not a perceptual one that stems from metrical speech; pause is treated as a datum from metrical structure. A more perceptual approach to rhythm, defined as the recurrence of the thesis, taking a more phonetic approach to pause, is found in the concept of metarrhythmisis*. Koster 1953 gave new life to metarrhythmisis (known from antiquity), but was not followed by West. Metarrhythmisis is the shift of one metrical rhythm to another, usually closely related, for example, from iambs to trochees, or from dactyls to anapaests. Metarrhythmisis is triggered by anaclasis* or by catalexis. As it stems from the way word types start and terminate within the metrical phrase, metarrhythmisis depends on assumptions also shared by the third type of rhythm (*Rhythmical word type recurrence* below), as indicated in the introductory remark to this section; it will therefore receive full treatment in the section on this third type of rhythm below.

1.2.2 Colon recurrence

The second concept of rhythm, the recurrence of subsequent metrical cola, is recently advocated in the overviews of Homeric prosody by Clark 2004 and Edwards (in Finkelberg 2011). Both use the terminology outer metrics for meter on the level of the syllable (the actual prosody) and inner metrics to indicate colometry. Inner metrics is easily understood as rhythm, as it answers to the three basic requirements of rhythm: the stimulus of repetition, the creation of coherence, and the possibility of variation. Dactylic rhythm in Homer is defined as the grouping of metrical feet in cola of varying size. Rhythmical variation is the alternation of variously formed metrical cola, a variance that is guaranteed for each and every verse thanks to the differently shaped hemistichs. Start on the foot's arsis or thesis determines the rhythmisis*, the direction of the rhythm. Rhythm is understood as rising*, when the colon starts from the arsis, as descending* when the colon starts from the thesis. Ending in the thesis, rhythm is called blunt*, whereas ending on the arsis turns it pendant*. Similar terminology is used for the rhythmical word type*, as used in the third concept of rhythm.

1.2.3 Rhythmical word type recurrence

The third concept of rhythm, found in (amongst others) Ruijgh 1987 and 1989, refers to an approach known from antiquity: the identification of rhythmical word types, the ῥυθμοί. Manuals from antiquity mainly deal with ῥυθμοί in their analysis of metrical text on a level beyond the individual syllable. In this approach, rhythm is understood as the perceptible recurrence of certain rhythmical word types, like the iamb (⌣ –), the trochee (– ⌣), the dactyl (– ⌣ ⌣), the anapaest (⌣ ⌣ –), the choriamb (– ⌣ ⌣ –), or the molossus (– – –). The rhythmical recurrence of word types is audibly perceptible when the start or the completion of the word is perceptibly demarcated in performance. In his list of ῥυθμοί, Dionysius of Halicarnassus[36] cites exemplary κῶλα that often, but not necessarily,[37] equal metrical cola or periods, that is, verses. Dionysius carefully chooses examples that start with the rhythmical word type that gives its name to the metrical phrase as a whole. In specific cases, he quotes an example that completely consists of one single rhythmical word type.[38] In his example of the dactyl, however, Dionysius quotes a Homeric line *without* any dactylic word type (rhythmical word types separated by commas):

(27) Ἰλιόθεν με φέρων ἄνεμος Κικόνεσσι πέλασσεν

Odyssey ix 39

– ⌣ ⌣ –, ⌣, ⌣ –, ⌣ ⌣ –, ⌣ ⌣ – ⌣, ⌣ – –,

On the way from Troy a storm wind carrying me drove me to the Cicones

---

[36] Dionysius of Halicarnassus *On literary composition* 17/68.7–73.8 (Usener-Radermacher).
[37] Cf. an important exception discussed in Ruijgh 1987:319.
[38] As in his example of the molossus word type: ὦ Ζηνὸς καὶ Λήδας κάλλιστοι σωτῆρες (Page *PGM* 1027c) "excellent saviours, of Zeus and Leda" (– – –, – – –, – – –, – – –,).

Basset suggests that Dionysius might have cited, although he need not have, *Iliad* I 214:[39]

(8) ὕβριος εἵνεκα τῆσδε σὺ δ' ἴσχεο πείθεο δ' ἡμῖν

Iliad I 214

‒ ◡ ◡, ‒ ◡ ◡, ‒ ◡, ◡,   ‒ ◡ ◡, ‒ ◡ ◡,   ‒ ‒,

Because of this affront; control yourself, and do as we tell you

A phenomenon that is related to this approach to rhythm, and more important for a discussion concerning rhythmical pause, is metarrhythmisis, already mentioned above. Metarrhythmisis, the shift from one rhythmical word type to another, is rationalized as a shift in the distribution of heavy and light syllables. In Homer, metarrhythmisis implies a change in the direction of the rhythmisis of dactyls and spondees. On the level of the rhythmical words, this has implications for the way words terminate: as blunt (ending on the thesis) or as pendant (ending on the arsis). The choice between the two types of termination seems in part a matter of taste and preferences. Dionysius of Halicarnassus (*On literary composition* 17) describes rhythmical words containing more heavy syllables in more favorable terms than those with more light syllables. Still, he considers the dactylic word type "noble," despite the preponderance of light syllables in the line he cites to illustrate dactylic ῥυθμός (*Odyssey* ix 39, quoted above).[40] Furthermore, Dionysius distinguishes between word end that is masculine (following the foot's thesis) and feminine (following the foot's trochee).[41] Just as heavy syllables are preferred over light ones, so word end in a heavy syllable is considered better than word end in a light syllable. As the localization of metrical word types (O'Neill 1942) and the avoidance of spondaic word end show, word end in a heavy syllable often coincides with word end in a heavy syllable on the thesis in Homer. In the following examples (28–29), word end on the thesis is underlined:

(28) <u>τῶν</u> ἕν' ἀειραμέ<u>νη</u> Ἑκά<u>βη</u> φέρε δῶρον Ἀθήνῃ

Iliad VI 293

Having lifted one of these Hecabe carried it as a gift for Athene

---

[39] Basset 1938:142. Or *Iliad* II 484 ἔσπετε νῦν μοι μοῦσαι Ὀλύμπια δώματ' ἔχουσαι, "Now please list for me, goddesses, in possession of Olympian dwellings." This example, the start of the Catalogue of Ships, is not haphazardly chosen. In his discussion of Dionysius's choice, Ruijgh 1987:322 points at the special value of *Odyssey* ix 39 as the start of Odysseus' autobiography, the first lines of the *Iliad* and the *Odyssey* being unsuitable.

[40] Rossi 1963:42n100; Ruijgh 1987:322.

[41] No specific terminology is being used for word end at the metron dieresis.

(29) Λαοδόκ<u>ῳ</u> Ἀντηνορί<u>δῃ</u> κρατε<u>ρῷ</u> αἰχμητῇ

Iliad IV 87

Laodocus the son of Antenor, a mighty spear fighter

Word end in a heavy syllable on the thesis brings out a different metrical pattern: that of the anapaest. Manuals from antiquity speak of τὰ μέτρα μεταρρυθμίζεσθαι; with regard to pause, the shift is from one metrical pattern (dactyl) to another (anapaest), so that different possibilities for word termination can be exploited.[42] Aristides Quintilianus labels the dactyl ἀνάπαιστος ἀπὸ μείζονος (*a maiore*, cf. the ionicus), and the anapaest ἀνάπαιστος ἀπὸ ἐλάττονος (*a minore*).[43] Basic rhythm remains unaltered as the cola take their beginning and termination from different metrical positions.

Metarrhythmisis in dactylic verse treats rhythmical pause as an aural effect. Preferences concerning the position and quantity of the word-final syllable are phonetic indicators of pause.

1.2.4 Timing mechanism of speech

The fourth treatment of rhythm in ancient Greek pays most attention to the phonetics of pause (Allen 1973, 1987; Devine and Stephens 1994). In their *The Prosody of Greek Speech*, Devine and Stephens explain rhythm as the timing mechanism of speech. They take meter as their cue to reconstruct the phonetics of the language. Meter reflects the mapping of language onto temporal patterns of linguistic origin:

> The position taken in this work is that metrics is a subdivision of rhythmics in the broad sense of that term. Metrics can be viewed as the central segment of a hierarchy. Above metrics in the hierarchy lies the highly abstract rhythmics that is the ontogenetic basis of metre, and below it lies the surface phonetic rhythmics that are generated in the performance of verse. Metrics is assumed to share a common property with rhythmics: the rules of metrics and the rules of rhythmics belong

[42] As described in Dionysius of Halicarnassus *On literary composition* 4/15.3–23.13 (Usener-Radermacher); cf. the comments *ad loc.* in Robert 1910, and Aujac and Lebel 1981; metarrhythmisis is analyzed in Koster 1953:25. The scholia regularly comment on the phenomenon.

[43] Anapaests may be studied as a rhythmical word type too. In the anapaest-example Dionysius gives, he carefully chooses a line with a metrically "pure" appearance (holo-anapaestic), and with an anapaestic initial phonetic word: βαρύ μοι κεφαλῆς ἐπίκρανον ἔχειν (Euripides *Hippolytus* 201), "It is hard for me to wear a hear-net on my head." Ruijgh 1989:311 considers the description in Aristides Quintilianus p. 35.8–12 W-I of the dactyl as *anapaest a maiore* versus the anapaest as *anapaest a minore* as an indication of the longer duration of the thesis compared to that of the arsis.

to one and the same system because they work together towards a single final objective, namely a degree of rhythmic regularity that neither could achieve alone. The relationship of Greek metre to the Greek language is also a topic of considerable disagreement. The view implicit in some modern work is that rhythms of Greek verse are of primarily non-linguistic origin and that versification involves searching through language for phonetic categories that can appropriately be mapped onto these extraneous rhythmic patterns and categories. It is tacitly assumed that while verse has rhythm, language–or at least pitch accented languages – have only intrinsic durations: segments and syllables just have the durations that they have, and those sequences that coincidentally fit the verse pattern are metrical. According to this conception of metre, the durational categories of language do not necessarily correlate with those of verse and are not organized into rhythmical patterns at all (or, if they are, it is into rhythms different from and unrelated in any direct way to the rhythms of verse). This view is not well supported by evidence from other languages.[44]

In accordance with the assumption that the properties of Greek conform to the expectations of general linguistics and psychology, Devine and Stephens quote Sapir[45] when they state that "the position taken in this work is that verse is 'merely the language itself, running in its natural grooves.'" They further assume that "the rhythms of Greek verse are simply more highly constrained versions of rhythms already existing in Greek speech." The rhythm of Greek speech is then analyzed (p. 101) as a temporal pattern comparable to stress feet:

Whatever the importance of literary convention, in principle Greek verse rhythm is born of the rhythm of Greek speech, and the former is consequently a valuable source of information about the latter. Just as an analysis of the distribution of words like *Tennessee* in English verse will show that in English speech they have primary stress on their final syllable or, under certain conditions, on their initial syllable but never on their medial syllable, so, for instance, a study of the distribution of fourth paeon-shaped words in the trimeter will indicate which rhythmic organizations of that word shape were possible in Greek speech and which were not, and which were usual at a certain speech

---

[44] Devine and Stephens 1994:100–101.
[45] Sapir, E. 1921. *Language: An Introduction to the Study of Speech*. New York.

rate and which less so. Finally, it is our position that however abstract the phonological terms in which metrical rules are stated and interpreted, most metrical rules reflect some form of measurable acoustic correlate at some rate of (prose) speech, not excluding artificially slow rates and styles. Whereas metrical rules can, and often do, abstract away from physically existing distinctions, it is reasonable to ask for empirical confirmation of the converse assumption, namely that some nonconventionalized metrical rules reflect a distinction that has no measurable surface correlate in any type of speech. The extent to which this position can be defended depends critically on the appropriate formulation of metrical rules.

In poetry, the submoraic adjustment of *prima facie* mora count is more restricted than in non-metrical speech: compared to non-metrical speech, the possible realizations for what Lidov 1989 (see §1.1.1) calls the changeable position of the foot, better known as the arsis, are restricted in Homer. The distribution of syllable structures over the verse also shows that towards the verse end less heavy syllables are used.[46] Devine and Stephens argue that all words come into the mind with syllable weights, and that speech has a number of mechanisms for submoraic modification in order to fit the different weights to the patterning that implies a binary opposition based on quantitative temporal contrast. Submoraic modification adjusts the actual performance duration of syllables if the weight-contrast does not automatically provide the necessary durational contrast. Devine and Stephens list a number of studies on different languages all providing empirical evidence for audibly noticeable modification of submoraic duration. They stress the need for an empirical answer to the question to what extent differences in syllable duration are systematically relevant for the rules of Greek meter, as "there is no reason to believe that poets are not consciously or intuitively aware of such differences and able to exploit them":[47]

> Greek verse is sensitive not only to the intrinsic weight or mora count of a syllable but also to its syllabic context. The distribution of heavy and light syllables in the metres of Greek verse cannot be accounted for without the additional principle that syllables are systematically different according to the position they occupy in the various word shapes in which they are embedded. Greek verse does not treat the syllables of Greek words as sequences of monomoraic and bimoraic

---

[46] Devine and Stephens 1994:401–402.
[47] Devine and Stephens 1994:49–52, citation from p. 50.

units following one another according to an equipollent mora or syllable timing scheme within the domain of the word; rather, there must be some sort of temporal organization below the level of the word domain that is reflected in the metre.[48]

Devine and Stephens follow Dionysius of Halicarnassus when he explicitly recognizes the systematic metrical relevance of the two categories of syllable weight and the phonetic reality of multiple durations arising from the differences between syllables in the way they are structured, and from the position the syllables occupy in the various word shapes. Devine and Stephens list the scholars who have sought to compute syllable weight like Aristides Quintilianus did, and those who explained restrictions, such as bridges, as due to submoraic differences. Following Wifstrand 1933, Devine and Stephens emphasize the nonresolution of the *longum* in the hexameter. Differences in submoraic duration led Ruijgh 1987 to the identification of six different syllable quantities, West 1970 to seven different quantities, and others even up to twenty. Without fixing the exact number of syllable quantities, Devine and Stephens note that:

> it was either explicitly claimed or implicit in their assumptions that the segmentally longer types of heavy syllable are preferred in the biceps and the shorter types in anceps, while the longer types of light syllable are preferred in resolutions and the longer type of anceps. It would follow that metrical distribution could be exploited as a valuable source of evidence not merely for moraic but also for submoraic and segmental duration in Greek.

I fall in with Devine and Stephens when they claim that, not unlike the practice in other natural languages, the syllables of ancient Greek have a wide range of quantities, that are categorized into a binary division *heavy-light* in rhythm, and *longum-breve* in meter. Quantity in meter is a rationalization of syllable structures representing more or less sonority. Syllables are "adjusted" (lengthened or shortened, elided or assimilated) within the limits of the two rhythmical categories (*heavy* and *light*) in order to be compatible with their position within the timing mechanism of speech. In the case of poetry the compatibility of syllables also serves the compatibility of metrical feet in an ongoing rhythmic regularity.[49]

---

[48] Devine and Stephens 1994:156.
[49] Arvaniti 2009; Rathcke and Smith 2015.

1.2.5 From pause in prosody to pause in performance

The ubiquitous compositional pauses in meter and rhythm frame the metrical phrase and the rhythmical phrase respectively. The identification of metrical and rhythmical phrase boundaries as pauses in prosody and rhythm depends on the identification of metrical and rhythmical phrases. The rhythmical pause at verse end is generally accepted, but within the line, metrical and rhythmical pauses are identified on various grounds. Sometimes syntactical considerations come in. Metrical pauses within the line are arbitrarily considered pauses in performance, often for other than prosodic reasons. Phonetic considerations concerning the possibility of metrical and rhythmical pause appear in the analysis of rhythm as rhythmical word type recurrence and language's timing mechanism.

The submoraic adjustment of *prima facie* mora count, and its restrictions, are my fundament for the reconstruction of the phonetics of pause. I will show that it is possible to derive from the rules of metrics and rhythmics some clues for the identification of possible performative pauses, next to the compositional pauses of the metrical surface structure and the rhythmic regularity. If the premises are accepted that (I) rhythm is the regulating timing mechanism of speech, and that (II) metrical speech is just like natural unplanned speech only more so,[50] submoraic adjustment can be studied by means of phonology, the metrical surface structure. Up to this point, Devine and Stephens' approach to rhythm and pause in rhythmics has developed into an approach determined by phonology. Chapter 3 further investigates the consequences of submoraic adjustment for the pause in phonology and phonetics.

[50] There is a danger of circularity here: Devine and Stephens assume, on the basis of cross linguistic evidence, that Greek speech rhythm is comparable to rhythm in other quantitative languages, and that Greek metrical rhythm does not differ in principle from the rhythm of natural unplanned speech. Then they reconstruct the rhythm of Greek speech on the basis of the metrical evidence.

2

Pause in Syntax and Sense

*Technical terms followed by * on their first occurrence in this chapter are in the glossary.*

2.0   Introduction

The subject of Chapter 2 is the compositional pause* in syntax. Syntactical pause is commonly treated as a pause suggested by common sense: the semantics of the utterance are determined upon completion of syntactical requirements—and so is pause. Printed punctuation in modern editions is in accordance with such commonsensical pause. The study of Homeric syntax treats pause as a compositional feature, which underlies and reflects the composer's juxtapositional adding of formula and single words. Where this compositional pause coincides with metrical boundaries like the main caesura* or the verse end, West 1982 speaks of sense-pause. When the verse end seemingly disrupts ongoing syntactical development, the line is enjambed (Parry 1929; Kirk 1966; Bakker 1990; Higbie 1990; Clark 1997; Edwards 2002). Both notions, sense-pause and enjambment*, rely on implicit assumptions concerning pause in performance*. Studies on Homeric discourse, like Chantraine 1953 and Bakker 1997b/2005, differ in their understanding of the compositional pause in syntax, as it may demarcate single words, word groups, constituents, phrases, clauses, and utterances depending on the approach to discourse.

There is no denying the compositional pause in syntax: syntactic unities start and end, and their completion may well be considered a compositional, pausal feature. Identification of the pause in syntax as a performative feature causes problems: like the metrical pauses in Chapter 1, pauses in syntax are ubiquitous—they cannot all be realized as rest in performance. In this chapter, I will show that the identification of the compositional pause in syntax as a pause in performance has incited arbitrariness in the treatment of pause as an audible phenomenon, as has the identification of the pause in sense. Without denying the possibility of a pause in syntax doubling as a performative pause, I will conclude this chapter with the advice to my reader to continue reading, as Chapters 3–5 will explore the phonetic conditions that allow compositional pauses to double as audible rest of some duration in performance.

2.1   Pause in Loose Syntax

Analysis of Homeric discourse is based on the concept of the paratactic juxta-positioning of words, word groups, and formulaic expressions, that occupy smaller or larger portions of the verse. The concept of paratactic juxtaposition lays great weight on compositional pauses: their occurrence makes juxtaposition possible. Compositional pauses occur at fixed positions within the line and between lines: composition is the art of creating syntactical wholes through adding phrases that fill the metrical space between two frequently recurring compositional pauses. As the words, word groups, or constituents that occupy the metrical phrase between compositional pauses vary amongst each other in syntax and semantics, so the compositional pauses separating the phrases have different values: a pause between two word groups within a single clause has a different syntactical and semantic contribution than a pause separating two clauses.

Within the verse, Homeric discourse seems to feature various compositional units: single words, word groups, constituents, phrases, clauses, and utterances. The variety of discourse units is the result of varying levels of syntactical organization, as well as of varying sizes of metrical cola. In many verses, the Homeric epic features a syntax that seems to reflect a high level of grammatical segmentation. Chantraine (1953:12–21, 351–364) describes Homeric syntax as characterized by apposition* and autonomy. Apposition, because Homer's utterance seems to take shape through constant adding: adding of subjects, attributes, epithets, and whole clauses. In his analysis of Homeric syntax, Chantraine (1953:351) uses the description "construction appositionelle":

> Un des traits qui commandent les procédés de la syntaxe homérique est la construction appositionelle ... Selon une structure héritée de l'indo-européen, chaque mot portrait en lui-même la marque du rôle qu'il jouait et les mots conservaient ainsi une grande autonomie. ... L'ordre des mots est libre et les termes de la proposition sont définis par des *appositions* qui se présentent sous des formes diverses et autonomes. ... L'autonomie de chaque terme a pour conséquence que l'aède peut, à l'occasion, perdre de vue le mot auquel il se réfère, d'où des libertés dans les règles d'accord, d' où aussi l'intervention de groupes de mots qui ne se rattachent pas strictement à ce qui précède ou à ce qui suit.

This appositional character of Homeric syntax is evident from the paratactic organization of the discourse. Devine and Stephens (2000:142) consider the "rather flat, as opposed to hierarchical, phrase structure" of the Homeric epic as illustrative for the nonconfigurationality* of ancient Greek, the fact that there is hardly any hierarchical phrase structure. Characteristics of nonconfigurationality[1] can be found everywhere in the *Iliad* and the *Odyssey*. The following contains eight of these characteristics, each illustrated with one or more examples from the Homeric epic:

1.   (Grammatically) free word order:

    (30) <u>τὸν</u> δ' αὖτ' ὀτρηρὴ ταμίη <u>πρὸς</u> μῦθον <u>ἔειπεν</u>

Iliad VI 381

    Then <u>to him</u> the bustling housekeeper <u>spoke</u> the following word:

2.   Pronouns that are implied in the verb:[2]

    (31) πολλὰς δ' ἰφθίμους ψυχὰς Ἄιδι <u>προΐαψεν</u>

Iliad I 3

    And many excellent souls <u>(he/she/it) sent forth</u> into Hades

3.   Dislocation of constituents and their replacement by clitic pronouns:

    (32) αὐτίκα δ' Ἠὼς ἦλθεν ἐΰθρονος ἥ <u>μιν</u> ἔγειρε
    <u>Ναυσικάαν εὔπεπλον</u>

Odyssey vi 48–49

    Immediately came Dawn on her beautiful throne, who woke <u>her,</u> | <u>well-dressed Nausicaa</u>

4.   Failure of agreement:[3]

    (33) ὣς φάτο <u>τῆς</u> δ' αὐτοῦ λύτο γούνατα καὶ φίλον ἦτορ
    σήματ' <u>ἀναγνούσῃ</u> τά οἱ ἔμπεδα πέφραδ' Ὀδυσσεύς

Odyssey xxiii 205–206

    Thus he spoke, and <u>her</u> knees gave way on the spot, as well as her heart | <u>as she had recognized</u> the signs which Odysseus had incontrovertibly listed for her

---

[1]   Devine and Stephens 2000:142–148. Nonconfigurationality points at Indo-European origin (Chantraine 1953:12; cf. Matthews 1981), but is not a sign of primitivism; cf. Bakker 1997b:284.
[2]   Also known as pro-drop. The dropped pronouns ("null anaphora") are partly suggested by the endings of verb forms (so-called "inflectional affixes").
[3]   Cf. Chantraine 1953:322. Some MSS read ἀναγνούσης in 206.

5. Restricted use of prepositional phrases. In Homer, the apposition* is regularly better analyzed as an adverb,[4] or as a morphological prefix to verb or adjective (examples 34–36):

> (34) <u>ἀμφὶ</u> δὲ χαῖται
> ὤμοις ἀίσσονται
>
> *Iliad* VI 509–510

<u>On both sides</u> his manes | spring out on the shoulders

> (35) σόον δ' ἀνένευσε μάχης <u>ἐξαπ</u>ονέεσθαι
>
> *Iliad* XVI 252

But he did not allow [him] to come <u>back</u> safe from the battle

> (36) μένεος δὲ μέγα φρένες <u>ἀμφιμέλαιναι</u>
> πίμπλαντ'
>
> *Odyssey* iv 661–662

And full of rage his heart, black <u>on both sides,</u> | became

6. Lack of definite article. In Homer, the definite article has "embryonic status":[5] when applied, it rather functions as demonstrative.[6]

> (37) οὕνεκα <u>τὸν</u> Χρύσην ἠτίμασεν ἀρητῆρα
>
> *Iliad* I 11

Since he had dishonored <u>that</u> [man], Chryses, his priest

7. Comitative adposition instead of noun phrase coordination. Nouns can be coordinated to be the subject of a verbal form, together: "A and B walked to school":

> (38) Βοιωτῶν μὲν Πηνέλεως καὶ Λήιτος ἦρχον
>
> *Iliad* II 494

Peneleus and Leitus commanded the Boeotians

In Homer, such noun phrase coordination has an alternative in comitative adposition: "A walked to school, and so did B" (example 39) / "A walked to school, and B with him" (example 40) / "A walked to school, ánd B" (example 41):

---

[4] Cf. Horrocks 1981.
[5] Devine and Stephens 2000:146.
[6] Chantraine 1953:162–168, but cf. Kirk 1985:54 on the use of the article in *Iliad* I 11.

(39) Βοιωτῶν μὲν Πηνέλεως καὶ Λήιτος ἦρχον
      Ἀρκεσίλαός τε Προθοήνωρ τε Κλονίος τε

Iliad II 494–495

Peneleus and Leitus commanded the Boeotians | and so did Arce-silaus, Prothoenor, and Clonius

(40) ἦλθ’ ὁ γέρων Δολίος σὺν δ’ υἱεῖς τοῖο γέροντος

Odyssey xxiv 387

The old man Dolius came, and with him the sons of that old man

(41) τῶν ἦρχ’ Ἀσκάλαφος καὶ Ἰάλμενος, υἷες Ἄρηος

Iliad II 512

Ascalaphus commanded them, ánd Ialmenus, sons of Ares

8. Parataxis. In Homer, parataxis is most remarkable in instances of gram-matical prolepsis, when a constituent is put first, separated from its clause by an intervening clause. Thus the constituent is "externalized," isolated from the clause in which it had an important, but unmarked semantic function:

(42) Τυδείδην δ’ οὐκ ἂν γνοίης ποτέροισι μετείη
      ἠὲ μετὰ Τρώεσσιν ὁμιλέοι ἦ μετ’ Ἀχαιοῖς

Iliad V 85–86

As for the son of Tydeus: you could not have discovered among which of the two parties he was: | whether he fought amidst the Trojans or the Greeks

The syntax of the Homeric epic is quite different from the syntax found in post-Homeric literary works. As opposed to the syntax of either poetry (for example, Hellenistic poetry) or prose (for example, Plato), Homeric syntax is rather flat and paratactic.[7] It consists of highly autonomous words, word groups, and clauses. The autonomy on these various levels is represented by the description of Homeric style as *adding* style: adding more words, word groups, and clauses is almost always possible, but the additions themselves are hardly ever necessary for proper understanding. Single words define their own role in the discourse,[8] and grammatical governance is not the standard. When put on a par with metrical pauses, compositional pauses in syntax reflect the

---

[7] Chantraine 1953:351–364; Notopoulos 1949; Bakker 1997b; Devine and Stephens 2000:142.
[8] Bakker 1997b.

additive style and the autonomy of the words and word groups. At the same time, the persistent recurrence of compositional pauses in syntax strengthens the notion of additive style when compositional syntactical pauses are understood as pauses in performance. The verse end is the best example, but all other metrical pauses equally qualify; a compositional pause like the verse end is judged as a syntactical pause, and syntactical pauses are considered pauses in performance (Parry 1929; Daitz 1991). I argue, however, that such considerations are arbitrary: one compositional pause doubles as pause in performance, and the next may not.

As discussed in §1.1, various studies concerned with colometry* assume syntactically coherent units between all the compositional pauses of meter. Fränkel 1926, Porter 1951, Kirk 1966, and Ingalls 1970/1972 discuss the coincidence of metrical boundaries and indicators of sense-structure or, alternatively, of cognitive structure. The question appears to be: what came first? Syntax or metrical cola? I appreciate the discussion, as it highlights the relevance of compositional pauses, but this approach does not provide any clue for the identification of performative pause. Such clues are, however, suggested by the approach that has been given new life by the study of Homeric discourse as spoken language: the appositional juxtaposition of metrical cola resembles the natural chunking of speech.

2.2   Pause in Special Speech

The analysis of the syntactical structure of the *Iliad* and the *Odyssey* is based on the implicit assumption that the syntactical structure of classical Greek prose may serve as the starting point. In recent years, more objections have been made against this comparison of the Homeric epic with the syntax of classical Greek. Starting from Chantraine's work in the field of Homeric syntax, Bakker, in a series of publications (Bakker 1990, 1997a, 1997b, 1999, 2005), discusses a large number of syntactical and stylistic issues in Homer, like enjambment, discourse markers, and the sentence.

For Bakker, the starting-point of the study of Homeric syntax is the study of Homeric discourse as *speech*, or *spoken language*. With spoken language, Bakker refers to the *medium aspect* of language, as distinct from the *conceptional aspect*: language is about linguistics (the conceptional aspect) *and* communication (the medium aspect). He agrees with linguists like Halliday and Hassan 1976 and Chafe 1994, who, in the words of Oesterreicher 1997:

> use—more or less systematically—the terms spoken versus written
> to mark the medium-opposition, and terms like oral versus literate,

> informal versus formal, or unplanned versus planned to denote aspects
> of the linguistic conception. ... The necessity of making a distinction
> between medium and conception becomes evident when scholars play
> with the ambiguity of the generic terms oral and literate.[9]

The conceptional aspects of orality can be illustrated by marking the differences with the conventions of written discourse. Doing so for Homer's *Iliad* and *Odyssey* would suggest that both epics were composed in an environment in which there were written texts as well as oral compositions. Since it is not probable that this is the case, there is no opposition between Homer's "oral style" and contemporary written literature.[10]

Parry, whose work[11] made the concept of Homer as oral poetry widely acceptable, focused on the compositional aspects of the formula as oral poetry's building block.[12] His observations have nourished the persisting notion of "primitive parataxis"[13] as a description of Homeric syntax, but Parry already showed that the formula is not the product of naivety.[14] Still, for Parry the conventions of written literature were the touchstone to judge the syntax of the Homeric epics. Bakker, on the other hand, stresses the receptional aspects of the language of the *Iliad* and the *Odyssey*. As he analyzes Homeric discourse as *spoken* language (speech), he applies the findings of general discourse analysis, as presented by, among others Chafe 1994, to the *Iliad* and the *Odyssey*.

In the analysis of Chafe, spoken language is the verbalization of consciousness. The cognitive terminology "consciousness" is defined as *focus on a little piece of what the brain knows in relation to the egocentric model of the environment.*[15] This focus changes constantly, and rapidly. In time, consciousness is a mental process consisting of a *flow of foci of consciousness.* Spoken language reflects the speaker's mental processes and, inevitably, the constraints of consciousness. Most important of these constraints is the *one new idea constraint.*[16] This cognitive constraint limits the size and the span of verbalization to the single focus of consciousness. The resulting "one-idea-unit" is "most typically characterized

---

[9] Oesterreicher 1997:191–192; cf. Bakker 2005:38–42.
[10] Bakker 2005:43: "in such a society poets may well exist, but in the absence of literate poets they cannot be oral poets."
[11] Gathered and republished in Parry 1971, after Lord 1960 furthered the study of oral poetry.
[12] Cf. discussion in Bakker 2005:44–46.
[13] Thalmann 1984:4–6.
[14] Cf. his remarks in Parry 1971:22–23.
[15] Chafe 1994:28.
[16] Chafe 1987:1; 1994:108.

prosodically," according to Chafe.[17] Based on physically realized properties of the unit like rhythm* and intonation, Chafe coins it *intonation unit.*

In Chafe's view, intonation units consist of four to five words,[18] and their beginning and end are marked by intonation boundaries. The intonation boundary may or may not coincide with exhalation and inhalation.[19] In verbalizations of foci of consciousness in spoken language, the intonation units appear as the *spurts* that, as shown by the study of the phenomenon in modern spoken languages, characterize unplanned speech.[20] Spoken discourse is a process with a very communicative purpose. Characteristic for unplanned speech on the *conceptional* level, however, is that its syntax not so much *organizes,* but *"reflects the speaker's mental processes."*[21] As these processes are equivalent to shifts in focus of consciousness, spoken language is "chunked," both from the receptional (audible "spurts") and the conceptional point of view (lack of larger scale syntactical organization). The syntactical structure of spoken language often resembles, at least partly, a "checklist."[22]

In applying the findings from linguistic research such as Chafe's to the *Iliad* and the *Odyssey,* Bakker shows that the Homeric epics have much in common with unplanned spoken language chunked into intonation units by discourse analysis. As an example, he presents *Iliad* I 1–7 (example 10 in the Introduction) as chunked text (Bakker 1997b:291–292):

---

[17] Chafe 1994:56.

[18] Bakker 2005:48 fixes the size of the intonation unit at 4 to 7 words; cf. Goldstein 2014.

[19] The notion of intonation raises questions concerning larger scale syntactical organization. Is intonation the key to sentence structure? Bakker's description of *Iliad* 1.1–7 as "a series of island-like ideas" underlines his doubts concerning the usefulness of the terminology sentence for the description of Homeric syntax. In an earlier article (Bakker 1990:3, cf. the remarks concerning the sentence in Chafe 1994:139–144), he links sentence to intonation patterns: "one of the consequences of ... related research in conversation analysis is that the concept of 'sentence' loses much of its importance when we are dealing with ongoing language production. When what we call the typical sentence-final falling intonation can occur at the end of any idea (intonation) unit, even when the syntax has not been brought to completion, it is not so clear anymore what a sentence is. ... Instead of being related to the productive aspect of texts, sentences may be seen as the result of a speaker's decisions as to the *presentation* of a narrative; they are thus a matter of rhetoric, of style, rather than of the cognitive activation of idea units in the speaker's mind." The concept of sentence seems hardly fit to describe the way in which the Homeric discourse is organized internally. Comparative studies have shown that the principles guiding the additive style of verse-making in Homer are similar to those underlying oral poetry from other centuries and cultures. Like these other products of poetry, the *Iliad* and the *Odyssey* present their narrative to the listening audience in a *chain-of-thought-style.* This style, which resembles a checklist, is the result of the chunking of information, as described below.

[20] Examples in Chafe 1994 and Bakker 1997b.

[21] Bakker 1997b:290.

[22] Bakker 1997a:100–121.

(10)

a	μῆνιν ἄειδε θεά
b	Πηληιάδεω Ἀχιλῆος
c	οὐλομένην
d	ἣ μυρί᾽ Ἀχαιοῖς ἄλγε᾽ ἔθηκε
e	πολλὰς δ᾽ ἰφθίμους ψυχὰς
f	Ἄιδι προιαψεν
g	ἡρώων
h	αὐτοὺς δὲ ἑλώρια τεῦχε κύνεσσιν
i	οἰωνοῖσί τε πᾶσι
j	Διὸς δ᾽ ἐτελείετο βουλή
k	ἐξ οὗ δὴ τὰ πρῶτα
l	διαστήτην ἐρίσαντε
m	Ἀτρείδης τε ἄναξ ἀνδρῶν
n	καὶ δῖος Ἀχιλλεύς

Iliad I 1–7

a	Sing, Goddess, of the wrath
b	Of Achilles, son of Peleus
c	So destructive
d	It bestowed innumerable pains on the Greeks
e	Many excellent souls
f	It sent to the house of Hades
g	Of heroes
h	But their bodies it turned into loot for the dogs
i	And all birds
j	The will of Zeus gradually became fulfilled
k	From the very first moment
l	The two of them stood opposite one another in anger
m	Atreus's son, the lord of men
n	And godlike Achilles

In Bakker's analysis, the text of the first seven lines of the *Iliad* is chunked "with the units into which the passage easily divides."[23] The resulting units correspond to Chafe's intonation units according to the *one new idea constraint*. The syntax of *Iliad* I 1–7 corresponds to the audible structure of the spurts: it resembles

---

[23] Bakker 1997b:292.

a checklist, in this case a "preview." Bakker calls *Iliad* I 1–7 "a series of island-like ideas,"[24] with "orientation" as main purpose. The checklist-structure can be found in many verses in the *Iliad* and the *Odyssey*, often in the shape [A — verbal form — B || addition to A || addition to B]. The apparent checklist-structure is further strengthened by the autonomous usage of words and word groups: words define their own role in discourse independent of "governance" by other words; intonation units can often be considered elliptic clauses.[25] Autonomy of words and word groups results in appositional style—as can be expected in unplanned spoken language. Bakker asserts, however, that the discourse of the *Iliad* and the *Odyssey* cannot be fully put on a par with spoken language in general. The use of formulas and the restrictions due to meter turn the spoken language of the *Iliad* and the *Odyssey* into "special speech" or "marked speech."[26] The intonation units that Bakker identifies are practically identical to the metrical cola that Fraenkel identified as the structural units of the hexameter. Bakker thus puts the structural unit of meter on a par with the compositional unit of discourse. The metrical shape of the Homeric epic is to be considered as a presentation of intonation units, albeit a stylized presentation.[27]

Bakker points out[28] that the localization of the chunks of information fits the metrical patterns of cola between positions of frequently occurring word end.[29] In his view, there is a correspondence between the cognitive restraints on the intonation unit, and the size of phrases. In poetry, stylization regularizes the phrases, the metrical cola of the single hexameter:

> The segmentation of Homeric discourse, as evidenced by the length of the linguistic units of which it consists, can be seen as the manifestations in speech of the flow of the speaker's consciousness, each unit being the verbalization of a focus of consciousness. The length and duration of the units fits the acoustic short-term memory of the performer, or in other words, that ability to process linguistic expressions as wholes.[30]

---

[24] Bakker 1997b:292.

[25] Bakker 1997a:54–122; 2005:50.

[26] Bakker 1997b:300–303.

[27] Bakker 2005:48: "The intonational and prosodic properties of the unit can be *stylized* into *metrical* properties. The intonation units of ordinary speech become the metrical units of special, poetic speech"; see, further, Bakker 2005:68; 1997a:146–155. Goldstein 2014:253 equates the intonational phrase to the clause in syntax; cf. Nespor and Vogel 1986; Cruttenden 1997:68–73; Gussenhoven 2004:22–23; Gussenhoven and Jacobs 2011:155–156; Blankenborg 2016:74–77.

[28] Bakker 1997b:302; cf. Edwards 2002:9–13.

[29] Bakker 2005:68.

[30] Bakker 1997a:57.

That is why the units that Bakker mentions are "stylized into metrical pro‐perties."[31] The syntactical "segmentation" of the Homeric discourse can hence be clearly felt. The units that are strung together to represent Homeric syntax are still recognizable as individual intonation units; their shape responds to frequently used metrical patterns.[32] The stylization of intonation units into metrical properties visualizes Homeric discourse as the equivalent of metrical colometry. An example can be found in *Odyssey* xvi 181–191 (example 43):

(43)

ἀλλοῖός μοι ξεῖνε	φάνης νέον	ἠὲ πάροιθεν
ἄλλα δὲ εἵματ' ἔχεις		καί τοι χρὼς οὐκέθ' ὁμοῖος
ἦ μάλα τις θεός ἐσσι		τοὶ οὐρανὸν εὐρὺν ἔχουσιν
ἀλλ' ἵληθ'		ἵνα τοι κεχαρισμένα δώομεν ἱρὰ
ἠδὲ χρύσεα δῶρα	τετυγμένα	φείδεο δ' ἡμέων
τὸν δ' ἡμείβετ' ἔπειτα	πολύτλας	δῖος Ὀδυσσεύς
οὔ τίς τοι θεός εἰμι		τί μ' ἀθανάτοισιν ἐΐσκεις
ἀλλὰ πατὴρ τεός εἰμι		τοῦ εἵνεκα σὺ στεναχίζων
πάσχεις ἄλγεα πολλά		βίας ὑποδέγμενος ἀνδρῶν
ὣς ἄρα φωνήσας	υἱὸν κύσε	κὰδ δὲ παρειῶν
δάκρυον ἧκε χαμᾶζε		πάρος δ' ἔχε νωλεμὲς αἰεί

Odyssey xvi 181–191

As a totally different man to me, stranger, you appeared just now, compared to before: | you have different clothes, and your skin is not the same anymore; | you are a god for sure, who hold the wide heaven; | please come to our aid, that we may present you with pleasing offerings, | and golden gifts, carefully made; please, spare us! | And he replied to him then, much-enduring, godlike Odysseus: | I am not at all a god: why do you compare me to the immortals? | No, I am your father, because of whom you moan, | and suffer numerous pains, weighed down by men's cruel treatment. | Having spoken thus, he embraced his son, and down from his cheeks | he shed tears to the ground; until this moment he constantly held them back

Like Porter 1951 and Ingalls 1970, Bakker accepts the premise that any smaller scale phrase within the hexameter must be characterized prosodically. He does not state, however, that the prosodic characterization of the metrical colon or

---

[31] Bakker 2005:48; cf. 1997a:146–155.
[32] Cf. the division of *Odyssey* xix 445b–454 in half-verses in Bakker 2005:69.

intonation unit provides any clue for the identification of performative pause. Bakker's approach, starting from prosodically characterized discourse units, in my view does not differ from other approaches that do not account for the phonetics of pause. The demarcations of Bakker's intonation units, ubiquitous like other compositional pauses, are syntactical pauses, too numerous to be realized as pauses in performance. Performative pause may well coincide with the demarcation of an intonation unit, but we need phonological criteria to determine where.

2.3   Pause in Syntactical Movement

Nonconfigurational syntax (§2.1) and special speech (§2.2) both consider pause as a compositional feature. The characteristics of pause are referred to as prosodic, but no clue is offered as to when and where pauses are realized in performance. Both approaches to Homeric discourse postulate that compositional pauses are very frequent since the compositional units of Homeric discourse are small in size and all demarcated by compositional pauses. In the identification of larger scale grammatical structure or syntactical development (involving two or more metrical cola), the compositional pause in syntax as a performative feature is neglected, with the exception of the pause at verse end and, when used as a sense-pause, the main caesura.

The requirements of grammar are secondary to the existence of the linguistic units: Bakker 2005:21 states that grammar "emerges as a response to a recurring task." What is this recurring task? Bakker argues that metrical unities consist of a nucleus* and one or more fillers*. Fillers are (1) context neutral, (2) metrical variable, and (3) interchangeable.[33] Fillers facilitate the nucleus of a metrical unity to extend towards a metrical boundary, a position of frequent word end like the caesurae following position 3, 5, 7, or 9, or the dieresis following position 8 or 12. The result is some level of grammatical governance. Between metrical boundaries within the verse or even the hemistich, metrical fillers allow the semantically more important constituents, often the verb, to occupy the position their metrical shape restricts them to.[34] Bakker[35] demonstrates this compositional principle by means of the well-known smaller scale narrative pattern "A kills B" in the *Iliad*. Such a pattern requires a killer, a

---

[33]   Bakker 1993:15–25; 2005:5–6.

[34]   Bakker and Fabricotti 1991 use the terminology nucleus to indicate the semantically required constituents of the smaller scale units between metrical boundaries. Bakker 2005:11 focuses on fillers as extensions of the <u>verb</u> towards the nearest metrical boundary.

[35]   Bakker and Fabricotti 1991; Bakker 2005:1–21.

victim, and a verb expressing the action of the killing (fillers are underlined in example 44):

(44) Ἀστύαλον δ' ἄρ' ἔπεφνε <u>μενεπτόλεμος</u> Πολυποίτης
Πιδύτην δ' Ὀδυσεὺς <u>Περκώσιον</u> ἐξενάριξεν
<u>ἔγχει χαλκείῳ</u> Τεῦκρος δ' Ἀρετάονα <u>δῖον</u>
Ἀντίλοχος δ' Ἄβληρον ἐνήρατο <u>δουρὶ φαεινῷ</u>
<u>Νεστορίδης</u> Ἔλατον δὲ <u>ἄναξ ἀνδρῶν</u> Ἀγαμέμνων

Iliad VI 29–33

So <u>warlike</u> Polypoetes killed Astyalus, | and Odysseus finished off Pidytus <u>from Perkote</u> | <u>with his bronze spear</u>, as did Teucer <u>the shining</u> Aretaon, | and Antilochus slew Ablerus <u>with his shining spear</u>, | <u>son of Nestor</u>, as did Agamemnon, <u>lord of men</u>, Elatus

All verses in the cluster *Iliad* VI 29–33 contain metrical fillers like the weapon, an epithet, or a patronymic/toponymic. The filler expressing the weapon itself contains another filler: the epithet χαλκείῳ / φαεινῷ.

Discussing particles and discourse markers,[36] Bakker shows that on a larger scale Homeric syntax is a *movement* that demands the audience's attention for what is to follow, with only little regard for what has already been said. I infer that the periodic sentence of written discourse regularly requires the addressee to interpret, or even re-interpret, the subordinate clause upon engaging the subsequent main clause. In spoken discourse, on the other hand, intonation units reflect the speaker's mental processes. The emerging grammar does not necessarily organize the units according to a logical or hierarchical principle. To illustrate movement of discourse in Homer, Bakker[37] presents two types of *discourse-relations*. On the one hand, there are *additions* (genitive attributives, participles used as adjectives, nominatives as appositions), on the other, *continuations* (connective δέ, *additives*). The various discourse-relations keep the narrative going: they facilitate continuation. Bakker consistently translates the Homeric text while maintaining his division in intonation units.[38]

Grammar emerges from the combination of intonation units or *chunks* into larger wholes.[39] Together, a series of chunks may result in a clause that meets certain grammatical requirements, for example, the use of a verb. The chunks themselves, especially those *without* a verbal form, are either *preparatory* or *additive* to preceding and subsequent clauses. As grammar emerges from the

---

[36] Bakker 1997a:54–71.
[37] Bakker 1997a:54–71; 1997b:292–295.
[38] Cf. the remarks on Bakker's way of translating Homer in Edwards 2002:9–13.
[39] Bakker 2005:21; cf. Blankenborg 2018.

alignment of intonation units, so the appositional alignment itself emerges from the *movement* of Homeric discourse. The movement has a preference for extension of semantically important constituents, like the verb, towards the nearest verse end, so that larger grammatical wholes do not cross the verse end metrical boundary. According to Bakker, unities crossing the verse end are only allowed at "emotional" moments in the narrative: reducing verse-internal word boundaries to (*my* terminology) compositional pauses (Fränkel 1926 considered them all sense-pauses), Bakker follows West (1982:36) in maintaining the verse end as the most important sense-pause. He does not comment on the realization of the sense-pause in the performance of emotionally more demanding passages of the *Iliad* and the *Odyssey*. I do not agree with Bakker here: there are more unities crossing the verse end than merely the emotionally more demanding passages, and in each instance the value of the compositional verse-end metrical pause as a pause in performance ought to be evaluated. In order to do so we will need to take phonological criteria into consideration.

2.4   Pause in Out-of-Line Composition

Studies on enjambment do comment on the verse-end sense-pause in performance, as they sometimes take an alternative view on the verse-end compositional pause: postulating the verse end compositional pause as a performative feature *for poetic effect*, they do not focus so much on the effect of compositional pause on syntax, but rather on the effect of syntax on the verse-end pause. Where the approach of Bakker (1990 and 1997b) considers out-of-line composition as a deviant treatment of the verse-end compositional pause (as do, most of the time, enjambment studies, such as Parry 1929; Kirk 1966; Higbie 1990; and Clark 1997), Edwards (2002) sometimes takes his starting point from the concept of the verse end as a performative pause. In Chapter 6, I argue that without a set of criteria to identify verse end as a performative feature, any approach to sense-pauses on the assumption of verse end as a performative feature leads to arbitrariness in the identification of special poetic effect at verse end. In this section I will show that the assumption that verse end is a performative feature leads to a debatable concept of the verse end as a pause in syntax: the verse-end syntactical pause in out-of-line composition has been described as a perceptible break in clause and sentence composition and judged in accordance with the syntactical disruption the verse end compositional pause causes. My overview of the study of enjambment and the examples in this section will show that the syntactical approach to verse-end pause results in the notion of a hiccup in out-of-line composition. In my opinion this hiccup does not represent a remarkable feature in performance, as long as the verse-end compositional pause is not established as a performative pause on phonological grounds.

2.4.1 Enjambment

The concept of enjambment in Homer is built on the idea of verse end as the logical termination of a unit. As the performative consequences of termination at verse end are being taken for granted—studies on enjambment focus on the verse as a syntactical unit—the approach of termination at verse end is that of a compositional pause, a position of frequently occurring word end (Parry 1929 [1971]; Kirk 1966; Higbie 1990; Bakker 1990; Edwards 2002) or *pausa**. Frequently occurring word end reflects the structural norms of hexametric poetry (§1.2). These structural norms have been interpreted as the frame for the compositional norms as evidenced by semantic phrasing (Chantraine 1963; Bakker 1997b).

Enjambment is defined as continuation of the utterance over the verse end. Enjambment is the acknowledgement of the disparity of two forms of termination: that of the metrical unit that is the single verse, and of the utterance. For Homerists who assume or expect the termination of the utterance at verse end and the start of a new utterance (through a sentential connector or asyndeton) with the start of a new hexameter, enjambment is a mismatch: the sentence or clause does not end where it is supposed to. Syntactical or grammatical requirements of the sentence or the clause have not been met, or turn out not to have been met, whereas they should, or could, have been at verse end. Runover* words occupy positions that they cannot occupy without consequences: at the start of the hexameter (Kahane 1997), a position reserved for the sentential connector or clause start in asyndeton. The special qualities of the runover word are heightened because of expectation: expectation concerning the fulfilment of syntactical and grammatical requirements that were not met at the preceding verse end. Fulfilment of expectations at verse-initial position results in emphasis; Edwards 2002 speaks of affective prosody* in case of enjambment.

The approach of enjambment as a special phenomenon in the Homeric epic starts with Parry's idea that "the easiest formula for the oral poet to handle is that which is both a whole sentence and a whole verse" and that "the art of the oral poet is largely that of grouping together whole fixed verses."[40] As Clark (1997:23) puts it: "the methods of composing oral poetry can be expected to produce a preponderance of lines consisting of one complete clause apiece."

The whole-line sentence is seen as the basis of oral composition and as the traditional, compositional unit that provides the oral singer with his necessary formulas. More recent enjambment studies agree with this analysis and approach. In their own subsequent approach to enjambment in Homer, they

---

[40]   Reprinted in Parry 1971:389.

follow Parry in considering enjambment at the verse end to be the result of the whole-line formula expanding "beyond the limits of a single hexameter." When discussing enjambed lines with unenjambed doubles, Higbie (1990:76) says:

> chronologically the unenjambed examples preceded the enjambed and were used as models for their creation. ... a certain amount of ability or sophistication is necessary to expand beyond the verse end.

Clark (1997:26) agrees:

> Enjambed lines ... involve the oral poet in compositional difficulties, since they cannot simply be added on, one after another, like whole-line formulas; and the difficulties are only increased when we see that the length of the enjambment can vary from a single syllable to a complete line.

Their acceptance of verse-end enjambment in Homer is based on the premise that at a certain early stage in the development of the *Iliad* and the *Odyssey* as oral narratives, the verse end was the syntactical and performative boundary of choice. It was seldom, or perhaps never, crossed to continue the syntactically coherent unit into the next verse. At that stage, most, if not all, lines were end-stopped and consisted of one single sentence.

Trading the sentence for the *clause*, as Parry suggested and as scholars working on his legacy adopt, widened the scope. Understanding "whole-line formula" to mean both whole-line sentence and whole-line clause, increases the total number of whole-line formulas considerably: Parry (1971:254) claims that "nearly one half of the verses finish where the sentence ends." Parry (1971:376–390) already uses whole-line clauses as examples of whole-line formulas:[41]

---

[41] Parry 1971:376–390. Higbie 1990:70 and Clark 1997:22 do the same when they refer to a "succession of eight whole lines (*Odyssey* xxi 269–276)" as a "series of unenjambed verses": ὣς ἔφατ' Ἀντίνοος τοῖσιν δ' ἐπιήνδανε μῦθος | τοῖσι δὲ κήρυκες μὲν ὕδωρ ἐπὶ χεῖρας ἔχευαν | κοῦροι δὲ κρητῆρας ἐπεστέψαντο ποτοῖο |νώμησαν δ' ἄρα πᾶσιν ἐπαρξάμενοι δεπάεσσιν | οἱ δ' ἐπεὶ οὖν σπεῖσάν τ' ἔπιόν θ' ὅσον ἤθελε θυμός | τοῖς δὲ δολοφρονέων μετέφη πολύμητις Ὀδυσσεύς |κέκλυτέ μευ μνηστῆρες ἀγακλειτῆς βασιλείης | ὄφρ' εἴπω τά με θυμὸς ἐνὶ στήθεσσι κελεύει, "Thus spoke Antinous, and for them it seemed like a good idea: | for them the heralds poured water over the hands | and servant boys filled the vessels to the rim with wine; | they handed them duely to all having started with the cups; | as for the others, when they had poured a libation and drunk as much as their heart desired, | resourceful Odysseus, hiding his real intentions, addressed them: | 'Listen to me, suitors of the famous queen, | that I may utter what my heart in my chest commands me.'" Clark (1997:22) expects his readers to consider correlative couplet formulas (e.g., *Iliad* VIII 66–67 ὄφρα μὲν ἠὼς ἦν καὶ ἀέξετο ἱερὸν ἦμαρ | τόφρα μάλ' ἀμφοτέρων βέλε' ἔπτετο πῖπτε δὲ λαός, "As long as it was morning, and the sacred day still increased, | so long the projectiles from both sides flew to and fro, and the men fell"), in addition to the list

(45) αὐτὰρ ἐπεὶ πόσιος καὶ ἐδητύος ἐξ ἔρον ἕντο

Odyssey iii 67

But when they had overcome their craving for drink and food

2.4.2 Classification of enjambment-types

Classifications of enjambment-types show to what extent the various types of enjambment are distinguished by looking at the grammatical completeness at the enjambed verse end. Such classifications, I argue, illustrate the various and, in my opinion, misleading ways to approach the pause in syntax as a performative feature as a result of the unjustified assumption that verse end is a performative feature. In Higbie (1990:29) we read:

> The primary factor determining enjambment is the degree of expectation of or grammatical need for what follows the verse end: if the sentence could have ended with the verse end but did not, then the next verse follows in adding enjambment; if the sentence is incomplete at verse end, then the enjambment is clausal, necessary or violent.

To date, Higbie's classification of all the types of enjambment is the most elaborate; Clark uses it as his starting point. The development of Higbie's system out of those by Kirk and Parry is best presented in a table:

Parry	Kirk	Higbie
Unenjambed verse	→ Unenjambed verse	→ Unenjambed verse
Unperiodic enjambment	→ Progressive enjambment	→ Adding internal enjambment
		→ Adding external enjambment
Necessary enjambment	→ Periodic enjambment	→ Clausal external enjambment
	→ Integral enjambment	→ Clausal internal enjambment
		→ Necessary enjambment
	→ Violent enjambment	→ Violent enjambment

---

of whole-line formulas (both whole-line clauses and whole-line sentences or whole-sentence lines). This couplet occurs again at *Iliad* XI 84–85. The lines from the couplet make their appearance separately at *Odyssey* ix 56 and *Iliad* XVI 778.

Different types of enjambment are classified based on what it is exactly that the verse end separates. In violent enjambment (example 46) the verse end separates words that belong to a single word group:

(46) μήτε σύ γ' Ἄρηα τό γε δείδιθι μήτέ τιν' ἄλλον
ἀθανάτων τοίη τοι ἐγὼν ἐπιτάρροθός εἰμι

Iliad V 827–828

Do not fear Ares on that account, or any other | of the immortals; such a stimulus I am for you

In necessary enjambment (example 47), the verse end separates constituents that need each other to form a grammatically complete clause. Such constituents consist of single words or word groups:

(47) τίφθ' οὕτως ἠθεῖε κορύσσεαι ἦ τιν' ἑταίρων
ὀτρύνεις Τρώεσσιν ἐπίσκοπον

Iliad X 37–38

Why are you donning your armor at this time, brother? Does it concern one of the comrades | you order to go to the Trojans as a scout?

In clausal internal enjambment (example 48), the verse end separates constituents that need each other to form a grammatically complete clause, as in cases of necessary enjambment. The only difference is that in clausal internal enjambment the verse end separates constituents that are tied together by correlative adverbs:

(48) δῆμον ἐόντα παρὲξ ἀγορευέμεν οὔτ' ἐνὶ βουλῇ
οὔτέ ποτ' ἐν πολέμῳ σὸν δὲ κράτος αἰὲν ἀέξειν

Iliad XII 213–214

[As it is absolutely unbecoming |] that a man from the people opposes you, neither in the assembly, | nor ever on the battlefield; he is supposed to always make your power grow

In clausal external enjambment (example 49) the verse end separates grammatical clauses*, the first of which is accompanied by a constituent suggesting hierarchical syntactical organization in combination with the subsequent line. This means that the first clause is a subordinate clause, or that the main clause in the enjambed line prepares for the subordinate clause, or another main clause, by means of a correlative adverb. Two clauses thus tied together need not immediately follow one another: there may be more subordinate clauses, parentheses, and independent main clauses in between:

(49) αὐτὰρ ὅτ᾽ ἂψ ἄρχοιτο καὶ ὀτρύνειαν ἀείδειν
(Φαιήκων οἱ ἄριστοι ἐπεὶ τέρπουντ᾽ ἐπέεσσιν)
ἂψ Ὀδυσεὺς κατὰ κρᾶτα καλυψάμενος γοάασκεν

Odyssey viii 90–92

But the moment he would start again, and they would encourage him to sing, | (the best of the Phaecians, as they enjoy the stories,) | Odysseus immediately hid his head under his cloak and mourned

In adding internal enjambment (twice at verse end in example 50), the verse end separates words belonging to a single clause, though the clause met all its grammatical requirements before the verse end. What follows the verse end can be left out without affecting the grammatical completeness of the preceding line:

(50) τώ μοι Τηλέμαχος πάντων πολὺ φίλτατος ἐστιν
ἀνδρῶν οὐδέ τί μιν θάνατον τρομέεσθαι ἄνωγα
ἔκ γε μνηστήρων θεόθεν δ᾽ οὐκ ἔστ᾽ ἀλέασθαι

Odyssey xvi 445–447

That is why Telemachus to me is by far dearest of all | men, and I assure him that he need not fear death | as caused by the suitors; it is impossible to avoid when it comes from a god.

Finally, in adding external enjambment (example 51) the verse end separates grammatical clauses that turn out to be hierarchically organized only after crossing the verse end: the developing sentence met all its grammatical requirements before the verse end of what turns out to be an enjambed clause. As in adding internal enjambment, what follows the verse end can be left out without affecting the grammatical completeness of the preceding line:

(51) ὅππως δὴ μνηστῆρσιν ἀναιδέσι χεῖρας ἐφῆκε
μοῦνος ἐών οἱ δ᾽ αἰὲν ἀολλέες ἔνδον ἔμιμνον

Odyssey xxiii 37–38

How then did he lay hands on the shameless suitors | as he was all alone, and they were always waiting inside all together

The above enjambment-classification in Higbie 1990 is based on (i) observance of the verse end as a natural boundary, and (ii) the identification of the grammatically coherent unit with the metrical phrase that is the single verse.

2.4.3 Acknowledgement of out-of-line composition

Clark 1997 follows Higbie in not automatically allowing for emphasis on the first constituent of the Homeric hexameter following enjambment, not even if it is, grammatically, a *mot-en-rejet*. Basset (1938:141–172), the basis for criticism of the Parryan "one-verse utterance," had been fundamental for its critique of the notion of emphasis resulting from metrical boundaries in general. Clatman and Nortwick 1977 revived the idea that rhetorical colometry, based on syntactical coherence, should be more important in determining the units of meaning than metrical colometry. Clayman 1981 concluded that the sentence as a larger scale unit of meaning may develop in spite of metrical colometry. As in other studies on enjambment following the principles of Parry (1971:251–265), Clark 1994 maintained the terminology of enjambment, but accepted that run-over composition is the result of paratactic juxtaposition of metrical phrases. Clark (1997:4) argues that such a "complex and elegant technique" is "consistent with oral formulaic composition." He uses the terminology enjambment as the acknowledgement that the verse end does not double as a syntactical boundary. His focus is not on grammatical completeness at verse end. He points at the frequency and ease with which Homeric composition is extended beyond the hexameter. In fact, this extension takes place so often that a model can be reconstructed in accordance with which specific run-over words and verse-final anticipations* provide the composer with formulaic material with which to continue his clause or sentence. A runover or an anticipation (for example, the verse-final constituent following position 8, the bucolic dieresis) is part of a formulaic verse: using the runover-word or the anticipation always extends the formulas used backwards or forwards towards the nearest verse end. A few examples (52–55) from Clark 1997:

Runover-word:

(52) ὁ δ' ἀνστήσει ὃν ἑταῖρον
Πάτροκλον τὸν δὲ κτενεῖ ἔγχεϊ φαίδιμος Ἕκτωρ
Iliad XV 64–65

Runover-word:

(53) ὁ δ' ὕστερος ὄρνυτο χαλκῷ
Πάτροκλος τοῦ δ' οὐχ ἅλιον βέλος ἔκφυγε χειρός
Iliad XVI 479–480

Anticipation:

(54) δὴν δέ μιν ἀμφασίη ἐπέων λάβε τὼ δέ οἱ ὄσσε
δακρυόφι πλῆσθεν θαλερὴ δέ οἱ ἔσχετο φωνή
Iliad XVII 695–696

Anticipation:

(55) θρυλίχθη δὲ μέτωπον ἐπ' ὀφρύσι <u>τὼ δέ οἱ ὄσσε</u>
      δακρυόφι πλῆσθεν θαλερὴ δέ οἱ ἔσχετο φωνή

Iliad XXIII 396–397

I think that, just like the formulaic material that can be used to compose whole-line verses or parts thereof, the runovers and anticipations of Clark's model provide formulaic material to compose beyond the boundaries—the metrical, but from a diachronic point of view the syntactical boundaries as well[42]—of the individual hexameter. Runovers and anticipations function as semantic hooks* to link formulas over the verse end. As this process has been productive in creating out-of-line composition over the centuries, the value of compositional pauses (like the verse end) as audible phenomena in performance needs to be reconsidered.

2.4.4 Affective prosody?

Despite the value attributed to the start of the hexameter by Kahane 1997, and the affective prosody of Edwards 2002, Bakker (2005, especially 53–54), argues that the terminology enjambment is best abandoned for many instances of run-over composition without any detectible poetic purpose (emphasis, for example). Dik (2007:249–254), though approaching the issue from another angle,[43] reaches roughly the same conclusion, thus avoiding the prosodic arbitrariness that stems from the acceptance of compositional pauses as performative features for poetic effect only. I agree with both: there is no reason to assume any poetic effect for the acknowledgement of out-of-line composition, as long as the value of the verse end as a performative pause has not been established on phonological grounds.[44]

---

[42] Clark 1997:23: "the frequent occurrence of whole-line formulaic clauses in the epics should be no surprise: the methods of composing oral poetry can be expected to produce a preponderance of lines consisting of one complete clause apiece. ... At times these whole lines, rather than individual words, seem to be the real units of composition."

[43] In the conclusion to her study on word order in Greek tragic dialogue, Dik summarizes her argument for the attribution of pragmatic functions Topic and Focus to constituents in the clause. She ends her conclusion with a few remarks on "old chestnuts of the metrical approach," notably emphasis by place and pause. In her view, line-end emphasis may be an issue in the case of necessary enjambment only. Emphasis is, then, rather due to the combination metrical position + pragmatic function than to metrical position + syntactical function.

[44] Blankenborg 2016.

3

Pause in Phonology and Phonetics

*Technical terms followed by * on their first occurrence in this chapter are in the glossary.*

3.0   Introduction

In this chapter I aim to draw conclusions on the pause* as an audible phenomenon. In order to do so, I will combine observations from studies on Greek phonology* and phonetics* into a new, coherent concept of audible pause. I label this new concept *phonetic pause**. As opposed to the metrical and the syntactical pause, both compositional pauses, pause as an audible phenomenon depends on the reconstruction of the phonetics of pause, instead of on the repetitive pattern of metrical phrasing, or on the common-sense pause of syntax. I will define phonetic pause as the termination of phonation due to the lengthened and sandhi*-free phonetic word-final syllable. It comes in two qualities and depends on localization within the hexametric line.

Pause as an audible phenomenon is a requirement for performative pause, but not automatically to be put on a par with it. Rate of speech (Chapter 5) determines when and where phonetic pause is realized as a rest in performance.

3.0.1 Audible phenomena in a dead language?

It is difficult to reach conclusions on the details of phonetics, the sound act of speech, in a language that is no longer represented by native speakers. Ancient Greek is such a language; no matter how abundant the testimonies of the language, and *on* the language, in writing, the disappearance of native speakers of ancient Greek makes it very difficult to say what the language sounded like, and to what extent the written testimonies reflect what actually reached the ears of its users. There are manuals from antiquity, written in ancient Greek, on the shape and the sound of the language itself. Such manuals are as close as anyone can get to the perception of a language by its users. Given, however, that the written testimonies span a period of more than two thousand years (in which Greek, like any other language, kept developing), and that only few such manuals survive, it would only be safe to assume that the manuals' observations on language do not apply, and should not be applied, to the whole two millennia of ancient Greek's development. Linguistic observations by scholars like Aristotle, Zenodotus, Aristarchus, Dionysius of Halicarnassus, or Hephaestion, are to be taken seriously as well as cautiously, but even more caution is required in the analysis of the scholars' methods and terminology, as well as the applicability of their findings over time. Their observations are drawn from the study of materials that may have differed greatly in wording and presentation both from the materials as they were in use centuries before and from those used by scholars today. Things become even more difficult when it comes to phonetics.

In the case of Homer, the distance in time between the origin of his *Iliad* and *Odyssey* and the linguistic scrutiny of the ancient scholars is at least several centuries. From Aristotle onwards the scholars of antiquity analyzed the remnants of epic narratives of which no one knew the exact sound many centuries earlier. The scholars of antiquity approached the pronunciation and performance of Homer's *Iliad* and *Odyssey* from the point of view of practices in their own time; practices that may have differed substantially from those in the ninth or eighth century BCE. Valuable as their analyses may be, their works would not even suffice for a full reconstruction of the phonetics of the Greek of their own times.

Steps have been taken, however, to face the difficulties that the reconstruction of phonetics in ancient Greek presents us with. In recent years much work has been done in attempts to reconstruct what ancient Greek sounded like. Due attention has been paid to the pronunciation of vowels and consonants, to accentuation, and to rhythm*. On the basis of recent studies, I will present an overview of the various aspects of ancient Greek phonetics pertaining to pause. My main focus will be on Homer. There is no overview of Homeric phonetics available yet: my overview combines the results and observations of existing studies in the fields of Greek meter and rhythm with those on phonology. Prosody and phonology are treated extensively by Allen 1973/1987 and Devine and Stephens 1994. Their work can be considered the basis for the reconstruction of Greek phonetics in general. My reconstruction of the phonetics of pause in Homeric poetry does not merely use the metrical surface structure to draw conclusions on phonetics; it draws conclusions from the notion that surface structure is sensitive to phonetic reality.

3.1   Pause in Phonology

In its written form, language abstracts away from physical and audible realities: similar phonemes, syllables, and clusters of consonants are not automatically the expression of similar or identical auditory sensations. Language's written form is the agreed-upon orthography of its phonology, the structure of its acoustic system. Such a structure strives to present its users with a recognizable and transferable set of characters to encode the meaning of spoken language. Phonology systematizes sound, but it cannot always react instantaneously to changes in the sound system. As phonology is itself largely based on conventions, its adaptability to sound change is limited, as is its perspicuity for those outside the group of language users. There may thus be a huge gap between the phonology, the sound system of a language, and its phonetics, the sound act of speech (Clark et al. 2007).

The phonology of a dead language like ancient Greek is even more abstract, as it is harder to reconstruct the sound act of Greek speech than to analyze the sound act of a modern language. Henderson 1973 and Allen 1973 have analyzed the segments, phonemes, and morphemes of ancient Greek, but their analysis leaves some aspects of prosody untreated. Recent study of prosody as a phonetic aspect of Greek, such as Devine and Stephens 1994, focuses on the reconstruction of the sound act of Greek speech. They consider meter (see §1.1) as an essential part of evidence in this reconstruction, as its rules, surface structure, and system rationalize the underlying phonology.[1] One level up from metrics, rhythm (see §1.2) is its ontogenetic basis: meter, it is assumed, works the way it does, because it works towards the same final objective as does rhythm, namely a degree of rhythmic regularity.[2] One level down from metrics, phonology reflects the phonetics of rhythmics: the phonological evidence for rhythm-based meter shows the surface rhythmics in the performance of verse.[3] The relationship phonology-metrics-rhythmics may be seen as hierarchical:

---

[1]   Devine and Stephens (1994:101) accept that verse is merely the language itself, running in its natural grooves. Lehiste 1990: "If one wants to study rhythm, one will do well to look where rhythm can be expected to be found—in the metric structure of poetry developed in a given language over the years."

[2]   Devine and Stephens 1994:101: "The rhythms of Greek verse are simply more constrained versions of rhythms already existing in Greek speech: the ῥυθμιζόμενα of verse are a selection of the most amendable ῥυθμιζόμενα of prose. The basic principles of the two systems are the same, as are their basic units of organization. Whatever the importance of literary convention, in principle Greek verse rhythm is born of the rhythm of Greek speech, and the former is consequently a valuable source of information about the latter."

[3]   Devine and Stephens 1994:99–101.

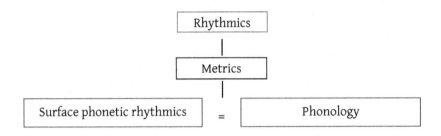

The phonology of the Homeric epic shows (A) the surface structure of metrical syllabification* (see §1.1.1), and (B) the coherence of the phonetic word through apposition*. A study of both A (§3.1.1) and B (§3.1.2) will illustrate how phonology counts as evidence for the *impossibility* of phonetic pause. It contributes to the analysis of the possibility of phonetic pause as well; from phonology the phonetic consequences can be analyzed of hiatus*, shortening*, prodelision*, elision*, crasis*, *brevis in longo*, phrase-final lengthening*, light syllable prolongation* on the anceps, heavy syllable subordination* on the arsis, and heavy syllable prolongation* on the thesis.[4]

3.1.1 Metrical syllabification

With regard to (A), the mapping of heavy and light syllables shows where metrical syllabification differs from orthographical syllabification:

> (56) τὸν δ' αὖτε προσέειπε συβώτης ὄρχαμος ἀνδρῶν
>
> *Odyssey* xvi 36
>
> To him in turn the swineherd spoke, the men's leader

> (56a) τὸν.δαῦ.τε.προς.έ.ει.πε.συ.βώ.της.ὄρ.χα.μος.ἀν.δρῶν
>   (orthographical syllabification)

> (56b) τὸν.δαῦ.τεπ.ρο.σέ.ει.πε.συ.βώ.τη. σόρ.χα.μο.σαν.δρῶν
>   (metrical syllabification)

The syllable structures are such that they correspond to the weight* required by the metrical positions they occupy. The rules of orthographical and linguistic syllabification (dividing the word into morphemes, such as prefix, stem, and suffix) are subordinate to the division of the words according to metrical

---

4   All are instances of submoraic adjustment*, the phonetically required adaptation of phonology. Golston and Riad 2000 show that the conscious disregard of phonetic adjustment results in a lack of rhythmical periodicity for most meters, except the anapaestic dimeter.

syllabification: into syllables determined by sonority's* peak and slope (§1.1.3). From the metrical positions the exact syllabification as it was produced by speakers and perceived by listeners, can be deduced. Thus it is clear that syllables .CV. featuring a short vowel as nucleus* are light, whereas syllables .CV. featuring a long vowel or diphthong as nucleus count as heavy, as well as syllables .CVC.[5] Syllable structures correspond to the weight required by metrical position, so when perceived, metrical syllabification does not match orthographical syllabification,[6] as some consonants have to move from coda* to onset* or vice versa. This may happen within the word, but also at the word juncture: the coda consonant of a word may be treated as the next syllable's onset. Or (part of) the onset (cluster) of a word is used to close the final syllable of the preceding word. In the example (56b above), three sigma's moved from coda to onset (as a result, the preceding syllable remained light), and a π changed from onset to coda (so that the sonority slope of the new syllable .τεπ. carried enough weight to make it heavy), all without any regard for word boundary. Devine and Stephens 1994 speak of resyllabification*: either as *onset to coda shift*, the right to left movement of a consonant[7] (ἔ.να.ρα.βρο.τό.εν.τα > ἔ.να.ραβ.ρο.τό.εν.τα), or as *coda to onset resyllabification*. This phenomenon can be compared to that of consonantal liaison both within and between words, attested by authors in antiquity (Ruijgh 1987:347n76).

Like liaison, resyllabification confirms the phonetic coherence of syllables and of words. Phonetic coherence in metrical syllabification is expressed as either liaison of consonants (συνάφεια, synaphy), or as vowel coalescence (συναλοιφή; elision, prodelision, crasis, and shortening); in my opinion, both preclude the possibility of audible pause and therefore performative pause. Together, consonantal liaison and vowel coalescence as markers of phonetic coherence are referred to as sandhi*. Scansion shows that the verse is its domain.

3.1.2 Apposition

Phonology also provides proof for (B) the coherence of word groups. Such coherence, it is generally accepted, usually arises from syntactic cohesion and/or accentual clisis*, the "leaning" of non-accented words onto the accented

---

[5]   In phonological terms syllables are not long by position, but heavy due to consonantal sonority slope (coda).

[6]   In 1.1.3 the following hierarchy of decreasing sonority was presented for ancient Greek: open vowels > closed vowels > glides > central liquids > lateral liquids > nasals > voiced fricatives > voiced stops > voiceless fricatives > voiceless stops. The consonants will appear in this order in the syllable's coda; in the onset they appear in reversed order. The spirans carries least weight: in colliding consonant clusters, the spirans is always the juncture, itself carrying so little weight that in orthography it regularly disappears (as in the perfect passive infinitive).

[7]   Devine and Stephens 1994:243–248.

word preceding or following it. Word groups are identified as all words are classified into two categories: lexical words* and nonlexical words*. Lexical words, or content words, are those words that are expandable into phrases that they head. Their category contains a vast number of members, and new members can be added by neologism (open class words). In prosody*, lexicals are not easily reduced or minimized. Nonlexical words, or function words, cannot be expanded like lexicals. Their category contains fewer members, and new members arise as the result of the semantic bleaching of erstwhile lexicals (closed class words). Prosodically, they are susceptible to reduction in continuous speech.[8] Word groups are formed as lexicals expand into phrases containing other lexicals and nonlexicals. This dependency of nonlexicals (and some lexicals, notably adjectives) on the lexical head of the word group is called phonological clisis* or apposition (Devine and Stephens 1994). Accentual clitics are always nonlexicals, but nonlexicals are not necessarily non-accented. Not all nonlexicals are appositive, and not all appositives are nonlexical (notably adjectives). In the hierarchy of word group coherence, accentual clisis and phonological apposition outweigh syntactical cohesion: the latter is more easily disrupted or left incomplete than the former.

In Greek, there are both accented (μέν, δέ, γάρ, ἄρα, οὖν) and non-accented nonlexicals.[9] Whereas most lexicals are at least bimoraic, monosyllabic nonlexicals tend to be monomoraic (ending in a short vowel: με, σε, ἑ, σφε, γε, τε τι, δέ, ὁ, τό, τά, σύ, ἄ, πρό). Any consonantal coda is made extrametrical through sandhi. Prosodically, nonlexicals do not have their own stable thesis*: their mapping varies, and when monosyllabic, they may easily be mapped on the arsis*. Polysyllabic nonlexicals without a stable thesis are considered appositives. An appositive that coheres with what follows is a prepositive*; cohering with what precedes turns the appositive into a postpositive*. The combination of the host lexical word and one or more nonlexicals is called an appositive group* or phonetic word*.[10] In Greek, where accent and rhythm are not obviously correlated, it is useful to distinguish the appositive group as a rhythmic domain from the clitic group as an accentual domain. Word location rules,

---

[8] Devine and Stephens 1994:291–292.

[9] Koster 1953:51–52 and Devine and Stephens 1978 demonstrate the prosodic characteristics of nonlexicals. Devine and Stephens (1994:354–355) discuss the possibility of clisis for the particle. Clisis seems to be well possible at higher rates of speech. At lower rates, as evidenced in the musical settings, the grave accent of the non-lexical appositive does not seem to be part of the rising trajectory, as opposed to other word-final grave accents (cf. §1.1.2).

[10] Devine and Stephens 1994:306–307. They stress that not all appositives lose their rhythmical autonomy, nor do those who lose rhythmical autonomy all have an equal propensity to do so in all environments or at all rates of speech.

like Wackernagel's Law[11] (enclitic appositives occupy second position in the clause) and, in my opinion at least, metrical bridges confirm the theory of Greek appositives. Metrical bridges find their origin in phonological realities. They are maintained where apposition ties the phonetic word together and breached where apposition terminates or starts the phonetic word. I argue that metrical bridges confirm the phonological cohesion that precludes phonetic word end and phonetic pause.

3.1.3 Coherence and pause in larger phonological domains

I argue that phonology provides the key to the identification of both coherence and phonetic pause within the discourse. Both stem from the phonetic consequences of elision (and prodelision), hiatus, shortening, crasis, gemination, *brevis in longo*, phrase-final lengthening, light syllable prolongation on the anceps, heavy syllable subordination on the arsis, and heavy syllable prolongation on the thesis. Many of these phenomena are exemplary for sandhi, the visible disparity of orthographical and metrical syllabification, where the sonority slope of the metrical syllable is maintained through liaison and vowel coalescence (§4.1.1). Sandhi points at coherence within domains that may be substantially larger that the single word or the phonetic word (§4.1.2). The same goes for bridges: though often treated as metrical phenomena, bridges are rhythmic-phonological indicators of phrase-internal coherence (cf. Devine and Stephens 1994:271–284).

Metrical surface structure is sensitive to the categorized weight of syllables (light — heavy). The phonological phenomena in metrical surface structure serve as examples of submoraic adjustment, the adjustment of categorized syllable weight to phonetic circumstances, so that all syllables' weight can be labelled either light or heavy—and nothing in between. Phenomena pointing at vocalic coalescence (elision, prodelision, shortening, and crasis), as well as light syllable prolongation and heavy syllable subordination, are indicators of phonological synizesis, just like phonological synaphy: in my opinion, they reflect the coherence, and with it the impossibility of audible pause, within a phonological domain. *Brevis in longo*, final lengthening, heavy syllable prolongation on the thesis, and hiatus are indicative of termination of the phonological domain, and hence of the possibility of audible pause. I must stress that there is a difference between phonological and phonetic indicators here. *Brevis in longo*

---

[11] Goldstein 2016 argues that enclitics constitute the right-hand boundary of the "intonational phrase" (cf. Goldstein 2014); see further the Appendix, pp. 266–68.

is a phonological clue; final lengthening, heavy syllable prolongation on the thesis, and hiatus are valued as phonetic indicators of termination.

Together, the indicators of internal coherence and phrase demarcation are the product of the analysis of phonological phrasing. The importance of phonological phrasing for this study thus lies in the clues it offers for the phonetics of termination and the possibility for performative pause. I will discuss these clues in the next three sections.

3.1.3.1 Vowel coalescence in larger domains

Vowel coalescence—elision, prodelision, shortening, and crasis—presupposes cohesive phonological phrasing. Audible pause is thereby excluded, as is evidenced by elision.

Elision

Elision looks like the coda to onset type of resyllabification, but is, in fact, reduction of a syllable to onset. In the discussion concerning the disappearance or suppression of the elided vowel, I fall in with Ruijgh and Devine and Stephens who argue for the reduction of the elided vowel. West (1973:226–229) considers elision as disappearance of the vowel without a trace. He points at light syllables as the result of elision where crasis results in heavy syllables. Ruijgh (1987:348n78) concludes that elision only affects the syllable-initial realization of consonants (cf. Devine and Stephens 1994:255–256) and not that of syllable-initial vowels: elision has no effect on the mora* count of the syllable following elision. Elision itself is always the disappearance of a single mora in mora count, though traces of the elided vowel remain present in phonetics as a *schwa*. Devine and Stephens (1994:256–266) express the same notion when they state that elision creates a syllable-initial consonant, but accept that the elided vocalic sound is still present, though severely reduced. Elision affects the pitch pattern in case of an elided accented syllable (*Odyssey* viii 550: εἴπ' (< εἰπὲ) ὄνομ' ὅττι σε κεῖθι κάλεον μήτηρ τε πατήρ τε, "speak the name that yonder your mother and father called you"). In case of an elided monosyllable, the remaining consonant turns into an orthographic onset, that is, the syllable-initial consonant(s) (*Iliad* XXII 25: τὸν δ' ὁ (τὸν.δό) γέρων Πρίαμος πρῶτος ἴδεν ὀφθαλμοῖσι, "old man Priam saw him first with his eyes"). Ruijgh's concept of the elided vowel as a *schwa* is evidenced, in my opinion, by the observation that elision makes it possible for a penultimate syllable ending in a short vowel to maintain its phonetic realization (as if elision prevents further syncopation of syllables, type *Iliad* I 2 μυρί' Ἀχαιοῖς ἄλγε' ἔθηκεν, "numerous pains it bestowed on the Greeks," where the underlined syllables do not suffer elision). Elision can

be avoided by moveable *nu** as an instance of coda to onset syllabification. In
example (57), elision at position 5½ is avoided through the movable *nu* that is
resyllabified to .χερ.σί.νὲ.πεὶ:

(57)   ἠὲ φίλων ἐν χερσίν ἐπεὶ πόλεμον τολύπευσε

Odyssey xiv 368

or in the hands of friends after he had survived the war

Elision avoids hiatus, the nonelidable vowel juncture. Elision thus precludes
audible pause and strengthens cohesion, and appears to be mainly used within
the domain of the syntactic phrase; hiatus, on the other hand is used to demarcate syntactic phrases. Shortening and gliding* equally result in the avoidance of hiatus. Shortening and gliding are features of phonological synizesis in
Greek. Shortening (correption) of long vowels, found in epic (*correptio epica*; epic
correption), in some lyric, and in comedy's catalectic anapaestic tetrameters,
may be interpreted as the avoidance of hiatus through elision of the long vowel's
second mora (as if word final -ω. is analyzed as -o'. before a vowel) or, alternatively, as gliding of the vowel's second mora (as if word final -ω. is analyzed as
-o°.). Gliding (examples 58–59) means that the last mora of the vowel is treated
as a consonant, thus facilitating the sequential syllable structure. Gliding is
common in diphthongs, both short (with, for example, -οι. analysed as -o'.) and
long (with -ῳ. analysed as -o°'. before a vowel):[12]

(58)   ἔχθιστος δέ μοί ἐσσι θεῶν οἳ Ὄλυμπον ἔχουσιν

Iliad V 890

But for me you are most hated of the gods who hold the Olympus

(59)   ἡμεῖς δ' εἰμὲν τοῖοι οἳ ἄν σέθεν ἀντιάσαιμεν

Iliad VII 231

But we are such men that we are able to oppose you

West (1982:11) notices that correption is almost always followed by a short
word-initial vowel.

Hiatus

Hiatus in Homer has been discussed by many (among others, Monro 1891:355–
356; Parry 1971:191; Lejeune 1972:225–231; West 1982:39; Van Raalte 1986:93;

[12]   Bakker 1988.

Hoekstra 1989:9; Bakker 1988). Devine and Stephens 1994 zoom in on its phonetics, which seem to differ depending on the domain in which it is found. Hiatus, though it is generally avoided in verse, is less unacceptable at weak word junctures in fixed phrases and appositive groups where the syllable organization most resembles that found word internally (where hiatus is not uncommon). As elision excludes hiatus, slow rates of speech constrain elision (resulting in hiatus), and high rates of speech constrain hiatus. In prose, hiatus involving elidable vowels may be seen as orthographic hiatus, not necessarily as phonetic. It is not clear to what extent this assumption is applicable to verse, where hiatus is linked to phonetic pause:

> Another aspect that is unclear is whether the avoidance of hiatus in both verse and prose is simply and directly avoidance of hiatus as such, that is avoidance of difficult sequential syllable structure, or whether it is avoidance of boundary marking properties that are potentially an indirect reflex of hiatus. The former assumption is theoretically quite acceptable ... . However, if hiatus between lexical words were consistently eliminated by elision, prodelision and synizesis within a prosodic domain, then its occurrence would signal a boundary between domains, which is the hypothetical premise of the latter theory.[13]

Hiatus serves as an indicator of phrase termination.

3.1.3.2 Lengthening, prolongation, and subordination in larger domains

Vowel coalescence and synizesis are phonological reflections of assumed surface rhythmics; assumed, because I understand metrical surface structure as the rationalization of phonetic realities. Lengthening, prolongation, and subordination are to be approached differently because all three are phonological phenomena that provide clues for the reconstruction of Homeric phonetics, especially concerning audible pauses. In these cases, it is not phonology adapting to rhythmic requirements, but allowing for the reconstruction (as several scholars have tried) of phonetic realization. In the light of the present study, reconstruction focuses on the phonetic realization of pause, suggesting the extent of its audibility as opposed to its occurrence as a purely compositional feature.

---

[13] Devine and Stephens 1994:255.

Lengthening

Lengthening may refer to (i) metrical, and (ii) phonetic lengthening. Metrical lengthening (Wyatt 1969) is the phonological explanation given to the occurrence of single light syllables on the foot's thesis. A light syllable on the thesis does not meet the requirements of the position, so lengthening is assumed, analogous to the lengthening expressed in printing, such as gemination* (ἔλλαβε, – ◡ ◡), the application of moveable *nu*, and protraction* of short vowels (ἀθάνατος, – ◡ ◡ –; οὐλύμπονδε, – – – ◡). Alternatively, the metrical requirements of the dactylic thesis are questioned; it has been noted by scholars (Bakker 1988; Steinrück 2005) that several theses in the hexameter appear to be ancipitia, considering the ease with which they may be occupied by either a light or a heavy syllable. Especially the first, the third, and the sixth thesis regularly feature light syllables. The sixth-foot thesis of the στίχος μείουρος* is an anceps (examples in Leaf 1900–1902,ap.D,C3); in this verse-type, the final thesis is occupied by a light syllable. The verse-initial thesis in στίχος ἀκέφαλος* is also occupied by a light syllable, as in *Iliad* XXI 379 ἐπεὶ δὴ τόνδ' ἄνδρα θεοὶ δαμάσασθαι ἔδωκαν, "as the gods have finally granted me to restrain this man," and *Iliad* XXIII 2 ἐπεὶ δὴ νῆάς τε καὶ Ἑλλήσποντον ἵκοντο, "as they had reached the ships and the Hellespont" (further examples in Leaf 1900–1902:ap.D,C1).[14] Metrical lengthening is commonly considered a license on the thesis of the third foot, and compared to the verse-final lengthening of the sixth arsis (*brevis in longo*): as *brevis in longo* reflects the prosodic neutrality of the verse-final element (Lejeune 1972, Van Raalte 1986:17), so metrical lengthening of the third-foot thesis bears witness to some prosodic neutrality of the element before the main caesura. Lidov 1989 states, however, that any comparison of metrical lengthening to *brevis in longo* is mistaken: *brevis in longo* is the rhythmical consequence of metrical anceps. If the foot's thesis is not considered an anceps element, the explanation for metrical lengthening cannot be similar to the explanation for *brevis in longo*: the latter is considered a rhythmical license due to the proximity of verse termination; the former may often be phonologically defensible (for example, with syllabification -ος) *if* termination *is assumed* at the penthemimeral caesura. *Brevis in longo* is better compared, I suggest, to phonological lengthening, below.

Phonetic lengthening (ii) is deduced from phonology, and partly based on cross-linguistic assumptions. The first of these assumptions is that, in ancient Greek, tempo of speech slows down towards the end of utterances, just like it does in modern, natural languages. This slackening is due to respiratory movement

---

[14] Both the verse-final and the verse-initial foot of the hexameter give rise to the assumption of an earlier stage in which both feet only had to comply with Aeolic isosyllaby (cf. Nagy 1979, Steinrück 2005).

and a gradual relaxation of the speech and breathing musculature. Ruijgh 1987 and 1989 refer to the slowing down of speech, or final-syllable lengthening, to account for the durational equation of metron-final syllables in march-anapaests. Devine and Stephens (1994:76–84) relate final lengthening not exclusively to the word-final syllable,[15] but to the utterance as a whole: they also point at Milman Parry's observation (1971:93–94) that towards the end of the hexameter, syllable structures, especially those of heavy syllables, tend to become relatively less heavy. Not all studies on syllable duration and weight acknowledge the relevance of syllable structures for phonological lengthening though. In my opinion, there is no significant difference in weight between heavy syllables .CV. and .CVC. I will argue (§3.2) that final lengthening in Greek metrical text must be identified on other criteria; I do, nonetheless, assume that the crosslinguistic final lengthening is a feature of the performance of Greek metrical text.

In an overview of the literature on final lengthening, Devine and Stephens present final lengthening as "a sort of drawling at the end of a group of articulatory events" and an example of the "deceleration that is typical of various types of human motor activity." Final lengthening is hence a signal of *close to termination of the domain*, but not necessarily of demarcation of the domain. Devine and Stephens (1994:146) describe the relationship between final lengthening and demarcation as follows:

> The timing of speech is programmed within domains, and these domains are commonly demarcated by a lengthening of terminal elements. It is a general perceptual principle that longer intervals tend to demarcate.

They note that additional lengthening may be considered as an indicator of termination of a domain:

> Later segments are lengthened more than earlier segments, and the vowel closing gesture is lengthened more than the vowel opening gesture, which suggests that final lengthening works inwards from the end of the domain.[16]

---

[15] Spare remarks from antiquity comment on the phenomenon. Aristides Quintilianus, for example, says that the prosodic realization of syllables does not only depend on their metrical position, but on their position within the word as well: word-final position results in additional lengthening of both short and long word-final syllables: ἡ γὰρ μεταξὺ διάστασις τῆς τε τοῦ προτέρου τελευτῆς καὶ τῆς ἀρχῆς τοῦ δευτέρου μῆκος τῇ συλλαβῇ παρέχεται, "for the in-between separation of, on the one hand, the completion of the first, and, on the other, the start of the second provides the syllable with duration" (p. 43.2-4 in the edition of Winnington-Ingram).

[16] Additional lengthening is not by itself a correlate of pause, as it is not independent of stress ("Final lengthening and lengthening under stress have results tending in the same direction") but is produced by different mechanisms. Informally, "final lengthening is a sort of drawling at

Additional lengthening provides the speech producer with time to think and plan, but may also show the characteristics of human motor activity:

> The primary motivation of final lengthening is presumably related to the overall pattern of acceleration followed by deceleration that is typical of various types of human motor activity .... In addition to deceleration, final lengthening may perhaps reflect a partial temporal allowance for a "deleted" pause or for a "gapped" constituent.

The above quotation hints at the second cross-linguistic assumption concerning final lengthening: lengthening may account for some or all of the value of a phonetic pause. Final lengthening is an indicator for some temporal allowance.

Prolongation

Devine and Stephens also comment on heavy syllable prolongation on the thesis. Such prolongation characterizes the thesis of iambic or trochaic (sometimes dochmiac) meter when the thesis constitutes a monosyllabic foot, due to syncopation of the arsis in the same foot. The result of the syncopation, the monosyllabic thesis, is preferably word-final.[17] On the basis of metrical evidence and evidence of the musical documents, Devine and Stephens assume that heavy syllable prolongation on the thesis mirrors any lengthening in speech (Devine and Stephens 1994:135):

> Since the rhythm of Greek song was so closely tied to the rhythm of speech, one interpretation of the musical evidence is that prolongation in song reflects some degree of prolongation in speech. It could also be assumed that prolongation in song had a purely musical basis; in that case, one would still expect the prolonged syllable to be the same syllable that would undergo any independent linguistically motivated lengthening in speech.

In Homer's hexameter, heavy syllable prolongation on the thesis would apply to the theses that are word final.[18] In case of metarrhythmisis* on the second, third, and fourth thesis the word-final heavy syllable gets isolated from the arsis in the same foot (Koster 1953 and cf. §1.2). Prolongation would also apply to

---

the end of a group of articulatory events, while stress is an actuation of the rhythmic beat. Final lengthening is a feature of the temporal organization of the prosodic domain and not merely a correlate of pause, since it often occurs in the absence of pause. However, the lengthening may be greater before a pause than otherwise" (Devine and Stephens 1994:147).

[17] Devine and Stephens 1994:129.

[18] O'Neill 1939:271.

the verse-final anceps in case of metarrhythmisis of the second hemistich to a catalectic anapaestic dimeter (| ‿‿ – | ‿‿ – | ‿‿ – | ^ – |). I consider the frequent anapaestic word end (with the word-final heavy syllable on the thesis and, as a result, a relatively isolated arsis within the same foot) as a phonological clue for metarrhythmisis to anapaests; the non-resolution of the hexametric thesis and the sixth-foot arsis are reminiscent of the non-resolvable word-final thesis in rising rhythm. From these observations, as from those concerning light syllable prolongation, follows my phonetic reconstruction of the heavy word-final sylla- bles as allowing for a specific temporal allowance: the heavy word-final syllable allows for additional word-final lengthening and possibly for (partial) assimila- tion with the audible pause.

Subordination

Finally, and related to the prolongation of heavy syllables on the thesis, there is subordination of heavy syllables on the arsis. With regard to the audibility of pause, prolongation and subordination have opposite results: prolongation, I argued, has a correlate to audible pause, whereas Devine and Stephens show that subordination is a phonetic adjustment in order to avoid such pause. The theory of subordination (Devine and Stephens 1994:131–132) assumes that heavy syllables are the preferred choice for theses. As each foot has only one thesis to fill, a sequence of three heavy syllables needs readjustment. A series of three subsequent theses ([T][T][T]) is not possible. In nondeliberate speech the heavy syllable between two theses is defooted so that it can be subordi- nated within an alternative foot structure [TA][T] in the hexameter. Devine and Stephens make two additional observations with regard to phonetics: (i) the duration of the subordinated heavy syllable on the arsis is less than that of the surrounding theses, and (ii) the heavy syllable on the arsis is not the preferred location for word end. For Homer, the first observation provides the theoretical basis for metrical theories that claim that $T^{duration} > A^{duration}$ regardless of syllable structure (see §1.1.1 above), a point of view I agree with; the second observation is, in my view, sufficiently confirmed by metarrhythmisis to anapaests and the restriction on spondaic word end. The restriction on spondaic word end is also a restriction concerning the possibilities for audible pause.

3.1.3.3 Bridges

Often called metrical, bridges are primarily signals of phonological coherence: a bridge ties together syllables at metrical positions where phonetic word end would be too disruptive to rhythmic regularity. Too disruptive means that phonetic word end would not meet the durational requirements of element and foot: the duration of the word-final syllable would be lengthened to such an extent that the perceptible footing of words becomes endangered. Two types of word final syllables are restricted most severely: light syllables because they run the risk of being perceived as heavy, and heavy syllables that mirror the anceps at verse end (and thus suggest premature verse end). Bridges thus reflect the impossibility of audible pause; such a pause would result in unwanted and untimely disruption. In the dactylic hexameter,[19] Hermann's Bridge* and the avoidance of spondaic word end are the most important bridges.

Hermann's Bridge postulates that word end is avoided between the two light syllables of the hexameter's fourth foot. Bridging by means of apposition within the phonetic word counts as bridging as well.

The avoidance of spondaic word end is only observed *within* the dactylic hexameter; at verse end, spondaic word end is allowed and frequent. Ruijgh 1987 rightly explains the avoidance of spondaic word end (formulated under Hilberg's Law* for the second foot, and Naeke's Bridge* for the fourth) with reference to Porson's Law in the iambic trimeter. In accordance with the observations of others (like Snell 1962), he explains both Porson's Law and the avoidance of spondaic word end in the hexameter introducing final lengthening (see §3.1.3.2). Ruijgh claims that final lengthening is an actual, absolute lengthening of syllables that may disrupt the balanced podic structure of metrical rhythm: word-final syllables would become too long due to additional lengthening. He uses the existence and persistence of metrical bridges as evidence: the occurrence of metrical bridges proves this disrupting effect of untimely final lengthening. Porson's Law, for example, forbids word end after a heavy anceps as final lengthening causes too serious disruption to rhythm. As does Parker 1966, Ruijgh extends Porson's Law to the arsis of the hexameter: Homer avoids spondaic word end, as final lengthening would disrupt dactylic rhythm.[20] In their reconstruction of the rhythm of Greek speech, Devine and Stephens (1994:124) state as a rule, rightly in my view, that the final syllables of a word ending in two heavy syllables can be mapped TT or AT, but not TA: spondaic word end cannot be prepausal.

---

[19] Outside the dactylic hexameter: Wilamowitz' Bridge and Knox' Bridge in the iambographs; Porson's Law after heavy anceps at the penthemimeres in the iambic trimeter; Havet and Porson's Bridge for the first and third anceps of the trochaic tetrameter. Cf. Snell 1982:11; Ruijgh 1987:325n27.

[20] From this, Ruijgh concludes that, in general, the duration of a *longum* surpasses that of a biceps, and that the duration of a word-final *longum* surpasses that of a word-final double *breve*. His conclusion, drawn especially from the seventeenth and twentieth chapters of *On literary composition* contradicts the dominant view (as in West 1982:20; Wefelmeier 1994) that the dactylic double *breve* has longer duration than the single-syllable arsis. Furthermore, Ruijgh concludes that any *longum* has more duration than double-*breve* (*contra* Wifstrand 1933:26–34, who considers the double *breve* longer than any single *longum*, especially in dactylic verse); see §1.1.1 above.

3.1.4 Pause in phonological phrases

As evidenced by sandhi (consonantal liaison, vowel coalescence), submoriac adjustment, and bridges, phonological coherence ties words and word groups together into phrases that are demarcated by pauses. In existing studies, the status of these pauses is interpreted in various ways: some are understood as merely compositional, others as audible features. Phonological criteria will have to be applied to judge the value of pauses as audible phenomena. First, the extent of the phonological phrases between the pauses has to be established.

Phonological phrases have been identified in Greek, though not specifically in Homer, by Devine and Stephens (1994), who distinguish minor and major phonological phrases. Their description of the minor phrase shares most of the characteristics of Homer's intonation unit, as identified by Bakker (see §2.2 above):

> In general, it is not surprising that phonological phrasing is more sensitive to constituency than it is to category: phrasing involves segmenting phonological substance into chunks which largely correspond to syntactic chunks, so it relates more to the beginnings and end of structures than it does to their internal composition. Whereas the appositive group serves to join nonlexical words with a host word into a single prosodic unit, the minor phonological phrase serves to unite certain combinations of lexical words and clitic groups into a single prosodic unit. Minor phonological phrases are not constructed randomly out of any adjacent words, but, as might be expected, they are made up of syntactically related words, typically the syntactic head and its modifiers. ... Various factors condition this process. The phonology will tend to phrase adjacent items together provided that neither of them belongs more closely to a third item. This intuition underlies the well-known effect of syntactic branching on phonological phrasing.[21]

Devine and Stephens identify the minor phrase as a prosodic unit first, and only then as a syntactic unit. They point at the positions of frequent word end, the occurrence of sandhi, and the minor phrase boost of the accent (phrase-initial tonal adjustment, as evidenced in the musical settings of the Delphic hymns) as proof of the prosodic coherence within the minor phonological phrase. Minor phrases team up to form larger scale phrases, referred to as major phonological phrases:

---

[21] Devine and Stephens 1994:377. By "syntactic branching" Devine and Stephens refer to the hierarchy of syntactical relations.

It is probably a general rule that the larger the verse structure, the more likely it is to end with a major syntactical boundary. In particular, sentence end is common at the end of stichoi and even more so at the end of couplets and stanzas, and conversely less common in other positions than it would be with random distribution. ... It is not the syntactic unit (sentence, clause, etc.) but its implementing phonological unit, or more precisely prosodic unit, that is involved in the rule constraining mismatch of verse unit and syntactic unit. This rule, which is naturally liable to artistic manipulation by the poet, is related to the disruption caused by pause and its associated prosodic features when verse unit and linguistic unit are mismatched, as is quite clear at the paragraph-stanza level, particularly in sung verse. ... Presumably, listeners tend to discard prosodic clues to syntactic boundaries immediately after another prosodic boundary, since the likelihood of a prosodic boundary increases as the phonological distance from the preceding boundary grows. This may be one of the reasons why those bridges in Greek verse which contain false division of the stichos are less strictly observed at the beginning of the line. Major phrases are apparently important not only as phonological cues to syntactic, and consequently semantic, structure, but also as cues to processing units. Our brains seem to process the utterances we hear in clausal chunks ... Verbal memory seems to be replaced by semantic memory clause by clause.[22]

Devine and Stephens thus identify both the minor and the major phonological phrase in ancient Greek. One of the phonetic aspects in the identification of phonological phrases is final lengthening. In general, they state, the larger or higher ranked the domain, the greater the final lengthening (Devine and Stephens 1994:148):

Lengthening at the end of an utterance is often greater than at the end of a major phrase; lengthening at the end of a major phrase tends to be greater than at the end of a minor phrase; and lengthening at the

---

[22] Devine and Stephens 1994:410. Among the prosodic clues demarcating the major phrase, Devine and Stephens list intonation, additional duration (final lengthening), pauses (audibly stronger disruptions at normal rates of speech), intensity (stress), and pitch (tone). Intonation is difficult to gauge in ancient Greek phonological phrases. Important as it may have been in performance, the melodious contour of phrases largely remains guesswork (see further Chapter 4). It seems reasonable to suppose that phrases had an intonation pattern terminating in tonal downtrend. On the basis of musical documents, Devine and Stephens (1994:409–410) point at the audible difference in downtrend between the major and minor phonological phrase; cf. Pierrehumbert 1980; Nolan 2014.

end of a minor phrase is greater than lengthening at the end of a word. When a word is uttered in isolation, its last syllable is not only word final, but also phrase final, sentence final and prepausal, and consequently undergoes significant final lengthening.

Lengthening is considered not only a phonetic signal of termination, but also a marker of hierarchy of prosodic domains (Devine and Stephens 1994:272):

> Evidence has already been cited that the amount of final lengthening is related to the hierarchy of prosodic domains; evidence has also been cited that in fluent speech prosodic domains encompass a larger span of phonosyntactic substance than in slow speech; it follows from these two premises that final lengthening is not merely physically reduced as speech becomes more fluent but is also adjusted to reflect the progressively more extensive prosodic domains. This argument may be restated in concrete terms as follows. It was found that nonbranching subject noun phrases in simple sentences had less final lengthening than branching subject noun phrases, which suggest that, at normal rates of speech, the nonbranching noun phrase was not processed as a separate phonological phrase but was joined with the following verb phrase into a single phonological phrase, whereas the branching noun phrase was accorded the status of an autonomous phonological phrase. Final lengthening was less at the end of words that were not the last word of the phonological phrase. To the extent that this branching distinction governs phonological phrasing at normal rates of speech but not at slow rates of speech, it illustrates the mechanism of readjustment.

Applying general linguistic data to ancient Greek, Devine and Stephens identify demarcation of the minor phonological phrase on the basis of metrical evidence (Devine and Stephens 1994:401–402):

> Evidence has already been cited that a minor phrase boundary may be foot internal, and that there is no necessary theoretical conflict between lengthening at the end of the minor phrase and foot structure assignment in the domain of the major phrase. Not only are longer items preferentially located at the end of domains, but phrase final lengthening tends to be proportionately greater on intrinsically or contextually long segments than on short ones: lengthening before voiced consonants in English is greatly exaggerated in prepausal position; ... It follows that any trend to prefer intrinsically longer syllable

structure in metrical positions corresponding to the end of the minor phrase can be taken as evidence of phrase final lengthening. By the second half of the third century B.C. a long-term diachronic trend is discernible for increasingly strict regulation of the syllable structure preceding the caesura and diaeresis. The fact that this trend is hard to identify in earlier texts is a reflection of the generally more stringent rules of Hellenistic and later versification.

Devine and Stephens continue by listing the metrical evidence for the strictness of syllabic structure preceding the, in principle, phonological boundaries. When dealing with the termination of the major phonological phrase, they temporarily lose sight of phonological criteria, and start from the concept of "true pause"; from there they include the aspect of final lengthening (Devine and Stephens 1994:432–433):

> Final lengthening or drawling may be substituted for a true pause. Grammatical pauses occur between prosodic units, generally of the rank of the phrase or higher. The occurrence and duration of a grammatical pause depend among other factors on the hierarchy of the prosodic domains as it reflects the hierarchy of syntactic structure. ... Inhalation requires more time than simply ceasing phonation, and consequently breathing pauses have greater duration than nonbreathing pauses, approximately twice the duration at most rates of speech; since longer pauses occur at deeper constituent boundaries, respiration occurs preferentially at major syntactic divisions.

After listing some examples, they continue with remarks on the phonetics of pause:

> Speakers prefer to balance the phonological length of constituents in the output, which can introduce a disparity between syntactic and prosodic domains. Subjective listening often leads to perceived pauses when there is no actual pause, merely phrase final lengthening. Both normal and time compressed speech is easier to understand when pauses are inserted periodically without reference to syntactic structure, even in the absence of other phrasal prosodic cues.

In conclusion, Devine and Stephens identify the boundaries of the phonological phrase with the aid of phonetic clues like final lengthening. Discussing final lengthening in relation to metrical bridges, they stress that final lengthening relates to demarcation in the hexameter (Devine and Stephens 1994:115–152):

Iteration of word end coinciding with metron end or trochaically dividing the metron is also avoided in the hexameter, and the requirement that the medial division be a caesura rather than diaeresis helps to reduce word boundary patterning. Patterned iteration of word boundary replicating caesura or diaeresis is even more strongly avoided. Such rules presuppose that word final syllables are prosodically differentiated from word medial syllables, and demarcation typically has just this function.

Final lengthening is evident both in phonology (though it may not disrupt the phrase-internal foot structure of the prosodic domain) and in phonetics (as an indication for audible termination). Nonetheless, Devine and Stephens include the notion of syntactic boundary in their identification of major phrases. I work from the notion that demarcation of minor and major phonological phrases is a matter of both meter and apposition (for the minor phrase) and phonetics (for the audible phenomena demarcating the major phrase). My assumption is hence that, despite the intuition to expect major phrase termination at compositional pauses (like the metrical boundary and the sense-pause at verse end), coincidence of demarcation of major phrases with syntactic divisions is not necessary. From the observations concerning phonological phrases I conclude that the identification of phrases is useful for the reconstruction of phonetic pause when phrases are identified on phonological grounds only.

3.2   Pause in Phonetics

In this section, I will argue that pause in phonetics is termination of phonation as evidenced in phonology. Having investigated the pause in phonetics as it has been explored in the work of others, I will now rely on that work for the larger part of the following analysis that is my own: pause has not been dealt with yet as a phonetic phenomenon evidenced in phonology. Such an approach places great value on the written text, the phonological representation of flawlessly maintained metrical surface structure.

The importance of maintenance of the surface structure stems from the assumption that metrical syllabification be understood as reflecting the perceived syllable division in natural speech (§1.1.1). It is more difficult to gauge the division of the verse, as both colometry and intonation units cannot be considered clues for prosodic contours (§2.2). Tonal patterns are suggestive of phonetic coherence in the application of the grave accent and secondary rise (§1.1.2). The contribution of weight to Homeric phonetics is the analysis of syllables of similar structure as syllables of various sonority (§1.1.3), depending on their localization on the thesis or on the arsis. The way thesis and arsis allow for syllables of varying sonority is the basis for the direction of rhythm (§1.2). This direction is an important contribution to the reconstruction of the phonetics of pause, as it evidences phonetic word end. It is also illustrative of the importance of submoraic adjustment, the phonetic adaptation of the weight of syllables, categorized as either heavy or light, to the circumstances of performance. Phonology provides the evidence for submoraic adjustment of syllable weight: phonology alone cannot account for the regularity of rhythm, but it shows how phonetic adaptations can. The phonetic reality of metrical syllabification is reflected in phonology (§3.1.1), as is the status of the appositive group as a phonetic word (§3.2.2). In addition to the treatment of elision as resyllabification rather than suppression (§3.1.3) of movable *nu* as a phonological, not an orthographical, coda and of hiatus, lengthening, and shortening as synchronic phonetic realities regardless of any diachronic explanation, I accept the submoraic adjustment of subordination and prolongation (§3.1.3) as surface phonetic rhythmics.

With regard to phrase formation (§3.1.4), I accept the phonetic word as the smallest unit demarcated by prosodic contours. The minor and the major phrases are understood as phonological substance demarcated by the possibility of additional lengthening; syntactical divisions may or may not coincide with the boundaries of the major phrase. The internal coherence of phonological substance as evidenced by sandhi and bridges is not considered the mere interplay of words and word groups between positions of frequent word end: I assume that where phonological legato crosses metrical boundaries, it may have done so in any stage of composition or at any performance of the Homeric epic.

3.2.1 The phonetics of pause

Pause is termination, the ending of a metrical, phonological, or syntactic unit. Termination of all these various units does not automatically coincide in Homer; metrical cola end at the metrical boundaries, phonological phrases end where phonation breaks off, and the completion of syntactic units is suggested by printed punctuation. The termination of the metrical unit is studied as the position of frequent word end; the termination of the syntactical unit is determined with reference to the completion of grammatical structure and syntactical requirements. Bakker's description of Homeric discourse, using the metrical cola and phrases as the building blocks of special speech, acknowledges the many instances of both the metrical and the syntactical termination. Any model of Homeric composition that starts from the notion of building blocks and apposition points at the relatively small size of those building blocks and hence, unavoidably, at the many compositional pauses between metrical cola, syntactical constituents, and appositional word groups. My approach to pause as an audible phenomenon starts from the assumption that not all the terminations reflected in metrical and syntactical boundaries were realized as audible, true pauses in performance.[23] What is a phonetic pause? Does it have to do with verse end and main caesura? If so, or if not, are there specific metrical and phonological circumstances for phonetic pause? These are the questions I will try to answer in this section. Related issues—Is the phonetic pause a performative pause? What is the relation between word group building blocks and phonetic pause? And between syntactical completion and phonetic pause?—will be dealt with in later chapters.

Phonetics from phonology

I will interpret Homeric phonology as the key to surface rhythmic phonetics, as phonetic pause is primarily a rhythmic phenomenon. In defense of such an approach, I start from the distinction between phonology and phonetics, as it is likened to the distinction between metrics and rhythm by Devine and Stephens.[24] They draw attention to the fact that twentieth-century durational approaches to Greek meter have developed some awareness for the durational differences between segmentally longer and shorter types of heavy and light syllables. Mora count does not run counter to the metrical pattern of light and heavy syllables, despite durational differences between the various heavy and the various light syllables. As mentioned in §1.2, such differences are referred to as differences in submoraic duration. Devine and Stephens point out that in the philological tradition there has been a tendency to assume that differences in submoraic duration arising from differences in segmental structure (subcategorical syllable duration) are relevant to the analysis of meter. They list a number of metrical phenomena to illustrate the metrical relevance of durational difference in the philological tradition (1994:102–117) and point out that differences in subcategorical and intrinsic syllable duration have been used to explain the possibilities of, and restrictions on, resolution, and to explain the occurrence of specific segmental structures at specific metrical positions. I will approach differences in submoraic duration as relevant to the analysis of phonological phrases, be it only to the analysis of phrase demarcation. Within the phonological phrase, I consider the durational differences between various syllable structures hardly relevant. Syllable structures represent sonority; within the categories heavy and light, syllable duration is adapted to rhyth-

---

[23] An assumption defended by Sturtevant 1921 and 1924, and O'Neill 1939.
[24] Devine and Stephens 1994:51; cf. the distinction *framing-rhythm* in Lidov 2010.

mical circumstances, and sensitive to the maintenance of rhythmic regularity. Perceptible durational differences are only to be expected at metrical positions that allow for phonological lengthening without disrupting rhythmic regularity. Such lengthening is a phrase-final phonetic reality for which phonology has to account. The approaches summarized in the overview by Devine and Stephens turn out to be relevant to phonological phrase structure: they all derive concrete phonetics from observations concerning syllable structures at phrase end.

No room for syntactic considerations

My hypothesis will be that phonetically realized pauses demarcate phonological phrases. I am looking for what makes phrases audible in the continuous flow of dactyls. Syntactic considerations should be neglected for now. In his discussion of phrasing, Porter 1951 relied on an *a priori* notion of the normative effect on meaning when he discussed the rhythmical unity looking for its demarcations. Kirk took a further step when he started looking for demarcation of unities that are "semantically coherent": in such an approach (cf. §1.2), the identification of the desired unity precedes the consideration of the criteria to identify points of termination. In the reconstruction of the phonetics of pause, syntactic considerations should be left out, as clauses and phrases may differ from each other in the way they terminate.

It is possible, I think, to identify the audible markers of phrase termination in our written version of the Homeric epic. Looking for the surface rhythmic phonetics of phrase termination means looking for opportunities for submoraic adjustment within the parameters—the restrictions, that is, of metrical formalism. The first restriction to deal with is that of the unavoidability of verse end and of the main caesura: does it have to do with phonetic pause?

3.2.2 Frequent word end and pause

Existing models of Homeric phrasing (metrical, syntactical, rhetorical) do not claim that all metrical boundaries are phonetically realized pauses. Metrical boundaries are treated as instances of pausa*, phonological demarcation through frequent word end. Not many studies comment on the phonetics of pausa: those that do (Korzeniewski 1968; Allen 1973; West 1982) rely on the analysis of metrical formalism as phonology. Such analysis considers verse-end phonetic disruption, and often allows for phonetic disruption at the main caesura. The pausa is hence treated as performative pause, especially at verse end. Illustrative for this approach, and an interesting contribution to the suitability of phonological pausa as phonetic pause, is the 1991 article by Daitz. As the title of the article ("On Reading Homer Aloud: To Pause or not to Pause") demonstrates, Daitz investigates "the pause at various points in the recitation and the possible effects that pause can produce on the listener's perception of the poetic rhythm." His "pause" is audible: "By pause I mean a temporary interruption of phonation by the performer which is perceived by the listener as a temporary silence." As evidence for an automatic pause at verse end, Daitz refers to the prosodic neutrality of the verse-final syllable (metrical indifference[25]), hiatus at verse end, and the clausular closure of the hexameter;[26] testimonies from antiquity are taken from Latin authors, including Cicero. Concerning the verse-internal pause, Daitz supposes that rhythmic disruption is unwanted, and he finds evidence for lines without internal pause, again, in Cicero.

Daitz cites Cicero on the issue of performative pauses, but to gauge the Homeric phonological phrase, and the audible pause at the metrical boundary with it, I also point at some helpful comments of the ancient ῥυθμικοί, as opposed to the μετρικοί. The latter group of scholars from antiquity, the μετρικοί, study what is now called outer metric*. To them, the realization of metrical rhythm is purely a regularized pattern of light and heavy syllables. Every single syllable is either heavy or light: both are absolute durations in accordance with the mora of the metronome. There is nothing in between. For the μετρικοί, the positions of frequent word end frame the metrical colon as a repeated sequence. Grouped together, the repeated metrical sequences form metrical periods, or metrical strophes. The theories of the μετρικοί are presented by Hephaestion.[27]

On the other hand, there are the ῥυθμικοί, whose ideas can be traced back to Aristoxenus. These scholars approach the issue of meter and rhythm with the aid of phonological tools that are very similar to those used in modern phonological research. Aristotle already stressed the importance of termination's phonetics (*Rhetoric* 1409a: ἀλλὰ δεῖ τῇ μακρᾷ ἀποκόπεσθαι καὶ δήλην εἶναι τὴν τελευτήν μὴ διὰ τὸν γραφέα μηδὲ διὰ τὴν παραγραφὴν ἀλλὰ διὰ τὸν ῥυθμόν, "but the strong pause ought to be introduced by a long syllable and the end clearly marked, not by the scribe nor by a punctuation mark, but by the rhythm"). The ancient ῥυθμικοί describe the phonetic phenomenon now known as lengthening* of final syllables (LFS). The additional lengthening of the word-final syllable (τονή)[28] is partly due to assimilation of the phonetic pause to the word-final syllable. Lengthening affects the final syllables of rhythmical word types*. Aristides Quintilianus adds that the prosodic realization of syllables does not only depend on their metrical position (light/heavy), but on

---

[25] Or rhythmic indeterminacy.

[26] Understood as catalectic verse.

[27] *Enchiridion* (Ἐγχειρίδιον περὶ μέτρων), second century CE.

[28] Musical term denoting "prolongation" (Cleonides *Introduction to Harmonics* 14).

their position within the word as well: word-final position results in additional lengthening of both light and heavy word-final syllables.[29] At word end, lengthening is described as διάστασις "separation" and κενὸς χρόνος "empty unit of time." Other terminology indicating the same phenomenon is μεταξὺ χρόνος "in-between unit of time," χρόνος μέσος "middle unit of time," and σιωπή "silence" or rather "sound stop."[30] None of our sources explicitly says so, but it is tempting to assume that such terminology indicates a true pause of measurable duration.[31] Dionysius[32] comments on audible pause as phonetic disturbance: the "reset[33] of durations" (ἀναβολὴ χρόνων) is caused by a "clashing of syllables" (ἀνακοπὴ συλλαβῶν) that is the result of "blockades formed by articulate sounds" (ἀντιστηριγμοὶ γραμμάτων).

Phonetic pause may have to do with the positions of frequent word end. Phonetic pause definitely has to do with the termination of the phonological phrase. So what is the relation between positions of frequent word end and phrase termination? Where do the two coincide?

3.2.3 The phonetics of termination

I argue that the phonetics of pause are the phonetics of word end, and that they have nothing to do with the orthography of word end. In line with the aspects of phonetics described so far, the phonetics of pause comprise of two aspects: (i) termination and (ii) lengthening. Termination demands that auditory features that suggest coherence be absent. Termination of the appositive group requires the absence of phonological clisis at word end. Termination of the phonetic word requires the absence of accentual clisis at word end, in addition to termination of phonation. Termination of the minor phonological phrase requires the absence of both accentual clisis and phonological clisis at word end, in addition to termination of phonation. Termination of the major phonological phrase requires the termination of phonation at word end and the possibility for additional phonetic lengthening.

---

[29] ἡ γὰρ μεταξὺ διάστασις τῆς τε τοῦ προτέρου τελευτῆς καὶ τῆς ἀρχῆς τοῦ δευτέρου μῆκος τῇ συλλαβῇ παρέχεται, "for the in-between separation of, on the one hand, the completion of the first, and, on the other, the start of the second provides the syllable with duration," Aristides Quintilianus (p. 43.2-4 in the edition of Winnington-Ingram).

[30] As in Dionysius of Halicarnassus *On literary composition* 22/101.19 and 22/109.2 (Usener-Radermacher), and in his *Demosthenes* 38; Rossi 1963:63–76 and 93–98.

[31] As the term is used in music, cf. Aristides Quintilianus p. 38.28–39.2 (Winnington-Ingram). Nicanor's punctuation system at least suggests that the term refers to a "measurable" duration of silence.

[32] Dionysius of Halicarnassus *On literary composition* 16/61.20–68.6 (Usener-Radermacher).

[33] Cf. Devine and Stephens 1994:449–450.

Termination

Termination of phonation means that the word-final syllable is free from the influence of sandhi: liaison of consonants (or συνάφεια), and vowel coalescence (or συναλοιφή). Hiatus and *brevis in longo* have been discussed as sandhi-free features (§3.1.3.1): hiatus resists elision despite vowel coalescence, and *brevis in longo* is a rhythmic license due to the absence of sandhi. Termination of the phonological phrase is hence found at the appearance of sandhi-free phonetic word-final syllables. Such syllables may be found both on the arsis and on the thesis. When on the arsis, sandhi-free syllables will regularly be light, as the spondaic bridge precludes spondaic word end on the arsis. On the thesis, sandhi-free syllables must count as heavy. Metrical analysis is helpful for the identification of word end as phonetic pause, as it rationalizes syllable structure.

Rationalization of syllable structures puts sandhi-free termination on a par with phonetic pause. Example (60) implies that the caesura at position 5 is treated as a phonetic pause, since the structure of the underlined syllables requires phonetic word end *following* position 5 if the syllable *on* position 5 is to meet the requirements of this metrical position:

(60) ὁ ξεῖνος ἐμέ<u>θεν</u> ἐθέλω δέ μιν ἐξερέεσθαι

Odyssey xix 99[34]

[that] the stranger [may listen] to me; I wish to interrogate him

Assumption of phonetic pause is restricted, however, to a limited number of heavy word-final syllables, and should not be extended to word-final heavy syllables in general: comparison of word-final heavy syllables CV and CV̆C shows that the latter elicits the assumption of pause, but that phonology provides evidence against such assumption. The requirements of the prepausal heavy syllable on the thesis are more easily (and according to statistics much more often) met by a syllable CV(C) with a long vocalic nucleus than by CV̆C. The latter would only be heavy *because* of an assumed, subsequent phonetic pause: phonation needs to terminate with the coda (CVC.) for the syllable to count as heavy, regardless of the segment (vocalic /V-/ or consonantal /C-/) that starts phonation after the pause. This observation, the irrelevance of subsequent start of phonation, has consequences for the word-final heavy syllable that is "long by position" (CV̆C). I argue that the resulting rest in performance is severely restricted, even to the extent that phonetic word end in CV̆C does not lead to subsequent phonetic pause: metrical syllabification implies that the syllable-final coda is resyllabified *unless* the postpausal syllable starts with a consonantal onset. In the case of

---

[34] Cf. the remarks on the metrical lengthening in Russo et al. 1992:79.

word-final CV̆C, the consequences of postpausal restart of phonation can only be of influence when phonetic word end does not allow for rest in performance: subsequent phonation ought to start with a very sonorant onset, as is the case with non-word-final .CV̆(C). Non-word-final .CV(C). is non-prepausal, so it does not run the risk of coda to onset resyllabification; word-final .CV̆C. does run that risk, therefore phonetic word end, maintaining the required rhythmical weight, also requires phonological coherence over the word-juncture. Word-final .CV̆C. is, in other words, not sandhi-free. It does not allow for termination. For that reason example (60) is exceptional in the assumption of phonetic pause, as are well-known expressions ending in CV̆C like τὸν δ' ἀπαμειβόμενος, occupying the first half of the verse, and sharing the verse with other, very frequently used expressions (e.g., ἔπεα πτερόεντα προσηύδα).

Lengthening

Sources from antiquity comment on the other aspect of phonetic termination: phonetic lengthening. The possibility of additional lengthening and the absence of phonological phenomena to avoid such lengthening (like elision or shortening) is described as a phenomenon occurring in the presence of pause by Devine and Stephens.[35] "In the presence of pause" is still rather vague. Does this mean that phrase-final lengthening is mainly to be found on the prepausal syllable? Or is it on the preceding syllables, and may the prepausal syllable not be its primary indicator? I argue that word-final lengthening is primarily found on the word-final syllable. For evidence, I turn to the discussion in Ruijgh 1987 on the "perfect" *longum*: from his treatment of this so-called μακρὰ τελεία, I deduce observations that point at additional lengthening as a feature of the word-final syllable.

In his article, Ruijgh defends the position that the perfect *longum*, as identified by Dionysius of Halicarnassus in *On literary composition*, is in fact the heavy word-final syllable—τελεία may also translate "final." Its phonetic duration, Ruijgh argues, is longer than that of the non-final heavy syllable, taking into account that final here means phonetic-word final. The non-final heavy syllable is then the "immeasurable" heavy syllable of Dionysius. Ruijgh invents the "perfect" and the "immeasurable" light to match the long syllables: the "perfect" light is the non-final, the "immeasurable" the word-final light syllable. In case of light syllables, word-final lengthening thus results in "immeasurability." With these technical terms, Ruijgh is able to establish a correspondence between the usage of "immeasurable" by Dionysius, Aristoxenus, and Aristides Quintilianus; a correspondence sought for since Boeckh (1811), who posited a

---

[35] Cf. Devine and Stephens 1994:79–82, 143–145.

durational adjustment of both arsis and thesis to account for the "immeasurable" proportion of arsis to thesis as a result of durational adjustment of heavy syllables in anceps positions.[36] Ruijgh's explanation of "immeasurable" still has to do with foot-internal proportion* of thesis and arsis, but not primarily with the realization of the anceps element as a heavy syllable. He rather includes the occurrence of non-final syllables into his account: if one of the two constituent elements of the foot, the arsis, is occupied by at least one "immeasurable," that is, by non-final heavy or by a word-final light syllable, the foot-internal proportion of arsis to thesis is by definition immeasurable. In Ruijgh's view, phonetic final lengthening is not evidenced by syllable structure: the preference for lighter syllable structures to account for the submoraic adjustment that is final lengthening. Ruijgh claims that final lengthening is an actual, absolute lengthening of syllables that may disrupt the balanced podic (foot) structure of metrical rhythm. He uses the existence and persistence of metrical bridges as evidence: the occurrence of metrical bridges proves this disrupting effect of untimely final lengthening. Porson's Law, for example, forbids word end after a heavy third anceps, as final lengthening causes too serious a disruption to rhythm. As does Parker (1966), Ruijgh extends Porson's law to the biceps of the hexameter: Homer avoids spondaic word end, as final lengthening would disrupt dactylic rhythm. From this, Ruijgh concludes that final lengthening applies to the word-final syllable. As I assume that phonetic lengthening applies to the performance of Greek metrical text (3.1.3.2) and that phonetic lengthening cannot disrupt rhythmic regularity, I agree with Ruijgh's conclusion.

Conclusion and consequences

From the observations concerning (i) termination and (ii) lengthening, I conclude that the phonetic pause in Homer may be identified as the lengthened and sandhi-free phonetic word-final syllable. The lengthened and sandhi-free phonetic word-final syllable is thus a prerequisite for performative pause, though not automatically its equivalent.

As is rhythm, so phonetic pause is subject to restrictions in metrical text. Metrical and phonological circumstances at word end are reflected in meter's surface structure, and so is phonetic pause. At the same time, phonetic pause may not disturb the surface structure and the implicit rhythmics it represents. In Chapters 4 and 5, I will discuss the possibilities for, and restrictions on, phonetic pause. I will argue that the combination of the syllable's phonological

---

[36] Such is the explanation of "immeasurable" proportion of arsis to thesis according to Westphal 1867, after Hermann had pointed out that there was no ancient evidence for the explanation by Boeckh. Devine and Stephens 1994:117 do not include Ruijgh's explanation.

realization and metrical position may allow for either a stronger or a milder phonetic pause: metrical location, on the thesis or the arsis, reflects the phonetic realization of termination: the more phonetic disruption metrical location allows, the stronger the audible pause at word end. Discussion of the possibilities for phonetic pause will bring out to what extent phonetic pause is identifiable as performative pause.

4

Possible Pause in Performance

*Technical terms followed by * on their first occurrence in this chapter are in the glossary.*

4.0   Introduction

This chapter deals with what Nagy 1998 describes as the performative perspectives of pause. He distinguishes between compositional and performative perspectives in the application of the term pause. My aim in this chapter is to explore the possibilities for, and restrictions on, the pause to be realized as a true pause, a silence due to the termination of phonation, in performance*. I will argue that the possibilities for such audible pause* depend on the phonological realization of the word-final syllable with regard for its metrical position.[1] The avoidance of disruption of the metrical surface structure is to be considered the most important restriction on pause as a performative phenomenon; the underlying rhythmic regularity cannot be disrupted by the temporal allowance that is a correlate of audible pause. Surface rhythmics of metrical text (like metrical bridges*, shortening*, elision*) show that the maintenance of rhythmic regularity is the decisive factor in the application of audible pause, instead of the markers of compositional pauses, like the metrical boundary or the syntactical sense-pause. Having explored the pause in meter (Chapter 1), syntax (Chapter 2), and phonology (Chapter 3), I take the final step towards a reconstruction of performative pause with the analysis of the possibilities for pause in performance. As does Nagy (1998), I will start from the distinction between compositional and performative perspectives in the application of the term pause.

---

[1]   In Chapter 5, I will argue that pause is an option in composition and a choice in performance.

Pause as a compositional phenomenon is identified as the recurrence of positions of frequent word end. The recurrence of metrical cola is derived from the positions of frequent word-end colometry* (Clark 2004). From the recurrence of metrical cola stems the notion of the sense-pause* (West 1982), the metrical equivalent of printed punctuation. Sense-pauses are identified in response to the need to structure a text that reflects the oral composition and performance of narrative. For the modern reader, the printed punctuation of a text furthers comprehension of its contents; understanding spoken language demands an ability to interpret what is being transmitted that is different from the ability to understand a printed text. Experienced readers are trained in self-structuring the soundless mental process of reading through recognition and processing of various means of punctuation. The punctuation of a printed text makes the text accessible to a reader. In spoken language, the person speaking may use differences in intonation, tempo, and articulatory prominence to further the audience's comprehension of what is being said. Punctuation in printed texts mimics to a certain extent the purpose of such audible differences in spoken language. It may, however, not cover all the nuances these differences add in spoken language.

The punctuation of the Homeric text does not receive much attention from commentators. The ancient scholia, especially those related to Nicanor, comment on rhetorical punctuation in a limited number of lines.[2] Comparison of the recent commentaries on the *Iliad* and the *Odyssey* shows that few if any critical remarks are made on the differences in punctuation between, and even within, various text editions.[3] At the same time, printed punctuation seems to be (understood as) the clue to performative pauses. To assess whether or not it really is, colometry and printed punctuation should be analyzed with regard to the *Iliad* and *Odyssey* as performable and performed text. Analysis of the Homeric epic as performance throws light on the performative perspectives of compositional pauses as well (§4.1). In §4.2, I will argue that the performative perspectives of phonetic pause, the pause I identified in Chapter 3, may equally be taken into account: the results of my analysis will show where phonetic word end offers the possibility for pause in performance.

---

[2] Erbse 1983:482 for the *Iliad*. Erbse 1988:135-144 lists all the words in the *Iliad* that are followed by some form of punctuation according to the scholia. The list does not account for all the punctuation used in modern editions of the Homeric epic.

[3] Covering the entire *Iliad*: Kirk 1985–1993, and, though only the first installments are yet available, Latacz 2000– ; covering the entire *Odyssey*: Heubeck et al. 1988, Heubeck and Hoekstra 1989, and Russo et al. 1992.

4.1   Performance and Pause

Parry 1929 (reprinted 1971) and Lord 1960 provide the framework for the application of cross-cultural observations concerning oral poetry* to the Homeric
epic. They do not formulate an oral theory centered around Homer, but draw
parallels between the Homeric epic, on the one hand, and oral traditions outside
the Greek world (notably in former Yugoslavia), on the other. The observations
in Lord 1960 are largely based on fieldwork: performances of Guslari (traditional
singers who accompany their recitative on a *guslar*, a guitar-like instrument)
serve as a model for the assumed Homeric performances. Nagy (1996:14–27)
presents performance as the key element in oral poetry. In the triad of composition, performance, and diffusion, it is performance that makes oral poetry truly
oral. Oesterreicher 1997 points out that performance is also an essential feature
of the medial aspect that defines oral literature and distinguishes oral literature
from written language. Foley (2002:82–93) presents a performance theory: a
performer "is there"; he uses special formulas, repetition, and appeals to tradition in front of an audience that actively participates. Martin (in Finkelberg
2011) defines performance as a significant enactment or expression for which
the initiator takes responsibility before a critical audience that can judge his
skill. In his definition, performance covers both the act of poetic composition in
an oral culture and (speech) acts by characters depicted in the Homeric poems.
Martin points out that performance practices *in* the Homeric epic (like *Odyssey*
i 325–353, viii 62, viii 83, viii 256–380) are to be considered archaizing projec-
tions and partial reminiscences of later reciters. If the *Iliad* and the *Odyssey*
provide any clue to the performance practice of Homeric poetry at all, Martin
offers the authoritative speech act performed prominently by heroes as the
most appropriate analogue. Beck 2012 argues in favor of performance practice
in the *Odyssey* (notably Demodocus) as analogous to that of Homeric poetry
in general: she considers especially Demodocus' second song as free indirect
speech, whereas other songs in the *Odyssey* take the shape of reported speech.
Demodocus' second song is thus a reflection of the way Homeric poetry itself
may have been performed.

For the study of pause as performative pause the distinction between the
performance of oral poetry as recitation (poetry read aloud) or as song is an
important one. Bonifazi and Elmer 2012 draw conclusions on the performative
aspects of pause, which will return in §4.2 below:

> Within the performative genre of South Slavic epic, the line works as
> the fundamental engine that drives the movement of song. The metrical
> shape and the melodic contour of the line serve both discontinuity

and continuity: on the one hand, each verbal unit is semantically and syntactically bounded by the meter and fits into a quantitatively undetermined sequence of hierarchically equal units; on the other hand, melody is constructed in such a way that each melodic unit joins the concluding verbal unit to the subsequent one, thus creating a sense of flow and forward momentum.

4.1.1 Poetry recited

In their description of performance of the Homeric epic, Daitz 1991 and Nagy 1998, 2000, 2010 draw parallels with poetry that is recited. Daitz refers to comments in Latin authors like Cicero on the recitation of Greek verses. Nagy points at the various selective markings in papyri of Bacchylides, which he interprets as guidelines for reciting the verses; he then explicitly broadens his observations concerning Bacchylides' verses as recitation to other works of poetry, especially those written in dactylic hexameters.

Both authors reach very similar conclusions with regard to the value of colometry. In the analysis of the hexameter, they apply the terms period* and colon as they are understood from Boeckh's approach of Pindar. The colon is the smaller metrical unit; the period the larger metrical unit (containing cola) that ends with word end allowing for hiatus* and/or *brevis in longo**. West 1982 rephrases the definition of period to the self-contained unit of metrical composition within which there is prosodic continuity and at the end of which prosodic connection is interrupted. Colon and period end commonly coincide with word end. Where colon end does not coincide with word end, Nagy (2000:13) uses the term *hyphenation*. The idea of more-or-less self-contained units of metrical composition leads both Daitz and Nagy to assume (and look for) coherence within the separate cola and within the period as a whole. For the dactylic hexameter this assumes coherence within the hemistichs and within the verse. Nagy 2000 uses the term rhythm* for the cola-internal and period-internal coherence. Their assumptions concerning the value of colometry have an effect on the way they argue that poetry is to be recited. Both Daitz and Nagy state that period end ought to coincide with a (breathing) pause and that any termination of phonation be avoided within the verse (cf. Hagel 2002: "pauses within the verse are incompatible with Greek versification").

As the title of Daitz' article ("On Reading Homer Aloud: To Pause or not to Pause") demonstrates, he investigates "the pause at various points in the recitation and the possible effects that pause can produce on the listener's perception of the poetic rhythm." As mentioned above at §3.2.1, his "pause" is audible: "By pause I mean a temporary interruption of phonation by the performer which is perceived by the listener as a temporary silence." Daitz is not very happy with the rhetorical punctuation that has permeated classical texts as we read them. Rhetorical punctuation relies mainly on the second-century CE Nicanor, "the Punctuator,"[4] Daitz claims that at least fifty percent of printed punctuation is wrong or misleading from the viewpoint of performance. Fortunately, he claims, there are external sources on the question of pause. Basically, Daitz deals with two questions: 1) is there always a pause at the end of the line? and 2) is there ever a pause within the line? As evidence for an automatic pause at verse end, Daitz refers to the prosodic neutrality* of the verse-final syllable (metrical indifference[5]), hiatus* at verse-end, and the clausular closure of the hexameter;[6] testimonies from antiquity are taken from Latin authors. From Cicero (*De Oratore* 1.61.261) he understands that the usual practice was to recite a single verse on a single breath. Furthermore, Homer does not present hypermetric verses* (against twenty in Vergil). Finally, the written practice of beginning each verse on a new line is a reflection of performance practice.

Concerning the possibility of a verse-internal pause in performance, Daitz supposes that rhythmic disruption is unwanted, and he finds evidence for lines without internal pause, again, in Cicero. He then adds phonological synaphy* and vowel coalescence as additional arguments against internal pause: liaison, shortening, and elision all nullify the possibility of audible pause. Daitz allows for internal pause under specific circumstances: to avoid hiatus, to handle *brevis in longo*, or after certain heavy syllables, for expressive purposes. As rhetoric overcame rhythm, Daitz concludes, the scholarly procedure for semantic and grammatical analysis was unhappily transformed into a performance practice:

> In the Homeric hexameter we have a form of poetry in which each verse was originally felt to be an integrated unit, centripetal in nature, knit together by the procedures of elision, correption, consonantal assimilation, and syllabic liaison. This poetry was normally read without pause from the first to the last syllable, but with a pause after the *last* syllable of each verse, and with sufficient flexibility of tempo and pitch to clearly convey meaning and expression without distortion of the

---

[4] Ὁ Στιγματίας (Eustathius 10.12). Various scholia on the *Iliad* mention issues concerning punctuation (Erbse 1983:482; 1988:135-144), but their main concern is syntactical phrasing. Devine and Stephens (1994:420–422) show that any prosodic element stems from a reconstruction of a hierarchy of pause durations based on Nicanor's system of punctuation in descending rank order, relying on mora count and only applicable in the purely metrical approach; cf. Schironi in Finkelberg 2011.

[5] Or rhythmic indeterminacy.

[6] Understood as catalectic verse.

rhythm. The overall aural effect would come closer to the rhythmic regularity and strictness of music than we are used to hearing in modern renditions of poetry. It would therefore be further removed from the rhetorical cadences of prose which we are accustomed both to hear and to see reflected in the printed punctuation of our texts, and which we unconsciously and erroneously tend to employ in our reading of ancient poetry.

Daitz's analysis is, in many respects, illustrative of the study of pause in the Homeric epic: in its conclusion; in its use of the phonological approach (and hence of *pausa**) for the identification of pause; in its argumentation, which is largely built on a specific interpretation of seemingly randomly chosen fragments from Latin authors; and in its consideration of phonetics—at best, "shown when wished for."[7] Nagy points at hyphenation (evidenced in the continuing coherence through avoidance of word end and accentuation) to account for the absence of pause within the verse; Daitz only allows for verse-internal pause "for emotional effect" Nagy (2000:13). shows his sharpest regard for colometry when he lists the advice he gives his students on reading hexametric poetry aloud:

- Try not to stop between words until you reach the end of the line.

- If you have to stop in order to catch your breath before you reach the end of the line, allow yourself to do so only at the caesura* or at the dieresis*.

With these instructions he aims to give his students a "feel" for the performative perspective of pause,[8] not unlike the conclusions that Daitz draws from the remarks by Cicero. I regret to say that Nagy's advice for reciting hexametric

---

[7] Still, I find issues in Daitz' work that are relevant for the study of phonetic pause: the consideration of coherent phonological phrasing as a hindrance for audible pause, the questioning of ancient written punctuation to identify audible pause, the "disappearance of recognisable meter" as the result of "rhetorical" colometry, and, most importantly of all, raising the issue of "to pause or not to pause." Like others before him, Daitz refers to the Danae-passage in *On literary composition* 26/140.18–142.13 U-R, and to Roman authors contradicting his quotations from Cicero (Daitz 1991:159n18): "W. S. Allen has suggested in private correspondence and also implicitly in his book, *Accent and Rhythm* (Cambridge 1973) 335–42, that Latin poetry, and particularly the hexameter, was read aloud as *prose*. This would accord with Quintilian's suggestions for reciting Vergil with pauses appropriate to prose, but would be at variance with Cicero's observation." I find the recent approach to these various issues in relation to Simonides in Lidov 2010:34–38 very stimulating.

[8] Cf. the comments in Brooks 2007:50–51 concerning reading aloud Latin poetry.

poetry has taught yet another generation of classical students and scholars to recite verses in an unnatural way, which cannot be accounted for on the basis of evidence for the performance of Greek verse. Unfortunately, Nagy's recommendations arise from the larger approach to performative features; though these features, which have pedagogic consequences in the teaching of Greek prosody* and rhythm*, lack a basis in theory, the assumptions underlying the pauses in performance die hard.

4.1.2 Song

Alternatively, the performance of the Homeric epic is described in terms of song. Often, the performance of poetry as song, accompanied by dance movement in *Odyssey* viii 256–380, is taken as a parallel for the performance practice of Homeric poetry in general. Song and music presuppose a more rigid rhythmical regularity than recitation, when rhythm in music is understood (as it often is) as a beat in accordance with the metronome. When performed poetry is considered song performed to music, the metrical and rhythmical regularity is not only seen as reflecting the regularization of the act of speaking, but also the regularity of the dance movement that accompanies that act.[9] David 2006 takes the consequences of this approach furthest when he reconstructs the origins of the dactylic foot* as a series of dance steps. In the process, he maintains the verse and the cola as the units of performance. As with performance as poetry recited (§4.1.1), there is neither reason nor evidence to assume that rhythm as a timing mechanism for speech followed the metronome, or musical rhythm according to the metronome; to this I add that intuition and cross-linguistic evidence rather opposes the metronome-approach of Greek verse performance. Ford (in Finkelberg 2011) cautions against any attempt to reconstruct the performance of song in the Homeric epic. Beck 2012 does not comment on the performative aspects of song.[10]

4.2 Performance and the Phonetics of Pause

My discussion of pause as a feature of performance requires a relation with the phonetics of pause, which has not been found in prior treatments of the compositional pauses of the *Iliad* and *Odyssey*, whether understood as recited text or as

---

[9] Such an equation was already present in the identification of the structural metrical elements thesis* and arsis* as the "lowering" and "lifting" of the foot (as in Hardie 1920, and any other study that labels the stable element of the foot arsis and the changeable element thesis).

[10] Samples of Homeric performance as song can be heard in a link in Hagel 2002 and of reconstructed Greek music comparable to Homer's in a link in D'Angour 2013.

song. Homeric performance as song furthermore presupposes, without proper argument in my opinion, that language's rhythmic regularity be synchronous with the regularity of musical rhythm. It is not my aim to propose a third concept of Homeric performance, next to recitation and song; in the face of the ungrounded assumptions underlying poetry as song, I understand Homeric performance as recitation. Within the concept of recitation, I focus on the possibilities and requirements for a rest of duration.

In existing studies, performance of the *Iliad* and *Odyssey* is studied from two different points of view. The first (starting from Lord 1960) considers performance a *datum*, so that discourse, style, composition, and technique are studied as reflections in writing of an original performance. Every single aspect in the study of the *Iliad* and the *Odyssey* is approached from the notion that the features in the text of the Homeric epic can and should be explained in accordance with cross-cultural observations concerning oral literature. The alternative point of view (which follows in the footsteps of Allen 1973) considers performance of the *Iliad* and the *Odyssey* a *possibility*: the text of the Homeric epic may or may not be similar to, or representative of, a version of the narrative that was orally performed. This second approach studies the text of the *Iliad* and the *Odyssey* for clues that may illustrate the occurrence of phenomena that are comparable to those observed in oral traditions from other cultures and periods. Although some mix-up of both approaches seems hard to avoid, in this section I will focus mainly on the second approach in order to establish the validity of phonetic pause—defined as the lengthened and sandhi-free phonetic word-final syllable—in performance.

Studies on performance of the Homeric epic do not regularly focus on the phonetics of pause. In general, the verse is seen as the unit of performance (Daitz 1991; Bakker 1997a; Nagy 2000; Edwards 2002; Finkelberg 2011; cf. Bonifazi and Elmer 2012, who claim the line as the basic unit of performance for the Serbo-croatian decasyllabic line); as a consequence, pause is assumed at every verse end. The analysis of enjambment* as affective prosody* is based on the concept of the verse as the unit of performance (Parry 1929; Kirk 1966; Higbie 1990; Clark 1997; Hagel 2002; cf. §2.4). The approach of Homeric discourse as special speech allows for the cola within the verse to function as intonation units (Bakker 1997b, 2005; cf. §2.2), suggesting prosodic contours that result in pauses between cola, like those between verses. At the same time, syntactic structure has provided a basis for the identification of pauses in performance: since many verses feature a syntactic break at verse end, Parry 1929 pointed at verses that do not as aberrations. Others, like Porter 1951, argued that cola were units of sense as well. West 1982 values positions of regular word end in Homer as sense-pauses, thus claiming identification as sense-pause for thirty-six percent of all instances of verse end—without regard to the phonetics of pause. Even in studies that do pay attention to pause as "termination of phonation" and its opposite (phonological legato; Nagy 2000 speaks of *hyphenation*), continuation of such legato over the metrical boundaries of the cola is not considered, nor is the cessation of phonation within the colon (and sometimes not even within the verse). Hiatus and *brevis in longo* are commonly treated as indicators of pause (as is any metrical indifference or rhythmical indeterminacy), but the same phenomena commonly receive different treatment *within* the line or the colon. A purely phonetic approach to the pause (based on phonology* and the acceptance of submoraic adjustment*) has not yet been applied to Homer. My analysis is the first to consider the performative perspectives of phonetic pause.

Outside the dactylic hexameter, the coincidence of the verse, its cola, and the units of performance is not considered to be as strict as in the analysis of Homeric performance (Lidov 2010): my aim is to approach the pause in Homer as a phonetic pause, a termination of phonation, and then, in later chapters, to investigate the consequences of such treatment on the many compositional pauses (Chapter 6), and on the resulting units of performance, rhythm, and sense (Chapter 7). In the remainder of this chapter, I will therefore analyze two aspects of phonetic pause: the possibilities for, and restrictions on, phonetic pause in performance.

4.2.1 Phonological perspectives of phonetic pause in performance

The phonetic pause has been defined as the lengthened and sandhi-free phonetic word-final syllable (§3.2). Termination of phonation can only be assumed under such circumstances.

Consonantal synaphy and vowel coalescence reflect the opposite of termination of phonation: phonological coherence within the verse. In Homer, this coherence is always broken at the metrical boundary of the verse end: shortening, liaison, and elision do not occur there. Coherence may also be broken at word end within the verse.

Phonological coherence facilitates metrical syllabification, the division of the line into vowel-centered sounds that do not correspond either with morphological or orthographic syllables (§1.3.1). The units of quantity are clusters of phonemes, groupings of sounds that have certain significance regardless of morphology:[11]

---

[11] Henderson 1973.

(56)   τὸν δ' αὖτε προσέειπε συβώτης ὄρχαμος ἀνδρῶν

Odyssey xvi 36

To him in turn the swineherd spoke, the men's leader

(56a)   τὸν.δαῦ.τε.προς.έ.ει.πε.συ.βώ.της.ὄρ.χα.μος.ἀν.δρῶν
(orthographical syllabification)

(56b)   τὸν.δαῦ.τεπ.ρο.σέ.ει.πε.συ.βώ.τη. σόρ.χα.μο.σαν.δρῶν
(metrical syllabification)

Phonological coherence is also indicated through the appositive group*, the combination of the lexical word* and its phonological clitics (including adjectives; §1.3.2). To illustrate the way phonology keeps the words together, I present four examples (61–64) of verses cut up into appositive groups (in brackets). Arrows indicate the direction in which phonological clitics (which may be accentual clitics as well) "lean" on their lexical and, in the case of accentual clitics, their accentual head:

(61)   δῦ δὲ χιτῶν' ἔλε δὲ σκῆπτρον παχύ βῆ δὲ θύραζε

(δῦ ← δὲ)(χιτῶν')(ἔλε ← δὲ)(σκῆπτρον παχύ)(βῆ ← δὲ)(θύραζε)

Iliad XVIII 416

He put on a cloak, grabbed a sturdy stick, and stepped outside

(62)   ὡς δ' ὅτ' ἂν ἀίξῃ νόος ἀνέρος ὅς τ' ἐπὶ πολλὴν

(ὡς ← δ')(ὅτ' ← ἂν)(ἀίξῃ)(νόος)(ἀνέρος)(ὅς ← τ')(ἐπὶ → πολλὴν)

Iliad XV 80

Like when a man's thoughts leap quickly who over a large stretch [of land has travelled]

(63)   εἰ δέ κε σίνηαι τότε τοι τεκμαίρομ' ὄλεθρον
      νηί τε καὶ ἑτάροις αὐτὸς δ' εἴ πέρ κεν ἀλύξῃς

(εἰ ← δέ ← κε)(σίνηαι)(τότε ← τοι)[12](τεκμαίρομ')(ὄλεθρον)
(νηί ← τε)(καὶ → ἑτάροις)(αὐτὸς ← δ')(εἴ ← πέρ ← κεν)(ἀλύξῃς)

Odyssey xii 139–140

---

[12]   Or (τοι → τεκμαίρομ'); cf. Devine and Stephens (1994:365–366) on the possible reversal of phonological clisis in combination with metrical boundary.

But if you harm them, then I assure you, I predict total ruin | for the ship and your comrades; and as for yourself, even if you would escape

(64)   πρίν γ' ὅτε δή με σὸς υἱὸς ἀπὸ μεγάροιο κάλεσσε

(πρίν ← γ')(ὅτε ← δή ← με)(σὸς → υἱὸς)(ἀπὸ → μεγάροιο)(κάλεσσε)

Odyssey xxiii 43

Before the moment when, finally, your son called me from the great
hall

On a different level, the words in examples 61–64 are also kept together through vowel coalescence (elision) and consonantal synaphy. Together sandhi* and phonological clisis evidence the coherent phonological phrase* (§3.1.4). Conversely, absence of both sandhi and phonological clisis indicates the possibility for phonetic pause.

It seems reasonable to assume, I argue, that phonetic pause appears in two qualities, as there are two types of coherent phonological phrases: the minor and the major phonological phrase (§3.1.4). The minor phrase is the combination of appositive groups (and clitic groups) into a single prosodic unit subject to sandhi. Phonology phrases adjacent items together, provided that neither of them belongs more closely to a third item (due to clisis* or apposition*).[13] In other words, clisis, apposition, and sandhi together keep the minor phrase together. The examples 61–64 are presented again, now reflecting both the appositive groups and the minor phrases, the latter of which are indicated using the symbol · (raised dot):

(61)   δῦ δὲ χιτῶν' ἕλε δὲ σκῆπτρον παχύ βῆ δὲ θύραζε

(δῦ ← δὲ) · (χιτῶν')(ἕλε ← δὲ) · (σκῆπτρον παχύ) · (βῆ ← δὲ) · (θύραζε)

Iliad XVIII 416

He put on a cloak, grabbed a sturdy stick, and stepped outside

(62)   ὡς δ' ὅτ' ἂν ἀίξῃ νόος ἀνέρος ὅς τ' ἐπὶ πολλὴν

(ὡς ← δ')(ὅτ' ← ἂν)(ἀίξῃ) · (νόος)(ἀνέρος)(ὅς ← τ')(ἐπὶ → πολλὴν)

Iliad XV 80

Like when a man's thoughts leap quickly who over a large stretch [of
land has travelled]

---

[13]   Devine and Stephens 1994:303.

(63) εἰ δέ κε σίνηαι τότε τοι τεκμαίρομ' ὄλεθρον
      νηί τε καὶ ἑτάροις αὐτὸς δ' εἴ πέρ κεν ἀλύξῃς

(εἰ ← δέ ← κε) · (σίνηαι) · (τότε ← τοι)[14] · (τεκμαίρομ')(ὄλεθρον)
(νηί ← τε) · (καὶ → ἑτάροις) · (αὐτὸς ← δ')(εἴ ← πέρ ←κεν) · (ἀλύξῃς)

Odyssey xii 139–140

But if you harm them, then I assure you, I predict total ruin | for
the ship and your comrades; and as for yourself, even if you would
escape

(64) πρίν γ' ὅτε δή με σὸς υἱὸς ἀπὸ μεγάροιο κάλεσσε

(πρίν ← γ')(ὅτε ← δή ← με) · (σὸς → υἱὸς) · (ἀπὸ → μεγάροιο) ·
(κάλεσσε)

Odyssey xxiii 43

Before the moment when, finally, your son called me from the great
        hall

The major phonological phrases of Devine and Stephens are defined as
syntactic wholes framed by phonetic pauses. This definition implies that
minor phrases team up to form major phrases on the principle of sentential
clisis*: the expectations that syntactical constituents raise with regard to
the scope of the major phrase—when does the major phrase come to completion? Such expectations are based on the requirements of the syntactically
complete utterance. If major phrases are made visible in the examples 61–64,
using [...] to visibly frame them, minor-phrase boundaries coinciding with
major-phrase boundaries disappear:

(61) δῦ δὲ χιτῶν' ἕλε δὲ σκῆπτρον παχύ βῆ δὲ θύραζε

[(δῦ ← δὲ) · (χιτῶν')(ἕλε ← δὲ) · (σκῆπτρον παχύ)][(βῆ ← δὲ) ·
(θύραζε)]

Iliad XVIII 416

He put on a cloak, grabbed a sturdy stick, and stepped outside

---

14 Or · (→ τεκμαίρομ').

(62)   ὡς δ' ὅτ' ἂν ἀίξῃ νόος ἀνέρος ὅς τ' ἐπὶ πολλὴν

[(ὡς ← δ')(ὅτ' ← ἂν)(ἀίξῃ) · (νόος)(ἀνέρος)(ὅς ← τ')(ἐπὶ → πολλὴν) ...]

Iliad XV 80

Like when a man's thoughts leap quickly who over a large stretch [of
land has travelled]

(63)   εἰ δέ κε σίνηαι τότε τοι τεκμαίρομ' ὄλεθρον
        νηί τε καὶ ἑτάροις αὐτὸς δ' εἴ πέρ κεν ἀλύξῃς

[(εἰ ← δέ ← κε) · (σίνηαι)][(τότε ← τοι)[15] · (τεκμαίρομ')(ὄλεθρον)
(νηί ← τε) · (καὶ → ἑτάροις)][(αὐτὸς ← δ')(εἴ ← πέρ ← κεν) ·
(ἀλύξῃς) ...]

Odyssey xii 139–140

But if you harm them, then I assure you, I predict total ruin | for
the ship and your comrades; and as for yourself, even if you would
escape

(64)   πρίν γ' ὅτε δή με σὸς υἱὸς ἀπὸ μεγάροιο κάλεσσε

[(πρίν ← γ')(ὅτε ← δή ← με) · (σὸς → υἱὸς) · (ἀπὸ ← μεγάροιο) ·
(κάλεσσε)]

Odyssey xxiii 43

Before the moment when, finally, your son called me from the great
hall

The major-phrase boundaries are understood by Devine and Stephens (1994:412–
414, 432–433) as pauses in performance. I do not agree with their identification for two reasons: (i) minor-phrase boundaries qualify as phonetic pauses
as well (so what is the difference between the way both types of phrases terminate?), and (ii) the completion of the major utterance is not primarily a matter
of phonetics (according to Devine and Stephens), but rather of completion of all
the syntactical requirements.

In their opinion intonation or melodic patterning may be suggestive of major
phrase completion. In terms of phonetics, such a concept of the phonological
major phrase is not very useful: it presupposes pauses to frame the phrase, just
like melodic patterning presupposes framing pauses. Such framing pauses are

---

[15] Or [... · (→ τεκμαίρομ') ...].

not that different from the pauses framing the verse or the cola—*compositional* pauses that accommodate the identification of units on a different level, in case of the verse and the colon on the level of metrics. Devine and Stephens's major phrase is a form of coherence that is based on syntactical considerations and assumes that prosodic contours will have aligned with syntactical units. This may or may not have been the case as far as I am concerned, but if the major phrase is to be of any use in the reconstruction of phonetics, its framing pauses must stem, I argue, from phonological instead of syntactical considerations, regardless of any coincidence of the former with the latter. Under such conditions, phonological phrasing, through sandhi and apposition, remains useful for my identification of performative pause ,as the phrase-internal coherence reflects the restrictions on pause in performance.

4.2.2 Phonological restrictions on phonetic pause in performance

Possibilities for phonetic pause are restricted by sandhi (consonantal liaison and vowel coalescence) and apposition. Sandhi and apposition can only be applied within the phonological phrase: together, they form the compositional principle behind the minor phrase. Alternatively (and turning the definition around), one might say that the minor phrase is the domain of sandhi and apposition. Sandhi and apposition regularly straddle the metrical boundaries, the positions of frequent word end that frame the metrical cola. Below, I present examples (65–68) of sandhi and apposition (→) straddling positions of frequent word end on the thesis (at the caesura following positions 3, 5 ,7 and 9):

> Straddling due to (apposition and) resyllabication at the caesura following position 3:
>
> > (65)   καί οἱ ὑπὸ σκήπτρῳ λιπαρὰς τελέουσι θέμιστας
> > (ὑ.πὸ → σ.κήπ.τρῳ.)
>
> > > > > > > *Iliad* IX 156
>
> And under his scepter they will pay him rich dues

> Straddling due to resyllabification at the caesura following position 5:
>
> > (66)   ὄψου τ' ἄσαιμι προταμὼν καὶ οἶνον ἐπισχών
> > .τ'ἄ.σαι.μιπ.ρο.τα.μὼν.
>
> > > > > > > *Iliad* IX 489
>
> I gave you enough meat after cutting it and holding wine to your lips

Straddling due to (apposition and) resyllabification at the caesura following
position 7:

> (67) Ἰδομενεὺς δ' Ἐρύμαντα κατὰ στόμα νηλέι χαλκῷ
>   (κα.τὰ → σ.τό.μα.)

> *Iliad* XVI 345

> Idomeneus [hit] Erumas in the mouth with the pitiless point

Straddling due to resyllabification at the caesura following position 9:

> (68) ὣς εἰπὼν ἐς δίφρον ἑλὼν ἔναρα βροτόεντα
>   .νἒ.να.ραβ.ρο.τό.εν.τα.

> *Iliad* XVII 540

> Having spoken thus and after putting the bloodstained armor in the
> chariot

Straddling in these four examples is due to resyllabification as onset to coda shift
(§3.1.1), the right to left movement of a consonant over the boundary between
words. In metrical syllabification, the shift may also be in the opposite direction: from coda to onset. This shift may cause syllabification to straddle, for
example, the trochaic word end (following position 5½) in the hexameter's third
foot. Realization of an audible pause following the third trochee would lead to
a serious disruption of rhythm. A phonetic pause would result in a prepausal
closed (= heavy) syllable in the third foot in the following examples (69–72). A
prepausal heavy syllable would occupy position 6, frustrate a main caesura alto-
gether, and lead to spondaic word end* on the third foot:

> (69) ἠὲ φίλων ἐν χερσίν ἐπεὶ πόλεμον τολύπευσε

> *Odyssey* xiv 368

> (as prepausal –.σίν. would be a heavy syllable)

> or in the hands of friends after he had survived the war

> (70) ἔσσεται ἦμαρ ὅτ' ἄν ποτ' ὀλώλῃ Ἴλιος ἱρή

> *Iliad* IV 164

> (as prepausal .ποτ'. would be a heavy syllable)

> The day will come when finally sacred Troy must fall

(71) Τρωιάδος τῆς εἵνεκ' ἐγὼ πάθον ἄλγεα θυμῷ

Odyssey xiii 263

(as prepausal –.νεκ'. would be a heavy syllable)

The Trojan (spoils) for which I endured pains in my heart

(72) δρηστοσύνη οὐκ ἄν μοι ἐρίσσειε βροτὸς ἄλλος[16]

Odyssey xv 321

(as prepausal .μοι. would be a heavy syllable)

In handiness no other mortal would be able to compete with me

In these four examples, only resyllabification (coda to onset shift) maintains the rhythmical regularity and in doing so it precludes the possibility for audible pause.

The phonological restriction on phonetic pause through coda to onset shift in syllabification may be seen most clearly in Homer by means of the movable (or ephelcystic) *nu**, whose application demonstrates the continuation of the phonological phrase over the third-foot word end in example (69) above (*Odyssey* xiv 368). Movable *nu* is interesting, as its application is optional: the manuscript tradition shows that it may or may not be included. Inclusion of movable *nu* may hence clarify not only its contribution to orthography, but also the reasoning behind its reflection of syllable weight*. In example (69) movable *nu* must contribute to phonological coherence, as it cannot contribute to the syllable weight of -σιν. In this and other examples, it becomes clear that movable *nu*, despite being optional, is not without consequences: there is a difference between movable *nu* used as a orthographic coda, and movable *nu* used for other reasons. As orthographic coda, movable *nu* is optional and regularly printed to avoid hiatus, for example, in *Odyssey* xxii 416:

(73) τῷ καὶ ἀτασθαλίῃσιν ἀεικέα πότμον ἐπέσπον

Odyssey xxii 416

Precisely because of their misbehavior they met a shameful death

Optional as movable *nu* may be, the choice to print it implies more than merely to choose between manuscript readings. In example (73) orthography implies quite the opposite of hiatus (without the insertion of movable *nu*) at the trochaic word end.[17] The movable *nu* at the caesura suggests a prepausal coda. This would

---

16 The actual shift is by means of a glide*: μο.ιε.ρίσ.σει.ε (Devine and Stephens 1994:255–256).

17 Cf. the reasoning in West 1998:xxv–xxvi.

result in a heavy syllable -.σιν. and is hence impossible at this metrical position. Meter and rhythm can only be maintained through resyllabification .σῐ.
να. The consequence of printing *nu* is the impossibility of a phonetic pause,
whereas leaving the *nu* out would result in pause-indicating hiatus.[18] The decision to print movable *nu* on the arsis means that a third-foot phonetic pause in
performance is not possible.

Movable *nu* as a contribution to syllabic weight can only be found in combination with the possibility of a pause in performance (so that the *nu* is prepausal
at word end) when the word-final syllable occupies a position that is metrically
long. The foot's thesis is the preferred location:[19]

(74)   ἀλλ' ἐρέω μὲν ἐγὼν ἵνα εἰδότες ἤ κε θάνωμεν

Odyssey xii 156

But I will tell you, so that, in full understanding, we may either die
   [or flee]

The possibility of pause appears to be only theoretical though. The heavy thesis
does not require movable *nu* for its rhythmical weight, and when it adds the
nu, the movable coda is resyllabified (as it is in example 74, and regularly with
ἐγὼν in "prepausal" location). A superheavy syllable on the prepausal thesis
featuring movable *nu* is thus avoided. When movable *nu* contributes to the
rhythmical weight of the syllable on the thesis, and there is no need to assume
metrical lengthening, phonetic pause is precluded: movable *nu* (like any coda
in word-final heavy CVC) only contributes to weight because of the absence of
phonetic pause:

(75)   ἷζεν ἐπ' ἐσχαρόφιν ποτὶ δὲ σκότον ἐτράπετ' αἶψα

Odyssey xix 389

He sat at the fireplace, and quickly turned away towards the shadow

---

[18]   Though not more than indicating: allowing hiatus in the arsis would not necessarily have been a
correlate for pause. In a line like *Iliad* XV 402 σπεύσομαι εἰς Ἀχιλῆα ἵν' ὀτρύνω πολεμίζειν, "I will
hurry to Achilles, that I may urge him to join the battle," hiatus and pause may coincide at position 5½. Within word groups that are semantically tied together, orthographic hiatus is common
at the trochaic caesura and often, even phonetically, not explained as hiatus but as sandhi due to
the influence of a consonantal sound that has disappeared in writing (e.g., *Iliad* XVI 600 πάντες
ἐπεὶ βασιλῆα ϝἴδον βεβλημένον ἦτορ, "All of them, as soon as they had seen their king, mortally
wounded").

[19]   With the exception of the verse end, movable *nu* is used on the heavy arsis once in the first 100
lines of the *Iliad* (*Iliad* I 66) versus five times on the thesis (see the sample that concludes Chapter
5). For the first 100 lines of the *Odyssey*, the ratio is 1 (*Odyssey* i 71) :1 (*Odyssey* i 88).

On the thesis, movable *nu* can be the consonantal coda and allow for a subsequent pause in performance. It may still be a coda without a subsequent pause, or not a coda at all. The application of movable *nu* at the two different third-foot caesurae (position 5 and position 5½) shows that inclusion of the orthographic coda into the rime* of the syllable cannot be as easily accounted for on the arsis as on the thesis. Inclusion of the movable *nu* on the arsis in the manuscript tradition suggests awareness of its consequences for phonetic word end.

4.2.3 Metrical perspectives of phonetic pause in performance

Metrical surface structure, maintained by phonology, reflects underlying rhythmic regularity (Chapter 3). This regularity is meter's ontogenetic basis. Meter therefore strives to maintain the rhythmic regularity, both within the foot and the larger rhythmical phrase. It is not clear what role melody and intonation play in the process of rhythmic regularity. Meter's role is evident though: meter will not disturb the regularity. Meter's most visible reflection of this avoidance of disturbance are the so-called bridges and the avoidance of spondaic word end (§3.1.3.3).[20] In this section, I will follow the combined lead of Ruijgh 1989 and Devine and Stephens 1994 when I take phonetic, word-final lengthening of phonetic-word final syllables as an indication for phonetic pause in a metrical text (as I already announced in §4.2): the need to maintain metrical surface structure produces the possibilities for phonetic pause in performance. From this observation, only one more step is required to identify the possibilities for performative pause in a metrical text.

Devine and Stephens 1994 assume that metrical composition remains sensitive to the rhythmical properties that words have in normal speech. Ruijgh's conclusion (1987, and see §3.2) that the foot's metrical thesis is longer than the metrical arsis, even when thesis and arsis have the same weight, corresponds to the durational ratio of the rhythmical thesis and arsis in speech. As word-rhythm shows a resistance to putting heavy final syllables in metrical arsis positions, so final heavy syllables in verse are rhythmical theses.[21] Ruijgh 1989 explores the consequences of the foot-internal durational proportion*

---

[20] Bridges and the avoidance of spondaic word end show that prolongation of both light and heavy word-final syllables on the arsis is much more restricted than on the thesis, the non-resolvable structural element of the foot. Porter (1951:20) and Ruijgh (1987:335–339), amongst others, consider this as evidence supporting an intrinsically longer duration of the thesis when compared to the arsis, but such scholars as Wifstrand (1933:26–34), Irigoin (1965:224–231), and West (1982:20, 36) argue that the arsis has longer duration when it is realized as a double-*breve*. In his 1998 edition of the *Iliad*, West states (xxv): "*in bicipitibus, ubi tempus paullo maius quam in thesi pedis implendum erat*"; cf. §1.1.1.

[21] In §3.2, I explained my reasons for accepting Ruijgh's argumentation in favor of accepting final lengthening as *final-syllable* lengthening.

(conclusion: T ≥ A) in relation to the maintenance of podic metrical structure in Homer's hexameter.[22]

Ruijgh 1989 advocates comparison of dactylic verse, like Homer's hexameter, with anapaestic dimeter,[23] as opposed to march-anapaests. He points out that march-anapaests ought to be analyzed κατὰ διποδίαν, in metrical units of a two feet each. The medial pause, a dieresis κατὰ διποδίαν, he says, facilitates the marching rhythm by equalizing the durations of the two half-verses;[24] the possibility for equalizing lies in the prolongation of the prepausal thesis.[25] In march-anapaests, the exact time-value of phonetic word-final syllables depends on the amount of final-syllable lengthening required to maintain the rhythmical march-beat.[26] In anapaestic dimeter, used in a system, there is no medial pause: the possibility for word-final lengthening is limited, especially on the arsis.[27] Ruijgh suggests comparison with the dactylic third-foot feminine caesura (following position 5½) where phonetic disruption is equally limited. Thus he differentiates between a "first" word end, in order to evoke phonetic disruption, and a "second" choice for word end, not too far from the preferred location but nonetheless phonetically far less disruptive. The

---

[22] As he announced in his 1987 article cited above, Ruijgh published a second article on final-syllable prolongation. As the numbering of the sections shows (the 1989 article starts with §22), the 1989 article is meant as *part II*. The issues dealt with in the 1989 article are reminiscent of the discussion concerning heavy syllable prolongation* on the thesis in Devine and Stephens 1994:129; their discussion concentrated on heavy syllable prolongation due to syncopated feet in iambic and trochaic meter.

[23] Dactyl and anapaest are both γένος ἴσον; their thesis and arsis have almost similar duration. The ancient ῥυθμικοί, Ruijgh points out, noted that the thesis often had a little more duration than the arsis (Aristides Quintilianus 33.26–28 in the edition of Winnington-Ingram). They labeled the dactyl ἀνάπαιστος ἀπὸ μείζονος (*a maiore*, cf. the ionicus), and the anapaest ἀνάπαιστος ἀπὸ ἐλάττονος (*a minore*). Their description makes it tempting to explain the dactylic-anapaest metarrhythmisis* as a form of metrical anaclasis*.

[24] Ruijgh 1989:313: "c'était donc le diérèse entre deux dipodies successives qui permettait de synchroniser le rythme du débit avec celui de la marche: en manipulant la durée supplémentaire de la syllabe longue finale de chaque dipodie, on pouvait égaliser les durées des dipodies"; cf. Korzeniewski 1968:88.

[25] Ruijgh 1989:314 claims that, at the same time, the analysis κατὰ διποδίαν allows for non-repetitive realizations of the various arses and theses, under the influence of final-syllable lengthening, within the διποδία. He demonstrates this by referring to the higher frequency of spondees in march-anapaests compared to dactylic verse.

[26] Such application of final-syllable lengthening seems incompatible with the lengthening resulting from, or rather indicating, a strong phonetic disruption. In anapaestic systems, for example in comedy, it becomes evident that there is no such relation between lengthening and phonetic disruption The anapaestic system itself leads to πνῖγος "suffocation," only to be released by a *catalectic* dimeter—in other words, by lengthening *and* a phonetic disruption.

[27] Heavy non-final syllables on the first thesis of both dipodies of the anapaestic dimeter thus contribute to what is called κυκλικός-rhythm; Ruijgh 1989:320; Korzeniewski 1968:43; Goodell 1901:181; Rossi 1963:45, 90.

combination of the 1987 and 1989 articles presents Ruijgh's clues for the word-final syllable undergoing final lengthening on specific positions within the metrical foot.[28]

What Ruijgh's work justly calls attention to is a mismatch between the footing of speech and the footing of the continuous line. I consider it likely that this mismatch plays an important role in the application of phonetic pause in performance. The effect of the mismatch is that the rhythmisis*, the direction of the rhythm, in the hexameter seems to change to another metrical patterning: rising word end on the thesis seems to orphan that thesis from its accompanying arsis in favor of some sort of attachment to the preceding arsis. Within the line, however, the thesis must form a foot together with the following arsis, even if that arsis belongs to the next word. Words ending in a heavy syllable on the thesis (rhythmical word types with rising end, like the iamb, anapaest, molossus, or choriamb) may have this effect in the dactylic hexameter: their word-final heavy syllable is more closely attached to the preceding arsis than to the following arsis. Depending on the amount of additional lengthening, rising* word end may exaggerate the separation from the arsis in the same metrical foot. In that sense, word-types ending in a heavy syllable on the thesis are at odds with the footing of the dactylic line: their occurrence makes it look as if the direction of the line's footing has changed. Below I present some examples (76–79) of change of rhythmisis due to an anapaestic word end on positions 3, 5, 7, and 9. In all the examples, the rhythmisis changes from pendant* (thesis » arsis) to blunt* (arsis » thesis) at word end. The rhythm at word end is not perceived as dactylic (with word end on the changeable element of the foot |– ◡ ◡| before the caesura indicated as /), but as anapaestic (with word end on the stable, nonresolvable element |◡ ◡ –|/, as at the median caesura of march-anapaests):

---

[28] As shown in §3.2, the ancient ῥυθμικοί considered the "perfect" long (μακρὰ τελεία) characteristic for anapaests and the "immeasurable" long (μακρὰ ἄλογος) for dactyls. The ῥυθμικοί are talking about the anapaestic and dactylic *word-type* (ῥυθμοί), not about the anapaestic and dactylic *verse*. The μακρὰ τελεία is hence characteristic for word-internal rhythm as in κεφαλῆς, the μακρὰ ἄλογος for a word like τεύχεσιν. Ruijgh (1987:324–326) concludes that the μακρὰ τελεία is a word-final heavy syllable, the μακρὰ ἄλογος a non-final heavy syllable. In march-anapaests, every dipody ends in μακρὰ τελεία (Ruijgh 1987:325); in the κυκλικός anapaest-rhythm, every dipody, like the first and third (word-final) heavy-syllable thesis, ends in μακρὰ ἄλογος.

On position 3 (⏑ ⏑|– / perceived as |⏑ ⏑ –|/):

> (76) τῇ δ' ἑτέρῃ ἔθεν ἆσσον ἐρύσσατο φώνησέν τε
>
> *Odyssey* xix 481

But with the other hand he pulled her closer, and spoke

On position 5 (–|– ⏑ ⏑|– / perceived as |– –|⏑ ⏑ –|/):

> (77) οἵ δή μοι καμάτῳ θυμαλγέι γούνατ' ἔλυσαν
>
> *Odyssey* xx 118

Who make my knees weaken because of painful weariness

On position 7 (⏑ ⏑|– ⏑ ⏑|– / ⏑ ⏑|– / perceived as |⏑ ⏑ –|⏑ ⏑ –|/ ⏑ ⏑ –|/) :

> (78) τὸν δ' ἀπαμειβόμενος προσέφη πολύμητις Ὀδυσσεύς
>
> *Odyssey* xi 354

To him in reply spoke resourceful Odysseus

On position 9 (–|– / ⏑ ⏑|– / ⏑ ⏑|– / perceived as |– –|/ ⏑ ⏑ –|/ ⏑ ⏑ –|/):

> (79) παῖδά τ' ἀποκτείνεις ἐμὲ δὲ μεγάλως ἀκαχίζεις
>
> *Odyssey* xvi 432

You try to kill my son, and you hurt me severely

Similar examples can be given for all rhythmical word types* ending in a word-final heavy syllable mapped on the thesis within the hexameter (the opening of example 76, τῇ δ' ἑτέρῃ, can be analyzed as a choriamb |– ⏑ ⏑ –|/). Word-final lengthening of all such words results in a word-final monosyllabic foot, as if the arsis is detached from its thesis (T[A]).

Starting from the assumption that metrical surface structure maintains rhythmic regularity,[29] the combined lead of Devine and Stephens and Ruijgh brings me to observations on the possibilities for phonetic pause in the poetry of a quantifying language like ancient Greek. The possibility for phonetic pause depends on the opportunity meter offers for realization of syllables as word-final. As shown in this section, the metrical thesis offers much more opportunity, that is, much more room for word-final lengthening, than the arsis. The value of word-final syllables as phonetically prepausal is thus determined by phonology and meter together: in order to be phonetically prepausal a syllable

---

[29] Suggested by the results from cross-linguistic studies in refooting over compositional pauses, cited in Devine and Stephens 1994:433–434.

has to be sandhi-free, and localized at a metrical position that allows for final-syllable lengthening.

4.2.4 Metrical restrictions on phonetic pause in performance

Meter determines the possibilities for phonetic pause. At the same time, meter provides the restrictions on phonetic pause, as additional word-final lengthening is not allowed at every metrical position. From the phonological and metrical perspectives combined, it follows, I argue, that the likeliest position for pause in performance is a phonetic word-final *heavy syllable* that is *mapped on the thesis*. Word end in a heavy syllable on the thesis brings out a different metrical pattern: often it brings out an anapaestic pattern:

(28) τῶν ἕν' ἀειραμένη Ἑκάβη φέρε δῶρον Ἀθήνη

Iliad VI 293

|‒|◡ ◡‒|◡ ◡‒|/ ◡ ◡‒|/ ◡ ◡‒|◡ ◡ ‒|‒|‖

Having lifted one of these Hecabe carried it as a gift for Athene

Due to phonetic word end and the possibility of phonetic lengthening, such word end gives the thesis the chance to equalize its duration to the *preceding* arsis (ἕν' ἀειραμένη ἑκάβη) and surpass it at phonetic word end. At the same time, any additional word-final lengthening exaggerates the separation of the orphaned monosyllabic thesis (T[A]) from the following arsis that belongs to the same metrical foot. On the level of the phonetic word, and of the phonological phrase, the orphaned thesis is heard as rising word end in rhythm. In §1.2, I described the resulting change of rhythmisis as metarrhythmisis (τὰ μέτρα μεταρρυθμίζεσθαι): the orphaned thesis becomes attached to the preceding arsis, thus suggesting a change in foot-structure. At the same time, example 28 shows that the metarrhythmisised, anapaestic rhythmical structure has *one foot more* than the dactylic metrical structure (rhythmical structure: [T][AT] [AT]/[AT]/[AT][AT][T] = seven feet in anapaestic rhythm). Metarrhythmisis to anapaests shows the possibility for additional word-final lengthening (indicated as L) of the heavy syllable on the thesis:

(28)	τῶν ἕν' ἀειραμένη Ἑκάβη φέρε δῶρον Ἀθήνη
Dactylic rhythm	[T A][T A][T A][T A] [T A][T A]
Metarrhythmisized	[T][A T][A T/L][A T/L][A T] [A T][T/L]

Word end in a light syllable (φέρε, δῶρον) will also carry extra duration (διάστασις) as it undergoes word-final lengthening. Additional lengthening as submoriac adjustment of light word-final syllables is mapped onto the arsis and hence more severely restricted than word end on the thesis:[30] word-final -ρε (φέρε) and -ρον (δῶρον) cannot be lengthened with the same temporal allowance as the heavy syllables mapped on the thesis.

There are two types of phonetic word end, depending on the additional lengthening the prepausal syllable may carry: the word-final heavy syllable may carry substantially more additional lengthening than the word-final light syllable, which often does not seem to allow for any additional lengthening at all. This variance in word end is reminiscent of Ruigh's first (*coupe primaire*) and second word end (*coupe secondaire*), but his labels for the two kinds of word end refer primarily to the frequency of occurrence. My approach aims at the identification of phonetic word endings that differ in the phonetic disruption they cause.

4.2.5 Two types of sandhi-free word end — two types of phonetic pause

The two types of sandhi-free word end in Homer differ with regard to their final-syllable lengthening, due to localization on the thesis or on the arsis. What the two types of word end have in common is that both imply termination of phonation: both imply phonetic pause. As sandhi-free phonetic word end on the thesis allows for considerable submoraic adjustment (additional, phonetic lengthening) of the prepausal syllable, I will refer to it as the primary pause. The primary pause, suggested by (...), can be realized at various positions in the verse:

Following position 3 (trithemimeres*):

> (80) Ἀργεῖοι (...) καὶ δ᾿ αὖτε μεθίετε Ἕκτορι νίκην
>
> > *Iliad* XIV 364
>
> Greeks, do you grant Hector victory again

Following position 5 (penthemimeres*):

> (81) ὧδε δὲ μυθέομαι (...) Ζεὺς δ᾿ ἄμμ᾿ ἐπὶ μάρτυρος ἔστω
>
> > *Iliad* VII 76
>
> That is what I think, and Zeus must be here for us, present as witness

---

[30] Ruijgh (1987:346) suggests that lengthening of a light final syllable may result in approximately half the additional lengthening compared to a heavy syllable: "syllabe longue finale, dont la durée supplémentaire était probablement le double de celle d'une syllabe brève finale."

Following position 7 (hephthemimeres*):

(82)   νῦν δ' ἅμα τ' αὐτίκα πολλὰ διδοῖ (...) τὰ δ' ὄπισθεν ὑπέστη

Iliad IX 519

But here and now he gives many, and others he promised in due
course

Following position 9 (ennehemimeres*):

(83)   σοὶ γὰρ ἐγὼ καὶ ἔπειτα κατηφείη (...) καὶ ὄνειδος

Iliad XVI 498

For I [will bring] from now on disapproval and shame for you

The primary pause stems from the phonetic lengthening of word-final syllables
containing a long vowel or a diphthong (examples 85, 86), or the word-final
superheavy syllable* (examples 84, 87):

(84)   ἦν δέ τις Εὐχήνωρ (...) Πολυΐδου μάντιος υἱός

Iliad XIII 663

There was a certain Euchenor, son of the seer Polyidus

(85)   σχέσθε φίλοι (...) καί μ' οἶον ἐάσατε κηδόμενοί περ

Iliad XXII 416

Don't, my friends, and please allow me alone, concerned though you
are,

(86)   οὔ τι κατακτείνει (...) πλάζει δ' ἀπὸ πατρίδος αἴης

Odyssey i 75

He does not kill him, but makes him wander far from his native land

(87)   τίς πόθεν εἶς ἀνδρῶν (...) πόθι τοι πόλις ἠδὲ τοκῆες

Odyssey xix 105

Who are you? From where among men are you? Where are your city
and parents?

Primary pause may also stem from the word-final closed syllable containing a short vowel, when mapped on the thesis and followed by a vowel (§3.2.3):[31]

(60) ὁ ξεῖνος (...) ἐμέθεν (...) ἐθέλω δέ μιν ἐξερέεσθαι

Odyssey xix 99

[that] the stranger [may listen] to me; I wish to interrogate him

(88) οἴκαδε νισσόμενον (...) ὃ δ' ἔβη μετὰ πατρὸς ἀκουήν

Odyssey iv 701

On his return home; he went searching for word of his father

(89) ἐλθὼν ἐξ ὄρεος (...) ὅθι οἱ γενεή τε τόκος τε

Odyssey xiv 175

Having come from the mountain, where his origin is and his offspring

I will refer to the sandhi-free word-final syllable on the arsis as the secondary pause. As a phonetic disruption, secondary pause results in limited (if any at all) word-final lengthening. Contrary to the primary pause, secondary pause cannot "increase" so easily; it is rather more likely that it does not result in phonetic disruption. The secondary pause may only be applied as an audible feature when its occurrence does not disturb the rhythmic regularity; in the pattern of regularity, featuring theses with more sonority* and arses with less, secondary pause has to adapt to what happens on the thesis. The primary pause, however, uses the orphaned thesis to equalize to the preceding feet, with hardly any regard for the arsis that is still to follow—let alone any other subsequent feet. There is no need to restrict the primary pause to what preceded it; for the maintenance of rhythmic regularity, it is merely necessary to adapt the subsequent, separated arsis to the preceding primary pause.

Phonetic word end in a light syllable is a necessary condition for secondary pause. As light syllables are restricted to the foot's arsis, so is the phonetic adjustment that is secondary pause. A metrical position often used for secondary pause is the feminine third-foot caesura (following position 5½):

---

[31] My suggestion is that the frequency of *metrical* lengthening in the thesis (especially the thesis of the third foot) points at a license due to *rhythmical* lengthening (submoraic adjustment) in prepausal mapping; see §3.1.3.2.

(90) ῥώοντ᾽ ἄσβεστος δὲ (...) βοὴ γένετ᾽ ἠῶθι πρό

Iliad XI 50

They swarmed; endless shouting arose before dusk

Sandhi-free means that the shortened word-final syllable (οἱ in example 91) does not qualify, nor does the elided syllable (τόδ᾽ in example 91), nor the resyllabified syllable (-.σο.ν and -.λὲ.ς in example 91), leaving (91) without secondary phonetic pause:

(91) καί οἱ ἐγὼ τόδ᾽ ἄλεισον ἐμὸν περικαλλὲς ὀπάσσω

Odyssey viii 430

I will even give him this cup of mine, most beautiful

At this point I am still dealing with (both the primary and the secondary) pause as phonetic pause, the termination of phonation; termination of phonation does not make clear what the effect of phonetic pause is in performance. I will discuss the conditions for, and the extent of, phonetic pause as performative pause in Chapter 5. In the current section, I have not made any distinction between the pause as phonetic disruption and as pause in performance: so far phonetic pause has been treated as a possibility for performative pause. I have treated the phonetic disruption as submoraic adjustment of the word-final syllable, not as a measurable pause (or silence) as a perceptible phenomenon. The latter depends on criteria (notably, the rate of speech) outside the realm of phonology.

5

Performative Pause

*Technical terms followed by * on their first occurrence in this chapter are in the glossary.*

5.0   Introduction

In this chapter I aim to show the conditions for, and extent of, phonetic pause* as pause in performance*. This chapter argues, in other words, for the reconstruction of performative pause*: under what conditions does phonetic word end become audible as a rest of some duration in performance (§5.1)? In Chapter 4, I have argued that phonetic pause, the prerequisite for performative pause, comes in two qualities, as primary and secondary word end. It will be my working hypothesis that primary and secondary pause make phrases audible in the continuous flow of dactyls of the Iliad and the Odyssey. In §5.2, the concept of performative pause is applied to the Homeric epic. The consequences of the application of performative pause to the Homeric epic, as if it were some form of audible punctuation in Homeric performance, are discussed in §5.3. A sample from the Homeric epic, presented in §5.4, shows the mosaic-like pattern of phrases that emerges from the application of performative pause to the Iliad and the Odyssey.

5.1   Performative Pause

The possibilities for, and restrictions on, phonetic pause have been described in outline in Chapter 4; so far, this description explained nothing about the perceptibility of phonetic pause in performance. Section 5.1 explores the performative perspectives of phonetic pause: the conditions for pause as a perceptible termination of phonation in performance.

Phonetic pause implies the termination of phonation. It does not automatically imply performative pause (§4.2.5). Performative pause is defined as a rest of some duration in performance due to the termination of phonation. Rest may mean either a drawling of speech due to the slackening of speech tempo resulting in termination of phonation, or a true silence. In the case of the former, termination of phonation coincides with the completion of word-final lengthening*. In the case of silence, the rest may have a measurable duration that does not need disturb the ongoing rhythmic regularity of speech in the performance of metrical speech.[1]

The language aspect that determines the realization of phonetic pause in performance is tempo of speech. In a deliberately slow tempo of speech virtually every phonetic word end is free of sandhi*: consonantal liaison is frustrated and hiatus* goes unnoticed. Elision* is absent. As a result, there is a performative pause after each and every phonetic word*. At high rates of speech the situation is reversed: elision is omnipresent at the cost of hiatus. At high rates of speech phonetic pause is much less frequent: the intervals between pauses widen with the increase of speech tempo (Allen 1973; Devine and Stephens 1994). The higher the tempo of speech, the more chance that speakers will insert audible pauses at regular intervals for no other reason than the need to take a breath regularly; under such circumstances, there seems to be hardly any regard for the use of pause as a device to structure the discourse along lines of syntactical units or units of sense. At normal rates of speech, pauses suggest patterns that remind us of the hierarchical constituency of spoken language:[2] there are stronger pauses, pauses of longer duration (including phonetic lengthening*, as the result of drawling of speech), which mark the boundaries of the major phonological phrase*, and milder pauses, of less or no perceptible duration, which mark the boundaries of the minor phonological phrase*. Milder pauses are regularly non-breathing pauses; stronger pauses are breathing pauses. Slow speech turns every pause into a potential breathing pause; higher speech rates only allow for breathing pauses at regular intervals at the expense of non-breathing pauses.[3]

Within the context of Homeric performance, I refer to the primary and the secondary phonetic pause (§4.2.5). The description of the phonological and metrical restrictions on pause in performance leads to my conclusion that the primary pause may double as the breathing pause, and the secondary pause as the non-breathing pause in performance. The underlying assumption is, of

---

[1] Devine and Stephens (1994:421) mention Nicanor's (reconstructed) punctuation system as it has been used for the measurement of pause in rhythmic units, but they point out that the reconstruction only deals with phonological categorization.

[2] Devine and Stephens 1994:376–378, 384–385, 412–420.

[3] Cf. Devine and Stephens 1994:148, 272.

course, that the speech tempo of the performed *Iliad* and *Odyssey* falls within the parameters of normal rates of speech, as lower and higher rates allow for one type of pause only. I see no reason to assume beforehand that the two types of pause in Homer are applied to frame units of sense or syntactical units. If the application of the primary and secondary phonetic pause in Homeric performance suggested patterns that were reminiscent of the hierarchical constituency of spoken language, this constituency was first and foremost on the level of rhythm* and phonology*. The pauses demarcate phonological phrases, not necessarily units of sense or syntax. With this caveat in mind, I find the terms minor and major phonological phrase very useful to describe the hierarchical constituency of phrases; I stress at this point that I consider the major phrase too, like the minor phrase, primarily as a rhythmical and phonological unity. I do not follow Devine and Stephens when they define the major phrase on syntactical grounds, whereas their approach of the minor phrase was primarily on the basis of prosody and phonology. In my definition the major phrase is a phonological unity framed by primary pauses. I assume that the phonological unity is probably strengthened by prosodic patterning through melody and intonation.

Having established the phonetic word end as the possible performative pause appearing in two qualities and having claimed that the realization of phonetic pause as performative pause depends on rates of speech to be determined by the performer, I can now discuss the options for performative pause based on my analysis. The composer determines these options for pause, but in the end it is the performer who decides to exploit options in performance.

5.1.1 Options for performative pause

The verse end was commonly thought to qualify as the performative pause *par excellence*. Studies on Homeric epic as poetry read aloud or as song commonly take the metrical boundary of the verse end as the termination of rhythm, meter, syntax, and phonation. The special phonological circumstance at verse end (the possibility of hiatus and *brevis in longo*, for spondaic word end*; the impossibility of elision) is seen as the *raison d'être* of this performative pause; verse-internal avoidance of the special metrical circumstance as proof of the impossibility of verse-internal pause. Verse-internal positions of frequent word end are treated as pausae*, compositional pauses in caesural zones (§1.2), joints between units of composition like the cola. Next to the verse end, only the main caesura* is regularly considered a possible performative pause, although only when the need to take a breath is taken into account, or, alternatively, when a Homeric verse deals with highly emotional peaks around the third foot ("expressive purposes," §4.1.1). This outlook on performative pause in Homer (always at verse end and hardly ever verse-internal) finds its basis—and, in my opinion, a weak one at that—in remarks by Roman authors, and the increasing stylization of post-Homeric hexametric poetry.[4] The phonetic approach of pause that I have introduced and analyzed in §3.2, calls for a very different treatment of all positions of word end in Homer. Word end, I argue, ought to be analyzed with regard to (i) the possibility of sandhi, and (ii) the temporal allowance of rhythm.

At every position of frequent word end and at every possible localization for a pause in composition, performative pause seems to be an option. An option in composition, that is, because in the process of composition it is the composer who decides on how to start phonation again after phonetic word end. It makes a difference whether phonation starts with a consonant or with a vowel, and both ways to start affect what preceded. The decision of the composer determines surface rhythmics at the start and completion of phrases and the size of phrases. As the start of phonation influences the way preceding phonation terminates, the composer marks phonetic word end as a possible performative pause through the way he restarts phonation. As long as rhythmic regularity and footing onto theses and arses is maintained, the composer may turn any compositional pause into a possible performative pause.

Performative pause is hence sought for at positions of frequent word end: following the first-foot arsis* (position 2), the second-foot thesis* (position 3: at trithemimeral word end), the third-foot thesis (position 5: at penthemimeral word end), the third-foot trochee (position 5½: at the trochaic caesura), the fourth-foot thesis (position 7: at hephthemimeral word end), the fourth-foot arsis (position 8: at the bucolic dieresis*), the fifth-foot thesis (position 9: at ennehemimeral word end), and following the sixth foot arsis (position 12: at verse end). Some of these positions (3, 5, 7, 9) immediately follow the stable element on the thesis; others, the diereses (positions 2, 8, 12), occur in the transition from the arsis to the thesis, a position whose temporal allowance is most severely restricted by the maintenance of dactylic rhythm. Within the arsis (when realized as a double *breve*) there may be phonetic word end following the first light syllable. Phonetic word end is not allowed after the fourth trochee (position 7½; Hermann's Bridge*).

Hermann's Bridge is one of the indicators that performative pause is subject to a rule: it is only allowed on the condition that disturbances to the flow of dactyls, due to the word-final phonetic lengthening or silence, are avoided. This rule underlies both the localization of the limited number of metrical word-types[5] and the various metrical bridges. It also extends to the impact of word

---

[4]   The development of the hexameter actually leads to a strong preference for third-foot word division at the trochaic caesura* in Nonnus (Van Raalte 1986:73), thus avoiding metarrhythmisis* in the third foot.

[5]   O'Neill 1942.

end on the arsis. Word end on the arsis is potentially much more restricted with respect to phonetic final lengthening than is word end on the thesis. Within the third foot, different options for performative pause are not dependent on the emotional evocation (cf. Daitz 1991), but on the metrical position: a penthemimeral caesura (following position 5) would allow for much more word-final lengthening or silence than a trochaic word end (following position 5½) without disrupting rhythmic regularity (§4.2.5). The alternation of main caesura following position 5 and 5½ is the alternation between two possible positions of word end, only one of which (following position 5) may double as a strong, primary pause. The alternation does not provide rhythmical variation for the third foot: rather, it marks the difference between a third foot *with* the option of a strong pause and a third foot *without*.

In my phonetics-based approach to performative pause, options are defined in terms of sandhi and metrical position at every position of frequent word end in the hexameter, including the verse end. Performative pause is never taken for granted on the basis of compositional pausing (metrical or syntactical termination) only. Having thus claimed the thesis of the dactyl as an option for primary pause in performance, I call for special attention for those positions in the hexameter that do feature licensed spondaic word end. In the case of position 12, spondaic word end elicits the question whether or not the metrical circumstance unavoidably results in performative pause. At other, verse-internal positions spondaic word end is supposedly avoided, as it could be understood as premature verse end. As performative pause ought to be avoided verse-internally, premature verse end would lead to hiccups in performance. In my approach the situation is reversed: spondaic word end at positions 2 and 8 provides clues as to what extent, and under what circumstances, the verse end may be possibly pause-avoiding in performance. To that end, I will discuss the permission for spondaic word end at position 2 (so-called στίχος λαγαρός*) in §5.1.2, and at position 8 (under the circumstances known as Wernicke's Law*) in §5.1.3. In §5.1.4, I discuss the options for performative pause at verse end, resulting from the analysis of spondaic word end at positions 2 and 8.

5.1.2 Options at position 2 (στίχος λαγαρός)?

The dieresis after the first foot may be labelled a secondary pause if the arsis is occupied by two *brevia*. In case of a bisyllabic first foot, the dieresis has a remarkable resemblance to the verse end: hiatus after long vowel or diphthong occurs regularly,[6] and the so-called στίχος λαγαρός (metrical indifference before

---

[6]   Bakker 1988:2n3.

the first-foot dieresis) copies the verse-final foot.[7] Steinrück 2005 explains the στίχος λαγαρός as a relic from the time dactylic repetition still had to be normalized throughout the hexameter.[8] Such an early stage of hexametric development must have had a relatively autonomous first foot, loosely tied to the subsequent foot by prosody and syntactic organization. If this reconstruction of the early stage of hexametric poetry is valid, Homer's first foot shows signs of both normalization of the foot in accordance with the rest of the hexametric line and a rather non-disturbing compositional pause at the first-foot dieresis.

The trisyllabic first foot is the easiest way to fulfil the requirement of the undisturbed flow of dactyls throughout the verse. Preceded by a trisyllabic first foot, the dieresis following position 2 (indicated as :) marks a compositional pause after a run-over* phonetic word, as in example 92 (twice):

(92)   ἐς δ' ἑκατόμβην
θείομεν : ἂν δ' αὐτὴν Χρυσηίδα καλλιπάρῃον
βήσομεν :

Iliad I 142–144

Let us place the offering | in the ship; and let us make beautiful Chryseis herself | embark

Combined with a compositional pause at the preceding verse end, the first foot dieresis features an extended imperative in, for example, *Iliad* I 32 (ἀλλ' ἴθι, "but come on") and *Iliad* I 37 (κλῦθί μευ, "please listen to me"). Alternatively, the dieresis may single out the transition to, or the completion of, a vocative as in *Iliad* I 334 (χαίρετε κήρυκες, "welcome, heralds"). In all these examples a phonetic pause following position 2 may be realized as a secondary performative pause at most.

A phonetic pause coinciding with spondaic word end (as in *Iliad* I 39 Σμινθεῦ, and many other examples) seems to be well allowed in Homer's hexameter.

---

[7] Leaf 1900–1902:app.D C2; Steinrück 2005.

[8] Steinrück (2005:495) analyzes the hexameter as an *asynartetic* verse: the third-foot caesura separates a dactylic basis (hemiepes) from a choriambic expansion. Koster (1953:26) suggests that the trochaic sixth foot of the hexameter might be considered as a metarrhythmisis of the dactyl (cf. the dactyl as metarrhythmisis in the trochaic tetrameter). This analysis presents the sixth foot as a logaoedic (λογαοιδός; dactyl + trochee) expansion to a dactylic pentapodic basis. It does not exclude that the sixth-foot thesis of the στίχος μείουρος* is an anceps (examples in Leaf 1900–1902, ap.D,C3); in this verse-type, the final thesis may be occupied by a light syllable, just like the verse-initial thesis in στίχος ἀκέφαλος*, as in, e.g., *Iliad* XXII 379 ἐπεὶ δὴ τόνδ' ἄνδρα θεοὶ δαμάσασθαι ἔδωκαν, "as the gods have finally granted me to restrain this man," and *Iliad* XXIII 2 ἐπεὶ δὴ νῆάς τε καὶ Ἑλλήσποντον ἵκοντο, "as they had reached the ships and the Hellespont" (further examples in Leaf 1900–1902, ap.D,C1). Both the verse-final and the verse-initial foot of the hexameter give rise to the assumption of an earlier stage in which both feet only had to comply with Aeolic isosyllaby.

Current explanations for the frequent occurrence of the coincidence often presuppose that the rhythmic disturbance due to resemblance to verse end is less significant in the first foot than it would be in other feet of the hexameter.[9] Taking seriously Ruijgh's observation that secondary phonetic word end is characterized by high frequency of elision, the status of the compositional pause is confirmed by examples like *Iliad* I 335 (ἆσσον ἴτ', "come closer") and well-known ὣς ἔφατ', "thus he/she spoke." Realization of the first-foot dieresis as, at most, a secondary pause[10] will throw light on the options for performative pause at verse end (§5.1.4).

5.1.3 Options at position 8 (under Wernicke's Law)?

Just as in the word rhythm of speech, there is a resistance to putting heavy final syllables in metrical arsis position. It is commonly assumed that spondaic word end is avoided to prevent resemblance with the sixth-foot arsis (premature verse end). On statistical grounds, Devine and Stephens (1994:74–75, 131) further develop the hypothesis that heavy syllables CV are less resistant to shortening and subordination (§3.1.3.2), and thus more easily accommodated on the rhythmical arsis than heavy syllables CVC; for spondaic word-final heavy syllables, this means that a distinction has to be made between spondaic word end in heavy word-final CV versus heavy word-final CVC: though avoided in general, spondaic word end would then still be more likely in word-final CV than in CVC. Similar considerations should apply to "indeterminate" verse end.

As I have given other grounds for the identification of prepausal word end in performance (favoring phonetic word end on the thesis), the spondaic verse end attracts special attention. The question presents itself whether spondaic word end doubles as a phonetic and performative pause as well. The relevance of this question stems from the status of the verse end as a pause. It is clear that the verse end is a compositional pause, but in studies on Homeric performance its status as performative pause is taken for granted. I will analyze its closest parallel within the line, spondaic word end at position 8 under Wernicke's Law, to illustrate which phonetic conditions lie at the basis of the prepausal word end at verse end.[11] From the analysis of the phonetics of verse end, conclusions

---

[9] West (1982:39) argues that the tempo of speech in the first foot is so high, that phonetic lengthening of a final syllable would hardly be noticeable, let alone disturbing to the rhythm.

[10] Contra the identification of the punctuation following initial vocatives as "4 morae" (in the summary of Nicanor's system quoted by Devine and Stephens 1994:421).

[11] Judging from the sample (§5.4), spondaic word end is found in position 2 in 7% of the verses of the *Iliad*, and 12% of the *Odyssey*. The third-foot internal word end makes spondaic word end in the third foot virtually impossible; verses in which the third-foot caesura is not being observed do not feature spondaic word end on the third foot. Homer hardly ever allows spondaic word end in the fifth foot. If he does, the explanation lies in the replacement of word endings with

may be drawn concerning the performative perspectives of pause following position 12.

The restriction on spondaic word end following position 8 (Naeke's Bridge*) is lifted under certain conditions under Wernicke's Law: spondaic word end is allowed when in a syllable containing a vowel that is long "by nature." If the syllable ends in a vowel, the word-final vocalic sound is therefore a long vowel or a diphthong. The metrical shape of the word featuring spondaic word end is concluded by | – – |, and cannot be modified by resyllabification into | – ◡ . | through a different localization in the hexameter. Localization in the second or the fourth foot of the Homeric hexameter allegedly widens the usage of the specific metrical word type: this word type might otherwise only be localized at verse end.[12]

In §5.1.2, it was pointed out that spondaic word end is common in the first foot. It has nothing to do with widening the possibilities of localization for a restrictive metrical word type. In the following examples (93–95), the word type on the first foot could have been placed elsewhere in the verse (with word end on the thesis):

(93) <u>κείνοις</u> ἀγγείλωσι θοῶς οἶκόνδε νέεσθαι

Odyssey xvi 350

That they may order them to return to their home quickly

(94) <u>κούρη</u> Ἰκαρίοιο περίφρων Πηνελόπεια

Odyssey xx 388

Daughter of Icarius, clever Penelope

(95) <u>νωμᾷ</u> ἔνθα καὶ ἔνθα κακῶν ἔμπαιος ἀλήτης

Odyssey xxi 400

He checks it from every angle, master of mischief, beggar

---

younger formations (ἠῶ δῖαν < *ἀϜόα δῖαν). For positions 4 and 8, the percentages are 1% (both *Iliad* and *Odyssey*) and 5% (*Iliad*) and 1% (*Odyssey*) respectively. The occurrence of metrically spondaic word end at position 12 (verse end) shows significant difference: 41% of the lines of the *Iliad* feature verse-final spondaic word end, against 78% of the *Odyssey*.

12 Word-final long vowels and diphthongs followed by hiatus on the arsis do not need the special condition of Wernicke's Law in order to be allowed at word end, as their metrical shape does not inevitably end in | – – |: they are usually phonetically shortened. Shortening* implies that the resulting syllable is one of the two light syllables on the arsis. In the absence of shortening, the conditions of Wernicke's Law must be invoked to help account for the permission of spondaic word end. In later hexametric Greek poetry, spondaic word end as permitted under the conditions of Wernicke's Law gradually disappears altogether.

In other feet of the hexameter, especially in the fourth, the same may occur: the deliberate creation of spondaic word end as the result of localization of a rhythmical word type that may as well be localized so as to *avoid* spondaic word end. It is possible, after all, to avoid it. The first book of the *Iliad* provides the following examples (96–104) of spondaic word end on position 8 that might have been avoided by different mapping of the word:[13]

(96) κλῦθί μευ ἀργυρότοξ᾽ ὃς <u>Χρύσην</u> ἀμφιβέβηκας

Iliad I 37 = *Iliad* I 451

Hear me please, Silverbow, who stand protectively over Chryse

(97) ἔκλαγξαν δ᾽ ἄρ᾽ ὀϊστοὶ ἐπ᾽ <u>ὤμων</u> χωομένοιο

Iliad I 46

The arrows rattled on the shoulders of the enraged

(98) οἴῳ φαινομένη τῶν <u>δ᾽ ἄλλων</u> οὔ τις ὁρᾶτο

Iliad I 198

Appearing to him alone; of the others no one saw her

(99) οὔτέ ποτ᾽ ἐς πόλεμον ἅμα <u>λαῷ</u> θωρηχθῆναι

Iliad I 226

And not ever to arm yourself for battle together with the soldiers

(100) ἀλλ᾽ ὅδ᾽ ἀνὴρ ἐθέλει περὶ <u>πάντων</u> ἔμμεναι ἄλλων

Iliad I 287

But this man here wants to be high above all others

(101) καί σφωιν δὸς ἄγειν τὼ <u>δ᾽ αὐτω</u> μάρτυροι ἔστων

Iliad I 338

And please give her to them to take; let the two of them be
wittnesses themselves

---

[13] If the word juncture following the prepositive after position 6 is hardly felt in examples 97, 100, 102, and 104, the localization of the prepositive + lexical* may better be compared to the metrically restricted bacchiac word type: in that case, the possibilities for localization are as restricted as those under Wernicke's Law.

(102) δίπτυχα ποιήσαντες ἐπ' <u>αὐτῶν</u> ὠμοθέτησαν

Iliad I 461

Having made it into a fold they put the pieces of raw meat on top of
    it

(103) νεικείῃσι πατήρ σὺν <u>δ' ἡμῖν</u> δαῖτα ταράξῃ

Iliad I 579

Lest father resorts to scolding and disturbs the meal for us with it

(104) ῥῖψε ποδὸς τεταγὼν ἀπὸ <u>βηλοῦ</u> θεσπεσίοιο

Iliad I 591

He grabbed me by the leg and threw me from the divine threshold

Under Wernicke's Law, bacchiac word shapes, or words ending in bacchiac
meter (‿| – – |),[14] may be possible before the bucolic dieresis. Their localization
cannot be altered as to map word end on the thesis. Instances in the *Iliad*'s first
book are the following:

2	οὐλομένην ἣ μυρί' <u>Ἀχαιοῖς</u> ἄλγε' ἔθηκε
44	βῆ δὲ κατ' Οὐλύμποιο <u>καρήνων</u> χωόμενος κῆρ
71	καὶ νήεσσ' ἡγήσατ' <u>Ἀχαιῶν</u> Ἴλιον εἴσω
89	σοὶ κοίλῃς παρὰ νηυσὶ <u>βαρείας</u> χεῖρας ἐποίσει
91	ὃς νῦν πολλὸν ἄριστος <u>Ἀχαιῶν</u> εὔχεται εἶναι
121	τὸν δ' ἠμείβετ' ἔπειτα <u>ποδάρκης</u> δῖος Ἀχιλλεύς
159	τιμὴν ἀρνύμενοι Με<u>νελάῳ</u> σοί τε κυνῶπα
244	χωόμενος ὅ τ' ἄριστον <u>Ἀχαιῶν</u> οὐδὲν ἔτισας
278	ἀντιβίην ἐπεὶ οὔ ποθ' <u>ὁμοίης</u> ἔμμορε τιμῆς
371	ἦλθε θοὰς ἐπὶ νῆας <u>Ἀχαιῶν</u> χαλκοχιτώνων
384	πάντῃ ἀνὰ στρατὸν εὐρὺν <u>Ἀχαιῶν</u> ἄμμι δὲ μάντις
412	ἣν ἄτην ὅ τ' ἄριστον <u>Ἀχαιῶν</u> οὐδὲν ἔτισε
430	τήν ῥα βίῃ ἀέκοντος <u>ἀπηύρων</u> αὐτὰρ Ὀδυσσεύς
551	τὸν δ' ἠμείβετ' ἔπειτα <u>βοῶπις</u> πότνια Ἥρη (cf. 568)
567	ἆσσον ἰόνθ' ὅτε κέν τοι <u>ἀάπτους</u> χεῖρας ἐφείω
571	τοῖσιν δ' Ἥφαιστος κλυ<u>τοτέχνης</u> ἦρχ' ἀγορεύειν

One (*Iliad* I 551/568) is not in accordance with the special feature that is the
most important condition for word end under Wernicke's Law: the length of the

---

[14] Metrical word shape as opposed to rhythmical word type, as the final heavy element of the
bacchiac counts as a thesis and cannot be resolved.

vocalic nucleus. In all other instances, the heavy syllable mapped on the hexameter's fourth arsis contains a long vowel or diphthong so that the word-final syllables take bacchiac shape before the dieresis. The formula βοῶπις πότνια Ἥρη (fourteen times in the *Iliad*, never in the *Odyssey*) contains a spondaic word end due to a consonantal coda ("through position"), instead of the natural length of the vocalic nucleus. In the analysis of Devine and Stephens, testing their hypothesis concerning the heavy syllable's resistance to shortening on the arsis, βοῶπις πότνια Ἥρη resists shortening more than the other examples, because of word end in heavy CVC (βοῶπις). The formula βοῶπις πότνια Ἥρη suggests that the more restrictive condition to allow for spondaic word end under Wernicke's Law postdates the localization of certain formulas.[15] It also suggests that subsequent permission for spondaic word end (that is, after the localization of certain formulas) has to do with the level of heavy syllables' resistance to shortening on the rhythmical arsis.

It is more significant that hardly any of the examples, both of rhythmical-spondaic word types *and* (final-)bacchiac word-shapes coinciding with metrical-spondaic word end, are phonologically indicative of phonetic word end. Overwhelmingly most of the examples feature a word-final syllable that is subject to sandhi. Devine and Stephens (1994:131) suggest as much when they point out that mapping on the arsis is much more likely for a syllable ending in a long vocalic nucleus (possibly as the result of coda-to-onset resyllabification*) than for a syllable that is heavy due to position.[16] This strikes me as peculiar since spondaic word end under Wernicke's Law is interpreted as a *permission* under specific conditions: the rhythmical closure of the verse-final spondaic word end with word-final lengthening is being duplicated at another, verse-internal position. The resulting disturbance of hexametric rhythm (premature verse-end) is then taken for granted.[17] Such disturbance, I reckon, would originate from any word end possible under the conditions of Wernicke's Law. The law would allow for word end with final lengthening—disrupting dactylic rhythm due to non-observance of submoraic adjustment (adjustment should have resulted in a shortening effect on the foot's arsis). The underlying premise is then that the metrical boundary following position 8 inevitably doubles as a phonetic disruption. I do not think it does: phonology shows that there is no phonetic word end.

---

[15] That the only exception is found in a noun-epithet formula bears some significance: I think it points at the possibility that spondaic word end under the conditions of Wernicke's Law is itself a license with regard to an older permission concerning spondaic word end due to position (word end in heavy word-final CVC). Of course, one formulaic example is insufficient proof.

[16] They speak of subordination* when discussing the mapping of heavy syllables on the arsis; see glossary, §3.1.3.2 above, and §5.1.4 below.

[17] Devine and Stephens 1976; cf. Van Raalte 1986:94. Basset 1938:144 credits the bucolic pause with the possibility to "restore the dactylic rhythm."

Most of the instances of spondaic word end at position 8 are subject to sandhi in their syllabification. Metrically, the syllable is heavy word-final CV instead of superheavy*; phonologically, the syllable is nonprepausal instead of prepausal. The resemblance to verse end seems to be rather weak.

Of the (final-)bacchiac examples from the *Iliad*'s first book, three (44, 121, 371) contain a superheavy syllable in the fourth foot arsis: sandhi cannot turn the syllable-final consonant into a syllable-initial onset*. Of these three lines, two (121, 371) allow the use of a superheavy syllable in order to apply a widely applied formula (ποδάρκης δῖος Ἀχιλλεύς, Ἀχαιῶν χαλκοχιτώνων). My conclusion tends to be the same as the one concerning βοῶπις πότνια Ἥρη in *Iliad* I 551: the more restrictive condition to allow for spondaic word end under Wernicke's Law postdates the localization of certain formulas (like *Iliad* I 89).[18]

The remaining superheavy syllable at position 8, καρήνων in *Iliad* I 44, results in a phonetic closure. Word-final lengthening is realized before word end. Word-final -νων thus resembles the monosyllabic foot ([T]), a thesis that has been orphaned from its arsis in the preceding or in the following word (§4.2.4). Final-syllable lengthening of -νων exaggerates the separation from the following thesis in the fifth foot. At the same time, it makes the preceding thesis within the fourth foot look like a syncopated foot. The lengthened arsis on position 8 looks like the second in a series of three theses:[19] $[(A)T^7][T^8]$ $[T^9A^{10}]$. The phonetic word end suggests a phonetic pause following position 8: in this case, a pause separating finite verb forms. Any change of direction in the rhythm (indicating metarrhythmisis to anapaests here) is no longer metarrhythmisis on the level of the rhythmical word type; it is metarrhythmisis on the level of the *phrase*, as termination is not merely in an isolated thesis, but in catalexis.[20]

Finally, the first book presents its audience with at least two molossus-shaped words[21] ending on position 8: ἀλλ' ἄγε διογενὲς Πατρόκλεις ἔξαγε κούρην in *Iliad* I 337, and οἶσθα τί ἦ τοι ταῦτ' εἰδυίη πάντ' ἀγορεύω in *Iliad* I 365. Both molossus-shaped words (-|- -|) can be used in other positions within the hexameter (mapped |- -|-). The phonetic effect of their localization is the same as for spondaic and (final-)bacchiac word shapes ending at position 8.

---

[18] It is noteworthy that, with few exceptions, the use of these formulas is restricted to the *Iliad*.

[19] Devine and Stephens (1994:131–132) speak of a series of theses due to syncopated feet: the number of rhythmical feet thus differs from the number of metrical feet.

[20] Description of rhythm as *alternating* (cf. Lidov 1989:69) does not allow phrasal metarrhythmisis within a period, but "between periods {that is, at a "pause"] a break in the alternation should not be construed as an abnormality of special interest."

[21] Metrical word shape, as opposed to rhythmical word type. In the rhythmical word-type, the word-final syllable is mapped on the thesis, though some of the instances of the non-contracted prototype, Ionicus *a minore*, treat the word-final syllable as an arsis.

With only few exceptions, submoraic adjustment of spondaic word end allowed under Wernicke's Law maintains the podic structure of dactylic rhythm. It does not result in the severe phonetic disturbance that is so readily assumed in the case of spondaic word end at verse end. On the contrary, phonological circumstances at position 8 are such as to prevent rhythmic disturbance. Synchronically, Wernicke's Law appears to be a condition under which word end is permitted in order to deal with verse-end-resembling rhythmical patterns within the hexameter. Diachronically, the non-disruptive word end on the hexameter's arsis developed together with the arsis of the sixth foot. It is therefore tempting to assume the possibility of non-disruptive word end at verse end for at least a number of the Homeric hexameters.

5.1.4 Options at verse end

How disruptive is the verse end to rhythm? Must we assume, as is common, that the verse end is always a rhythmical termination? Studies that take termination at verse end for granted assume that performance of the *Iliad* and the *Odyssey* is per verse (§4.1). Supposedly every verse is one breath; every verse is presented as a coherent unity. Phonological terminology would then label every verse a major phonological phrase. Defining the major phrase as a syntactical whole framed by pauses (as do Devine and Stephens) would mean that the pause at verse end should double as a syntactical break; verse end in Homer, however, often does not coincide with fulfilment of all the verse's syntactical requirements (§2.4). I propose that we leave these assumptions behind and start from a different angle, leaving aside the exact definition of the major phrase for now. The analysis of spondaic word end within the line (§5.1.2 and §5.1.3) shows that the condition to allow for verse-internal spondaic word end is sensitive to the phonology and to the phonetics of word end. Spondaic word end is often applied under such phonological circumstances that disruptive effects to rhythm, due to word end in a long syllable on the arsis, are reduced or avoided. In this section I argue that analysis of the rhythmical and phonological circumstances of word end at verse end will show how disruptive phonetic word end at verse end is to rhythm. The phonological circumstances of word end are options in composition: the composer deliberately creates specific circumstances through the way he continues after phonetic word end. Continuation by means of a vowel leads to circumstances that differ from those created by continuation by means of a consonant. As the composer determines the phonological circumstances of word end, both at verse end and within the line, I present the disruption to rhythm caused by word end at verse end as options for phonetic word end.

5.1.4.1 Option 1: Metarrhythmisis due to a verse-final heavy syllable

I will start from the broadly accepted notion that word end at verse end is indeed disruptive. From the rhythmical perspective, word end at the hexameter's verse end results in performative pause due to metarrhythmisis to anapaests (§5.1.3), that is, if the phonological circumstances of word end at verse end allow for phonetic word end in a heavy syllable. As in the case of spondaic phonetic word end at position 8, metarrhythmisis at position 12 means metarrhythmisis on the level of the phrase instead of on the level of the rhythmical word: the verse-final metrical colon needs to end in catalexis (so that verse-final ◡ ◡|◡́ –‖ renders ◡ ◡ ◡́ |◡́ ‖) so that the metrical colon starting after position 5 is actually a catalectic anapaestic dimeter. Starting from another position, metarrhythmisis to anapaests is more gradual, within a metrical phrase. The following two examples (105, 106) feature both types of phrasal metarrhythmisis to anapaests. In both examples the metrical colon after position 5 is perceived as an anapaestic dimeter, whereas the metarrhythmisis is more gradual in the first metrical colon of the line, as it is on the level of the rhythmical word (the first colon of example 105 terminates in an orphaned thesis; the first colon of 106 opens with one; there are more rhythmical feet than metrical feet):

(105) ὣς ἔφατ᾽ εὐχομένη   ἀνένευε δὲ Παλλὰς Ἀθήνη

    [T A][T   A][T]   [A T][A T][A   T][T]

                                                      Iliad VI 311

Thus she spoke praying, but Pallas Athena shook her head in refusal

(106) τὴν δ᾽ ἀπαμειβόμενος   προσέφη πολύμητις Ὀδυσσεύς

    [T] [A T][A   T]   [A   T][A   T][A   T][T]

                                                      Odyssey xix 499

Answering her clever Odysseus spoke

5.1.4.2 Option 2: Subordination due to spondaic closure

Metarrhythmisis is not considered an option when the phonological circumstances of word end at verse end do not automatically allow for phonetic word end in a heavy syllable, for example when consonantal liaison over the verse end cannot be excluded, or when the syllable on the sixth-foot arsis can only meet the requirements of the heavy syllable "by position." The verse end is then not the closure of catalectic anapaestic rhythm but the spondaic closure of dactylic rhythm, due to metrical indifference on the sixth arsis. In that case, word end at verse end would facilitate a mild disruption to the flow of dactyls at the dieresis.[22] This is option 2: dactylic prepausal word end does allow for word-final lengthening, if the additional final lengthening would be minimal (as it is on the arsis). Above in section 5.1.3, spondaic word-final heavy CV proved to be much more frequent than CV̌C: the statistical evidence supports the hypothesis that CV̌C is more resistant than heavy CV to the submoraic shortening that allows heavy syllables to occupy the foot's arsis. The sample in section 5.4 below shows that the same tendency is to be expected with regard to spondaic word end at verse end: CV̌C | C- is found in *Iliad* I 14 and *Iliad* I 37, CV | C- is more frequent.

Qualification of the dieresis at verse end as secondary pause stems from the assumption of metrical indifference (anceps) at verse end. Korzeniewski (1968:9) considers anceps indicative of termination. Comparison, however, of the verse end with verse-internal spondaic word end suggests that its realization would not be prosodically neutral. It is rather reminiscent of what Devine and Stephens (1994:131) call the subordinated syllable: a syllable whose rhythmical prominence is kept in accordance with the foot-internal proportion* (see §5.1.3). Subordination describes the adjustments to heavy syllables to retain the unidirectional structure for stress feet in a phrase: heavy syllables are supposedly theses, so footing problems appear as soon as a series of heavy syllables (and hence a series of theses) appears. Such contiguous stresses, suggesting a sequence of theses [T][T][T], are replaced by a [TA] stress foot structure. The process involves adjustments to the defooted heavy syllable, the single thesis that, by itself, constitutes a rhythmical foot in the rhythmical sequence [T] [T][T]. An adjacent syllable is defooted in order to form a foot together with the subordinated heavy syllable that is preceded and followed by a thesis. The subordinated heavy syllable is consequently mapped onto arsis ([T][T][T] → [TA][T] or [T][AT]). Devine and Stephens (1994:131) note that "implicit in the hypothesis of subordination is the assumption that, when a heavy syllable is mapped onto arsis, it is pronounced with less duration than a heavy syllable mapped onto thesis." I argue that a similar treatment may be an option for the verse-final arsis. Having accepted the foot-internal proportion A ≤ T, I find the terminology subordination very useful outside the reconstruction of stress feet. Used for metrical feet, subordination also describes the restriction on

---

[22] The dieresis at verse end separates descending rhythm from descending rhythm, as the dieresis would within the line (Basset 1938:150). Mild demarcation is not unusual at the dieresis at position 8 (cf. the bucolic dieresis as the most common spot for printed punctuation in the hexameter).

prepausal mapping of heavy syllables onto the arsis to retain the unidirectional podic structure.[23]

Like the heavy syllable on position 8, the verse-final anceps offers word-end options that are comparable to the heavy syllable on the arsis in both the dactyl and the anapaest.[24] Like phrasal metarrhythmisis, realization of the verse-final syllable as a subordinated syllable is an example of phonetic adjustment: this time frustrating the realization of a prepausal syllable. As non-prepausal, the verse-final metrical anceps requires no more than maintenance of the dactylic foot (with its foot-internal proportion) and realization of the verse-final syllable as a metrically indifferent arsis. The thesis, as the first element of the sixth foot, must be the only stable element: only then can it be avoided that the verse-final element is mapped as a prepausal syllable. Evidence to support this observation can be found in the general avoidance of lexical monosyllables on the verse-final element of the hexameter.

As the sixth-foot anceps offers options, there is no reason to assume, as Ruijgh does,[25] that the sixth foot ends in a perfect long syllable (μακρὰ τελεία). Attractive as his assumption may seem from the metrical point of view, phrasal metarrhythmisis (to anapaests; option 1) cannot automatically be taken for granted. Within the line, phrasal metarrhythmisis is evidenced by spondaic word end in a superheavy syllable, that is, by an overlong syllable *without* the possibility of synaphy.[26] The parallelism between the condition under which such word end is allowed under Wernicke's Law and the Law's *raison d'être*, the verse end, proves that caution is equally required when considering the possible realization of position 12 as a μακρὰ τελεία. Option 1 may very well be possible (phrasal metarrhythmisis to anapaests; rhythmically orphaned verse-final thesis [τ]), but for most verse-final heavy syllables the metrical and phonological considerations presented so far are not sufficient to consider them as other than subordinated syllables. For these instances option 2, subordination, seems to be more easily defensible than option 1.

5.1.4.3 Option 3: Metarrhythmisis despite a verse-final light syllable?

There is yet another aspect of verse end that ought to be taken into account, as the phonological perspectives of verse end have not been completely accounted

---

[23] From Porter's notation of alternating rhythm (in Loomis 1972; cf. Lidov 1989:72n17), it becomes clear that the metrical anceps is the regular alternative *between* instances of double short (as the realization of the "more changeable expression," the arsis) in dactylo-epitrite.

[24] Rossi (1963:44–49) describes the subordinated heavy syllable on the arsis as a κυκλικός-element. The denomination κυκλικός refers to the non-disruptive character of the non-prepausal syllable.

[25] Ruijgh 1987:349: "Denys oublie de signaler que la syllabe finale en fin de vers est bien une μακρὰ τελεία."

[26] Or ambisyllabism, with the exception of [long vowel + ς].

for so far. Options 1 and 2 accounted for the heavy verse-final syllable, but not the metrically short syllable. As heavy anceps, the arsis of the sixth foot must have mora count of at least two: the mora count of the verse-final anceps is more or less equal to that of the non-final heavy syllable. What about the verse-final light syllable?

In modern approaches to Homeric meter, it is not uncommon to consider the verse-final syllable as heavy *per se*. The repertorium by Dee 2004 automatically scans *longum* at verse end in examples like (107) and (108):

(107) χάλκεον αὐτὰρ ἔπειτα σάκος μέγα τε στιβαρόν τε

Iliad XVI 136

Of bronze, and then the big and solid shield

(108) καί τέ με νεικείεσκον ἐγὼ δ' οὐκ αἴτιός εἰμι

Iliad XIX 86

And they keep casting it in my teeth, but I am not responsible

The automatism that presents position 12 as a *longum* is based on the indifference that characterizes metrical finality. This automatism makes it look like the verse-final foot inevitably resembles, or even takes, the shape of a spondee. The metrical indifference of the final syllable, including the light syllable, of the verse may result in a verse-final foot that might be labelled σπονδαιοείδης "resembling a spondee." A verse-final foot scanned |– –|| is spondaic because it features a monosyllabic arsis: the final syllable does not represent double light.[27] As the monosyllabic arsis is in no way the alternative for a resolvable element, its realization would not allow for a primary pause following it. If position 12 would be considered a *longum* due to *brevis in longo*, the *brevis in longo* itself is due to the identification of verse end as a performative pause.[28] Such pause may be compared to the verse-internal dieresis or to the trochaic caesura, both secondary pauses. Any word-final lengthening of the verse-final element is restricted: only about half that of the μακρὰ τελεία. Before the trochaic caesura, the metrical syllabification of word-final (short vowel + consonant) shows that the phonological constraints are stronger than the

---

[27] Van Raalte (1986:17) compares a double light ending for the hexameter with the final heavy element of the iambic trimeter as a license for *brevis in longo*. Apparently, she does not presume a correspondence between this license and the rhythmical closure (*blunt** versus *pendant**) of the metrical colon.

[28] Van Raalte (1986:17) explains such *brevis in longo* by saying "that the actual quantity of the verse-final syllable (i.e., the rhythmic realization of the final metric element) is irrelevant in virtue of its prosodic neutrality, the rhythmic series ... being interrupted as soon as the metric series has been rhythmically completed."

phonetic disruption. In such cases, word-final consonants must be considered as subject to resyllabification:

(109) μάψ ἀτὰρ οὐ κατὰ κόσμο<u>ν</u> ἐμοι δ' ἄχος οἱ δὲ ἔκηλοι

.κόσ.μο.<u>νε</u>.μοι

Iliad V 759

Recklessly and without restriction; for me it means sorow, but the
others calmly

The word-final light syllable preceding the secondary pause may be additionally lengthened, but lengthening cannot turn it into a heavy syllable. The appearance of movable *nu** at the trochaic caesura points in the same direction:

(110) τοῖσι δὲ βοῦν ἱέρευσε<u>ν</u> ἄναξ ἀνδρῶν Ἀγαμέμνων

βοῦ.νι.έ.ρευ.σε.<u>νά</u>.νακ.σαν.δρῶ.ν-

Iliad VII 314

And for them the lord of men Agamemnon immolated a bull

Movable *nu* is metrically harmless, phonologically useful, and phonetically non-disturbing. There is epigraphical evidence[29] of movable *nu* turning the trochaic caesura into a secondary pause, despite punctuation included in the inscription:

ἀλ(λ)όμενος νίκησεν : Ἐπαίνετος οὔνεκα τοῦδε: (from Eleusis)
ϙου[φαγόρας μ' ἀνέθη]κεν : Διὸς γλαυϙώπιδι ϙούρηι   (from Athens)

Brevis in longo may occur on the prepausal thesis, and the license is extended to word end on a thesis that is not prepausal (§3.1.3.2). *Brevis in longo* does *not* appear on the arsis preceding verse-internal dieresis. If I combine the observations concerning syllable duration and weight before various positions of word end in, or following, the arsis, I can reasonably postulate that *brevis in longo* is restricted to the completion of blunt rhythm. I argue that it is not a feature of the rhythm at verse end, unless metarrhythmisised on the level of the phrase. Otherwise, I conclude, the verse-final arsis is not a perfect long element.[30]

In order to exploit phrasal metarrhythmisis at word end in a verse-final light syllable, the composer has to allow for an audible pause at verse end. Phonology does not evidence this pause or metarrhythmisis in case of a verse-final light

---

[29] Examples from Usener 1887:38–40.

[30] Dionysius' comment that the hexameter example *Odyssey* xi 598 (αὖτις ἔπειτα πέδονδε κυλίνδετο λᾶας ἀναιδής, "Then, again, the shameless boulder rolled back to the plain") does not feature a perfect long element may be puzzling, but endorses this conclusion (line 599 starting αὐτὰρ ...). Dionysius does not forget (cf. Ruijgh 1987 and footnote 194) to count the verse-final syllable among the "perfect" long elements.

syllable though. Metarrhythmisis seems to be taken for granted, since the necessity for the verse-final *breve* to be realized as rhythmically heavy and phonetically lengthened requires *brevis in longo*, a phenomenon exclusive to the thesis, on the anceps element. I see no reason to postulate metarrhythmisis for the verse-final light syllable; its occurrence in the unidirectional podic structure elicits some phonetic lengthening due to temporal allowance and word end in a secondary performative pause.

Conclusion

The metrical anceps on the sixth-foot arsis is thus metrically indifferent, but not rhythmically indeterminate. Phonology allows for three types of realization. As (option 1) a heavy (example 111), or rather superheavy syllable (example 112), the sixth arsis equals the "perfect" long:

(111) πρῶθ' ἑκατὸν βοῦς δῶκεν ἔπειτα δὲ χίλι' ὑπέστη
 (Next line starts αἶγας ὁμοῦ καὶ ὄϊς ...)

Iliad XI 244

First he gave a hundred cows, and later he promised a thousand |
[goats and sheep together]

(112) ἴσχειν ἐν στήθεσσι φιλοφροσύνη γὰρ ἀμείνων
 (Next line starts ληγέμεναι δ' ἔριδος ...)

Iliad IX 256

Keep it in your heart: calmness is always to be preferred; | [refrain from strife]

As (option 3) a light syllable, the verse-final syllable results in a heavy verse-final element (resembling *brevis in longo*) due to metrical indifference:

(113) αὐτὸς δὲ κλάγξας πέτετο πνοιῆς ἀνέμοιο
 (Next line starts Τρῶες δ' ἐρρίγησαν ...)

Iliad XII 207

But he [the eagle] flew on the breaths of the wind, shrieking; | [the Trojans stood in horror]

Both realizations (option 1) and (option 3), however, take a performative pause at verse end for granted (in case of option 3, to turn what seems to be *brevis in longo* into phonetic lengthening). Option 3 elicits a milder pause: the verse-final light syllable is free from sandhi and from apposition, but its prolongation requires a mild rhythmical disruption. Option 1 requires phrasal metarrhythmisis. As the verse end cannot automatically be seen as metarrhythmisised unless phonology demonstrates the change in direction of the rhythm, many verse-final syllables remain nonprepausal: their structure does not allow phonetic word end (example 114) or pause (example 115, cf. § 4.2.5), or represents too little rhythmic weight (example 116) to make them count as heavy. I have argued that in those instances "dimming of the rhythm of the end of the hexameter"[31] through realization of an anceps element as (option 2) subordinated syllable at position 12 is likely:[32]

(114) ὀλλύντ' Ἀργείων πουλὺν στρατὸν αἰχμητά<u>ων</u>
       (Next line starts οὐ γὰρ πρὶν ...)

Iliad VIII 472

Destroying a large army of Greek spearfighters | (for no sooner)

(115) Αἰτωλῶν ὄχ' ἄριστον Ὀχησίου ἀγλαὸν υἱ<u>όν</u>
       (Next line starts τὸν μὲν Ἄρης ἐνάριζε ...)

Iliad V 843

By far the best of the Aetolians, shining son of Ochesios; | [him Ares killed]

(116) ἑσταότες παρ' ὄχεσφιν ἐύθρονον Ἠῶ μί<u>μνον</u>
       (Next line—and book—starts ὣς οἱ μὲν Τρῶες φυλακὰς ἔχον ...)

Iliad VIII 565

Standing next to the chariots they waited for golden-throne Dawn; | so the Trojans kept watch)

---

[31] Parry 1971:263. "Dimming of rhythm" is, in fact, the maintenance of podic structure and unidirectional rhythmisis over the verse end.

[32] From the analysis of *Iliad* I 1–100 and *Odyssey* i 1–100 in the sample at the end of this chapter the following statistics emerge:

Percentage of lines ending in:	Iliad	Odyssey
Perfect heavy after metarrhythmisis (option 1)	16%	18%
Subordinate syllable (option 2)	63%	66%
"*Brevis in longo*"* (option 3)	21%	16%

* The alternative would be to describe this possibility as "perfect heavy < light syllable after metarrhythmisis," taking metarrhythmisis for granted. Metrically, there is no distinction between the two ways to end the line. It is exactly the metrical resemblance that obscures the option of pause: the anceps allows for secondary pause, metarrhythmisis for primary pause. In case of *brevis in longo*, there is no *a priori* reason to assume metarrhythmisis, apart from the notion that *brevis in longo*, strictly speaking, is limited to the thesis.

Example 115 illustrates how a heavy verse-final syllable is maintained because there is no verse end pause: verse-end straddling υἱόν | τὸν makes verse-final -όν meet the requirements of the heavy syllable on the sixth arsis in a way similar to the verse- and word-internal syllable CVC on the arsis. Example 116 shows something similar, even over the book division: there is no reason to assume any serious phonetic disruption at verse end, since verse-final –vov is subordinated. Its rhythmical weight is not sufficient to account for a "perfect" heavy, even when assuming the possibility of phrasal metarrhythmisis.

5.1.5 Options at secondary word end

Unlike primary phonetic word end, secondary phonetic word end does not automatically allow for performative pause. Metrical surface structure cannot accommodate additional word-final lengthening when it disrupts rhythmic regularity. Despite the absence of accentual clisis*, phonological apposition*, and sandhi, secondary phonetic word end will feature hardly any perceptible syllable lengthening. Word end at verse end in movable *nu* (example 117) actually *requires* some phonetic disruption at verse end if the verse-final syllable is to retain the necessary rhythmical weight:

> (117) σὺν σφῆσιν κεφαλῆσι γυναιξί τε καὶ τεκέεσ<u>σιν</u>
> (Next line starts εὖ γὰρ ἐγὼ τόδε οἶδα ...)
>
> *Iliad* IV 162
>
> With their lives, their spouses and their children; | (for I know this well)

Additional lengthening of secondary phonetic word end on the heavy arsis needs to maintain the foot-internal proportion* $T^{duration} > A^{duration}$, and so must the double-*breve* arsis featuring phonetic word end in a light syllable. Generally, the perceptibility of secondary phonetic word end benefits from word end in an enclitic: the sharp accentual fall on, and the susceptibility to reduction of, the nonlexical* enclitic bring out word end as a sharper contour in prosody (example 118):

> (118) Ῥῆσός θ᾿ Ἑπτάπορός τε Κάρησός τε Ῥοδίος <u>τε</u>
>
> *Iliad* XII 20
>
> Rhesos and Heptaporos and Karesos and Rhodios

This prosodic contour is strengthened by mapping of the enclitic on the foot's thesis (example 119):

(119) Ἕκτωρ <u>τε</u> Πριάμοιο πάϊς καὶ χάλκεος Ἄρης
ἀντίθεον Τεύθραντ᾽ ἐπὶ <u>δὲ</u> πλήξιππον Ὀρέστην

Iliad V 704–705

[who did they kill first,] Hector, son of Priam, and bronze Ares? |
Godlike Teuthras and after him Orestes "horse-whip"

The composer does not only influence the phonological circumstances of word end by the way phonation restarts after phonetic word end, but also by the mapping of constituents that do not have a stable thesis.

Options for secondary word end to be realized as performative pause are options for minor phrase termination. Devine and Stephens (1994:303) state that phonology phrases adjacent items together into the minor phrase provided that neither of them belongs more closely to a third item. The tie with a third item can be accentual (due to clisis) or appositional. In the latter case, apposition is not only understood as phonological apposition, but as syntactical apposition as well. The inclusion of syntactical apposition seems, so I fear, to call a level of arbitrariness back into the identification of phonological phrases. I am not sure that such arbitrariness can be avoided in the identification of minor phrases in Homer: the major phrases appear to be rather long, and selection of (only) secondary word end in an enclitic or in a heavy syllable on the arsis as the boundary of the minor phrase makes the units of performance quite substantial.

5.1.6 Options and choice

I have described what options for pause the various metrical positions offer in case of phonetic word end. The transmitted text of the *Iliad* and the *Odyssey* has been treated as the reflection of a performable and performed text. It is the poet in his role as composer who chooses to mark options for phonetic word end: he decides on the phonological and phonetic consequences of word end through what he puts next. The way he continues with a new phrase within the framework of the meter determines the phonetics of the way he concluded the previous phrase. The choice for phonetic word end belongs to the domain of composition; the performer does not treat phonetic word end as a choice. In performance the only choice is the choice in rates of speech, in other words: the choice to turn options for pause into true pauses. It is this choice, in rates of speech, that determines the audible patterning of phrases in the flow of dactyls. At very slow rates of speech, phonetic word end becomes perceptible as a rest of some duration; at high rates of speech, phonetic word end tends to become perceptible as a breathing pause at regular intervals. At normal rates of speech, primary word end appears as a strong phonetic disruption, as an audible pause, in performance. Secondary word end results in a perceptible pause, but as a milder disruption than primary word end, notably in case of word end in an enclitic (the more so when mapped on the foot's thesis), or in a heavy syllable on the foot's arsis.

5.2   Performative Pause as Audible Punctuation

In Chapter 4 and §5.1, I have described the performative perspectives of phonetic pause. Against the background of Homeric performance, the performative aspects suggest where a performative pause may be possible and where not, where a performative pause is likely to occur and where not, where a performative pause may or may not reasonably be assumed. Assumption of performative pause is as close as one can get to audible punctuation, to termination of phonation and silence, in Homeric performance, until evidence is found from antiquity on performance. Such evidence is not readily available at the moment.

We may, however, find evidence concerning the feature that determines whether options for pause become a choice for pause: rates of speech. At first sight, it seems we are not very well informed when it comes to the rates of speech in Homeric performance. Plato's Socrates (in his *Ion*) discusses the Homeric content, but he does not enlarge on the actual performance of hexameters. On iambs, Aristotle (*Rhetoric* 1408b33) informs us that they resemble natural unplanned speech; the anapaestic system, on the other hand, is said to lead to "suffocation" (Scholion to Aristophanes *Acarnians* 659). Little is known about the enactment of the *Iliad* and the *Odyssey*: centuries after the first performance of the Homeric epic, we find the observation that a preponderance of spondees slows down the rate of speech, whereas dactyls are supposed to speed it up (Dionysius of Halicarnassus *On literary composition* 17). Dionysius of Halicarnassus comments on the drawling effect on speech of phonetically disruptive word end: word end on the arsis, in a light syllable, makes the line run more smoothly and regularly, he says. I argue that the occurrence of two types of word end in Homer, one more and one less disruptive to rhythm, is indicative of the application of normal rates of speech in performance. The two types of word end reappear in performance as milder and stronger phonetic disruptions. The milder disruptions allow for some word-final lengthening, but not for silence. There may have been a chance to take a breath, but the milder disruption is not the preferred moment to do so. Inhalation at secondary word end practically has to be voiced (sonorant) and the start of a syllable; secondary word end leaves no room for true silence. Such a stealthy breath at secondary word end seems to be easiest when the phonetic pause stems from prosodic markers of termination like apposition (in case of postpositives*) and accentual clisis (in case of enclitics); both markers are prosodically susceptible to reduction (§3.1.2). A stealthy breath seems less likely when the secondary word end concludes a subordinate syllable: subordinate syllables are heavy (§5.1.4) and their realization as word-final heavy syllable on the arsis leaves no temporal allowance within the framework of rhythmic regularity. Submoraic adjustment of subordinate syllables strives towards a minimal duration for the heavy syllable, without room for anything other than the minimal mora count (2). The stronger disruption may allow for considerable word-final lengthening, for silence and for taking a breath. Even stopping short at the stronger disruptions does not impede the podic structure and the unidirectional structure of the rhythm.

5.3 Repetition of Rhythmic Patterning

Having introduced the notion that the identification of audible punctuation is neither arbitrary nor based on metrical repetition, I must address the new punctuation pattern that emerges from variable and varying word end. I will do so referring to the sample that I add to this chapter (§5.4): the application of the two types of word end to the first 100 lines of the *Iliad* and the *Odyssey*. Does this new pattern evidence any form of repetition—or its avoidance?

Mention has been made of the resemblance of permission for spondaic word end under Wernicke's Law and at verse end (§5.1.3 and §5.1.4). On the one hand, under Wernicke's Law there is a possibility for the mapping of a specific type of word end that is otherwise found only or mostly at verse end; on the other hand, word end under Wernicke's Law depends on specific conditions that cause the verse to avoid audibly terminating too early. Both explanations, of the permission and of its restrictive use, are based on the assumption that phonetic disruption is repeated under similar metrical and phonological circumstances within one single hexameter. Such repetition is not a persistent phenomenon in Homeric poetry though, not even in verses featuring word end allowed under Wernicke's Law. In the sample below, 16% of the lines of the *Iliad* and 6% of the lines of the *Odyssey* show repetition of phonetic disruption under similar metrical circumstances within the line. Repetition is significantly clustered in and around direct speech: 62.5% and 67% of the verses featuring phonetic repetition in the *Iliad* and in the *Odyssey*, respectively, are found in direct speech. The combination of word end under Wernicke's Law, phonetic word end at position 8, *and* a primary pause at verse end, hardly ever occurs in Homer: in the *Iliad*'s first book, only lines 44 and 371 qualify as examples.[33] Performance strives towards avoidance of repetitive rhythmical patterns within the line: verses with word end at the bucolic dieresis, even in a secondary pause, do not feature secondary pauses both at the bucolic dieresis *and* the verse end.

5.4   A Sample (*Iliad* I 1–100, *Odyssey* i 1–100)

I present the result of my approach in a sample, which is representative for the Homeric epic as a whole, as is the statistical data derived from it. I have tried to visualize the mosaic-like pattern of phrases in performance through a proselike rendering: the main focus is not on the stichic hexameter, but on phonological phrases demarcated by primary pauses. Following a primary pause (i.e., primary phonetic word end), the phonological phrase begins in the left margin. After every secondary word end, a new phrase is indented two tab stops. I have indicated three different realizations of secondary word end to account for the realizations that indicate not only word end but termination of the minor phrase as well.

Legend to the sample

ᵒ	Primary phonetic word end
ᵒM	Primary phonetic word end due to phrasal metarrhythmisis to anapaests
·	Secondary phonetic word end (indicated by minimal phonetic adjustment at normal rate of speech)
··	Secondary phonetic word end indicated by enclitic
···	Secondary phonetic word end indicated by phonetic adjustment (at normal rate of speech) and by enclitic
1½ etc.	Metrical location of phonetic word end
(1)	Verse number

---

[33] Printed punctuation may suggest otherwise as in, for example, *Iliad* IV 364: ὣς εἰπὼν τοὺς μὲν λίπεν αὐτοῦ βῆ δὲ μετ᾽ ἄλλους, "having spoken thus he left them there, and went to the others." There is no reason, however, to consider the verse-final syllable a "perfect" heavy element, as *Iliad* IV 365 starts with a vowel: εὗρε δὲ Τυδέος υἱὸν ὑπέρθυμον Διομήδεα, "and he found the son of Tydeus, brave Diomedes."

Chapter 5

Iliad I 1–100

(1) Μῆνιν ἄειδε˙³½

θεά˙⁵

Πηληϊάδεω Ἀχιλῆος˙¹²

(2) οὐλομένην˙³

ἣ μυρί’ Ἀχαιοῖς ἄλγε’ ἔθηκε˙¹²

(3) πολλὰς δ’ ἰφθίμους˙⁵

ψυχὰς Ἄϊδι προΐαψεν˙¹²

(4) ἡρώων˙³

αὐτοὺς δὲ˙˙⁵½

ἑλώρια˙⁸

τεῦχε˙⁹½

κύνεσσιν˙¹²

(5) οἰωνοῖσί τε˙˙⁴

πᾶσι˙⁵½

Διὸς δ’ ἐτελείετο˙¹⁰

βουλή˙¹²

(6) ἐξ οὗ δὴ˙³

τὰ πρῶτα˙⁵½

διαστήτην ἐρίσαντε˙¹²

(7) Ἀτρεΐδης τε˙˙³½

ἄναξ ἀνδρῶν˙⁷

καὶ δῖος Ἀχιλλεύς˙ᵉᴹ¹²

(8) τίς τάρ σφωε˙³½

θεῶν ἔριδι ξυνέηκε˙⁹½

μάχεσθαι˙ᵉᴹ

(9) Λητοῦς καὶ Διὸς υἱός ὃ γὰρ˙˙˙⁷

βασιλῆϊ˙⁹½

χολωθείς˙ᵉᴹ¹²

(10) νοῦσον ἀνὰ στρατὸν ὦρσε˙⁵½

κακήν˙⁷

ὀλέκοντο δὲ˙˙¹⁰

λαοί˙¹²

(11) οὕνεκα τὸν Χρύσην ἠτίμασεν ἀρητῆρα˙¹²

(12) Ἀτρεΐδης˙³

ὃ γὰρ˙˙⁴

ἦλθε˙⁵½

θοὰς ἐπὶ νῆας Ἀχαιῶν˙ᵉᴹ¹²

(13) λυσόμενός τε˙˙³½

θύγατρα˙⁵½

φέρων τ' ἀπερείσι' ἄποινα˙¹²

(14) στέμματ' ἔχων ἐν χερσὶν ἑκηβόλου
      Ἀπόλλωνος (15) χρυσέῳ ἀνὰ
      σκήπτρῳ˙⁵

καὶ λίσσετο˙⁸

πάντας Ἀχαιούς (16) Ἀτρείδα δὲ˙˙˙³½
μάλιστα˙⁵½
δύω˙⁷

κοσμήτορε˙

λαῶν˙¹²

(17) Ἀτρεῖδαί τε˙˙³½
καὶ ἄλλοι ἐϋκνήμιδες Ἀχαιοί˙¹²
(18) ὑμῖν μὲν˙˙˙³
θεοὶ˙⁴
δοῖεν Ὀλύμπια˙⁸
δώματ' ἔχοντες˙¹²
(19) ἐκπέρσαι˙³

Πριάμοιο˙⁵½

πόλιν˙⁷

εὖ δ' οἴκαδ' ἱκέσθαι˙¹²

(20) παῖδα δ' ἐμοὶ˙³

λύσαιτε˙⁵½

φίλην˙⁷

τὰ δ' ἄποινα˙⁹½

δέχεσθαι˙¹²
(21) ἁζόμενοι˙³

Διὸς υἱὸν ἑκηβόλον Ἀπόλλωνα˙¹²

(22) ἔνθ' ἄλλοι μὲν˙˙˙⁴
πάντες ἐπευφήμησαν Ἀχαιοί˙¹²
(23) αἰδεῖσθαί θ' ἱερῆα˙⁵½
καὶ ἀγλαὰ˙⁸
δέχθαι ἄποινα˙¹²
(24) ἀλλ' οὐκ Ἀτρείδῃ Ἀγαμέμνονι˙⁸
ἤνδανε˙¹⁰
θυμῷ˙¹²
(25) ἀλλὰ κακῶς ἀφίει˙⁵

κρατερὸν δ' ἐπὶ μῦθον ἔτελλεν˙¹²

(26) μή σε γέρον κοίλῃσιν ἐγώ˙⁷

παρὰ νηυσὶ˙⁹½

κιχείω˙¹²

(27) ἢ νῦν δηθύνοντ' ἢ ὕστερον αὖτις ἰόντα˙[12]
(28) μή νύ τοι οὐ χραίσμη[°5]

σκῆπτρον καὶ στέμμα˙ [9½]

θεοῖο[˙12]
(29) τὴν δ' ἐγὼ οὐ λύσω[°5]

πρίν μιν[‴ 7]

καὶ γῆρας ἔπεισιν˙[12]
(30) ἡμετέρῳ ἐνὶ οἴκῳ ἐν Ἄργεϊ[˙8]
τηλόθι πάτρης   (31) ἱστὸν ἐποιχομένην[°5]

καὶ ἐμὸν λέχος ἀντιόωσαν˙[12]

(32) ἀλλ' ἴθι[˙2]
μή μ' ἐρέθιζε[˙5½]
σαώτερος ὥς κε νέηαι˙[12]
(33) ὣς ἔφατ' ἔδδεισεν δ' ὁ γέρων[°7]

καὶ ἐπείθετο[˙10]

μύθῳ[°M12]

(34) βῆ δ' ἀκέων[°3]
παρὰ θῖνα[˙5½]

πολυφλοίσβοιο˙[9½]

θαλάσσης[°M12]
(35) πολλὰ δ' ἔπειτ' ἀπάνευθε κιὼν ἠρᾶθ' ὁ γεραιός˙[12]

(36) Ἀπόλλωνι[˙3½]
ἄνακτι[˙5½]
τὸν ἠΰκομος τέκε˙ [10]
Λητώ[°M12]

(37) κλῦθί μοι[˙2]

Ἀργυρότοξ', ὃς Χρύσην ἀμφιβέβηκας
(38) Κίλλάν τε[‴3]
ζαθέην[°5]

Τενέδοιό τε[¨8]

ἶφι˙[9½]
ἀνάσσεις[°M12]

(39) Σμινθεῦ[˙2]

εἴ ποτέ τοι[°5]

χαρίεντ' ἐπὶ νηὸν ἔρεψα˙[12]

(40) ἢ' εἰ δή ποτέ τοι[°5]

κατὰ πίονα[˙8]

μηρί' ἔκηα˙[12]
(41) ταύρων ἠδ' αἰγῶν[°5]

τόδε μοι[°7]

κρήηνον ἐέλδωρ°M12
(42) τείσειαν Δαναοὶ °5
ἐμὰ δάκρυα·8

        σοῖσι βέλεσσιν·12
        (43) ὣς ἔφατ' εὐχόμενος τοῦ δ' ἔκλυε·8
        Φοῖβος Ἀπόλλων°M12

(44) βῆ δὲ···1½

        κατ' Οὐλύμποιο·5½
        καρήνων°M8

χωόμενος κῆρ°M12
(45) τόξ' ὤμοισιν ἔχων ἀμφηρεφέα τε···9½

        φαρέτρην· (46) ἔκλαγξαν δ' ἄρ' ὀϊστοὶ ἐπ'
          ὤμων°M8

χωομένοιο·12

        (47) αὐτοῦ κινηθέντος ὃ δ' ἤϊε·8
        νυκτὶ·9½
        ἐοικώς·12
        (48) ἕζετ' ἔπειτ' ἀπάνευθε νεῶν°7

μετὰ δ' ἰὸν ἕηκε·12

        (49) δεινὴ δὲ···3
        κλαγγὴ°5

γένετ' ἀργυρέοιο·9½

        βιοῖο·12
        (50) οὐρῆας μὲν···4
        πρῶτον ἐπῴχετο·8
        καὶ κύνας ἀργούς (51) αὐτὰρ ἔπειτ'
          αὐτοῖσι·5½
        βέλος °7

ἐχεπευκὲς ἐφιείς°M12
(52) βάλλ' αἰεὶ δὲ··3½

        πυραὶ°5

νεκύων°7
καίοντο·9½

        θαμειαί·12
        (53) ἐννῆμαρ μὲν··3½
        ἀνὰ στρατὸν ᾤχετο·8
        κῆλα·9½
        θεοῖο·12
        (54) τῇ δεκάτῃ δ' ἀγορήνδε·5½
        καλέσσατο·8
        λαὸν Ἀχιλλεύς°M12

(55) τῷ γὰρ¨¹½

       ἐπὶ φρεσὶ˙⁴
       θῆκε˙⁵½
       θεὰ°⁷

λευκώλενος Ἥρη˙¹²

       (56) κήδετο γὰρ¨¨³
       Δαναῶν°⁵

ὅτι ῥα¨¨⁷

       θνήσκοντας ὁρᾶτο˙¹²
       (57) οἳ δ' ἐπεὶ οὖν ἤγερθεν ὁμηγερέες τ'
         ἐγένοντο˙¹²
       (58) τοῖσι δ' ἀνιστάμενος μετέφη°⁷

πόδας ὠκὺς Ἀχιλλεύς˙ (59) Ἀτρεΐδη°³
νῦν ἄμμε˙⁵½

       πάλιν πλαγχθέντας ὀΐω˙¹²
       (60) ἂψ ἀπονοστήσειν εἴ κεν θάνατόν γε¨¨⁹½
       φύγοιμεν˙¹²
       (61) εἰ δὴ¨¨¹½
       ὁμοῦ°³

πόλεμός τε¨¨⁵½

       δαμᾷ°⁷

καὶ λοιμὸς Ἀχαιούς (62) ἀλλ' ἄγε δή¨³
τινα μάντιν ἐρείομεν ἢ ἱερῆα˙¹²

       (63) ἢ καὶ ὀνειροπόλον καὶ γάρ τ' ὄναρ ἐκ
         Διός ἐστιν˙¹²
       (64) ὅς κ' εἴποι ὅ τι τόσσον ἐχώσατο Φοῖβος
         Ἀπόλλων (65) εἴ ταρ¨¨¹½
       ὅ γ' εὐχωλῆς ἐπιμέμφεται ἠδ' ἑκατόμβης
       (66) αἴ κέν πως ἀρνῶν°⁵

κνίσης αἰγῶν τε¨¨ ⁹½

       τελείων°ᴹ¹²

(67) βούλητ' ἀντιάσας ἡμῖν ἀπὸ λοιγὸν ἀμῦναι˙¹²

       (68) ἤτοι ὅ γ' ὣς εἰπὼν°⁵

κατ' ἄρ' ἕζετο˙ ⁸

       τοῖσι δ' ἀνέστη (69) Κάλχας Θεστορίδης
         οἰωνοπόλων ὄχ' ἄριστος˙¹²
       (70) ὃς εἴδη°³

τά τ' ἐόντα˙ ⁵½

       τά τ' ἐσσόμενα πρό τ' ἐόντα˙¹²
       (71) καὶ νήεσσ' ἡγήσατ' Ἀχαιῶν Ἴλιον εἴσω˙¹²

(72) ἦν διὰ μαντοσύνην[5]
τήν οἱ πόρε·[8]

Φοῖβος Ἀπόλλων[12]
(73) ὅ σφιν ἐῢ φρονέων ἀγορήσατο[8]
καὶ μετέειπεν[12]
(74) ὦ Ἀχιλεῦ[3]
κέλεαί με[5½]

διίφιλε[8]
μυθήσασθαι (75) μῆνιν Ἀπόλλωνος[5]
ἑκατηβελέταο[9½]

ἄνακτος[12]
(76) τοὶ γὰρ[1½]
ἐγὼν ἐρέω[5]
σὺ δὲ[6]

σύνθεο[8]
καί μοι ὄμοσσον[12]
(77) ἦ μέν[2]
μοι πρόφρων ἔπεσιν[7]
καὶ χερσὶν ἀρήξειν (78) ἦ γὰρ[1½]
ὀΐομαι ἄνδρα[5½]
χολωσέμεν ὃς μέγα[10]
πάντων (79) Ἀργείων[3]
κρατέει[5]
καί οἱ πείθονται Ἀχαιοί[12]

(80) κρείσσων γὰρ[3]
βασιλεύς ὅτε χώσεται ἀνδρὶ[9½]
χέρηϊ[12]
(81) εἴ περ γάρ τε[3½]
χόλον γε[5½]
καὶ αὐτῆμαρ καταπέψῃ (82) ἀλλά τε[2]
καὶ μετόπισθεν ἔχει[7]
κότον ὄφρα τελέσσῃ (83) ἐν στήθεσσιν ἑοῖσι[5½]
σὺ δὲ[7]
φράσαι εἴ με σαώσεις[M12]
(84) τὸν δ' ἀπαμειβόμενος προσέφη[7]
πόδας ὠκὺς Ἀχιλλεύς[M12]
(85) θαρσήσας[3]
μάλα[4]

εἰπὲ[5½]
θεοπρόπιον[9]

ὅ τι οἶσθα˙¹²

    (86) οὐ μὰ γὰρ¨²

Ἀπόλλωνα˙⁵¼

διίφιλον ᾧ τε¨⁹¼

σύ˙¹⁰

Κάλχαν˙¹²

    (87) εὐχόμενος Δαναοῖσι˙⁵¼

θεοπροπίας°⁹

ἀναφαίνεις (88) οὔ τις¨¹¼

ἐμέο ζῶντος καὶ ἐπὶ χθονὶ˙⁸

δερκομένοιο˙¹²

    (89) σοὶ κοίλης°³

παρὰ νηυσί˙⁵¼

βαρείας χεῖρας ἐποίσει (90) συμπάντων°³

Δαναῶν οὐδ' ἢν Ἀγαμέμνονα˙¹⁰

εἴπης (91) ὃς νῦν˙²

πολλὸν ἄριστος ἐνὶ στρατῷ εὔχεται εἶναι

    (92) καὶ τότε δὴ˙³

θάρσησε˙⁵¼

καὶ ηὔδα μάντις ἀμύμων (93) οὔτ' ἄρ¨¹¼

ὅ γ' εὐχωλῆς ἐπιμέμφεται οὐδ'

ἑκατόμβης (94) ἀλλ' ἕνεκ' ἀρητῆρος

ὃν ἠτίμησ' Ἀγαμέμνων (95) οὐδ'

ἀπέλυσε˙³¼

θύγατρα˙⁵¼

καὶ οὐκ ἀπεδέξατ' ἄποινα˙¹²

(96) τοὔνεκ' ἄρ¨˙²

ἄλγε' ἔδωκεν Ἑκηβόλος ἠδ' ἔτι δώσει˙¹²

(97) οὐδ' ὅ γε¨²

πρὶν°³

λοιμοῖο˙⁵¼

βαρείας χεῖρας ἀφέξει (98) πρίν γ' ἀπὸ πατρὶ

    φίλῳ°⁵

δόμεναι ἑλικώπιδα˙¹⁰

κούρην (99) ἀπριάτην ἀνάποινον ἄγειν θ'

    ἱερὴν ἑκατόμβην (100) ἐς Χρύσην°³

τότε κέν μιν ἱλασσάμενοι°⁹

πεπίθοιμεν˙¹²

Odyssey i 1–100

(1) ἄνδρα ˙^{1½}

    μοι ἔννεπε ˙^{4}
    μοῦσα ˙^{5½}
    πολύτροπον ὃς μάλα ˙^{10}
    πολλὰ ˙^{12}
    (2) πλάγχθη ἐπεὶ ˙$^{'''3}$

Τροίης ἱερὸν πτολίεθρον ἔπερσεν ˙^{12}

    (3) πολλῶν δ᾽ ἀνθρώπων ἴδεν ἄστεα ˙^{8}
    καὶ νόον ἔγνω (4) πολλὰ δ᾽ ὅ γ᾽ ἐν πόντῳ ˙^{5}

πάθεν ἄλγεα ˙^{8}

    ὃν κατὰ θυμόν ˙^{12}
    (5) ἀρνύμενος ἥν τε ˙$^{'''5}$
    ψυχὴν ˙^{7}

καὶ νόστον ἑταίρων (6) ἀλλ᾽ οὐδ᾽ ὣς ἑτάρους ἐρρύσατο ˙^{8}

    ἱέμενός περ ˙^{12}
    (7) αὐτῶν γὰρ ˙$^{'''3}$
    σφετέρησιν ἀτασθαλίησιν ὄλοντο ˙^{12}
    (8) νήπιοι οἳ κατὰ βοῦς Ὑπερίονος Ἠελίοιο ˙^{12}
    (9) ἤσθιον αὐτὰρ ὁ τοῖσιν ἀφείλετο ˙^{8}
    νόστιμον ἦμαρ (10) τῶν ἁμόθεν γε ˙$^{''3½}$
    θεά, ˙^{5}

θύγατερ Διός εἰπὲ ˙^{9½}

    καὶ ἡμῖν (11) ἔνθ᾽ ἄλλοι μὲν ˙$^{'''4}$

πάντες ὅσοι φύγον αἰπὺν ὄλεθρον ˙^{12}

    (12) οἴκοι ἔσαν πόλεμόν τε ˙$^{''5½}$
    πεφευγότες ἠδὲ θάλασσαν (13) τὸν δ᾽ οἶον
     νόστου ˙^{5}

κεχρημένον ἠδὲ γυναικός (14) νύμφη πότνι᾽ ἔρυκε ˙^{5½}

    Καλυψώ ˙^{M8}

δῖα θεάων (15) ἐν σπέσσι γλαφυροῖσι ˙^{5½}

    λιλαιομένη ˙^{9}

πόσιν εἶναι ˙^{12}

    (16) ἀλλ᾽ ὅτε δὴ ˙^{3}

ἔτος ἦλθε ˙^{5½}

    περιπλομένων ἐνιαυτῶν ˙^{M12}

(17) τῷ οἱ ἐπεκλώσαντο ˙^{5½}

    θεοὶ ˙^{7}

οἰκόνδε ˙^{9½}

    νέεσθαι ˙^{12}

(18) εἰς Ἰθάκην οὐδ' ἔνθα˙⁵½
πεφυγμένος ἦεν ἀέθλων˙ᴹ¹²

(19) καὶ μετὰ οἷσι φίλοισι˙⁵½
θεοὶ δ' ἐλέαιρον ἅπαντες (20) νόσφι
    Ποσειδάωνος ὁ δ' ἀσπερχὲς μενέαινεν˙¹²
(21) ἀντιθέῳ Ὀδυσῆϊ˙⁵½
πάρος ἦν γαῖαν ἱκέσθαι˙¹²
(22) ἀλλ' ὁ μὲν¨²
Αἰθίοπας μετεκίαθε˙⁸
τηλόθ' ἐόντας˙¹²
(23) Αἰθίοπας τοὶ διχθὰ˙⁵½
δεδαίαται ἔσχατοι ἀνδρῶν (24) οἱ μὲν¨·²
δυσομένου Ὑπερίονος οἱ δ' ἀνιόντος˙¹²
(25) ἀντιόων˙³

ταύρων τε¨⁵½

καὶ ἀρνειῶν ἑκατόμβης (26) ἔνθ' ὅ γ'
    ἐτέρπετο˙⁴
δαιτὶ˙⁵½
παρήμενος οἱ δὲ δὴ¨¹⁰
ἄλλοι (27) Ζηνὸς ἐνὶ μεγάροισιν Ὀλυμπίου
    ἀθρόοι ἦσαν (28) τοῖσι δὲ¨²
μύθων ἦρχε˙⁵½
πατὴρ ἀνδρῶν τε¨·⁹½
θεῶν τε¨·¹²
(29) μνήσατο γὰρ¨·³

κατὰ θυμὸν ἀμύμονος Αἰγίσθοιο˙¹²
(30) τόν ῥ' Ἀγαμεμνονίδης˙⁵
    τηλεκλυτὸς ἔκταν' Ὀρέστης˙ᴹ¹²
(31) τοῦ ὅ γ' ἐπιμνησθεὶς ἔπε' ἀθανάτοισι˙⁹½
μετηύδα˙¹²
(32) ὢ πόποι, οἷον δή νυ θεοὺς˙⁷

βροτοὶ αἰτιόωνται˙¹²
(33) ἐξ ἡμέων γάρ¨⁴
φασι˙⁵½
κάκ' ἔμμεναι οἱ δὲ¨·⁹½
καὶ αὐτοὶ (34) σφῇσιν ἀτασθαλίῃσιν ὑπὲρ
    μόρον ἄλγε' ἔχουσιν˙¹²
(35) ὡς καὶ νῦν Αἴγισθος ὑπὲρ μόρον
    Ἀτρεΐδαο˙¹²
(36) γῆμ' ἄλοχον μνηστήν˙⁵

τὸν δ᾽ ἔκτανε˙⁸

    νοστήσαντα,˙¹²

    (37) εἰδὼς αἰπὺν ὄλεθρον ἐπεὶ˙⁷

πρό οἱ εἴπομεν ἡμεῖς (38) Ἑρμείαν πέμψαντες ἐΰσκοπον

        ἀργεϊφόντην˙ᴹ¹²

(39) μήτ᾽ αὐτὸν κτείνειν˙⁵

μήτε μνάασθαι ἄκοιτιν˙¹²

    (40) ἐκ γὰρ¨¹½

    Ὀρέσταο˙⁵

    τίσις ἔσσεται Ἀτρεΐδαο˙¹²

    (41) ὁππότ᾽ ἂν ἡβήσῃ τε¨⁵½

    καὶ ἧς ἱμείρεται αἴης (42) ὣς ἔφαθ᾽ Ἑρμείας

        ἀλλ᾽ οὐ φρένας Αἰγίσθοιο˙¹²

    (43) πεῖθ᾽ ἀγαθὰ φρονέων˙⁵

νῦν δ᾽ ἀθρόα˙⁸

    πάντ᾽ ἀπέτισεν˙¹²

    (44) τὸν δ᾽ ἠμείβετ᾽ ἔπειτα˙⁵½

    θεά˙⁷

γλαυκῶπις Ἀθήνη˙¹²

    (45) ὦ πάτερ ἡμέτερε Κρονίδη˙⁷

ὕπατε κρειόντων˙ᴹ¹²

(46) καὶ λίην˙³

κεῖνός γε¨⁵½

    ἐοικότι˙⁸

    κεῖται ὀλέθρῳ (47) ὡς ἀπόλοιτο˙³½

    καὶ ἄλλος ὅτις τοιαῦτά γε¨¹⁰

    ῥέζοι˙¹²

    (48) ἀλλά μοι ἀμφ᾽ Ὀδυσῆϊ˙⁵½

    δαΐφρονι˙⁸

    δαίεται ἦτορ (49) δυσμόρῳ ὃς δὴ δηθὰ¨⁵½

    φίλων ἄπο¨⁸

    πήματα˙¹⁰

    πάσχει (50) νήσῳ ἐν ἀμφιρύτῃ ὅθι τ᾽

        ὀμφαλός ἐστι˙⁹½

    θαλάσσης˙ᴹ¹²

(51) νῆσος δενδρήεσσα˙⁵½

    θεὰ δ᾽ ἐν δώματα˙¹⁰

    ναίει˙¹²

    (52) Ἄτλαντος θυγάτηρ ὀλοόφρονος ὅς τε¨⁹½

    θαλάσσης˙ᴹ¹²

(53) πάσης˙²

βένθεα˙⁴
οἶδεν ἔχει δέ τε¨⁸
κίονας αὐτὸς (54) μακράς˙²
αἳ γαῖάν τε¨⁵½
καὶ οὐρανὸν ἀμφὶς ἔχουσιν˙¹²
(55) τοῦ θυγάτηρ°³

δύστηνον ὀδυρόμενον κατερύκει˙¹²

(56) αἰεὶ δὲ¨¨³
μαλακοῖσι˙⁵½
καὶ αἱμυλίοισι˙⁹½
λόγοισιν (57) θέλγει ὅπως Ἰθάκης
   ἐπιλήσεται αὐτὰρ Ὀδυσσεύς (58) ἱέμενος
   καὶ καπνὸν ἀποθρήσκοντα˙⁹½
νοῆσαι˙¹²
(59) ἧς γαίης°³

θανέειν ἱμείρεται οὐδέ νυ¨¹⁰

σοί περ¨¨¹²
(60) ἐντρέπεται°³

φίλον ἦτορ Ὀλύμπιε˙⁸

οὔ νύ τ’ Ὀδυσσεὺς (61) Ἀργείων°³

παρὰ νηυσὶ˙⁵½

χαρίζετο˙⁸
ἱερὰ ῥέζων°ᴹ¹²

(62) Τροίῃ ἐν εὐρείῃ°⁵
τί νύ¨⁶

οἱ τόσον ὠδύσαο Ζεῦ °ᴹ¹²

(63) τὴν δ’ ἀπαμειβόμενος προσέφη°⁷
νεφεληγερέτα Ζεύς°ᴹ¹²
(64) τέκνον ἐμόν ποῖόν σε˙⁵½

ἔπος φύγεν ἕρκος ὀδόντων°ᴹ¹²

(65) πῶς ἂν ἔπειτ’ Ὀδυσῆος ἐγὼ°⁷
θείοιο˙⁹½

λαθοίμην (66) ὃς περὶ μὲν¨¨³
νόον ἐστὶ¨⁵½ βροτῶν°⁷

περὶ δ’ ἱρὰ˙⁹½

θεοῖσιν¹²
(67) ἀθανάτοισιν ἔδωκε˙⁵½
τοὶ οὐρανὸν εὐρὺν ἔχουσιν˙¹²
(68) ἀλλὰ Ποσειδάων°⁵

γαιήοχος ἀσκελὲς αἰὲν (69) Κύκλωπος κεχόλωται ὃν ὀφθαλμοῦ °9
ἀλάωσεν·12

    (70) ἀντίθεον Πολύφημον ὅου κράτος ἐστὶ·9½
μέγιστον (71) πᾶσιν·2
Κυκλώπεσσι·5½
Θόωσα δέ··8
μιν τέκε νύμφη (72) Φόρκυνος θυγάτηρ
    ἁλὸς ἀτρυγέτοιο·9½
μέδοντος·12
    (73) ἐν σπέσσι γλαφυροῖσι·5½
Ποσειδάωνι·9½
μιγεῖσα·12
    (74) ἐκ τοῦ δὴ·3

Ὀδυσῆα·5½

    Ποσειδάων ἐνοσίχθων (75) οὔ τι
    κατακτείνει°5
πλάζει δ' ἀπὸ πατρίδος αἴης (76) ἀλλ' ἄγεθ' ἡμεῖς οἵδε·5½
    περιφραζώμεθα·10
    πάντες (77) νόστον ὅπως ἔλθησι·5½
Ποσειδάων δὲ··9½
μεθήσει·12
    (78) ὃν χόλον οὐ μὲν γὰρ···3
τι δυνήσεται ἀντία·10
πάντων (79) ἀθανάτων ἀέκητι·5½
θεῶν ἐριδαινέμεν οἶος (80) τὸν δ' ἡμείβετ'
    ἔπειτα·5½
θεά°7

γλαυκῶπις Ἀθήνη·12
    (81) ὦ πάτερ ἡμέτερε Κρονίδη°7
ὕπατε κρειόντων°M12
(82) εἰ μὲν δὴ νῦν°M
τοῦτο φίλον μακάρεσσι·9½
    θεοῖσιν (83) νοστῆσαι Ὀδυσῆα·5½
πολύφρονα·8
ὅνδε δόμονδε···12
(84) Ἑρμείαν μὲν··3½
ἔπειτα·5½
διάκτορον ἀργεϊφόντην°M12
(85) νῆσον ἐς Ὠγυγίην ὀτρύνομεν ὄφρα τάχιστα·12
    (86) νύμφη ἐϋπλοκάμῳ εἴπῃ°7
νημερτέα·10

βουλήν˙ᵒᴹ12

(87) νόστον Ὀδυσσῆος ταλασίφρονος ὥς κε νέηται˙12

(88) αὐτὰρ ἐγὼν Ἰθάκην ἐσελεύσομαι ὄφρα
οἱ υἱὸν (89) μᾶλλον ἐποτρύνω˙ᵉ5

καί οἱ μένος ἐν φρεσὶ˙10

θείω˙12

(90) εἰς ἀγορὴν˙ᵒ3

καλέσαντα˙5½

κάρη˙ᵒ7

κομόωντας Ἀχαιοὺς˙ᵒᴹ12

(91) πᾶσι μνηστήρεσσιν ἀπειπέμεν οἵ τε˙¨9½

οἱ αἰεὶ (92) μῆλ᾽ ἀδινὰ σφάζουσι˙5½
καὶ εἰλίποδας ἕλικας βοῦς˙ᵒᴹ12

(93) πέμψω δ᾽ ἐς Σπάρτην τε˙¨5½

καὶ ἐς Πύλον ἠμαθόεντα˙12

(94) νόστον πευσόμενον πατρὸς φίλου ἤν
που ἀκούσηι˙12

(95) ἠδ᾽ ἵνα μιν κλέος ἐσθλὸν ἐν ἀνθρώποισιν
ἔχησιν˙12

(96) ὣς εἰποῦσ᾽ ὑπὸ ποσσὶν ἐδήσατο˙8

καλὰ πέδιλα˙12

(97) ἀμβρόσια χρύσεια˙5½

τά μιν φέρον ἠμὲν ἐφ᾽ ὑγρὴν (98) ἠδ᾽ ἐπ᾽
ἀπείρονα˙4

γαῖαν ἅμα πνοιῆς ἀνέμοιο˙12

(99) εἵλετο δ᾽ ἄλκιμον ἔγχος ἀκαχμένον
ὀξέι˙10

χαλκῷ˙ᵒᴹ12

(100) βριθὺ˙1½

μέγα στιβαρόν τῷ δάμνησι στίχας ἀνδρῶν
(101: ἡρώων˙ᵒ3 κτλ)

6

Audible Punctuation

*Technical terms followed by * on their first occurrence in this chapter are in the glossary.*

6.0 Introduction

Chapter 6 aims to show that the concept of phonetically variable and varying word end in Homer, previously labeled audible punctuation (§5.2), causes only a selection of the compositional pauses* to be exploited as a rest of some duration in performance*. This selective use of compositional pauses as performative features suggests a different approach towards several widespread concepts of "termination-mismatch," notably enjambment*.

6.1 Audible Punctuation in Performance

The audibility of punctuation has been taken more or less for granted in studies on Homeric performance: there is pause at the end of the hexameter, and none within the verse. Exceptions have been allowed for extraordinary circumstances: lines with a remarkably violent enjambment, or verse-internal moments of emotional outcry (Bakker 1990; Daitz 1991). Such an approach of audible punctuation in performance appears to be rather arbitrary, and based on a concept of constant rhythmical repetition. It also presupposes that metrical surface structure remains intact and unaltered despite the rather randomly realized rests in performance. But at least it shows that audible punctuation has little to do with printed punctuation. That is a first step.

The second step, the step I took with the reconstruction of phonetics* in Homer and of phonetic pause* in Chapter 5, shows that there is no reason to assume that every Homeric line ends in phonetic pause; nor is there ground to deny the possibility of phonetic pause within the line. Phonetic pause is the result of a sandhi*-free word-final syllable mapped on a metrical position that allows for word-final syllable lengthening*. As there are two types of endings in metrical text, there are possibly two types of phonetic pause: one allowing for considerable word-final lengthening (or even silence in performance), and one allowing for hardly any drawling of speech. Tempo of speech in performance determines whether both types of phonetic pause are realized as true audible pauses. At higher rates of speech, the milder phonetic word end, prosodically realized as accentual clisis* and/or limited final lengthening, may hardly have been noticed as a true phonetic pause, and hence not as a pause in performance. The more disruptive phonetic word end, due to considerable word-final lengthening, is then still perceptible as a pause in performance; at higher rates of speech it is realized as a breathing pause occurring at rather regular intervals in spoken discourse. There is presumably room for variation in performance.

6.1.1 Selective pausing in performance

Punctuation in performance depends on the localization of phonetic word end, and the continuation of phonation following phonetic word end. The latter choice is made in the process of composition as the poet decides on the exact wording and the resulting syllable structures. The rates of speech in performance determine whether audible punctuation comes in one quality or in two (§5.1.5). The criteria for the identification of performative pause have their basis in phonetics. The requirements for pause, the sandhi-free word-final syllable and the possibility of lengthening, may be met at several positions in the hexametric verse. There is no fixed metrical position for the fulfilment of these requirements, nor is there any *a priori* reason to assume that certain metrical positions cannot qualify to fulfill at least one of the requirements for performative pause.

In the localization of phonetic pauses in the sample (§5.4) no repetitive patterning or predictability of rests becomes apparent. Many different metrical positions allow for a subsequent rest in performance, but their appearance as prepausal is rather random and unpredictable: in some verses there is no rest at all.

The localization of performative pauses is a process of selection: selection of metrical positions, selection of syllable structures to continue phonation with after a rest, and selection of rates of speech. With the possible exception of unnaturally high rates of speech (harming the rhythmic regularity, as taking a breath is reduced to a necessity at certain intervals), rates of speech in performance enable practically every metrical position in the hexameter to be realized as prepausal. Theoretically that is, as composition has already marked the options, and performance relies on the exact rate of speech for its realization of audible rests. Regardless, however, of the composer's choices and the performer's rate of speech, almost every metrical position can be selected as pre- or postpausal. The sample shows that almost all positions do appear as such at a certain moment. There seems to be no other reason behind the random localization of rests than the preferences of the individual poet.

6.1.2 Straddling compositional pauses

Performative pause in Homer does not *a priori* have to do with syntactical wholes (Chapter 2), nor with repetitive metrical unities (Chapter 1). Both have been (and remain) objects of study among Homerists, but both are to be studied on their own account and only then in relation to the performative pause.

For now it suffices to conclude that where only few compositional pauses double as rests in performance, the vast majority of compositional pauses has no aural effect—not as the boundary of a metrical colon nor as a sense-pause*. Most compositional pauses remain compositional: it is clear that they have a role in the metrical surface structure and in the units of meaning of appositional style, but they do not audibly frame the units of performance, the units of phonation.

Pausing is selective, so there is no set rule for the localization of non-aural compositional pauses either. It is not beforehand decided which compositional pauses in the verse will be audibly straddled, or as Parry (1971:263) put it, dimmed. All compositional pauses may be dimmed, including metrical pauses, like the caesura* and the verse end, and sense-pauses as suggested by printed punctuation. Both markers of compositional pause, the metrical surface structure and the printed reflection of syntactical structure, do not have an automatic effect on the pauses in performance. Dimming of compositional pauses mirrors the continuation of phonation between performative pauses.

Existing approaches to pause assume that compositional pause may *at times* be straddled. Implicit in the identification of the verse end as an unavoidable pause in performance is the assumption that other metrical boundaries do not qualify as such. Exceptions are hardly ever made, unless for semantic reasons (like emotional outcry). The identification of sense-pause relies on printed punctuation: leads from antiquity are supplemented with modern analysis of sentence structure to distinguish between various forms of punctuation signaling different discourse relations. The concepts of appositional style, nonconfigurational* syntax, and intonation units highlight the compositional value of boundaries and pauses, but cannot avoid arbitrariness when it comes to their value in performance. Again, semantics are called in to help decide on the boundary or pause as an audible feature; when not evidenced by metrical predictability or printed punctuation, pauses are postulated as commonsensical, without regard to the disruption to rhythm. My approach to the dimming of compositional pauses does away with the arbitrariness that underlies existing approaches. Performative pause is identified without regard for patterns of compositional structure. Such patterns are not being denied, far from that; it is merely observed that the patterning of metrical boundaries and sense-pauses does not automatically match the localization of performative pauses.

6.2   Mismatching Punctuation

The selectiveness of performative pausing creates a mismatch between the pauses in performance and the compositional pauses of the metrical and syntactical patterning. Audible punctuation does not coincide with metrical repetitiveness nor with the pattern of printed punctuation. However, audible punctuation does coincide with metrical boundaries and may coincide with instances of printed punctuation. What happens when audible punctuation does not match with patterns of compositional pause? Is there any clue in phonology for some aural effect, some affective prosody* to compositional pauses that are being straddled?

Aural effect is sought for as a means to frame units of sense or meaning (Fränkel 1926; Porter 1951; Bakker 1997) and to strengthen the tone and atmosphere of the narrative. Affective prosody (Devine and Stephens 1994; Edwards 2002), a correlate of emphasis, is a notion that stems from the common approach of compositional pauses. As the verse end is considered the strongest boundary in meter and syntax, and the performative pause *par excellence*, any mismatch of metrical boundary and printed punctuation at verse end is seen as meaningful aberration: runover* of the sentence or clause at the start of the hexametric line turns the first syllables of the verse into a prosodically affective start, lending emphasis to the word localized onto this position (Kahane 1994). In my view, this identification of affective prosody is arbitrary and based on circularity: as the strength of the verse end as a boundary is assumed, so the assumptions of emphasis and of prosodic affectiveness strengthen one another. As emphasis derives from localization, so affective prosody derives from emphasis: outside the *mot-en-rejet*, the single runover word following enjambment, both affective prosody and emphasis seem to have no role to play. At the end of this section 6.2, I will argue that the punctuation mismatch does evidence a level of performative effect of prosody, a contribution of prosody to the perception of a remarkable break in syntax—albeit not a level resulting in emphasis. With reference to the, in my opinion, overrated notion of affective prosody, I will refer to this contribution of prosody as *prosodic affectiveness*.

6.2.1 Mismatched metrical pauses

The metrical boundary or pause that attracts most attention when mismatched with performative pause is the verse end—the more since the verse end is commonly considered the preferred boundary in performance.

6.2.1.1 Verse end

Verse end is, of course, not always straddled in performance nor is it always mismatched: numerous are the instances of verse end coinciding with performative pause (§5.4). If the verse end then also coincides with syntactical termination, it will not attract any special attention. Within a sentence that develops over the verse end, there is no mismatch in an example, as in example (120), where the performative pause at verse end separates two verb forms:

(120)   δόμον ὅν με κελεύεις
        δείξω

Odyssey vii 28–29

The house you ask me for | I will show

Sentences start at various positions in the hexameter, and their development may disregard the occurrence of the verse end. Both in the *Iliad* and in the *Odyssey*, whole passages consist of such diverging grammatical and metrical patterns. I will cite four larger scale examples (121–124) where sentences run over the verse end without, in my definition, being hampered by a performative pause. The first two are examples of character speech: they illustrate what Bakker calls the "fugal effect" of more emotional passages. Examples (123) and (124) do not have a similar excuse: they show the ordinariness of the non-alignment of the verse-end metrical boundary and performative pause. In the Greek text, I indicate the positions of ongoing development of the sentence without being hampered by performative pause at verse end as » :

(120) τοῖσι μὲν ἔμπεδα κεῖται ἐμεῦ δ' ἀπὸ μούνου Ἀχαιῶν »
        εἵλετ' ἔχει δ' ἄλοχον θυμαρέα τῇ παριαύων
        τερπέσθω τὶ δὲ δεῖ πολεμιζέμεναι Τρώεσσιν »
        Ἀργείους τὶ δὲ λαὸν ἀνήγαγεν ἐνθάδ' ἀγείρας »
        Ἀτρείδης ἦ οὐχ Ἑλένης ἕνεκ' ἠυκόμοιο
        ἦ μοῦνοι φιλέουσ' ἀλόχους μερόπων ἀνθρώπων »
        Ἀτρεῖδαι ἐπεὶ ὅς τις ἀνὴρ ἀγαθὸς καὶ ἐχέφρων
        τὴν αὐτοῦ φιλέει καὶ κήδεται ὡς καὶ ἐγὼ τήν »
        ἐκ θυμοῦ φίλεον δουρικτητήν περ ἐοῦσαν

Iliad IX 335–343

For them it remains untouched, but from me alone of the Greeks | he took, and he keeps my pleasing concubine for himself; let him sleep with her | and take his pleasure! But why was there need to fight the Trojans | for the Greeks? Why did he gather the army and bring it here, | Atreus's son? Was it not because of fair Helen? | Are we to understand that of mortal men the only ones who love their partners | are Atreus's sons? As every worthy and sensible man | loves his own and cares for her, so did I | love her from the heart, even if she were a mere prize of war

(122) κῆρυξ τῇ δή τοῦτο πόρε κρέας ὄφρα φάγῃσι »
       Δημοδόκῳ καί μιν προσπτύξομαι ἀχνύμενός περ
       πᾶσι γὰρ ἀνθρώποισιν ἐπιχθονίοισιν ἀοιδοὶ »
       τιμῆς ἔμμοροί εἰσι καὶ αἰδοῦς οὕνεκ' ἄρα σφέας »
       οἴμας Μοῦσ' ἐδίδαξε φίλησε δὲ φῦλον ἀοιδῶν

Odyssey viii 477–481

Herald, here then, take, that he may eat, this piece of meat | to Demodocus; I will even praise him despite my sorrows; | for in the eyes of all men who dwell on the land the singers | are entitled to reward and respect, as, obviously, to them | the Muse has taught her songs; she loved the race of singers

(123) ὣς φάτο Σαρπηδών ὁ δ' ἀνέσχετο μείλινον ἔγχος »
       Τληπόλεμος καὶ τῶν μὲν ἁμαρτῇ δούρατα μακρὰ »
       ἐκ χειρῶν ἤιξαν ὁ μὲν βάλεν αὐχένα μέσσον »
       Σαρπηδών αἰχμὴ δὲ διαμπερὲς ἦλθ' ἀλεγεινή
       τὸν δὲ κατ' ὀφθαλμῶν ἐρεβεννὴ νὺξ ἐκάλυψε
       Τληπόλεμος δ' ἄρα μηρὸν ἀριστερὸν ἔγχει μακρῷ
       βεβλήκειν αἰχμὴ δὲ διέσσυτο μαιμώωσα »
       ὀστέῳ ἐγχριμφθεῖσα πατὴρ δ' ἔτι λοιγὸν ἄμυνεν

Iliad V 655–662

Thus spoke Sarpedon; Tlepolemus had lifted his ashen spear | and simultaneously their long weapons | rushed from their hands; Sarpedon hit the other's neck in the middle; | the painful point ran right through; | black night covered the other's eyes; | Tlepolemus, however, had hit the left thigh with his long spear; | the point hastened on eagerly | grazing the bone, but his father still warded off death

(124) ἀλλ' ὁ μὲν ἔκφυγε κῆρα καὶ ἤλασε βοῦς ἐριμύκους »
    ἐς Πύλον ἐκ Φυλάκης καὶ ἐτίσατο ἔργον ἀεικὲς »
    ἀντίθεον Νηλῆα κασιγνήτῳ δὲ γυναῖκα »
    ἠγάγετο πρὸς δώμαθ' ὁ δ' ἄλλων ἵκετο δῆμον »
    Ἄργος ἐς ἱππόβοτον τόθι γάρ νύ οἱ αἴσιμον ἦεν »
    ναιέμεναι πολλοῖσιν ἀνάσσοντ' Ἀργείοισιν

Odyssey xv 235–240

But he escaped death and brought the lowing cows | from Phylake to Pylus and for his unfair deed he punished | godlike Neleus; a wife for his brother | he took home with him; he reached the house of others | in horse-feeding Argos; there then it was his fate | to live as a ruler over many Greeks

I do not propose to replace the automatic assumption of performative pause at verse end with a new assumption of no performative pause if the sentence develops over the verse end. Syntactical structure is not necessarily equal to the pattern suggested by phonological phrases* and phonetic pauses. The appearance and avoidance of performative pause at verse end stems from the choice that the options at verse end offer. The options at verse end find their basis in the phonology of the verse-final syllable and the subsequent verse-initial syllable.[1]

---

[1] In total, there would be *eighteen* phonologically different realizations of the indeterminate verse-final heavy element in cases where sentences develop over the verse end. Type 1, short vowel + hiatus: οὐδ' οἵ γ' ὁρμηθησαν ἐπ' ἀνδράσιν ἀλλ' ἄρα τοί γε ‖ οὐρῇσιν (*Odyssey* x 214–215), "And they did not attack the men, but these same beasts | with their tails"; type 2, short vowel + ‖ consonant: ὅς τ' εἶσ' ὑόμενος καὶ ἀήμενος ἐν δέ οἱ ὄσσε ‖ δαίεται (*Odyssey* vi 131–132,) "He makes his way vexed by rain and wind, and in his head both his eyes | burn"; type 3, short vowel + ambisyllabic* consonant + ‖ vowel: τὼ δ' αὖτις ξιφέεσσι συνέδραμον ἔνθα Λύκων μὲν ‖ ἱπποκόμου (*Iliad* XVI 337–338), "The two of them immediately attacked each other with swords; then Lyco | of the helmet"; type 4, short vowel + consonant + ‖ vowel: αἴτιοι ἀλλά ποθι Ζεὺς αἴτιος ὅς τε δίδωσιν ‖ ἀνδράσιν (*Odyssey* i 348–349), "Guilty, but I think Zeus is guilty: he bestows | on men"; type 5, short vowel + movable *nu* + ‖ consonant: ὡς Ὀδυσεὺς κούρῃσιν ἐυπλοκάμοισιν ἔμελλεν ‖ μίξεσθαι (*Odyssey* vi 135–136), "Similarly Odysseus was about to join the beautiful girls' | company"; type 6, short vowel + consonant + ‖ consonant: τέκνον ἐμόν τοῦτον μὲν ἐάσομεν ἀχνύμενοί περ ‖ κεῖσθαι (*Iliad* XIX 8–9), "My child, despite our grief we will let him | lie here"; type 7, short vowel + ‖ consonants: ὡς φάτο καί ῥ' ἵππους κέλετο Δεῖμόν τε Φόβον τε ‖ ζευγνύμεν (*Iliad* XV 119–120), "Thus he spoke, and he ordered that his horses, Deimus and Phobus, | be yoked"; type 8, long vowel + hiatus: ὑψόσε δ' ἄχνη ‖ ἄκροισι σκοπέλοισιν ἐπ' ἀμφοτέροισιν ἔπιπτεν (*Odyssey* xii 238–239), "And high up the foam | fell on the steep cliffs on either side"; type 9, diphthong with short vowel + ‖ vowel (The phonological realization of the consonantal sound of the diphthong, the glide, avoids hiatus): ὦ πόποι ἦ ῥα καὶ ἄλλοι ἐυκνήμιδες Ἀχαιοί ‖ ἐν θυμῷ βάλλονται ἐμοὶ χόλον (*Iliad* XIV 49–50), "O dear, surely the other well-harnessed Greeks | will foster a grudge against me in their heart as well"; type 10, diphthong with long vowel + ‖ vowel: ἀλλά τ' ἐπ' αὐτῷ ‖ ἔσσυτο καί τέ μιν ὦκα λαβὼν ἐξείλετο θυμόν (*Iliad* XVII 677–678), "But straight to him | he rushed, and snatching him quickly he took his life away"; type 11, long

167

Verse final phonology may not allow for elision*, shortening*, and apposition*, as does verse-internal phonology; it does allow, unlike the verse-internal situation, for hiatus and prolongation* on the arsis*. As a metrical boundary it is comparable with other arses within the line, and its capacity for performative pause should be compared with the other arses.

6.2.1.2 Main caesura

The third-foot caesura is the second-best performative pause in existing studies. I have listed four conditions for the third-foot caesura to be straddled and dimmed:

(i) The third foot caesura is not penthemimeral but trochaic.

(ii) The third foot caesura falls within an appositive group.[2]

---

vowel + ‖ consonant: τοῖσι δὲ Κίρκη ‖ πάρ ῥ' ἄκυλον βάλανον τ' ἔβαλεν (*Odyssey* x 241–242), "And to them Circe | threw walnuts and acorns"; type 12, diphthong with long vowel + ‖ consonant: δεκάτη δέ με νυκτὶ μελαίνῃ ‖ γαίῃ Θεσπρωτῶν πέλασεν μέγα κῦμα κυλίνδον (*Odyssey* xiv 315–316), "In the tenth night, on the dark | land of the Thesprots a great rolling wave disposed me"; type 13, diphthong with short vowel + ‖ consonant: σοὶ δὲ θεοὶ ἄλοχον τ' ἰδέειν καὶ πατρίδ' ἱκέσθαι ‖ δοῖεν (*Odyssey* viii 410–411), "May the gods | grant | you to see your wife again and to reach your home land"; type 14, long vowel + movable *nu* + ‖ consonant: ἠδ' ἔτι καὶ νῦν ‖ πείθευ (*Iliad* XIV 234–235), "And so this one more time | obey me"; type 15, long vowel + consonant + ‖ vowel: οὐδέ κε φαίης ‖ ἀνδρὶ μαχεσσάμενον τόν γ' ἐλθεῖν (*Iliad* III 392–393), "One would not have thought | this man as one who had come after doing battle"; type 16, diphthong with long vowel + consonant + ‖ vowel: εἰ δ' ἐθέλεις καὶ ταῦτα δαήμεναι ὄφρ' ἐὺ εἰδῇς ‖ ἡμετέρην γενεήν (*Iliad* VI 150–151), "If you wish to know that as well, that you may understand fully | my lineage"; type 17, long vowel + consonant + ‖ consonant: ὡς ὅτε μήτηρ ‖ παιδὸς ἔεργη μυῖαν (*Iliad* IV 130–131), "As when a mother | sweeps a fly from her child"; type 18, long vowel + ‖ consonants: ἡμῖν δὲ δὴ αἴσιμον εἴη ‖ φθίσθαι (*Iliad* IX 245–246), "And that it may be our fate | to perish." The examples quoted give rise to the notion of prosodic neutrality of the verse-final syllable: they do not prove that verse end may be a continuation of sandhi, both since hiatus is possible and since liaison, elision, and epic shortening are either non-existent or seemingly impossible to demonstrate. It is, however, possible to question the irrelevance of the metrical indifference of the verse-final syllable, and hence its prosodic neutrality. Examples of grammatical clauses that run over the verse end into the subsequent hexameter all feature verse-final syllables that are not only the completion of a stichic metrical shape (the hexameter), but also take their position *within* the metrical pattern of the grammatical clause (Basset 1938:147–148, 153–154 was one of the first to argue in favor of a continuing metrical pattern within the grammatical unity). The listening audience expects continuation of the metrical repetition within a clause (I agree here with Daitz 1991:153–154, who argues that despite the demarcating value of metrical boundaries, repetition of a recognizable metrical pattern underlies the continuation of grammatical clauses). The verse-final foot must be realized as a spondee to maintain the metrical repetition within the grammatical clause. In other words, any anticipatory metrical organization at verse end requires a spondaic verse-final foot.

[2] Consider examples like ἕζετ' ἔπειτ' ἀπάνευθε νεῶν μετὰ δ' ἰὸν ἕηκε (*Iliad* I 48), "Then he sat down at some distance from the ships, and he let go an arrow," Ἰφιδάμας δὲ κατὰ ζώνην θώρηκος ἔνερθε (*Iliad* XI 234), "But Iphidamas [stabbed him] on the belt beneath the corselet' καὶ ἑστήκει γὰρ ἐπὶ πρυμνῇ μεγακήτεϊ νηΐ (*Iliad* XI 600), "For he was standing on the stern of the huge ship." All three verses feature a preposition group that straddles the third-foot caesura. An audible

(iii) The word end in the third foot is subject to elision:[3]

> (125) ὣς ἔφαθ' ἡμῖν δ' αὖτ' ⁵ ἐπεπείθετο θυμὸς ἀγήνωρ
>
> *Odyssey* ii 103
>
> So he spoke, and for us the proud heart consented

(iv) The third foot contains a word that bridges at least the entire third foot:

> (126) Τηλέπυλον <u>Λαιστρυγονίην</u> ὅθι ποιμένα ποιμήν
>
> *Odyssey* x 82
>
> Laestrigonian Telepylus, where herdsman (calls to) herdsman

The third-foot caesura is phonologically as easily straddled (and rhythmically dimmed) as the verse end. Other metrical boundaries may then step in as the primary phonetic break within the line. Consider the realization of, respectively, position 7, 8, and 9 as phonetic pauses (marked by metrical position in superscript) in the following examples (127–129). The phonetic pause in these examples easily outdoes any disruption within the third foot:

> (127) σχέτλιος ἀλλ' ἀκέσασθε φίλοι :⁷ δύναμις γὰρ ἐν ὑμῖν
>
> *Odyssey* x 69
>
> So miserable; come, make us recover, please, friends; for you have that power

> (128) κείνου ὅπως δὴ δηρὸν ἀποίχεται :⁸ οὐδέ τι ἴδμεν
>
> *Odyssey* iv 109
>
> Because of him; remember how long he has been away by now; we do not even have a clue

> (129) ἀνέρες ἠρήσαντο παρεστάμεναι :⁹ δύναται γάρ
>
> *Odyssey* iv 827
>
> Men have begged her to stand by them; for she is able to do it

What these examples have in common (and many more can be added) is that the phonetic pauses suggest a pattern that disregards the guidance of the two

---

break at the third-foot caesura in performance is unlikely in these examples. The dimming of the metrical boundary is phonologically strengthened by trochaic word end and resyllabification*. The preposition group is not *audibly* cut up: the caesura is a mere *visible* word juncture. As a rhythmical boundary, the third foot pause is no more than theoretical in these verses.

[3] Arguments against prosodic disturbance at elision are summarized in Devine and Stephens 1994:256–266.

ἡμιστίχια of the hexameter. The force with which phonological boundaries, other than the third-foot caesura and verse end, determine the shape and internal organization of the phrases (*at the cost of* the alleged importance of the third caesura and verse end) can be mirrored by the use of printed punctuation. The use by modern editors of printed punctuation like colon, semicolon, and comma, if it is to be accepted, must be judged on the basis of their observance of audible pause. For this reason, Daitz 1991 considers fifty percent of all printed punctuation wrong or misleading. In addition to his general criticism, I would like to point out that one common application of printed punctuation, in particular, is questionable, the use of the comma following the second-foot trochee before a vocative as in *Iliad* I 1 μῆνιν ἄειδε θεά, "sing of the wrath, goddess," and *Iliad* XI 287 ἀνέρες ἔστε φίλοι, "prove yourself men, comrades." It seems that Meyer's Law* for the Callimachean hexameter is observed in Homer as well: in the examples quoted and as elsewhere, the synaphy of the developing phonological phrase frustrates the possibility of performative pause end at the verse's second trochee.

6.2.2 Mismatched syntactical pauses

Printed punctuation mirrors syntactical structure and hence the pause in syntax (see Chapter 2). Not all syntactical pauses are suggested by printed punctuation though. Depending on the model of syntax analysis, many more syntactical pauses may be suggested than shown in printed punctuation. Models that take their starting point from units of sense (Fränkel 1926; Porter 1951) assume that virtually all metrical boundaries demarcate organic word groups. Chantraine 1963 states that appositional style is sensitive to the demarcating value of metrical boundaries. Bakker 1997b/2005 describes metrical cola as intonation units in special speech, and shows how the colon, starting from the nucleus*, is extended by means of peripheral material to the nearest metrical boundary. All these models assume that the smaller scale units are phonetic phrases that are prosodically characterized; and so are their demarcations. The smaller scale phrases are hence more or less equal to minor phonological phrases*; for the larger scale syntactical unit, resemblance to the major phrase is suggested (Devine and Stephens 1994; cf. §3.1.4 above), though higher rates of speech may make the major phrase demarcation appear rather at random (dictated by the need to breathe).

Followers of Parry 1929 start from the metrical unity when identifying the units of syntax. The syntactical patterns of the text are judged considering their accordance, or mismatch, with the repetitive hexametric structure. There is an underlying presupposition here: the Homeric wording had to be molded into syntax within the already existing metrical shape. This underlying presupposition equally presupposes that the single hexametric verse is not just the metrical unity in the Homeric narrative, but also the unity whose prosodic characterization suggests audible coherence on the level of syntax. The prosodic pattern, the metrical shape, is regularly seen as pre-existing compared to the development of wording and syntax.

When compared to performative pauses, metrical boundaries are possibly overestimated as breaks in sense. Phonological phrases do not always terminate where (parts of) sentences terminate (§6.2.2.1), just as repetitive metrical units and sentences do not automatically terminate at the same position (§6.2.2.2). Sometimes they do, and sometimes they do not. The resulting mosaic-like pattern of metrical units, phonological phrases, and sentences will bring out possibilities for what I will label *prosodic affectiveness* (§6.3).

6.2.2.1 Pause and clause

Acknowledging the limited usefulness of "sentence" as a term in the analysis of Homer's units of syntax, Parry 1929 preferred clause, as did his followers. Bakker 1990 explains why the terminology sentence is best abolished in the study of Homeric discourse. Following his lead, I will present the mismatch of performative pause and pause in syntax as the mismatch between performative pause and pause framing the grammatical clause. First I will briefly define the characteristics and the extent of the grammatical clause in Homer so that its boundaries can be discussed as framing the clause.

Extension of the clause

Bakker 1997b argues for the approach of Homeric discourse as a movement (§2.3): metrical cola can be added onto each other to keep the developing clause continuing. In his 1991, 1993, and 2005 publications he shows that, underlying the development of the clause, there is the extension of the metrical colon towards the nearest metrical boundary: a semantic nucleus, the colon's core constituent, is extended by means of metrical fillers*. He demonstrates this compositional principle by means of the narrative pattern "A kills B" in the *Iliad* (fillers are underlined):

> (44) Ἀστύαλον δ' ἄρ' ἔπεφνε <u>μενεπτόλεμος</u> Πολυποίτης
> Πιδύτην δ' Ὀδυσεὺς <u>Περκώσιον</u> ἐξενάριξεν
> <u>ἔγχεϊ χαλκείῳ</u> Τεῦκρος δ' Ἀρετάονα <u>δῖον</u>
> Ἀντίλοχος δ' Ἄβληρον ἐνήρατο <u>δουρὶ φαεινῷ</u>
> <u>Νεστορίδης</u> Ἔλατον δὲ <u>ἄναξ ἀνδρῶν</u> Ἀγαμέμνων
>
> *Iliad* VI 29–33

> So <u>warlike</u> Polypoetes killed Astyalus, | and Odysseus finished off
> Pidytus <u>from Perkote</u> | <u>with his bronze spear</u>, as did Teucer <u>the</u>
> <u>shining</u> Aretaon, | and Antilochus slew Ablerus <u>with his shining</u>
> <u>spear</u>, | <u>son of Nestor</u>, as did Agamemnon, <u>lord of men</u>, Elatus

In the cluster *Iliad* VI 29–33, the usage of metrical fillers[4] shows the compositional
principle of extension towards the nearest metrical boundary, as explained by
Bakker.[5] The fillers prove to be (1) context neutral, (2) metrically variable, and
(3) interchangeable.[6] Variable fillers like ἔγχει / ἔγχει χαλκείῳ and δουρὶ / δουρὶ
φαεινῷ show both their metrical usefulness and their semantic superfluity and
redirect attention towards semantically more important constituents. The filler
ἔγχει χαλκείῳ also shows that extension of the clause may be over the verse end.
In this case the distribution of performative pause (none at the verse end of line
30 due to subordination*, and a primary pause following χαλκείῳ in 31) is in
accordance with the shape of the developing clause. The sample in §5.4 shows,
however, that more often it is not.

Fixed positions of start and completion

The usage of metrical fillers demonstrates the restrictions on the localization
of certain clauses, such as the start and completion of direct speech and the
resumption of an extended simile by means of ὡς. In both these cases, direct
speech and the extended simile, the transition over the verse end is the only
position from which the poet starts. That makes it necessary to fill out the line
before the start of direct speech by means of a filler (fillers are underlined in
examples 130–132):

> (130) Ἶριν δ᾽ ὤτρυνε χρυσόπτερον ἀγγελέουσαν
>   βάσκ᾽ ἴθι Ἶρι ταχεῖα
>
> > *Iliad* VIII 399–400a
>
> He urged Iris, <u>his gold-winged to carry a message</u>: | "Go, quickly,
> swift Iris,

When the verb "to speak" is confined to verse-final position,[7] fillers may bridge
the gap to the verse end:

---

[4] The fillers enable semantically more important constituents to occupy the metrical position
    they are restricted to without jeopardizing the comprehensibility of their syntactical func-
    tion: the epithet ἄναξ ἀνδρῶν in *Iliad* VI 33 makes it easier, not more difficult, to recognize
    Agamemnon as the subject of the clause in which Elatus is the object.

[5] Bakker 2005:11 focuses on fillers as extensions of the <u>verb</u> towards the nearest metrical boundary.

[6] Bakker 1993:15–25; 2005:5–6.

[7] In this example, because of the avoidance of verse-internal spondaic word end*.

(131) δή ῥα τότ' ἀμφιπόλοισιν <u>ἐυπλοκάμοισι</u> μετηύδα
κλῦτέ μευ ἀμφίπολοι λευκώλενοι

Odyssey vi 238–239a

Finally then she spoke to her <u>beautiful</u> maidservants: | "Listen to
me, maidservants with white arms

When grammatical completeness requires another constituent that must
be postponed to the following line (for example, the grammatical subject in
example 110), the subsequent line is still extended towards the verse end:

(132) εἰ μὴ ἄρ' Αἰνείαι τε καὶ Ἕκτορι εἶπε παραστὰς
Πριαμίδης Ἕλενος <u>οἰωνοπόλων ὄχ' ἄριστος</u>
Αἰνεία τε καὶ Ἕκτορ

Iliad VI 75–77

Had not rushed to Aeneas and Hector and spoken to them | Helenus,
son of Priam, <u>by far the best of the seers</u>: | "Aeneas and Hector,

Extension of the clause over the verse end leads to a verse not denoting the act
of speaking (which had already been introduced with μετέφη in example 133),
that in turn has to be extended towards the verse end:

(133) τοῖς δὲ βαρὺ στενάχων μετέφη κρείων Ἀγαμέμνων
χειρὸς ἔχων Μενέλαον ἐπεστενάχοντο δ' ἑταῖροι
φίλε κασίγνητε

Iliad IV 153–155a

Sighing heavily among them powerful Agamemnon spoke, | holding
his brother by the arm, and the comrades moaned together with
him: | "My dear brother,

What the various extensions have in common, regardless of their size and
exact metrical shape, is their usefulness in extending an utterance towards the
verse end. The extended simile (resumption of which is underlined in examples
134–135) seems to be equally restricted to the beginning of the hexameter:[8]

(134) ὡς δ' ὅτ' ἀπ' Οὐλύμπου νέφος ἔρχεται οὐρανὸν εἴσω
αἰθέρος ἐκ δίης ὅτε τε Ζεὺς λαίλαπα τείνῃ
<u>ὣς</u> τῶν ἐκ νηῶν γένετο ἰαχή τε φόβος τε

Iliad XVI 364–366

---

[8] With the possible exception of *Iliad* VI 146.

As when a cloud enters the sky from Mount Olympus | after bright weather, when Zeus starts a storm | <u>so</u> a panic and fear rose in them from between the ships

(135) <u>ὥς</u>⁹ δ' αὔτως καὶ κεῖνο ἰδὼν ἐτεθήπεα θυμῷ
       δήν ἐπεὶ οὔ πω τοῖον ἀνήλυθεν ἐκ δόρυ γαίης
       <u>ὡς</u> σέ γύναι ἄγαμαί τε τέθηπά τε

Odyssey vi 166–168

<u>In exactly the same way</u> I felt amazement in my heart when I saw it | and for a long time, as a tree like that one did not grow from the earth before, | <u>similarly</u>, I admire you, lady, and feel amazement

The extended simile shows the usefulness of additional constituents up until the verse end before resumption: constituents and even whole lines are freely added, as long as the addition as a whole, together with possibly required constituents,[10] ends with verse end (resumption of the extended simile is underlined in example 136):

(136) οἷον δὲ τρέφει ἔρνος ἀνὴρ ἐριθηλὲς ἐλαίης
       χώρῳ ἐν οἰοπόλῳ ὅ θ' ἅλις ἀναβέβροχεν ὕδωρ
       καλὸν τηλεθάον τὸ δέ τε πνοιαὶ δονέουσι
       παντοίων ἀνέμων καί τε βρύει ἄνθεϊ λευκῷ
       ἐλθὼν δ' ἐξαπίνης ἄνεμος σὺν λαίλαπι πολλῇ
       βόθρου τ' ἐξέστρεψε καὶ ἐξετάνυσσ' ἐπὶ γαίῃ
       <u>τοῖον</u> Πάνθου υἱὸν ἐϋμμελίην Εὔφορβον
       Ἀτρείδης Μενέλαος ἐπεὶ κτάνε τεύχε' ἐσύλα
       ὡς δ' ὅτε τίς τε λέων ὀρεσίτροφος ἀλκὶ πεποιθὼς
       βοσκομένης ἀγέλης βοῦν ἁρπάσῃ ἥ τις ἀρίστη
       τῆς δ' ἐξ αὐχέν' ἔαξε λαβὼν κρατεροῖσιν ὀδοῦσι
       πρῶτον ἔπειτα δέ θ' αἷμα καὶ ἔγκατα πάντα λαφύσσει
       δῃῶν ἀμφὶ δὲ τόν γε κύνες τ' ἄνδρές τε νομῆες
       πολλὰ μάλ' ἰύζουσιν ἀπόπροθεν οὐδ' ἐθέλουσιν
       ἀντίον ἐλθέμεναι μάλα γὰρ χλωρὸν δέος αἱρεῖ
       <u>ὣς</u> τῶν οὔ τινι θυμὸς ἐνὶ στήθεσσιν ἐτόλμα
       ἀντίον ἐλθέμεναι Μενελάου κυδαλίμοιο

Iliad XVII 53–69

Like the blossoming shoot of the olive that a man grows | in a secluded spot, where water surfaces in abundance; | it is beautiful and in

---

⁹ Actually a double resumption within three lines, cf. Edwards 1991:29.
¹⁰ Cf. Edwards 1991:68–69.

bloom, breezes of various winds rock it gently | and it is covered in white blossom; | but suddenly a wind has risen with heavy squalls, and | overthrown it from its pit, and knocked it down to the ground; | <u>like that shoot</u>, the spear-warrior Euphorbus, son of Panthous, | was being robbed of his armor by Menelaus, son of Atreus, after he killed him; | just as when a lion from the mountains, confident in his own strength, | snatched a cow from the grazing herd, precisely the very best; | clenching her between his mighty teeth he broke the animal's neck | first; then he laps up the blood and all the entrails | tearing it apart; all around him dogs and herdsmen | make a terrible noise from a distance, and they do not want | to come face to face with it; for sickening fear gets a firm hold on them; | <u>similarly</u>, for none of them the heart in the chest had the courage | to come face to face with famous Menelaus

The start, or completion, of direct speech, like the resumption of an extended simile, always coincides with verse end. The verse end functions as a sense-pause in the cases of direct speech and the extended simile. Maintenance of the verse end as a sense-pause—for example, by means of fillers to extend the sense-pause *towards* verse end—is not, however, automatically supported by a strong performative pause at verse end.[11] I think it is clear that in case of direct speech, the shift in discourse type is indicated by semantic markers[12] rather

---

[11] It is tempting to consider the absence of a strong performative pause at the start and the completion of direct speech an indication for the grammatical analysis of direct speech as an argument to the verb denoting "to speak" (as an object). The case is, however, especially difficult to prove in the Homeric epic: the status of direct speech (direct discourse) as a freely localized argument, or as embedded predication, cannot be sufficiently evidenced, since direct speech is never used as an argument to the verbal form *following* it: the completion of direct speech leads to resumption of the type "having spoken thus … ." A possible exception is *Iliad* VIII 373.

[12] Examples of semantic markers of discourse shift in the case of direct speech are the vocative (*Iliad* I 74 ὦ Ἀχιλεῦ κέλεαί με διίφιλε μυθήσασθαι, "Achilles, you, dear to Zeus, order me to fully explain"), imperative (*Iliad* I 37 κλῦθί μοι Ἀργυρότοξ᾽ ὃς Χρύσην ἀμφιβέβηκας, "Listen to me, Silverbow, who stands protectively over Chryse"), prohibitive (*Iliad* I 26 μή σε γέρον κοίλησιν ἐγὼ παρὰ νηυσὶ κιχείω, "Let me not find you here, old man, anywhere near the curved ships"; *Iliad* I 131-132 μὴ δ᾽ οὕτως ἀγαθός περ ἐὼν θεοείκελ᾽ Ἀχιλλεῦ || κλέπτε νόῳ ἐπεὶ οὐ παρελεύσεαι οὐδέ με πείσεις, "Do not in this way, fine as you are, godlike Achilles, | try to steal from me by thought, as you will not deceive me nor persuade me"), emotional outcry (*Iliad* I 149 ὤ μοι ἀναιδείην ἐπιειμένε κερδαλεόφρον, "No! You, clothed in shamelessness, so crafty"), shift to first or second person (*Iliad* I 207 ἦλθον ἐγὼ παύσουσα τὸ σὸν μένος αἴ κε πίθηαι, "I have come to put an end to your aggression, if at least you obey"; *Iliad* I 202 τίπτ᾽ αὖτ᾽ αἰγιόχοιο Διὸς τέκος εἰλήλουθας, "Why then, child of the aegisbearing Zeus, have you come?"; *Iliad* I 216 χρὴ μὲν σφωίτερόν γε θεά ἔπος εἰρύσασθαι, "It is necessary, goddess, to do as the two of you command") or asyndeton (*Iliad* I 15b-17 καὶ λίσσετο πάντας Ἀχαιούς || Ἀτρεΐδα δὲ μάλιστα δύω κοσμήτορε λαῶν || Ἀτρεΐδαι τε καὶ ἄλλοι ἐυκνήμιδες Ἀχαιοί, "And he begged all the Greeks, | especially the two sons of Atreus, the

than by performative features.[13] The same holds true for the discourse shift at the completion of direct speech.[14]

Variety in positions for start and completion

In his approach to Homeric discourse as a movement, Bakker 1997b reduced the stylistic feature referred to as adding. He allowed for grammatical governance and syntactical organization to develop over metrical boundaries, including over the verse end. Juxtaposition of metrical cola is not *per se* appositional, but regularly shows the mark of well-prepared linking of chunks to achieve more complex syntactical arrangements. The continuation of syntax over metrical boundaries is not coincidental, but requires careful anticipation by a poet who consciously composes his clauses in grammatically complete wholes comprising several metrical phrases. The grammatical anticipation reduces the importance of the compositional principles of adding style; I argue, rather, that it adds the concept of open-ended clause formation to the description of Homeric verse-making.[15] The start and completion of clauses is not necessarily and inevitably bound to fixed metrical position, but determined by semantic and syntactical factors. As is the case with clause start and completion from fixed positions (like direct speech or the extended simile), clause start and completion from alterna-

---

leaders of the army: | 'Sons of Atreus and you other well-harnessed Greeks'"). In many instances, as in the examples cited, various markers of discourse shift are combined. The discourse shift itself seems confined to verse-initial position.

[13] Some doubt might arise in the absence of verse-initial semantic markers of the shift, as in *Iliad* I 84–85 τὸν δ' ἀπαμειβόμενος προσέφη πόδας ὠκὺς Ἀχιλλεύς ‖ <u>θαρσήσας μάλα</u> εἰπὲ θεοπρόπιον ὅ τι οἶσθα, "Answering him swift-footed Achilles said | '<u>Take heart and</u> tell us the divine revelation that you know of'" or "Answering him swift-footed Achilles said | <u>having encouraged himself</u>: 'Tell us the divine revelation that you know of.'" Both analyzes seem to be equally possible. The strong performative pause at verse end in line 84, together with the absence of a performative pause following the second foot of line 85, favors the former analysis and translation.

[14] With the possible exception of a unique "quotation" of thought in *Iliad* XV 82. The constituent marking the shift back to the narrative is normally in verse-initial position: resumption (*Iliad* I 33 ὣς ἔφατ' ἔδδεισεν δ' ὁ γέρων καὶ ἐπείθετο μύθῳ, "Thus he spoke; the old man, however, became scared and obeyed the order"; *Iliad* I 304–305a ὣς τώ γ' ἀντιβίοισι μαχησαμένω ἐπέεσσιν ‖ ἀνστήτην, "Having fought thus with words of evident hostility both | rose from their seats"; *Iliad* I 528 ἦ καὶ κυανέῃσιν ἐπ' ὀφρύσι νεῦσε Κρονίων, "Said the son of Kronos and he nodded in assent with his brows"), emphatic use of the personal pronoun (*Iliad* I 68–69a ἤτοι ὅ γ' ὣς εἰπὼν κατ' ἄρ' ἕζετο τοῖσι δ' ἀνέστη | Κάλχας Θεστορίδης, "Now, having spoken thus, he sat down, and for them rose | Calchas, son of Thestor"; *Iliad* I 121 τὸν δ' ἠμείβετ' ἔπειτα ποδάρκης δῖος Ἀχιλλεύς, "To him then replied swift, godlike Achilles"; *Iliad* I 130 τὸν δ' ἀπαμειβόμενος προσέφη κρείων Ἀγαμέμνων, "Giving him an answer mighty Agamemnon spoke"), emphatic use of a narrative-structuring adverb (*Iliad* I 22 ἔνθ' ἄλλοι μὲν πάντες ἐπευφήμησαν Ἀχαιοί, "At that time, all other Greeks approved"; *Iliad* I 92 καὶ τότε δὴ θάρσησε καὶ ηὔδα μάντις ἀμύμων, "At that moment then the excellent seer took heart and said").

[15] As the rhythmical word type* necessarily fits the hexameter, so the clause-pattern has the stichic hexametric series as its phrasal domain.

tive and varying positions is not always highlighted by performative features. It will become clear, however, that performative pauses do play a role in marking the transitional constituents that link one clause to the next.

Start and completion of clauses in Homer is a matter of semantics and syntax, as the Homeric narrative tends to simply continue without much regard for the internal organization of complex sentences and the hierarchy of main and subordinate clauses. At first sight the continuation is facilitated by this lack of hierarchy (Chantraine 1963). Clauses follow one another with only a few markers of transition, like asyndeton, conjunctions (like ὅτε, αὐτάρ, εἰ), adverbs (like ἔπειτα, τότε, ὥς, ἔνθα, καί, τῷ), and sentential particles (μεν, δὲ, γάρ, ἄρ, ῥα, κε, ἄν). Often conjunctions, adverbs, and particles are combined into extended sense units of nucleus (the most important constituent) and fillers, regularly ending in an enclitic (δ' ἐπεὶ οὖν, δέ τε, δέ κε, ἦ ῥά νυ, ἀλλ' ἦ τοι μέν, πρίν γ' ὅτε δή).[16] Such extended transitional constituents mark the completion of a clause and are themselves the introduction to the next one. Transitional constituents play a role in the grammatical clause model of functional grammar: this model does not provide many clues for the performative aspects of pause, but is a very useful model to describe the dynamics of Homeric clause formation and clausal grammar.

A model for the grammatical clause in Homer

In the grammatical clause model of functional grammar,[17] the transitional constituent is not necessarily itself part of the clause: identification as extra-clausal

---

[16] A word group like, for example, δ' ἐπεὶ οὖν may be considered as an expansion of nuclear δέ, see Bakker 1993:15–25.

[17] Cf. Van Emden Boas and Huitink in Bakker 2010:134–150. The model was introduced into linguistics by Tesnière 1959, and adopted by Chafe 1970, Helbig 1971; Korhonen 1977; Lyons 1977:147–154, 434–438; Matthews 1981; Allerton 1982. The terminology used here is that of S. C. Dik 1997 and Pinkster 1990. For an overview of functional grammar in relation to the Homeric epics, see Edwards 2002:9–13. The most recent attempt to define the clause in ancient Greek is H. Dik 2007:22–28. I present a full application of the model to Homeric discourse, with examples, in the Appendix.

In this model, the central role in the grammatical clause is that of the predicate, the finite verb, because it is the verb form that dictates the further requirements for a grammatically correct and complete clause. The semantics of the predicate determine the predicate frame (or nuclear predication): the meaning of the finite verb creates, or requires, one or more valencies for arguments with a specific semantic value in relation to the predicate. In addition to the predicate frame, a grammatical clause may contain peripheral constituents (the terminology has been applied to the grammar within Homeric metrical units in Bakker and Fabricotti 1991) labelled satellites. In general, there are two types of satellites. On the one hand, we find the *adjuncts*: satellites that further specify the nuclear predication, with the semantic role *instrument, beneficiary, purpose, time, place, mode,* and *degree* (Bartsch 1972; Verkuyl 1972; S .C. Dik 1997:I,191–209), and the pragmatic function (S. C. Dik 1997:I,313–338, II,401–405) *setting*. On the other hand, the *disjuncts*, satellites that render *meta-communicative expressions*; for example: the point of view or opinion of either the writer or, as understood by the writer, of the audience. The scope of disjuncts is the predication as a whole. Examples of disjuncts are the *modal adverbs,*

follows from the identification of pragmatic functions: topic, focus, theme/tail
(= left-/right-dislocation) and setting.[18] Example (137) illustrates theme/tail,
examples (138) and (139) setting:

(137)   <u>Λητοῦς καὶ Διὸς υἱός</u> ὃ γὰρ βασιλῆι χολωθεὶς
        νοῦσον ἀνὰ στρατὸν ὦρσε κακήν ὀλέκοντο δὲ λαοί
        οὕνεκα τὸν Χρύσην ἠτίμασεν ἀρητῆρα
        <u>Ἀτρείδης</u>

                                                    Iliad I 9–12

<u>Leto's and Zeus' son [theme]</u>: for he felt angry towards the king and
| sent a foul plague over the army's camp–the soldiers perished–
| since he had dishonored him, Chryses, the priest, <u>he, that is,</u>
<u>Agamemnon</u> [tail]

(138)   <u>τοῦ ὅ γ' ἐπιμνησθεὶς</u> ἔπε' ἀθανάτοισι μετηύδα

                                                    Odyssey i 31

<u>thinking of him</u> he spoke the following words to the immortals

(139)   <u>εἰ μὲν δὴ νῦν τοῦτο φίλον μακάρεσσι θεοῖσι</u>
        νοστῆσαι Ὀδυσῆα πολύφρονα ὅνδε δόμονδε
        Ἑρμείαν μὲν ἔπειτα διάκτορον ἀργειφόντην
        νῆσον ἐς Ὠγυγίην ὀτρύνομεν κτλ.

                                                    Odyssey i 82–85

<u>if that [is] indeed dear to the blessed gods,</u> | that Odysseus returns
to what is his, to his home, | then let us send Hermes, the guide, the
slayer of Argus | to the island Ogygia ...

Pragmatic functions determine whether constituents are part of the clause
or not: S. C. Dik[19] labels constituents with function theme/tail and setting as

---

opinion-based adverbative elements, style disjuncts, pseudo-final subordinate clauses, parenthetic
conditionals, constituents with the pragmatic function *theme* and *tail* (Greenbaum 1969; Meier-
Fohrbeck 1978; Quirk 1972; S. C. Dik 1997:I,132–140) and in addition, I argue, the vocative (the
vocative is not regularly treated as a disjunct, but I would argue that comparison with, e.g., the
description of parenthetic verbal forms to identify *illocutive* functions and discourse types, justi-
fies the identification of vocatives as disjunct satellites; cf. Lyons 1977:738).

18 Extra-clausals are commonly quite short, though there are instances of combined noun-epithet
formulas occupying a hexameter (*Iliad* I 7 Ἀτρείδης τε ἄναξ ἀνδρῶν καὶ δῖος Ἀχιλλεύς). The
shorter extra-clausals appear occupying almost any metrical phrase between positions of
frequent word end. Their appearance reflects, like a negative, the highly variable sizing of the
intervening grammatical clauses.

19 S. C. Dik 1997:II,381: "[these constituents] are typically set off from the clause proper by breaks
or pause-like inflections in the prosodic contour."

extra-clausal.[20] Strictly clausal are the constituents with the function topic and focus, in addition to, of course, the predicate. Since theme, tail, and setting are extra-clausal, their appearance marks the boundaries of the grammatical clause. The metrical isolation (as a colon[21]) and prosodic characterization (terminating in an enclitic[22]) of the extra-clausal constituents suggest a relation between audible punctuation and the boundaries of the grammatical clause (see further below).

Anything in between—between the constituents with pragmatic functions inside and outside (especially *following*) the clause—is labelled "extra," but seen as part ("extension") of the clause.[23] Since the "extras" are normally found only following the pragmatically labelled constituents within the clause, their identification makes the clause highly "open-ended." In Homer, it extends the nuclear predication into an extended clause. The transitional constituent is left in between: between the *pragmatically confined* clause and the *semantically extended* predication. In examples 140–141, each clause, extra-clausal transitional constituent, and "extension" is preceded by a number that indicates the metrical position from which the clause, the transitional constituent, or the "extension" starts:

(140) ὦ φίλοι οὐκ ἂν δή τις ἀνὴρ πεπίθοιθ' ἑῷ αὐτοῦ
θυμῷ τολμήεντι μετὰ Τρῶας μεγαθύμους
ἐλθεῖν εἴ τινά που δηίων ἕλοι ἐσχατόωντα
ἤ τινά που καὶ φῆμιν ἐνὶ Τρώεσσι πύθοιτο
ἅσσά τε μητιόωσι μετὰ σφίσιν ἢ μεμάασιν
αὖθι μένειν παρὰ νηυσὶν ἀπόπροθεν ἦε πόλινδε
ἂψ ἀναχωρήσουσιν ἐπεὶ δαμάσαντό γ' Ἀχαιούς.

Iliad X 204–210

My friends, could there not be a man confident enough in his | daring heart to go amidst the courageous Trojans | to see if he might catch one of the foes on the outskirts | or gather some information even among the Trojans | what all they plan among themselves, whether they plan | to stay where they are, at some distance but near to the ships, or that they will retreat back to the city now that they have smitten the Greeks.

---

[20] To which I would like to add all *non-clausal appositions*, including the *vocative*.
[21] Schepper 2011; Bonifazi et al. 2016; Blankenborg 2018.
[22] Goldstein 2016.
[23] For the word order of the constituents *within* the clause, see H. Dik 1995; 2007.

12	[ὦ φίλοι] transitional constituent
2	[οὐκ ἂν δή τις ἀνὴρ πεπίθοιθ'] clause
9	[ἑῷ αὐτοῦ θυμῷ τολμήεντι μετὰ Τρῶας μεγαθύμους ἐλθεῖν] "extra"/"extension"
2	[εἴ] transitional constituent
3	[τινά που δήιων ἕλοι] clause
8	[ἐσχατόωντα] "extra"/"extension"
12	[ἤ] transitional constituent
1	[τινά που καὶ φῆμιν ἐνὶ Τρώεσσι πύθοιτο] clause
12	[ἅσσά τε] transitional constituent
2	[μητιόωσι] clause
5½	[μετὰ σφίσιν] "extra"/"extension"
8	[ἤ] transitional constituent
9	[μεμάασιν] clause
12	[αὖθι μένειν παρὰ νηυσὶν ἀπόπροθεν] "extra"/"extension"
8	[ἦε] transitional constituent
9½	[πόλινδε ἂψ ἀναχωρήσουσιν] clause
5½	[ἐπεὶ] transitional constituent
7	[δαμάσαντό γ' Ἀχαιούς] clause

(141) ἔνθ' ἐφάνη μέγα σῆμα δράκων ἐπὶ νῶτα δαφοινός
σμερδαλέος τόν ῥ' αὐτὸς Ὀλύμπιος ἧκε φόως δέ
βωμοῦ ὑπαΐξας πρός ῥα πλατάνιστον ὄρουσεν
ἔνθα δ' ἔσαν στρουθοῖο νεοσσοί νήπια τέκνα
ὄζῳ ἐπ' ἀκροτάτῳ πετάλοις ὑποπεπτηῶτες
ὀκτώ ἀτὰρ μήτηρ ἐνάτη ἦν ἣ τέκε τέκνα
ἔνθ' ὅ γε τοὺς ἐλεεινὰ κατήσθιε τετριγῶτας
μήτηρ δ' ἀμφεποτᾶτο ὀδυρομένη φίλα τέκνα
τὴν δ' ἐλελιξάμενος πτέρυγος λάβεν ἀμφιαχυῖαν

Iliad II 308–316

Then a great omen became apparent: a snake, blood-colored on the back, | terrible, that the Olympian himself had sent into the light, | having emerged from beneath the altar made his way to the plane-tree | where a sparrow's nestlings were, little youngsters, | crouching under the leaves on the highest branch, | eight of them, and number nine was the mother who raised the youngsters; | then he–wretched things–devoured them, as they were twittering, | and the mother flew around lamenting her young, | but coiling up he grabbed her at the wing, and she squeaked.

12   [ἔνθ'] transitional constituent
1   [ἐφάνη μέγα σῆμα] clause
asyndeton
5½   [δράκων] (part of clause)
7   [ἐπὶ νῶτα δαφοινὸς σμερδαλέος] "extra"/"extension"
3   [τόν ῥ'] transitional constituent
4   [αὐτὸς Ὀλύμπιος ἧκε] clause
9½   [φόως δέ] "extra"/"extension"
12   [βωμοῦ ὑπαΐξας] "extra"/"extension"
5   [πρός ῥα πλατάνιστον ὄρουσεν] clause
12   [ἔνθα δ'] transitional constituent
1½   [ἔσαν στρουθοῖο νεοσσοί] clause
8   [νήπια τέκνα ὄζῳ ἐπ' ἀκροτάτῳ πετάλοις ὑποπεπτηῶτες ὀκτώ] "extr'"/"extension"
1½   [ἀτὰρ] transitional constituent
3   [μήτηρ ἐνάτη ἦν] clause
asyndeton
8   [ἣ τέκε τέκνα] clause
12   [ἔνθ' ὅ γε] transitional constituent
2   [τοὺς ἐλεεινὰ κατήσθιε] clause
8   [τετριγῶτας] "extra"/"extension"
12   [μήτηρ δ'] transitional constituent
2   [ἀμφεποτᾶτο] clause
5½   [ὀδυρομένη φίλα τέκνα] "extra"/"extension"
12   [τὴν δ'] transitional constituent
1   [ἐλελιξάμενος] extra-clausal/setting
5   [πτέρυγος λάβεν] clause
8   [ἀμφιαχυῖαν] "extra"/"extension"

The open-endedness of Homer's grammatical clause is not linked to performative features one-on-one, but the introduction of the subsequent clause appears to be, as the transitional constituent introducing it regularly ends in secondary pause strengthened by clisis.*

Koster 1953:51–52 and Devine and Stephens 1978 describe the prosodic characterization of the clause-initial phonetic word as ending in clisis* as marking transition. Devine and Stephens (1994:354–355) discuss the possibility of clisis for the accented particle. Clisis seems to be quite possible at higher rates of speech. At lower rates, as evidenced in the musical settings, the grave accent of the non-lexical* appositive still does not seem to be part of the rising trajectory, as opposed to other word-final grave accents. The announcement through the extra-clausal transitional constituent is syntactically and phonetically isolated due to the combination of the additive usage and the appositive character of its concluding particle. The continuation, the movement of Homeric discourse, is thus *audible* in the isolating characterization of discourse markers. The audibility of discourse markers through audible punctuation is not exclusive for clause start—as if clause start is always audibly highlighted, or performative features always highlight clause start. Transitional constituents may end in elision (in examples 140–141, they often do), and thus become *intra*-clausal: this leaves no room for a performative feature signaling the transition from extra-clausal constituent to the clause proper. On the other hand, there are enclitics that conclude phonetic words (notably τε and γε) but do not necessarily herald the start of a new clause.

Isolated heralding and afterthoughts

As clause development and continuation over metrical boundaries is sensitive to the mismatch with performative features, I argue that the frequent "heralding" of a clause to come, or "afterthought" to the clause that has just been completed, by means of an isolated constituent at verse end ought to be reassessed with regard to performative pauses, instead of by grammatical governance or the frequency of word end. As just mentioned, the isolation of constituents is determined by prosodic characterization. In my opinion, the so-called dislocation of constituents, a characteristic of nonconfigurational language (§2.1), is better analyzed as ongoing development of the clause in enjambment,[24] when the verse ends in a subordinated syllable (as in examples 142 and 143). The isolation of the noun is metrical rather than performative. Enjambment, as the acknowledgement of ongoing clause development, describes the phenomenon better than heralding or dislocation:

(142)   αἱ δὲ γυναῖκες
        ἱστάμεναι θαύμαζον ἐπὶ προθύροισιν ἑκάστη
                                Iliad XVIII 495b–496

And the women | stood each at her door and marveled [enjambment]

And as for the women, | they stood each at her door and marveled [left-dislocation, "heralding"]

---

[24] Blankenborg 2016. Many instances of enjambment can then be recognized as ongoing and unhindered clause development over the verse end. The mismatch with metrical boundaries reflects a cognitive process: an implicit constituent is made explicit through left- or right-dislocation. This procedure is applied to Homeric Greek in Bakker 1990; in later publications, Bakker analyzes such constituents as instances of "staging" or "re-staging of characters," cf. Bakker 1997a:198–200; 1997b; 2005:13.

(143) οὕνεκα τὸν Χρύσην ἠτίμασεν ἀρητῆρα
      Ἀτρείδης

Iliad I 11–12a

Since | the son of Atreus | had done dishonor to Chryses, his priest [enjambment]

Since he had done dishonor to Chryses, his priest, | he, that is, the son of Atreus [right-dislocation]

Enjambment of dislocated discourse markers or sentential particles (examples 144–146) should be equally considered as ongoing and unhindered development of the clause over verse end in the case of a subordinated verse-final syllable (example 146):

(144) <u>αὐτὰρ</u> ὄπισθε
    νῶι μαχησόμεθα Τρωσίν τε καὶ Ἕκτορι δίῳ

Iliad XVII 718b–719

<u>But</u> behind you | we two will do battle with the Trojans and godlike Hector

(145) ἄλλοτε μέν τε γόῳ φρένα τέρπομαι ἄλλοτε <u>δ' αὖτε</u>
      παύομαι

Odyssey iv 102–103a

At times I satisfy my heart with weeping, <u>but then again</u> at others | I
    stop

(146) οὐδὲ τροφοῦ οὔσης σεῦ ἀφέξομαι ὁππότ' <u>ἂν</u> ἄλλας
    δμωιὰς ἐν μεγάροισιν ἐμοῖς κτείνωμι γυναῖκας

Odyssey xix 489–490

And I will not even spare you, though you are my nurse, when <u>later</u> upon the other | slave women in my palace I will execute the death-sentence

In these example, dislocation incorrectly treats the metrical boundary that separates the discourse markers and sentential particles from their clauses as a syntactical or sense boundary. Still, it is remarkable that so many discourse markers and sentential particles, often together with other constituents, are metrically isolated, as they constitute metrical phrases. Without a performative pause to separate them from their clauses, however, they do not comprise independent units of meaning. When separated from their clauses by performative pauses, metrical cola containing discourse markers and sentential particles are prosodically characterized as transitional: they continue from what was already said (sometimes by contrast), but need further elaboration, after a rest in performance, in subsequent syntactical development. Rests in performance may thus highlight transitional constituents, but not at fixed and predictably recurrent metrical positions.

Clauses and extra-clausals as equivalent of phonological phrases

The metrical shape of the Homeric grammatical clause is highly variable, open-ended, and rather free: the alternation and combination of grammatical clauses and extra-clausal constituents (with their specific shape) creates a metrical mosaic.[25] Transitional constituents are prosodically characterized at their termination. It is not to be automatically assumed, however, that the start and completion of the grammatical clause coincides with a phonological phrase boundary.

[25] The sample in §5.4 provides the following statistics on clause start from various metrical positions:

CLAUSE STARTS AFTER POSITION ...	*ILIAD*	*ODYSSEY*
1 [and start in ⏑⏑]	0.00%	0.00%
1 [and start in —]	0.89%	1.07%
1½	5.35%	4.30%
2	5.35%	7.53%
3 [⏑⏑]	2.68%	3.23%
3 [—]	8.93%	1,.8%
3½	2.67%	1.07%
4	3.57%	0.00%
5 [⏑⏑]	1.78%	0.00%
5 [—]	9.82%	6.45%
5½	7.14%	15.05%
6	5.36%	2.15%
7 [⏑⏑]	5.36%	2.15%
7 [—]	1.78%	1.07%
7½	0.89%	0.00%
8	3.57%	4.30%
9 [⏑⏑]	3.57%	2.15%
9 [—]	0.00%	0.00%
9½	1.78%	5.38%
10	0.89%	2.15%
11[⏑⏑]	0.00%	0.00%
11 [—]	0.00%	0.00%
11½	0.00%	0.00%
12	28.6%	30.10%
Total number of clauses*	112	93

*Predicatively used participles have not been counted as individual grammatical clauses

It may be reasonably expected that the major phonological phrase encompasses several smaller minor phrases, some of them clauses or parts thereof, some extra-clausal constituents. Devine and Stephens 1994 assume that major phrases, though demarcated by phonetic disruptions or rests, will tend to comprise syntactical coherent unities. In Chapter 4, I have argued against this assumption, in favor of a purely phonetic identification of major phrases. The sample in §5.4 showed that phonologically characterized major phrases do not correspond to grammatical clauses. Sometimes grammatical clauses are disrupted by strong performative pauses, at other times major phrases consist of more than one complete grammatical clause. As syntactical coherent unities are indicated by the application of printed punctuation, not all printed punctuation will be supported by performative pauses.

The sample also shows that the occurrence of transitional constituents appears to provide some coincidence of clausal structure and performative pauses. Syntactically, their appearance signals the completion of a grammatical clause; their completion the start of the next grammatical clause. As a performative feature, transitional constituents avoid taking a shape that resembles the major phrase: of the two phonetic pauses (on the left and on the right of the extra-clausal constituent), not more than one is realized as a primary pause. Such realization gives the transitional constituent a structuring role in performance as well: either the constituent may be preceded by a metrical position that allows for considerable additional lengthening or its own final syllable is mapped at such a position. If there is no primary pause, there is a fair chance that the transitional constituent features at least a secondary pause due to termination in an enclitic.[26] As pointed out before, this performative feature of the constituent is lost in case of elision:

(147) ... <u>τὸν δ'</u> εὖρ' ἀμφ' ὤμοισι τιθήμενον ἔντεα καλὰ
νηὶ πάρα πρυμνῇ ... <u>τῷ δ'</u> ἀσπάσιος γένετ' ἐλθὼν

Iliad X 34–35

And him he found busy putting the beautiful armor around his shoulders | near the ship's deck; for him his arrival was most welcome

Together, grammatical clauses and transitional constituents create a sequence of phrases in which hardly any metrical or phonological shape is being repeated instantly.

---

[26] Vocatives regularly start from an unmarked position and end in a position that allows considerable additional lengthening. Devine and Stephens (1994:418) speak of "parentheticals" as "right dislocated afterthoughts."

6.2.2.2 Pause and enjambment

Enjambment is a special feature in the discussion of mismatched syntactical pause. It deserves attention, as the approach of pause in enjambment-studies is diametrically opposed to that taken by studies on syntactical pause in general. Latter studies focus on sense-pause at metrical boundaries as evidenced by the division of the hexameter in units of sense and by printed punctuation. The role of words, word groups, constituents, and phrases in discourse is studied and only then compared with the metrical boundaries. Studies on enjambment (notably Parry 1929; Kirk 1966; Higbie 1990; Edwards 2002), however, assume that grammar and syntax developed within the metrical framework of the single hexameter (as the rhythmical unit: Parry 1929; Lejeune 1955; Van Raalte 1986; Daitz 1991; Nagy 2000; Finkelberg 2011, or as the breath: Bakker 1997b)[27] and tend to grant extra value in performance to syntactical development over the verse end. What exactly this extra value is does not become completely clear. Kahane 1997 and Edwards 2002 treat it as emphasis on the hexameter's first constituent after enjambment due to metrical position. Basset (1938:141–172), the basis for criticism of the Parryan "one-verse utterance," had been fundamental for its notion of emphasis resulting from metrical boundaries in general. Clayman and Nortwick 1977 and Clayman 1981 conclude that on a larger scale syntax may develop in spite of metrical colometry. Higbie 1990 finds it difficult to consider enjambment the mere acknowledgement of composition over the verse end: her label *violent* (see Chapter 2) betrays that the concept of enjambment is always prone to the idea of prosodic affectiveness.[28] I agree with Bakker

---

[27] Early in the history of the written transmission of the text, the *Iliad* and the *Odyssey* were presented *kata stichon*, one verse per line.

[28] The distinction between necessary enjambment and violent enjambment is often not easy to make, unless violent enjambment is understood as the *mot-en-rejet*, the single word in enjambment that completes the clause. Examples of necessary enjambment resulting in violent enjambment: *Iliad* IX 74–75 πολλῶν δ' ἀγρομένων τῶι πείσεαι ὅς κεν ἀρίστην ‖ βουλὴν βουλεύσῃ, "When many come together in assembly, you will listen to the one who has the best | advice to offer"; *Iliad* XIII 611–612 ὁ δ' ὑπ' ἀσπίδος εἵλετο καλὴν ‖ ἀξίνην εὔχαλκον, "But from under his shield he drew the beautiful | axe well-made in bronze"; *Iliad* XIII 709–710 ἀλλ' ἤτοι Τελαμωνιάδῃ πολλοί τε καὶ ἐσθλοὶ ‖ λαοὶ ἕπονθ' ἕταροι, "But in the wake of Telamon's son many and outstanding | soldiers followed as his brothers in arms"; *Iliad* XV 37–38 Στυγὸς ὕδωρ ὅς τε μέγιστος ‖ ὅρκος δεινότατός τε πέλει, "The water of the Styx, which is the strongest | and most terrible oath"; *Iliad* XVI 104–105 δεινὴν δὲ περὶ κροτάφοισι φαεινὴ ‖ πήληξ βαλλομένη καναχὴν ἔχε, "and around his temples the shining | helmet, taking hit after hit, gave a | terrible | row" (even more violent would be the hyperbaton δεινὴν ... καναχήν, only paralleled by Hesiod *Shield* 226–227); *Iliad* XVI 338–339 ἀμφὶ δὲ καλὸν ‖ φάσγανον ἐρραίσθη, "All around the beautiful | sword fell in shatters"; *Iliad* XXII 254–255 τοὶ γὰρ ἄριστοι ‖ μάρτυροι ἔσσονται καὶ ἐπίσκοποι 'For they will be the best | witnesses and supervisors"; *Iliad* XXIV 204–205 (≈ *Iliad* XXIV 520–521) ὅς τοι πολέας τε καὶ ἐσθλοὺς ‖ υἵέας ἐξενάριζε σιδήρειόν νύ τοι ἦτορ, "Who killed many and noble | sons of yours; surely your heart is made or iron": in some ancient texts, σιδήρειόν νύ τοι ἦτορ was a constituent in a phrase that straddled the verse end: σιδήρειόν νύ τοι ἦτορ ‖ ἀθάνατοι ποίησαν

(2005, especially 53–54) and H. Dik (2007:249–254) that the terminology enjambment is best abandoned for many instances of run-over composition without any detectible poetic purpose (Blankenborg 2016). In §6.3 I will discuss what is left of prosodic affectiveness, including the case of enjambment, in the application of performative pause.

Expectations based on semantics

Higbie's classification of the types of enjambment (see Chapter 2) is based on the expectations enjambment creates with the audience. These expectations are the result of the audience's ability to perceive the verse end as a point of termination of syntax, at least: types of enjambment are primarily classified according to the level of completion of grammatical and syntactical requirements at verse end. Expectations also depend on verse-final pause: if the audience cannot be brought to a level of expectation by a performative feature like pause, listeners cannot be expected to await a word to complete a word group, a constituent to complete the clause, or a clause to complete the sentence. From the point of view of the poet as composer, enjambment as the acknowledgement of out-of-line composition does not create expectations.[29] These stem from the guidance provided to the listening audience by performative features. Rests in performance are paramount in guiding the audience through performed text. Intonation may have been supportive of any expectations of the audience based on rests. Little, however, is known about intonation or the melodic pattern in Homeric performance. It suffices though, to observe that Higbie's enjambment classification takes supportive intonation for granted—that is for the verse end as a rest in performance.

Equally arbitrary as the acceptance of supportive intonation is the assumption of affective prosody based on metrical position. Affective prosody is assumed as the result of the mismatch between two compositional pauses, the metrical

---

Ὀλύμπια δώματ' ἔχοντες (Aristonicus in A) or σιδήρειόν νύ τοι ἦτορ ‖ ἀθάνατοι ποίησαν οἳ οὐρανὸν εὐρὺν ἔχουσιν (T); cf. Leaf 1900–1902:551; Erbse 1969; Richardson 1993:295).

[29] As there appears to be no set rule as to what follows the enjambed verse end: words completing an enjambed word group and constituents completing a clause do not have to be in first position in the verse after enjambment. Scholars react arbitrarily to the lack of rule. If words and constituents in enjambment are also in hyperbaton, commentators use such qualifications as "harsh" or "unusual enjambment." The breaking up of a word group in *Iliad* VI 498–499 κιχήσατο δ' ἔνδοθι πολλὰς ‖ ἀμφιπόλους τῇσιν δὲ γόον πάσῃσιν ἐνῶρσεν, "And inside she found many | maid-servants, and for them all she evoked mourning" is considered an "awkward enjambment" by Kirk (1990:225), who points out that other verses ending in a form of πολύς are smoother and wonders why an adverb like ἔνδοθι "inside" has priority over the object-noun. Verse 498 is grammatically complete ("and inside she found many") and might have been complete in meaning if Andromache were expecting only one type of women inside the house at this time. Was she? The question, of course, is not what Andromache (or the composing poet) might expect to find, but what the listening audience was expecting.

and the syntactical pause. Edwards 2002 explains affective prosody as an audible effect of the continuation of clause development over the verse end. In my view, it remains unclear what causes the effect: is it the alleged performative pause at verse end that does not allow for the lowering of tone since the clause keeps developing? If we were to assume that the performative pause at verse end is a prosodic reality in clauses developing over the verse end and that such a pause does not allow for lowering of tone, affective prosody means that the performed hexameter does not start with a tonal rise following enjambment, as it would if the start of the line coincided with clause start. Affective prosody is then a rhythmic irregularity, induced by the continuation of a clause over verse end. It follows that the clause may continue with any word or constituent at the start of the hexameter. Any poetic value to affective prosody, like emphasis, would be the result of semantics, as the emphasis is tied to the meaning of the first constituent after enjambment; the arbitrariness of this notion of emphasis is best shown by citing some examples (148–151, many more could be added) where the semantics of out-of-line composition do not give rise to the identification of emphasis. In terms of giving emphasis or building up tension, these instances of enjambment, regardless of the performative features at verse end, are disappointing:

(148) εἰσωποὶ δ' ἐγένοντο νεῶν περὶ δ' ἔσχεθον ἄκραι
       νῆες ὅσαι πρῶται εἰρύατο

                                                    Iliad XV 653–654

They got between the ships, and all around them stood the high |
ships that had been drawn up first

(149) θεσπεσίῳ δ' ὁμάδῳ ἁλὶ μίσγεται ἐν δέ τε πολλὰ
       κύματα παφλάζοντα πολυφλοίσβοιο θαλάσσης
       κυρτὰ φαληριόωντα πρὸ μέν τ' ἄλλ' αὐτὰρ ἐπ' ἄλλα[30]

                                                    Iliad XIII 797–799

---

[30] Line 798 supplies only one requirement for grammatical completeness, the subject. The predicate is missing, so ἐν in line 797 is to be understood as ἔνεστι, preferably written ἔν. The remarkable phenomenon of a particle used as an adverb to perform as the finite verb in the line ending in enjambment, supposedly prepares the audience for the subject in the next line. The even more remarkable fact that this occurs again with πρό and ἐπί in line 799, both acting as finite verbs for their subjects, suggests to me that the audience was waiting for only the subject to follow the verse end of line 797. Something similar (and again in a comparison/simile) happens in *Iliad* XXIII 520–521 οὐδέ τι πολλὴ ǁ χώρη μεσηγύς where there is no predicate: the audience only waits for the subject (χώρη) of the developing clause to appear in the subsequent line. In *Iliad* XXIII 520–521, it is difficult to decide whether πολλή was used attributively ("and there was not a big gap in between") resulting in "violent" enjambment or predicatively ("and the gap in between was not big"), resulting in "necessary" enjambment.

Three of the four words in line 798 appear four times in epic together as a word group, not interrupted by other words. The fourth word, παφλάζοντα, is separating the word group this

With deafening roar it mingles with the salt water, and in it many |
splattering waves of the dashing sea, | curling with white caps, some
in the front, others following

(150) ἀντίοι ἵστανται καὶ ἀκοντίζουσι θαμειὰς
       αἰχμὰς ἐκ χειρῶν

Iliad XII 44–45

They keep their opposite position, and they throw as a shower | the
spears from their hands

(151)   ἀκόντιζον δὲ θαμειὰς
       αἰχμάς

Iliad XIV 422–423

And they threw as a shower | their spears

Unlikely as the contribution of prosody to emphasis may be in these examples,
it is even harder to imagine a performative pause at verse end that is introduced via lowering of tone and followed by tonal rise in the case of necessary
or violent enjambment: such divergence of prosodic and syntactic patterns is
unparalleled in any known language. Is then the colon following the enjambed
verse end in any other way audibly different from other line-initial cola? What
would cause it to be different other than semantics? And at what price? The
result would be an awkward hiccup in performance. Emphasis, I argue, is not
likely to be the result of awkward hiccups; its origins lie in dynamic accent,
rising tonal patterns, or well-timed rests that do not disturb the pattern of intonation. Dynamic accent cannot be evidenced in Homer; with regard to tonal
patterns and rests, I have argued in this study that those cannot be assumed
merely on the basis of metrics or syntax. Phonetics has the greatest role to play.

Expectations based on the pattern of intonation

Then the alternative: what if there is not automatically a performative pause at
verse end? Does that mean that an intonation unit (regardless of its definition
and exact size) can continue over the verse end together with the developing
clause (cf. Hagel 2002, 2004; Nagy 2010; Goldstein 2014; Blankenborg 2016)?
Intonation, I argue, is best considered a feature of spoken language that is not
unrelated to the units of discourse. Intonation is a factor in the judgement that
grammatical completeness of the line ending in enjambed verse end is not by
itself decisive for identification of enjambment types. This becomes particularly

---

time, and happens to be a *hapax legomenon* in Homer: it occurs in Alcaeus (supp. 25.4) and is used
in Attic comedy (Aristophanes *Knights* 919, *Peace* 314).

clear in verses where the grammatical structure of the straddling clause at verse end leaves room for several options for continuation. In example (152) description focuses on the large number of ships and the hardly sufficient space on the beach to draw them all up:

(152) τῷ ῥα προκρόσσας ἔρυσαν καὶ πλῆσαν ἁπάσης
ἠϊόνος στόμα μακρόν

Iliad XIV 35–36

For that reason they drew them up like the theater's rows, and they filled the entire | beach's great mouth

The verb ἔρυσαν indicates the soldiers' action of drawing the ships onto dry land. Subsequently, the verb πλῆσαν indicates a soldiers' action as well.[31] Based on the grammatical completeness of line 35, the audience might understand the soldiers to have filled the ships with something "complete."[32] I do not believe that the poet deliberately misleads his audience into thinking that the soldiers had filled the ships with something, as readers, taking one verse at a time, might understand at first. I consider it much more likely that intonation prepared the listeners for more to follow in the next line than just the noun agreeing with ἁπάσης. It may have, in a similar way, kept words together in violent enjambment despite hyperbaton, in examples (153–165):

(153)   ἥ οἱ ἀπάσας
ἔσχ' ὀδύνας

Iliad XI 847–848

That | curbed | for him all | the pain

(154) δῶκε δὲ Δηϊπύλῳ ἑτάρῳ φίλῳ ὅν περὶ πάσης
τῖεν ὁμηλικίης

Iliad V 325–326

And gave them to his friend Deipylus, whom, more than the rest | he valued of his peer-group

(155)   πὰρ δέ οἱ ἄλλοι
ναῖον Βοιωτοί μάλα πίονα δῆμον ἔχοντες

Iliad V 709–710

---

[31] Which is to be preferred to taking the ships as subject.

[32] As ravines are being filled with corpses (ἐναύλους νεκύων *Iliad* XVI 72), human beings with courage (ἀμφοτέρω μένεος *Iliad* XIII 60, μένεος φρένες *Iliad* I 104, ἀλκῆς καὶ σθένεος *Iliad* XVII 212), a travel bag with provisions (πήρην σίτου *Odyssey* xvii 441), a river with horses and men (ῥόας ἵππων τε καὶ ἀνδρῶν *Iliad* XXI 16), a cup with wine (δέπας οἴνοιο *Iliad* IX 224) or, metaphorically, a heart with food and drink (θυμὸν ἀδητύος ἠδὲ ποτῆτος *Odyssey* xvii 603).

And next to him the other | Boeotians lived occupying very fertile territory

(156)   οὐ γὰρ ἔτ᾽ ἄλλη
         ἔσται θαλπωρή

Iliad VI 411–412

For not any other | hope will be left

(157)   οὐδὲ γὰρ οὐδ᾽ εὐρύς περ ἐὼν ἐδυνήσατο πάσας
αἰγιαλὸς νῆας χαδέειν[33]

Iliad XIV 33–34

For still, though it was wide, it could not for all, | that is the beach, for the ships provide enough space

(158)   δὸς νῦν μοι φιλότητα καὶ ἵμερον ᾧ τε σὺ πάντας
         δαμνᾷ ἀθανάτους ἠδὲ θνητοὺς ἀνθρώπους

Iliad XIV 198–199

Please give me the power of love now and that of longing, with which you bring all | under your control, immortals and mortal men alike

(159)   ἔνθα κ᾽ ἔτι μείζων τε καὶ ἀργαλεώτερος ἄλλος
         πὰρ Διὸς ἀθανάτοισι χόλος καὶ μῆνις ἐτύχθη

Iliad XV 121–122

---

[33]   αἰγιαλός stands in hyperbaton (εὐρύς περ ἐὼν ... αἰγιαλὸς) due to the verse-end straddling word group (πάσας ... νῆας) that stands in hyperbaton itself. There are only two other examples in Homer of verse end allowing a double hyperbaton. The first one is the already cited *Iliad* XVI 104–105, but at least there one of the divided word groups was divided only by the verse end (φαεινὴ || πήληξ). The second one is *Iliad* I 283–284 ὃς μέγα πᾶσιν || ἕρκος Ἀχαιοῖσιν πέλεται πολέμοιο κακοῖο, "Who, strong, for all, | serves like a bulwark for the Greeks against disastrous war." It is tempting to understand μέγα as an adverb ("highly") here, as it is used elsewhere, e.g., *Iliad* I 78–79 ὃς μέγα πάντων || Ἀργείων κρατέει καί οἱ πείθονται Ἀχαιοί, "Who highly over all | the Greeks wields the scepter, and whom the Greeks obey." On several, similar occasions the adverb is more closely attached to the verb (e.g., *Iliad* I 454, *Iliad* II 64, *Iliad* XVIII 162, *Odyssey* xxiv 402, *Odyssey* i 276, etc. Together with a verb, it also expresses the intensity of sound, e.g., *Iliad* II 784, *Iliad* XI 10, *Iliad* XIX 260, *Odyssey* xvii 239, *Odyssey* xvii 541, and the intensity of emotions, e.g., *Iliad* I 256, *Iliad* VI 362, *Odyssey* iv 30, *Odyssey* xvi 139). If *Iliad* I 78–79 is seen as a fortuitous combination of formulas, the translation may be more like "who, high above all, rules over the Greeks, and whom the Greeks obey." Such a translation is in accordance with a line-to-line approach as well. Still, neither *Iliad* I 283 nor *Iliad* I 78 will have left any doubt for the audience as to how μέγα was to be understood. For the poet and his audience, there must have been a significant difference in intonation at the end of the two verses (cf. Nolan 2014: "to indicate that they have had their say, or, conversely, that they are in full flow and don't want to be interrupted"). The latter prepares for the next line to continue the grammatical clause unhindered. The former includes the metrical break at verse end in the application of the hyperbaton. In other words, not only the audience was likely well aware of the grammatical function of μέγα as an adjective in *Iliad* I 283, but the poet in his role as composer as well.

Then yet an even bigger and more painful | rage and wrath from Zeus would have befallen the immortals

(160) ἀλλ' ὥς τε στάθμη δόρυ νήιον ἐξιθύνει
       τέκτονος ἐν παλάμησι δαήμονος ὅς ῥά τε πάσης
       εὖ εἰδῇ σοφίης ὑποθημοσύνησιν Ἀθήνης

Iliad XV 410–412

But similar to the way the plumbline straightens the ship's timber | in the hands of a crafty carpenter who in all respects | masters his profession thanks to the teachings of Athene

(161) γάστερα γάρ μιν τύψε παρ' ὀμφαλόν ἐκ δ' ἄρα πᾶσαι
       χύντο χαμαὶ χολάδες

Iliad XXI 180–181

For he hit him in the stomach close to the navel, and out all | the bowels came pouring on the ground

(162)   οὐδέ τι πολλὴ
       γίνετ' ἐπισσώτρων ἁρματροχιὴ κατόπισθεν

Iliad XXIII 504–505

And not much | was left of the wheels' rut behind the chariot

(163) εὗρε δ' ἐνὶ σπῆι γλαφυρῷ Θέτιν ἀμφὶ δέ τ' ἄλλαι
       εἵαθ' ὁμηγερέες ἅλιαι θεαί

Iliad XXIV 83–84

She found Thetis in a curved cave, and all around the other | sea-goddesses were sitting in an assembly

(164) εὗρον δ' εὐρύοπα Κρονίδην περὶ δ' ἄλλοι ἅπαντες
       εἵαθ' ὁμηγερέες μάκαρες θεοὶ αἰὲν ἐόντες

Iliad XXIV 98–99

They found thundering Zeus, and in his vicinity all other | ever-living, blessed gods were sitting in an assembly

(165) ἵκετο δ' αἰπὺν Ὄλυμπον ὁμηγερέεσσι δ' ἐπῆλθεν
       ἀθανάτοισι θεοῖσι Διὸς δόμῳ[34]

Iliad XV 84–85

---

[34] The adjective ὁμηγερέεσσι stands in hyperbaton with the agreeing noun, but is not the last word of the line, nor is the noun the first of the next. In his commentary on *Iliad* 13–16, Janko

> She reached steep Mount Olympus, and found the gathered |
> immortal gods in the palace of Zeus

If there is any emphasis on the runover constituent in examples (153–165), emphasis may be the product of the continuation of the intonation pattern over the verse end. Where does this leave the verse end as a perceptible and audible pause? If the intonation pattern develops over the verse end, the rhythmical indeterminacy on the sixth arsis will not be noticeable as a disturbance to continuing rhythm*. This leaves no room for affective prosody or emphasis as its result.

Expectations based on phonetic word end

The phonology of verse-end enjambment leaves no room for prosodic affectiveness either. Higbie's classification of enjambment types categorizes enjambment by looking at the grammatical break caused by the verse end. As enjambment rises from the concept of verse-internal grammatical completeness, the acknowledgement of grammatical incompleteness at verse end determines the strength of the enjambment. Her classification of enjambment types can be reorganized in accordance with the phonetic realization of the metrical verse end:

Type of enjambment in Higbie's system:	Phonetic realization:
* Adding internal enjambment	Phonetic-word boundary (possibly) Minor-phrase boundary
* Adding external enjambment	Minor-phrase boundary (possibly) Major-phrase boundary
* Clausal internal enjambment	Phonetic-word boundary (possibly) Minor-phrase boundary
* Clausal external enjambment	Minor-phrase boundary (possibly) Major-phrase boundary
* Necessary enjambment	Phonetic-word boundary (possibly) Minor-phrase boundary
* Violent enjambment	Phonetic-word boundary

(1992:237) points out that the word group ἀθανάτοισι θεοῖσι is "transposed from the verse-end," where it can be found thirty-eight times.

Higbie's classification disregards a) that the realization of phonetic-word boundary is not automatically perceptible as a pause, b) that the realization of minor phrase boundaries is in accordance with grammatical organization,[35] and c) that, within the phonological phrase, there is no affective prosody,[36] that is, no emphasis due to localization. Phonetically, violent enjambment resembles necessary, clausal internal, and adding internal enjambment. The only difference is that violent enjambment cannot coincide with a minor-phrase boundary. To the ear, necessary, clausal internal, and adding internal enjambment not coinciding with a minor-phrase boundary are exactly the same as violent enjambment.[37]

6.3   Prosodic Affectiveness

It is theoretically unsound to grant emphasis to words based on their *metrical* location. The poetic effect of prosody stems from the mismatch of grammatical / syntactical pausing and the phonetic disturbance caused by primary pauses. Dionysius[38] comments on such disturbance: the audible pause (ἀναβολὴ χρόνων, "delaying of durations") is a "clashing of syllables" (ἀνακοπὴ συλλαβῶν) like "blockades formed by articulate sounds" (ἀντιστηριγμοὶ γραμμάτων). I argue that, if such an ἀντιστηριγμὸς γραμμάτων evokes an audible pause *within* a grammatically coherent clause, poetically meaningful enjambment may be assumed, both at verse end and *within* the verse, as the phonological circumstances for primary pause at the various metrical positions do not differ substantially. I will refer to this poetic effect of prosody, the phonetically characterized disruption of ongoing clause or sentence development, as *prosodic affectiveness*.

Prosodically affective enjambment

The sample in §5.4 provides the data concerning this prosodically affective enjambment in Homer.[39] Here, I present two examples (166–167). The first,

---

[35]   Devine and Stephens 1994:377–382.

[36]   Devine and Stephens 1994:469–475.

[37]   The first constituent of the Homeric hexameter following enjambment does not automatically receive emphasis, not even if it is, grammatically, a *mot-en-rejet*. Looking at Higbie's classification and from her point of view, I find it advisable to change the label "violent": it is the only label that does not refer to what the word or words following the enjambment contribute to the grammatical (in)completeness of the line ending in enjambment at verse end.

[38]   Dionysius of Halicarnassus *On literary composition* 16/61.19–68.6 U-R.

[39]   Prosodically affective enjambment occurs twenty times in the *Iliad* sample, of which thirteen times are in direct speech (where direct speech is fifty-two percent of the sample). In the *Odyssey*, there are twenty-four instances, sixteen of which are in direct speech (where direct speech is fifty-nine percent of the sample). The twenty instances of enjambment in the *Iliad* all

example (166), deals with prosodically affective enjambment at verse end. Prosodic affectiveness is the result of a primary pause at verse end breaking up the grammatical clause:

(166) ἀφείλετο νίκην
    ῥηιδίως

Iliad XVII 177–178

He took away victory | easily

The second example, (167), features similar enjambment[40] verse internally, following position 5 after πασέων:

(167) ὅσσ' ἐμοὶ ἐκ πασέων Κρονίδης Ζεὺς ἄλγε' ἔδωκεν

Iliad XVIII 431

As many sorrows as to me, out of all, Cronus's son Zeus has given

I would like to stress that enjambment is *possible* considering the phonetic realization, not that it is *unavoidable*. The impact of enjambment depends on the choice of the performer to exploit the option for phonetic pause. In addition, I do not claim that prosodically affective enjambment at such positions lends emphasis to either the word preceding or the word following the phonological realization. I do not know what exactly the poetic effect of such enjambment might have been, but merely analyze the possibility for an audible pause that disturbs the grammatically coherent unit. There is, nonetheless, one specific aspect that I do want to point out: both at verse end, and verse internally, instances of phonetically characterized enjambment that possibly disturbs clausal grammar are rare, especially in the *Iliad*.[41]

---

    break up the clause, and all but one are verse-internal. A remarkable example is *Odyssey* i 82, where the enjambment is the result of phrasal metarrhythmisis* on position 4. Of the twenty-four instances of enjambment in the first 100 lines of the *Odyssey*, twenty-three break up the grammatical clause, and twenty are verse-internal. In *Odyssey* i 72, I see no enjambment, but a syntactical structure in which the apposition in nominative case is not tied to the preceding, but to the subsequent genitive case apposition. The only examples of prosodically affective enjambment that are in accordance with Higbie's system are *Iliad* I 66, *Odyssey* i 52 (integral enjambment), *Odyssey* i 18, *Odyssey* i 61 (adding external enjambment), *Odyssey* i 39 (clausal internal enjambment), *Odyssey* i 59 (clausal external enjambment), though *Odyssey* i 39 and *Odyssey* i 59 are verse-internal.

[40] Phonetic word end in [long vowel + ς], as in Κρονίδης at position 7 in example (167), does not necessarily lead to a superheavy syllable, cf. the syllabification of ς in consonant-clusters in Devine and Stephens 1994:43.

[41] The sample in §5.4 provides the following statistics on demarcation due to the primary rhythmical pause as percentage of total number of primary pauses:

Prosodically affective clause juncture

Prosodic affectiveness, at verse end or verse-internal, may be exploited as a clausal divider. In its development into larger size units, the Homeric complex sentence encompasses several cola and verses. In the transition from main to subordinate clause, or from subordinate to main clause, the verse end turns out to be the favorite localization for clause juncture. Prosody may be affective in such instances, given that the tonal pattern at, and over, the verse end differs from the pattern in verse clusters where every line ends in sentence termination. The sentence-internal lowering of tone at the completion of clauses is less than the lowering of tone at sentence end; sentence-internal clause start picks up from a higher tone than sentence start (Devine and Stephens 1994:429–455). Crosslinguistic observations suggest that the verse end as a clause divider results in a verse-final intonation pattern that differs from the verse end as sentence end. Prosody may well have been sensitive to the alternative intonation pattern.

The clause and sentence formation in Homeric discourse evokes the possibility of considerable prosodic affectiveness at the clause juncture. This affectiveness can be linked to the concept of audience expectation at the coincidence of various compositional pauses. In discourse where approximately a third of all verse ends coincide with sense-pause (West 1982:36), continuation of the intonation pattern over the verse end will not have been a very exceptional feature. An audience's attention may rather have been drawn to instances where the coincidence of sense-pause and intonational stop at verse end highlights the heralding of the start of the next line; this is prosodic affectiveness that does not stem from metrical position, but from the match of units in composition:

(168) τίς τ' ἄρ σφωε θεῶν ἔριδι ξυνέηκε μάχεσθαι
         Λητοῦς καὶ Διὸς υἱός

Iliad I 8–9

	Iliad			Odyssey		
	Clause end*	Affective enjambment	Other**	Clause end*	Affective enjambment	Other**
Pos. 3	8.10%	9.30%	8.1%	7.50%	12.50%	13.75%
Pos. 4	0.00%	0.00%	0.00%	0.00%	1.25%	0.00%
Pos. 5	17.44%	5.81%	3.49%	6.25%	7.50%	3.75%
Pos. 7	11.63%	5.81%	3.49%	5.00%	10.00%	2.50%
Pos. 9	2.32%	2.32%	1.20%	0.00%	3.75%	1.25%
Pos. 8	2.32%	0.00%	0.00%	0.00%	1.25%	2.50%
Pos. 11	0.00%	0.00%	0.00%	0.00%	0.00%	0.00%
Pos. 12	12.79%	3.48%	2.32%	7.50%	5.00%	7.50%

* Including the right branch demarcation of the predicatively used participle.
** The right branch demarcation of a transitional constituent or a cluster of transitional constituents.

Who then of the gods brought the two of them together to argue in strife? | The son of Leto and Zeus

Example (169) presents an interesting case, a variation on the standard direct speech clause start at the beginning of the hexameter. As with the start of direct speech, the unique quotation[42] that replaces direct speech here is heralded by the verse end:

(169) ὡς δ' ὅτ' ἂν ἀΐξῃ νόος ἀνέρος ὅς τ' ἐπὶ πολλὴν
γαῖαν ἐληλουθὼς φρεσὶ πευκαλίμῃσι νοήσῃ
ἔνθ' εἴην ἢ ἔνθα μενοινήῃσί τε πολλὰ[43]

Iliad XV 80–82

As when a man's thoughts leap quickly who over a large stretch | of land has travelled, and ponders in his agile mind: "if only I were[44] in this place or that," and reconsiders many things

To the ear, the demarcation in intonation at the verse end of line 81 resembles the audible pause of the colon (:) read aloud.[45]

---

[42] Unique also in not expanding into at least a full line. Compare half-line quotations as *Iliad* I 9 Λητοῦς καὶ Διὸς υἱός, "the son of Leto and Zeus," and (understanding the first half of line 85 as predicative with Ἀχιλλεύς) *Iliad* I 84–85 τὸν δ' ἀπαμειβόμενος προσέφη πόδας ὠκὺς Ἀχιλλεύς || θαρσήσας μάλα εἰπὲ θεοπρόπιον ὅ τι οἶσθα, "To him in reply spoke Achilles swift of foot | having taken heart: 'Speak of any oracle that you know.'"

[43] The present subjunctive μενοινήῃσι is the reading of Aristarchus. Most MSS and a papyrus read the aorist optative μενοινήσειε, probably under the influence of the optative εἴην. A present subjunctive following an aorist subjunctive is odd, and so is this specific form with assimilation of -ά- into -ή-; cf. Chantraine 1953:I,77.

[44] Aristarchus understood εἴην as optative of ἰέναι "to go," as it seems to be understood in *Iliad* XXIV 139 (cf. Macleod 1982:101) and *Odyssey* xiv 408 and *Odyssey* xiv 496. Chantraine (1953:I,285) argues for its origin in the verb εἶναι to be.

[45] There seems to be a connection between two successive cases of enjambment in two successive verses; in this instance an accumulation of the audience's expectations resulting in a surprising continuation after the second "enjambed" verse end. The mere suggestion of such a connection is not plausible, and almost unexplainable, in a model for Homeric verse-making that is based on the assumption of the whole-line formula as the compositional unit, and the subsequent explanation of enjambment as "expanding beyond the hexameter." It also runs counter to the idea "that the length of the enjambment can vary from a single syllable to a complete line" (Clark 1997:26). In this case, it develops into a second "enjambed" verse end and hence another subsequent line. Clark allows for some "planning ahead" in Homer, when he states: "I believe that passages ... demonstrate that the oral poet could plan at least a certain distance ahead and adjust the run of words to fit the requirements of the context" (p. 126) and: "Evidently the composition of these passages required some planning; again we see that the art of oral poetry requires forethought; it does not consist merely of adding one formula to another" (p. 165). This is the furthest that Clark disassociates himself from Parry's remark that "the singer of oral narrative rarely plans his sentences ahead, but adds verse to verse and verse part to verse part until he feels that his sentence is full and finished" (Parry 1971:414–418).

The force of the verse end as a clausal divider, especially when preparing for a main clause to follow a subordinate clause, is sometimes stronger than the compositional need for a logical and appropriate sentence. There are examples of verse-end straddling subordinate clauses without an apodosis, e.g., *Odyssey* iii 103, *Odyssey* iv 204, *Odyssey* vi 187,[46] *Odyssey* viii 236, *Odyssey* xiv 149, *Odyssey* xvii 185, etc. The structure of these syntactically rambling sentences varies: the subordinate clause is followed by a relative clause, another subordinate clause, a participle, a main clause in parenthesis, or a combination of any of the above. In all cases, the subordinate clause is followed by at least one other verse and the end of the incomplete sentence always coincides with the end of the dactylic hexameter. This suggests that the force of the verse end as a clausal divider has much in common with the force of the verse end as an intonation boundary. So much so, that the former can be mistaken for the latter and thus create a syntactically open-ended grammatical clause. Several such incomplete lines were maintained throughout the manuscript tradition. Example (170) provides an extreme version of a subordinate clause followed by a relative clause, an embedded relative clause, a parenthetic main clause, and a proper main clause. The proper main clause starts at the beginning of line 230, so the true "clausal enjambment" coincides with the verse end of line 229:

(170)   νῦν δ' ἐπεὶ ἤδη σήματ' ἀριφραδέα κατέλεξας
εὐνῆς ἡμετέρης ἣν οὐ βροτὸς ἄλλος ὀπώπει
ἀλλ' οἶοι σύ τ' ἐγώ τε καὶ ἀμφίπολος μία μούνη
Ἀκτορίς ἥν μοι δῶκε πατὴρ ἔτι δεῦρο κιούσῃ
ἣ νῶιν εἴρυτο θύρας πυκινοῦ θαλάμοιο
πείθεις δή μευ θυμὸν ἀπηνέα περ μάλ' ἐόντα

Odyssey xxiii 225–230

---

[46] Attractive as it may have seemed to attribute the anacolouthon to the girl's state of inexperience, the rambling syntax is in no way unique. In this specific case, Plutarch found it necessary to supply an extra line to amend the syntactical mess. The speaking character, Nausicaa, proceeds with a general statement (188 Ζεὺς δ' αὐτὸς νέμει ὄλβον Ὀλύμπιος ἀνθρώποισιν ... , "Olympian Zeus himself dispenses wealth to men ... ") that meets the syntactical requirement of the expected main clause, but should be explained as a parenthesis. In line 190 (καί που σοὶ τάδ' ἔδωκε σὲ δὲ χρὴ τετλάμεν ἔμπης, "I think he gave you this as well, and you must endure it till the end"), all hope of an appropriate main clause is lost since a new main clause starts. Nausicaa will actually start her ἐπεὶ -sentence once more, in line 191 (νῦν δ' ἐπεὶ ἡμετέρην τε πόλιν καὶ γαῖαν ἱκάνεις, "now since you have arrived at our citadel and country"), this time with a more appropriate continuation. Plutarch (*On progress in virtue* 82 e) cites, between 187 and 188, as 187a, οὐλέ τε καὶ μέγα χαῖρε θεοὶ δέ τοι ὄλβια δοῖεν, "greetings and be most welcome; may the gods grant you happiness." Plutarch almost quotes an existing line from the *Odyssey* (*Odyssey* xxiv 402 reads μάλα instead of μέγα [vulgate]). The line cited by Plutarch is identical to *Hymn to Apollo* 466, and suitable to end in an apodosis.

But now, since you have listed the unmistakable signs | of our bed, which no other mortal has seen, | but just you and me and one single maid-servant, | Aktoris, whom my father gave me long ago when I moved here— | she used to guard the doors of the well-built bed room for the two of us— | you finally convince my heart though it is very suspicious

This example goes to show what is evident throughout the *Iliad* and the *Odyssey*: when the subordinate clause precedes the main clause, the boundary between the subordinate clause and the main clause usually coincides with the verse end. The poet will postpone the start of the main clause until the start of a verse, thus making use of the continuing intonation pattern over the verse end. What Higbie 1990 labels clausal-external enjambment is a prosodic affectiveness comparable to that of the punctuation used in prose to mark the boundary between the subordinate and the main clause, and that of the audible pause in prose when read aloud and, in spoken language, the audible rise in tone at the beginning of the main clause after the audible fall of tone at the end of the subordinate clause. Clausal external enjambment serves the same structuring purpose as these phenomena in prose.[47] The intonation boundary is as audibly non-disruptive and—despite the verse end—as poetically insignificant as these prose phenomena.

Any preparatory effect of intonation would be the result of the application of a compositional pause as an audible feature. This effect of intonation is not restricted to verse end, as it may equally highlight the verse-internal clausal divider. In examples (171) and (172), verse-internal clause juncture is semantically and syntactically signaled by (underlined) resumption and phonetically introduced by a primary pause:

(171) οἵη περ φύλλων γενεή <u>τοίη</u> δὲ καὶ ανδρῶν

Iliad VI 146

Just as are the generations of leaves, <u>such</u> are those of men

(172) τρὶς μέν μιν πελέμιξεν ἐρύσσασθαι μενεαίνων
τρὶς δὲ μεθῆκε βίης <u>τὸ δὲ τέτρατον</u> κτλ

Iliad XXI 176–177

Thrice he made it quiver in his eagerness to pull it, | thrice he gave up the effort; <u>but the fourth time</u> etc.

---

47 According to this approach, clausal external enjambment occurs two times in the sample of the *Iliad* (§5.4), and three times in the *Odyssey*.

In example (173), the verse-internal clause start, following two preceding subordinate clauses,[48] is signaled by a primary pause (following position 5 in line 41) only:

(173) κλῦθί μευ ἀργυρότοξ᾽ ὃς Χρύσην ἀμφιβέβηκας
       Κίλλαν τε ζαθέην Τενέδοιό τε ἶφι ἀνάσσεις
       Σμινθεῦ εἴ ποτέ τοι χαρίεντ᾽ ἐπὶ νηὸν ἔρεψα
       ἢ εἰ δή ποτέ τοι κατὰ πίονα μηρί᾽ ἔκηα
       ταύρων ἠδ᾽ αἰγῶν τόδε μοι κρήηνον ἐέλδωρ

Iliad I 37–41

hear me please, Silverbow, who stand protective over Chryse | and holy Killa and over Tenedus rule with iron fist, | Smitheus, if ever I covered a temple with a roof pleasing to you, | or if ever I gave you full ration when burning the fat shanks | of bulls and goats: fulfil this one hope for me

The intonation pattern of line 41 in example (173) incorporates a primary pause within the juncture of a subordinate and a main clause. Prosodic affectiveness here is comparable to a similar audible feature at verse end and proof of the possibility of prosodically affective enjambment (in this case, clausal-external enjambment) within the line. The result of affective prosody due to enjambment is not emphasis, but the enforcement of audible punctuation as structuring device in performance.

---

[48] But compare the use of εἰ in such combinations as εἰ δ᾽ ἄγε, εἰ δ᾽ ἄγετε, εἰ δέ, reducing εἰ to an introduction of an imperative.

7

Between Performative Pauses

*Technical terms followed by * on their first occurrence in this chapter are in the glossary.*

7.0   Introduction

With phonetic pauses* audibly structuring performance*, attention is drawn towards what happens between these pauses. If the rests in performance are the opportunities for compositional pauses* to structure performance as audible features, units of performance appear that are not identical to the compositional units of meter or syntax. In this chapter, I will analyze the units of performance as phonological phrases* that encompass a coherent intonation pattern. I will argue that this prosodic coherence, which brings about the coherence resulting from rhythm*, has an effect on the progressive tendency that characterizes the open-endedness of Homeric discourse: it creates a mosaic of phrases that keeps the narrative going, while dimming the repetitiveness of the metrical surface structure in performance.

7.1   Intonation Between Pauses

Intonation is a characteristic of the prosodic domain. Prosodic domains are the spans within which the application of prosodic rules is motivated by fluency and across which application is blocked by prosodic demarcation (Devine and Stephens 1994:286). One of the naturally occurring, crosslinguistic rules of phrase prosody is the initial rise and terminal fall of tone, both within the phonetic word* and within the phonological phrase. The Delphic hymns provide evidence for initial rise and terminal fall within the phonetic word in ancient Greek and for rise and fall of an octave or more at the boundaries of the major phonological phrase. There is no reason to assume that tonal rise and fall are sensitive to, or coincide with, all the compositional pauses of meter and syntax; the patterns of intonational differences correspond with the spans of phonological phrasing. Crosslinguistically, intonational patterns show substantial lowering of tone as a correlate of phonetic word end and word-final lengthening, and rise of tone immediately following the performative pause*. They audibly support the coherence suggested by the phonetic boundaries of units that are restricted in performance, as shown by metrical surface structure.

Intonation belongs to the performer, and its use is the performer's way to guide the audience's expectations. Intonation, however, cannot be seen as unrelated to the structure of language. Any expectation that the performer creates using intonation is the result of the pattern of intonation within the units of Homeric discourse. Any remark with regard to the units of discourse is, in a way, a remark that takes some sort of independent phrasal intonation pattern for granted. The pattern of intonation is not necessarily the key to syntactical phrasing, but it does show that verse end enjambment* is not likely to be "strong" or "emphatic" (§6.2.2.2). Continuation of the intonation pattern, together with developing syntax, over the verse end does not create expectations because of enjambment as the acknowledgement of missing syntactical requirements, but because of required melodious elements. Seen as an audible phenomenon that is related to the structure of language, intonation, rather than grammatical completeness, would be a reason to label any enjambment *violent* or *necessary enjambment*. Intonation, I argue, is thus a factor in the judgement that grammatical completeness of the line ending in enjambed verse end is not by itself decisive for identification of enjambment types. This becomes particularly clear in verses where the grammatical structure of the clause straddling the verse end leaves room for several options for continuation.

7.2   Syntax Between Pauses

In the analysis of Homeric discourse, there is an abundance of discourse-unit structuring elements: sentence, clause, idea unit, intonation unit, utterance, phrase, mental picture. Clark 1997 is right, I think, in stating that the grammatically complete clause proves to be the most useful instrument, but then we must accept that grammatical completeness is not *per se* determined by recurrent metrical boundaries like the verse end. Terminology like enjambment, as it is used by Higbie 1990, accounts for the mere acknowledgement of a visible disparity between metrical phrases and syntax: it does not tell us anything about what the audience actually perceives—though the temptation to explain enjambment as poetically effective is never far away, as recent commentaries on the *Iliad* and the *Odyssey* show.

7.2.1 Continuation

Homeric syntax is not so much concerned with the due completion of sense in accordance with metrical phrasing. The frequent divergence of syntactical and metrical phrasing serves *continuation* despite metrical repetition. Such divergence is at least as frequent as the structuring of the discourse into metrically well-balanced, grammatically complete wholes. I do not deny that syntactical phrasing or completion of sense is regularly enclosed within metrical phrases like cola, hemistichs, and verses. I merely observe that there is a second type of syntactical, or rather sense phrasing: a type whose units do not seem to be restricted in size by the recurring metrical phrases.[1] The units of this second type are rather open-ended, as their termination is casually signaled by the start of the subsequent unit through asyndeton or a transitional constituent, regardless of metrical position.

This disregard for the structuring impulse of metrical repetition reflects the progressive movement that characterizes Homer's style: at first sight the nonconfigurationality* (Devine and Stephens 2000), so reminiscent of Chantraine's approach, of the merely paratactic structure seems to reflect the sense of Homeric narrative, but looks naïve when compared to the syntax of the complex periodic sentence of written language. But Homeric syntax is not naïve: its aim is not to progressively categorize the various units to form a larger-scale, well-ordered syntactical hierarchy—a hierarchy, though, whose sense often may only be understood from re-reading. On the contrary, Homeric syntax aims to retain the attention of the listening audience, without them having to rearrange previous chunks along the way. In Homer, grammar and syntax emerge from a progressive tendency (Bakker 2005). Listening to Homer, the audience must rely on their own ability to construct a mental picture of what is told from the order in which it is told. As Bakker assumes, prosodic phenomena characterize the units into which spoken language naturally divides. For Bakker, these prosodic phenomena are the recurrence and fixed shape of metrical phrases (§2.2). The resulting metrical-phrase chunks were labelled intonation units, but unfortunately meter does not provide us with clues for a prosodic phenomenon like intonation: intonation is related to the structure of language and, to an extent, syntactical phrasing, not to colometry. I have argued that the units of Homeric discourse, units of spoken language in performance, are characterized

---

[1]   This second type of phrasing inevitably leads to a higher level of grammatical organization than witnessed within the boundaries of the recurring metrical phrase. Descriptions of Homeric syntax like Chantraine's (1953) and Bakker's (1997b), who both stress the compositional principle of appositional alignment of words and metrical phrases, point in the right direction, but do not account for this emergence of larger scale grammatical organization.

as phonological phrases: discourse's progressive tendency is furthered by the way phonological phrasing presents the units of discourse in performance.

7.2.2 Compositional units teaming up

As much as the metrical cola resemble the spurts of unplanned speech, the Homeric epic cannot be described as "unplanned" speech. Certain stylized features, in addition to meter, turn the discourse of the *Iliad* and the *Odyssey* into special speech. Special speech is represented in the chunks (or spurts) of spoken language, but attains a different formal level, as it uses metrical formulas, not the units of intonation, as its chunks.[2] Grammar emerges from the combination of chunks into larger wholes.[3] Together, a series of chunks may result in a clause that meets certain grammatical requirements, for example, the use of a verb. The chunks themselves, especially those *without* a verbal form, are either *preparatory* or *additive* to preceding and subsequent clauses. As grammar emerges from the alignment of chunks, so the appositional alignment itself emerges from the movement of Homeric discourse. My approach shows that this effect of the movement of discourse is evidenced within the span of the phonological phrases.

The studies I have cited offer no way to accommodate, as the result of the appositional alignment, a level of syntactical organization that exceeds the grammatical governance of the syntactical unit that is the metrical phrase. A description of Homeric style as "adding" is in accordance with the concept of grammatical completeness at fixed and recurring metrical boundaries. Does such composition allow for, or does it lead to, a higher level of syntactical organization? An answer can be found in the discussion of the well-known phrasing of *Iliad* I 2 οὐλομένην ἥ, which is typically cited as an example of the frequently recurring model of an "emphatic runover-word cumulation developed in what follows."[4] Syntactically, the "development" seems to contribute to continuation in a way similar to the adjective. The development allegedly has, however, the advantage of a larger and more adaptable appearance; it is regularly labelled subordinate. It is not evident, at least in my view, that the syntactical qualification "subordinate" can be applied: transitional constituents, like the extra-clausal pronoun, merely keep discourse running; they do not organize clauses into complex sentences through hierarchy.

---

[2]   Bakker 1997b; 2005:38–55, especially 47.
[3]   Bakker 2005:21.
[4]   Kirk 1985:53; cf. Clark 1997:115.

7.2.3 Discourse between performative pauses

The units of performance, the phonological substance between performative pauses, do not necessarily coincide with grammatical clauses or parts thereof. Taking into account that major phonological phrases encompass several minor phrases, there is still no perfect overlap of phrases and syntactical units, with the exception of the minor-phrase extra-clausal constituent (§6.2.2.1). The major phonological phrase is not a sentence; the minor phrases it consists of may belong to a single syntactical unit, and they may (for example, in the case of extra-clausal constituents) signal continuation and more to come. As a unit in performance, the major phrase supports continuation of the discourse as movement.

7.2.4 Audible continuation

Support of continuation between performative pauses is found when a transitional constituent terminates in a secondary pause following an enclitic*, but was not introduced by an audible pause. The listener notices that the performer has started the heralding of a new syntactical unit, before having heard the completion of the preceding unit. In examples (174) and (175), the prosodic quality of δέ as a (possibly enclitic) postpositive* supports the heralding of a new (underlined) theme as well as the apparent completion of a clause preceding it:

> (174) ἀλλὰ πίθεσθ' <u>ἄμφω δὲ</u> νεωτέρω ἐστὸν ἐμεῖο
>
> > *Iliad* I 259
>
> But please listen to me: <u>both of you</u> are younger than I am

> (175) ὣς φάτο <u>Τυδείδης δὲ</u> διάνδιχα μερμήριξεν
>
> > *Iliad* VIII 167
>
> Thus he [Hector] spoke <u>and the son of Tydeus</u> considered the two
> alternatives

Support for continuation within coherent phonological substance is also found when constituents that appear to be syntactically added to what directly preceded them are phonologically characterized as more closely tied to what follows them. I will illustrate this claim with examples featuring a genitive case attributive element.[5] Example (176), the opening lines of the *Iliad*, features a

---

[5] As in *Iliad* I 7 Ἀτρείδης τε ἄναξ <u>ἀνδρῶν</u> καὶ δῖος Ἀχιλλεύς, "The son of Atreus, lord of men, and godlike Achilles," *Iliad* I 14 στέμματ' ἔχων ἐν χερσὶν <u>ἑκηβόλου Ἀπόλλωνος</u>, "Holding the ribbons in his hands of far shooting Apollo," *Iliad* I 34 βῆ δ' ἀκέων παρὰ θῖνα <u>πολυφλοίσβοιο θαλάσσης</u>,

genitive case attributive element Πηληιάδεω Ἀχιλῆος that is phonologically more closely tied to the participle in line 2 than to the noun it specifies: it is separated from μῆνιν by a primary pause following position 5, but together with οὐλομένην in a single phonological phrase that straddles the verse end:

(176) μῆνιν ἄειδε θεά Πηληιάδεω Ἀχιλῆος
          οὐλομένην

Iliad I 1–2a

Sing, goddess, of the wrath of Achilles, son of Peleus, so destructive

The genitive case word group specifies the wrath that is going to be the central theme, if not of the whole epic, then at least of its opening scene.[6] As long as more information is being added concerning the wrath of Achilles, the theme of the wrath is still being further and further elaborated.[7] In the words of Bakker (2005:5), the imperative ἄειδε "sing" is *extended* to the phonetic pause at position 5 by means of the vocative θεά "goddess." If attributive elements extend verbal forms, Πηληιάδεω Ἀχιλῆος does not further extend ἄειδε: it rather helps the participle οὐλομένην extend backwards, even crossing the verse end.[8] Forward extension is seen in examples (177–178), where the attributive element appears in a phonological phrase straddling the verse end; in both examples, primary pauses following the attributive element terminate the phonological phrase, whereas the preceding verse end is realized as phrase-internal:

(177)   ψυχὰς Ἄιδι προίαψεν
          ἡρώων

Iliad I 3–4a

The souls it sent to the house of Hades | of the heroes

"And he strode in silence along the shore of the roaring sea." Bakker 1997b lists these under the characteristics of adding style.

[6] That is how its meaning and location were interpreted by various authors of scholia (e.g., AT: ἤρξατο μὲν ἀπὸ μήνιδος ἐπείπερ αὕτη τοῖς πρακτικοῖς ὑπόθεσις γέγονεν); cf. Erbse 1969 *ad loc.*

[7] Kirk1985:52 "The wrath of which the goddess is to sing will persist throughout the entire poem and is to determine, in a sense, the fate of Troy; ... its immediate beginning is the subject of book 1 which follows."

[8] Backwards extension is also seen verse-internally: *Iliad* I 5 οἰωνοῖσί τε πᾶσι Διὸς δ᾽ ἐτελείετο βουλή, "And all the birds; the will of Zeus gradually became fulfilled." In *Iliad* I 9 Λητοῦς καὶ Διὸς υἱός ὃ γὰρ βασιλῆϊ χολωθείς, "The son of Leto and Zeus [it was]; for he, enraged with the king," genitive Λητοῦς καὶ Διὸς extends the missing verb backwards to the start of the line. This is a remarkable phrase, considering the further absence of elliptic answers to direct questions in Homer. When it comes to shape and position within the verse, the first hemistich of *Iliad* I 9 resembles Bakker's right-dislocation (Bakker 1990; 1997a:89–108; 1997b:293–297; 2005:12n33; cf. Devine and Stephens 2000:143–144). On the other hand, the answer, especially since it is in nominative case, resembles the parenthetic position of the nominative case, i.e. a parenthesis to τίς in *Iliad* I 8; cf. Bakker 1997a:198–200; 2005:13.

(178)   κατὰ πίονα μηρί᾿ ἔκηα
     ταύρων ἠδ᾿ αἰγῶν

Iliad I 40–41a

I have burnt fat thighs | of bulls and goats

Many genitive case attributive elements appear as the final word of a metrical colon or the verse. Their localization, especially with word end on the arsis* (type *Iliad* I 19 ἐκπέρσαι Πριάμοιο πόλιν ἐὺ δ᾿ οἴκαδ᾿ ἰκέσθαι, "To destroy Priam's citadel, and to return home safely"), contributes to the bridging of positions of frequent word end.[9] The result of the phonological organization of *Iliad* I 1–2a is a major phonological phrase that crosses the verse end: Πηληϊάδεω Ἀχιλῆος οὐλομένην. Syntactically, the adjective has a continuing effect similar to, for example, a relative clause. Phonologically, the participle οὐλομένην is more closely tied to the preceding verse-final words than the relative pronoun ἥ is to preceding οὐλομένην. The recurring phenomenon of the "run-over participle + relative pronoun"[10] (rhythmical result: muted verse end + audible pause following position 3[11]) is also an effective way to create rhythmical variety.

A third means to audibly support continuation, next to the prosodic shape of transitional constituents and attributive elements, is the shape of the grammatical apposition.[12] Its appearance regularly functions as an afterthought: the information in the apposition may well be meaningful in its own right, but the apposition itself does not prepare the audience for what is to follow.[13] In many similar instances, however, the apposition seems to be a break in a larger whole,

---

[9]   A remarkable case is the location under Wernicke's law of Ἀχαιῶν with word end at position 8.

[10] Clark 1997:35–40.

[11] Cf. the "clausal" division in Clark 1997:21–30.

[12] As opposed to the loosely applied term in the description of appositional style, cf. Chantraine 1953 II:12 "L'autonomie de chaque terme a pour conséquence que l'aède peut, à l'occasion, perdre de vue le mot auquel il se réfère, d'où des libertés dans les règles d'accord, d' où aussi l'intervention de groupes de mots qui ne se rattachent pas strictement à ce qui précède ou à ce qui suit," and the nonconfigurationality of Devine and Stephens 2000:142.

[13] Many of them, especially the epithets, have been described as compositional fillers, and thus as the building blocks of the oral compositional technique. Analysis as metrical filler might be functional: when the epithet is used to fill the remainder of a verse in order to facilitate the usage of an audible pause, for example, verse end, for discourse shift or sense-pause. The first examples the *Iliad* offers are *Iliad* I 16 Ἀτρείδα δὲ μάλιστα <u>δύω κοσμήτορε λαῶν</u>, "And especially the two sons of Atreus, <u>the two arrangers of the army</u>," *Iliad* I 21 ἀζόμενοι Διὸς υἱὸν <u>ἑκηβόλον Ἀπόλλωνα</u>, "With proper respect for the son of Zeus, <u>far shooting Apollo</u>," *Iliad* I 35–36 πολλὰ δ᾿ ἔπειτ᾿ ἀπάνευθε κιὼν ἠρᾶθ᾿ ὁ γεραιός ‖ Ἀπόλλωνι ἄνακτι <u>τὸν ἠύκομος τέκε Λητώ</u>, "And then, having arrived at a great distance, the old man spoke in prayer | to lord Apollo, <u>whom fair Leto had given birth to</u>." In personal communication, Joel Lidov points out that *Iliad* I 36 is very likely a case of "free indirect discourse." Change the dative to vocative, and *Iliad* I 36 is the start of a formal prayer, to be continued and turned into a complete prayer in line 37; cf. Lidov 1996:134 with references.

in something that still needs to be picked up *after* the apposition. Example (179) shows an (underlined) apposition that disrupts the developing grammatical clause. Phonetically, the disturbance in *Iliad* I 19 is minimal. *Iliad* I 19 does not contain a strong audible pause; the first primary pause is the word end following position 3 in *Iliad* I 20:

> (179) ὑμῖν μὲν θεοὶ δοῖεν <u>Ὀλύμπια δώματ' ἔχοντες</u>
>   ἐκπέρσαι Πριάμοιο πόλιν ἐὺ δ' οἴκαδ' ἱκέσθαι
>
>   *Iliad* I 19–20

> May the gods grant you, <u>the gods who have their houses on mount</u>
>   <u>Olympus</u>,
>   to destroy Priam's citadel, and to return home safely

The prosodic shape of other nominative case appositions makes them contribute to the syntactical movement in quite a different manner, as they are prosodically characterized as grammatical requirements of a clause, rather than true appositions (cf. §6.2.2.1).[14] Example (180) comes from the *Iliad*'s first lines. Within the phonological phrase, the patronymic Ἀτρεΐδης functions as the subject of *Iliad* I 11, extending the verbal form ἠτίμασεν "had dishonored" forwards to position 3 of *Iliad* I 12. Ἀτρεΐδης in *Iliad* I 12 may well have a pause preceding it, but the force of that pause is being muted compared to that of the word end following position 3:

> (180) οὕνεκα τὸν Χρύσην ἠτίμασεν ἀρητῆρα
>   <u>Ἀτρεΐδης</u> ὁ γὰρ ἦλθε θοὰς ἐπὶ νῆας Ἀχαιῶν
>
>   *Iliad* I 11–12

> As he had dishonored him, Chryses the priest,
>   <u>the son of Atreus</u>; for he had come to the fast ships of the Greeks

The phonological tie between the final words of *Iliad* I 11 and the run-over word Ἀτρεΐδης is stronger than that between Ἀτρεΐδης and the phonological

---

[14] In his analysis of Homeric syntax, Bakker (1997b:293–297) labels such nominative case appositions "additions." In his analysis, the verse end boundary renders such appositions *tail-constituents* to the preceding intonation unit (in his 1990 study, Bakker used the terminology *right-dislocation*). The main purpose of the nominative case apposition lies in the *staging* or *restaging* of persons or objects. The syntactical checklist-structure is characterized by a certain degree of looseness between consecutive intonation units. Such looseness occasionally requires nominative case appositions for the purpose of "disambiguation" (Bakker 2005:13; cf. 1997a:198–200; Bonifazi et al. 2016: "priming"). Ἀτρεΐδης in *Iliad* I 12 is identified as an apposition to the subject implicit in the verbal form ἠτίμασεν. The right-dislocation, or pragmatic function as tail-constituent, may soften the effect of the verse end enjambment, as may left-dislocation (cf. Bakker 1997b:303–303; 2005:53). In translation, *Iliad* I 11–12 may be something like "since he had dishonored him, | Chryses the priest, | <u>he, that is, the son of Atreus</u>; for he came to the fast ships of the Greeks."

phrase that follows it.[15] The rhythmical structure of the verse-end-straddling phonological phrase suggests that the grammatical tie between ἠτίμασεν and Ἀτρείδης is closer than merely that between *verb with implicit subject* and *apposition*. Involving other cases than merely nominative, example (181) shows that the distinction between "appositions" (term based on syntactical relations) and "true appositions" (based on phonetic word end) turns an emotional outburst of Achilles (as if he has lost his concentration) into a well-balanced speech. The (underlined) tail-constituents in 338, 339, and 341 are prosodically characterized as constituents of a phrase that develops over verse end:

(181)   τερπέσθω τὶ δὲ δεῖ πολεμιζέμεναι Τρώεσσιν
        Ἀργείους τὶ δὲ λαὸν ἀνήγαγεν ἐνθάδ' ἀγείρας
        Ἀτρείδης ἦ οὐχ Ἑλένης ἔνεκ' ἠυκόμοιο
        ἦ μοῦνοι φιλέουσ' ἀλόχους μερόπων ἀνθρώπων
        Ἀτρείδαι

Iliad IX 337–341

Let him take his pleasure! But why was there need to fight the Trojans for the Greeks? Why did gather the army and bring it here Atreus's son? Was it not because of fair Helen? Are we to understand that of mortal men the only ones who love their partners are Atreus's sons?

Finally, as a fourth means in which phrasing between performative pauses supports discourse continuation, there is the Homeric trend to localize discourse shift (to an imperative, a question, or direct speech) at the start of the hexameter. As the hexameter's start is not automatically a start from a pause in performance, discourse shift is not automatically signaled by means of a performative pause. The transition to direct speech is through semantic means. In §6.2.2.1, I suggested that the absence of a performative pause at the start or completion of direct speech supports the status of direct speech as an embedded predication, on a par with the object to the verbal form denoting *to say*.

---

[15] Along similar lines, the position of the predicative participle as an apposition should be valued. In highly paratactic syntax the participle does resemble the finite verb form: it can be extended forwards and backwards towards stronger phonetic disruptions. Predicative participles can be located either before the finite verb of a clause, or following it, like an "extra." From the observations on appositions above, I deduce that in order to be more or less a finite verb form, the participle has to appear in nominative case, it has to precede the true finite verb of the clause, and the phrasing of its prosodic domain must make audible that the participle-centered phonological phrase is not merely preparatory to the subsequent clause.

7.2.5 Expectations between pauses

The phonological phrase may easily straddle the verse end, or the third-foot word juncture. With it, Homeric discourse may extend over these metrical boundaries with equal ease: the units of discourse are rather open-ended, regularly at the expense of compositional pauses as meaningful grammatical or syntactical boundaries. The expectations of an audience, relying on its ears, depend on what is audible. The grammatical completeness of the sentence or clause does not have to be audibly suggested or frustrated by the verse end. I argue that the thought whose coherence is evident from grammatical organization is prosodically characterized as (part of) a phonological phrase. The phonological phrase is hence the domain for the grammatical clause.[16] The relatively "variable clause-length" is an original feature of Homeric poetry. Homeric clausal grammar is the grammar of the phonological phrase, not of the metrical phrase. This means that there is quite a distance between the expectation and the grammatical need for what follows compositional boundaries, including the verse end.

Later hexametric Greek poetry shows that the equation of metrical and sense-phrase gradually developed into a poetic norm. Latin hexametric poetry accepted the norm, but realized that there were exceptions. In Latin hexametric poetry, the spondaic verse-final foot is often deliberately created (Hardie 1920:5). As in later Greek poetry, affective prosody could be exploited to use enjambment for the purpose of emphasis and raising of expectations. In Latin prosody, the Homeric subordination* of word-final syllables (§5.1.4) could not be imitated by means of a verse-final metrical foot, as the nonresolvability of the foot's thesis is not linked to syllable structure but to dynamic accent in Latin; there is no possibility for realization of the verse-final syllable as rhythmically indeterminate (Brooks 2007:50–52 points at the coincidence of ictus and dynamic accent in especially the final feet of classical Latin hexameter). Furthermore, verse-final syllable CVC with short vocalic nucleus* in Latin is not metrically heavy.[17] Straddling the hexameter's verse end with a phonological phrase in Latin requires resyllabification: in other words, elision at the end of the hypermetric verse.[18]

---

[16] Cf. Clayman 1981.
[17] Hardie 1920:5.
[18] E.g., Vergil *Aeneid* I 46–47: *Iovisque* || *et soror et coniunx*.

7.3   Rhythm Without Beat[19]

Homeric rhythm is a regularization of the utterance in performance. It is the perceptibly regular recurrence of auditory stimuli, but not the rhythmical beat according to the metronome. Metrical surface structure suggests that there were quite a few means to perceptibly categorize syllables into the bipartition *more prominent* and *less prominent*, but there is no trace in phonology of the need or the wish to reduce syllable sonority to the production of sounds in syllables of absolute duration. Meter reflects the underlying rhythmics; it does not dictate them. The reconstruction of phonetics brings to light that the performance of the *Iliad* and *Odyssey* resembles natural speech and clause formation rather than a dull and awkwardly phrased recitation of single-verse sentences.

The *Iliad* and the *Odyssey* seem, however, to represent a transitional stage in the development of stichic hexametric poetry, as the poems feature both the whole-line sentence and the less restrictive type of clause formation. An interesting parallel for the developments in Homer can be found in hexametric inscriptions and the punctuation used in these inscriptions. Some of these inscriptions[20] are "run-over"-type hexameters. An example like (182) looks like a dactylic line, but not like a hexameter:

(182)   [Γ]λαυκατ[ίαι τόδε] μνᾶμα Κάλας [στῆσ' Ἀν]θίδα υἰὸς ⟩ παι[δί]

IG V 1.720

To Glaucatias, his son, Calas, son of Anthidas, set up this monument

It rather looks like a *hepta*meter. What makes it appear as a hexameter is the punctuation following υἱὸς. To Friedländer, the punctuation suggested that "παι[δί] seems to fall outside the verse." Comparison with other metrical inscriptions suggests that his conclusion may have been precipitate.

7.3.1 Breaking the measure

With a few examples from the corpus of metrical inscriptions, I will illustrate that the less restrictive clause formation stood in a tradition outside the works of Homer. The use of punctuation is a helpful means to draw parallels between what happens in these inscriptions and what we find in the *Iliad* and the *Odyssey*. In metrical inscriptions, punctuation is based on a variety of principles.[21] Sometimes punctuation is found at the end of the metrical period: in the case of *IG* V 1.720, cited above, that would suggest a hexameter. Then again,

---

[19]   The title of Blankenborg 2018.
[20]   Examples and their translation from Friedländer 1948.
[21]   Devine and Stephens 1994:400–401.

punctuation is sometimes linguistically based. For *IG* V 1.720 it is hard to decide which explanation is to be preferred. What is not so hard is to see that the grammatical clause extends beyond the hexameter and is phonologically phrased by means of word end at position 7 and 12: the metrical phrase στῆσ' Ἀνθίδα υἱὸς is followed by the run-over* παιδί. Whatever punctuation marks, it is *not* an audible pause. Examples (183–185) feature visible verse end:

(183) [ϙυλοίδας μ']ἀνέθηκε Ποτειδάϝωνι ϝάνακτι : αὐτοπόεια

IG IV 222

... dedicated me to Lord Poseidon | as the work of his own hands

(184) ['Ι]εροϕῶν μ' [ἀνέ]θη[κε Διὸς γλαυ]ρώπιδι [ϙ]ούρηι : [π]ολ[ι] ούχω[ι δ]εκ[ά]τη[ν]

IG I² 418

... dedicated me to the gleaming-eyed daughter of Zeus, | mainstay of the city, as a tithe

(185) Δειναγόρης μ' ἀνέθηκεν ἑκηβόλωι Ἀπόλλωνι : δεκάτην

IG XII 5.42

Deinagoras dedicated me to Far-Darter Apollo | as a tithe

The inscriptions vary "among hexameter, prose, and hybrid forms."[22] In all examples cited the verse end may function as a linguistically defensible minor phrase boundary. Such a minor phrase boundary, however, is impossible in example (186):

(186) [Δημοχάρη]ς ἀνέθηκε{ν} [Διὸς κρατερ]όϕρονι παιδί : ἀπαρχήν

IG I² 689

... dedicated to the mighty-willed Child of Zeus | the first-fruits

This inscription contains a formula familiar from prose dedications. Here, the run-over word ἀπαρχήν belongs to the predicate frame of ἀνέθηκε. There is no reason to assume affective prosody due to verse-end enjambment in this inscription. Compare example (187), an inscription on the Chest of Cypselus (cited by Pausanias 5.19.3): as in (186), syntactical development continues unhindered over the compositional pause that is indicated through punctuation (Pausanias comments on the shape of the verse: "a hexameter with a word added"):

---

[22] Friedländer 1948:22.

(187)   Τυνδαρίδα Ἑλέναν φέρετον Αἴθραν δ' ἑλκε(ῖ)τον : Ἀθάναθεν

The sons of Tyndareus carry Helen and drag Aethra | away from
  Athens

In example (188) grammatical clauses are formed as parts of hexametric lines.
The first line is itself not a hexameter: Γνάθωνος τόδε σημα is the start of a
hexameter, and θέτο δ' αὐτὸν ἀδελφὴ the completion, but in between there is
an iamb missing. The metrical phrase between positions 5½ and 7 is not there:

(188)   Γνάθωνος τόδε σημα· θέτο δ' αὐτὸν ἀδελφὴ : ἠλίθιον
       νοσηλεύσασα

                                                                    IG I² 975

This is the tomb of Gnatho; his sister buried him | after nursing him
  in mental disease

In Homer, this specific metrical phrase may be occupied by an extra-clausal
constituent.[23] If a Homeric example like (189) is compared with *IG* I² 975, the
inscription seems to disregard the need for maintaining podic structure[24] within
the metrical period:

(189)   σχέτλιός ἐσσι γεραιέ (5½) <u>σὺ μὲν</u> (7) πόνου οὔ ποτε λήγεις

                                                                    Iliad X 164

You are bold, old man, <u>you</u>, from labor you never refrain

The Homeric example, by contrast, shows the way in which maintaining podic
structure can be used to single out the phonetic demarcation between the
extra-clausal constituent and the subsequent grammatical clause (§7.2). In
Homer, localization of extra-clausals proves to be an antidote to stichic metrical
repetition. In the inscription, such appliance of an antidote is not required. The
metrical period is disregarded: θέτο δ' αὐτὸν ἀδελφὴ fills the metrical phrase
between positions 7 and 12, and ἠλίθιον νοσηλεύσασα cannot be analyzed as a
dactylic metarrhythmisis*.[25] The combination of prose-elements and dactylic
verse-patterns appears to be old and persistent. Compare the "enjambed" (and
underlined) dactylic (or anapaestic?) *clausula* to an otherwise prose inscription
in example (190):

---

[23] Two times in the sample of the *Iliad* (§5.4), four times in the *Odyssey*.
[24] Lidov (1989:83) warns against the assumption of pre-existence of the cola in the I-E tradition.
      I do not assume any such pre-existence in the comparison between Homer and verse inscriptions.
[25] Friedländer 1948:148 describes the inscription as "intermediate between verse and prose."

(190) Ἀντίδο[τός μ' ἐποίησεν αὐτὸ]ς καὶ παῖδες Πασιδίϟωι · τὸ δὲ
σᾶμ' Εὔνο[ος] ἔστασε καλὸν <u>κεχαρισμένον</u> : <u>ἔργον</u>

IG XII 178

Antidotus and his sons [made me] for Pasidicus, | Eunomus erected
the tomb, a fair <u>and acceptable</u> | <u>work</u>

The freedom in clause-formation in Homer disregards the metrical boundary
that is the verse end in a way comparable to the verse inscriptions. This slightly
resembles prose rhythm in that the phrase structure is more important than the
metrical structure in the experience of the verse. It is unwise, as I have shown,
to put hexametric meter on a par with hexametric phonological phrasing.
The former is clearly visible. The well-known metrical bridges* all show the
importance of retaining the podic structure of the hexameter. Phonological
phrasing, however, is not the product of the metrical hexameter. Not every
verse contains two phonetically demarcated hemistichs, or four cola, nor is
the verse automatically a phonological major phrase. Coherent phonological
phrasing is phonologically defined, regardless of metrical phrasing. If the
metrical phrasing corresponds with the phonological phrasing, the metrical
cola that characterize poetry appear as phonological phrases. If the two do
not correspond, meter has to give way to phonology. The result is a temporary
"breaking the measure," a dimming of meter (cf. §5.1.4); a step towards dactylic
rhythm without a beat, as even metrical repetitiveness is subordinated in favor
of a more prosaic movement. Or should we say, considering the increasing
rigidity in later Greek hexametric composition, that what we see in Homer is
actually beatless rhythm's last trace?

7.3.2 Rhythm from pause to pause

The prosodic pattern built by primary and secondary pauses reveals a level
of coincidence of hierarchical phonological and syntactical phrases. Metrical
phrasing, however, remains normative in existing studies: especially verse-end
enjambment and its poetic effectiveness are sought after. Section 5.4 above visualizes the coincidence of hierarchical phonological and syntactical phrases, the
patchwork of grammatical clauses and transitional constituents as the result of
the mapping of phonetic disruption. In addition to the observations presented
schematically in §5.4, the sample in §7.4 below (encompassing the same verses)
highlights what happens at, and between, pauses: embedded discourse shift and
prosodically characterized enjambment. The latter sample also shows where
printed punctuation is *not* supported by rests in performance.

As a lead-in to the sample presented in §7.4, I offer a finer-grained analysis of part of this sample, *Odyssey* i 88–92, as an example both of the results to

be expected from phonetic analysis, and of the confusion that may arise from fitting well-established formulas into a narrative that is presented between performative pauses. Example (191) shows the text of *Odyssey* i 88–92 without printed punctuation:

(191) αὐτὰρ ἐγὼν Ἰθάκην ἐσελεύσομαι ὄφρα οἱ υἱὸν
       μᾶλλον ἐποτρύνω καί οἱ μένος ἐν φρεσὶ θείω
       εἰς ἀγορὴν καλέσαντα κάρη κομόωντας Ἀχαιοὺς
       πᾶσι μνηστήρεσσιν ἀπειπέμεν οἵ τέ οἱ αἰεὶ
       μῆλ᾽ ἀδινὰ σφάζουσι καὶ εἰλίποδας ἕλικας βοῦς

Odyssey i 88–92

Now I shall go to Ithaca, that to his son | I may give more encouragement and put strength in the heart for him | to call to the place of assembly the long-haired Greeks | and to give notice to all suitors, who for him always | butcher the thick-thronging sheep and shambling, screw-horned cows

The whole-line utterance is not a persistent compositional device in these lines. Example (192) shows that rhetorical punctuation (Stanford 1950) already suggests as much:

(192) αὐτὰρ ἐγὼν Ἰθάκην ἐσελεύσομαι, ὄφρα οἱ υἱὸν
       μᾶλλον ἐποτρύνω, καί οἱ μένος ἐν φρεσὶ θείω,
       εἰς ἀγορὴν καλέσαντα κάρη κομόωντας Ἀχαιοὺς
       πᾶσι μνηστήρεσσιν ἀπειπέμεν, οἵ τέ οἱ αἰεὶ
       μῆλ᾽ ἀδινὰ σφάζουσι καὶ εἰλίποδας ἕλικας βοῦς.

Odyssey i 88–92

Are all the printed commas more or less the same in the way the word end they mark is phonetically realized? Does printed punctuation indicate the primary or the secondary pause? Or no pause at all? Is there no third-foot pause in 88, 89, 91, and 92? Is there no verse-internal pause at all in 90? Or does the inevitability of an audible third-foot pause create some sort of meaningful verse-internal enjambment in 90? And what about verse-end enjambment? The verse end of 89 may coincide with the transition from one embedded predication to another. The verse end of 88 and 91 falls somewhere halfway between the constituents of the developing grammatical clause. Why would the clause οἱ υἱὸν μᾶλλον ἐποτρύνω signal the metrical boundary following υἱὸν? Are we supposed to forgive Homer for the fact that καλέσαντα is attracted into the construction of accusative and infinitive (in line 90) instead of to οἱ (in line 89), precisely because "enjambment" at verse end in line 89 is more than a theoretical acknowledgement and a true break that elicits case-disagreement? Is the participle phrase εἰς ἀγορὴν καλέσαντα κάρη κομόωντας Ἀχαιοὺς expanded into a whole line to grant verse-initial position to πᾶσι μνηστήρεσσιν so that any emphatic position for the clause's verb ἀπειπέμεν would be further strengthened by the third-foot caesura? What is the use of identifiable "enjambment" here? This last question can be extended to other boundaries of metrical phrases, such as every third-foot caesura, made visible in example (193):

(193)   αὐτὰρ ἐγὼν Ἰθάκην / ἐσελεύσομαι, ὄφρα οἱ υἱὸν ‖
        μᾶλλον ἐποτρύνω,/ καί οἱ μένος ἐν φρεσὶ θείω, ‖
        εἰς ἀγορὴν καλέσαντα / κάρη κομόωντας Ἀχαιοὺς ‖
        πᾶσι μνηστήρεσσιν / ἀπειπέμεν, οἵ τέ οἱ αἰεὶ ‖
        μῆλ' ἀδινὰ σφάζουσι / καὶ εἰλίποδας ἕλικας βοῦς. ‖

Odyssey i 88–92

The answer to the question does not necessarily have to be found in further sifting of the rhetorical punctuation;[26] rather, we have to abandon the alleged paratactic juxtaposition of metrical phrases. After all, example (194) shows that rhetorical punctuation can be visualized with similar ease in prose:

(194)
αὐτὰρ ἐγὼν Ἰθάκην ἐσελεύσομαι, ὄφρα οἱ υἱὸν μᾶλλον ἐποτρύνω, καί οἱ μένος ἐν φρεσὶ θείω, εἰς ἀγορὴν καλέσαντα κάρη κομόωντας Ἀχαιοὺς πᾶσι μνηστήρεσσιν ἀπειπέμεν, οἵ τέ οἱ αἰεὶ μῆλ' ἀδινὰ σφάζουσι καὶ εἰλίποδας ἕλικας βοῦς.

Odyssey i 88–92

Together with metrical demarcation, rhetorical punctuation can be visualized when the text is divided into the chunks of spoken language. Example (195) presents *Odyssey* i 88–92 divided into Bakker's intonation units (a-l), as discussed in Chapter 2:

(195)
a   αὐτὰρ ἐγὼν Ἰθάκην
b   ἐσελεύσομαι,
c   ὄφρα οἱ υἱὸν
d   μᾶλλον ἐποτρύνω,
e   καί οἱ μένος ἐν φρεσὶ θείω,
f   εἰς ἀγορὴν καλέσαντα
g   κάρη κομόωντας Ἀχαιοὺς
h   πᾶσι μνηστήρεσσιν

---

[26] As Daitz 1991 suggests, or even in banning all printed punctuation from our texts.

i   ἀπειπέμεν,
j   οἵ τέ οἱ αἰεὶ
k   μῆλ' ἀδινὰ σφάζουσι
l   καὶ εἰλίποδας ἕλικας βοῦς.

Odyssey i 88–92

The syntactical structure is clearly built *despite* the metrical phrasing. Its resemblance to spoken discourse becomes visible not in metrical, but in phonological phrasing. Applying the criteria for primary and secondary phonetic word end brings out the phonological phrasing. I will start by marking all the minor phonological phrases in example (196), regardless of the strength of the phonetic disruption that starts or ends the phrase. As pointed out, phonetic disruption stems from phonetic-word end in a sandhi-free syllable:

(196)

i.   αὐτὰρ ἐγὼν Ἰθάκην ἐσελεύσομαι, ὄφρα οἱ υἱὸν μᾶλλον
      ἐποτρύνω,
ii.   καί οἱ μένος ἐν φρεσὶ θείω,
iii. εἰς ἀγορὴν
iv.   καλέσαντα κάρη
v.   κομόωντας Ἀχαιοὺς
vi.   πᾶσι μνηστήρεσσιν ἀπειπέμεν, οἵ τέ
vii. οἱ αἰεὶ μῆλ' ἀδινὰ σφάζουσι καὶ εἰλίποδας ἕλικας βοῦς.

Odyssey i 88–92

A number of issues call for extra attention. The first minor phrase is very long and includes what seems to be a complete subordinate clause that straddles verse end. The second minor phrase, καί οἱ μένος ἐν φρεσὶ θείω, is a complete and completed grammatical clause. The third, εἰς ἀγορὴν, appears to be isolated in the way one would expect an additive chunk to be isolated, just like the two phrases that follow. In the sixth minor phrase, the transitional constituent providing continuation is included. The seventh minor phrase is long again and encompasses a grammatical clause that straddles verse end. It ends in a single monosyllabic word, βοῦς, that is thrown into relief by the phonetic realization.[27] Whereas phonetic word end in a heavy syllable always results in an anapaestic word end, phrasal metarrhythmisis* to catalectic anapaests is twice in order here (compare the analysis in §5.4): at position 12 in *Odyssey* i 90 Ἀχαιοὺς ([AT] (A)[T]), and at position 12 in *Odyssey* i 92 βοῦς ((A)[T]). Applying the two different pauses to the minor phrases leads to the following visualization of the way they

---

27 Stanford (1950:218) comments: "perhaps H. deliberately intended to suggest the heavy movement of the cattle with this heavy monosyllabic ending."

217

phonetically start and end: in example (197) the primary pause is indicated as °, the secondary pause as ˙:

(197)
1.   ˙αὐτὰρ ἐγὼν Ἰθάκην ἐσελεύσομαι, ὄφρα οἱ υἱὸν μᾶλλον
       ἐποτρύνω,°
2.   °καί οἱ μένος ἐν φρεσὶ θείω,˙
3.   ˙εἰς ἀγορὴν°
4.   °καλέσαντα κάρη°
5.   °κομόωντας Ἀχαιοὺς°
°6.   πᾶσι μνηστήρεσσιν ἀπειπέμεν, οἵ τέ˙
˙7.   οἱ αἰεὶ μῆλ᾽ ἁδινὰ σφάζουσι καὶ εἰλίποδας ἕλικας βοῦς.°

Odyssey i 88–92

The primary pauses are the start and end of major phonological phrases. At normal rates of speech, minor phrases will be reorganized into subphrases of the major phrase. This leads to five major phrases in example (198):

(198)
1.   ˙αὐτὰρ ἐγὼν Ἰθάκην ἐσελεύσομαι, ὄφρα οἱ υἱὸν μᾶλλον
       ἐποτρύνω,°
2.   °καί οἱ μένος ἐν φρεσὶ θείω,˙εἰς ἀγορὴν°
3.   °καλέσαντα κάρη°
4.   °κομόωντας Ἀχαιοὺς°
5.   °πᾶσι μνηστήρεσσιν ἀπειπέμεν, οἵ τέ˙οἱ αἰεὶ μῆλ᾽ ἁδινὰ σφάζουσι
       καὶ εἰλίποδας ἕλικας βοῦς.°

Odyssey i 88–92

It is noteworthy that some grammatical clauses are tied together in, and by, a phonological phrase. Then again, if primary pause disrupting a grammatical clause is an indicator for (verse-internal and prosodically characterized) enjambment, there is a remarkable example of enjambment in a much-used formulaic expressions (κάρη κομόωντας Ἀχαιοὺς). Earlier,[28] I pointed out that phonological phrasing tends to lead to remarkable phonetic disruption in and around well-established formulas, particularly noun-epithet combinations. Especially in these combinations, I am inclined to lessen the disruptions caused by the primary pause somewhat, as the usefulness of the formula may have been felt as more important than the slightly awkward phonetics of the word group in performance.

---

[28] When dealing with the observance of Wernicke's Law in formulaic expressions in §5.1.3.

Rhetorical punctuation suggests the boundaries of smaller scale syntactical units that cannot be made audible as units. Printed punctuation, however, does not always indicate the start and completion of smaller units that *can* be made audible. The smaller scale units contribute to audible phrase variation: they are not characterized metrically, but phonologically. They do not reflect the coherence of the metrical unit, but organize metrical word-types along the lines of a different type of coherence. At times this coherence, determined by prosody, evidences the demarcation of larger scale units in Homer as visualized by means of rhetorical punctuation. Then again, *Odyssey* i 88–92 shows that we must remain careful not to attribute too much importance to larger scale demarcation in Homer.[29] Any larger scale demarcation that I have made identifiable is no more than the identification of major phonological phrases comprised of one or more minor phrases. Larger scale is not a division into sentences: it is a division into perceptible units of variable size and internal shape. The importance of meter suffers most from phonological phrasing. Example (199), the final rendering of *Odyssey* i 88–92, shows that a strict rhetorical colometry, including the abundant (verse-internal) enjambment, defies not only the verse end: there are other metrical boundaries that are observed or straddled, depending on syntactical analysis. Pure syntactical chunking (κατὰ διαστολάς) is confined between phonological boundaries, but seems to make the repetitive pattern of Homeric metrical phrasing less relevant:

(199)   αὐτὰρ ἐγὼν Ἰθάκην ἐσελεύσομαι, ὄφρα οἱ υἱὸν
          μᾶλλον ἐποτρύνω, καί οἱ μένος ἐν φρεσὶ θείω,
          εἰς ἀγορὴν ... καλέσαντα κάρη ... κομόωντας Ἀχαιοὺς
          πᾶσι μνηστήρεσσιν ἀπειπέμεν, οἵ τέ οἱ αἰεὶ
          μῆλ' ἀδινὰ σφάζουσι καὶ εἰλίποδας ἕλικας βοῦς.

7.4 *Iliad* I 1–100, *Odyssey* i 1–100 between Performative Pauses

In §7.4, I present the same sample of verses as in §5.4, this time without the markings that indicate the primary and secondary phonetic word end. Both word ends reappear in this sample, but are marked so as to represent the phonetic disruption they cause. Following a primary pause, the phonological phrase

---

[29] Bakker 1997b explains how the syntax of Homeric discourse is a movement due to continuation and addition. In antiquity, scholars describe the style of the Homeric narrative as "strung style" (Aristotle: λέξις εἰρομένη; Dionysius of Halicarnassus: λόγος εἰρόμενος), while pointing at the ease with which it keeps the narrative continuing.

begins as a new paragraph. Word end on the thesis in word-final CV̆C is not considered as prepausal (§3.2.3); on the arsis, word-final CV̆C is treated as subordinate (§5.1.4). When secondary phonetic word end is likely to be realized as an audible pause demarcating the minor phrase in performance at normal rates of speech, it is indicated as spacing (followed by ᵀ or ᴬ; see below) in the continuing line; this is the case when secondary word end is in a (lengthened) enclitic. It requires artificially slow rates of speech to make any other secondary word end audible as a pause, as the coherence within the phonological substance is too tight—especially when the word-final short syllable is accented. Such nonprepausal secondary word end will be marked with a comma.

Prepausal syllables undergo additional, phonetic lengthening. At the boundaries of the major phrase, this lengthening may be substantial. Within the major phrase, only limited lengthening is allowed: word end within the major phrase is sensitive to the resumption of rhythm together with resumption of phonation after the pause. Following disruptive pause within the major phrase, resumption of phonation is marked as ᵀ when the subsequent rhythm is descending* due to starting on the thesis structural element, and as ᴬ when it starts on the arsis (and is thus rising*). Rhythmical restart after a primary pause is rising following metarrhythmisis on the level of the rhythmical word, and descending following phrasal metarrhythmisis.

The sample in §7.4 highlights what happens at, and between pauses: embedded discourse shift and prosodically characterized enjambment. To that end I have made visible the contours of the grammatical clause and of the transitional constituents, both within the clause and extra-clausal. The result is a presentation of 200 lines of Homeric poetry as phrases in performance.

Legend to the analysis

[ ]	Domain of the grammatical clause (participles *not* always treated as finite verbs, see 7.2n259)
[[ ]]	Syntactically embedded predication (*Iliad* I 96; *Odyssey* i 11)
« »	Domain of direct speech
+	Major-phrase boundary breaching the grammatical clause (prosodically characterized enjambment)
<u>underlined</u>	Transitional constituent, both within the clause and extra-clausal
(1)	Verse number

Iliad I 1–100

(1) [Μῆνιν ἄειδε , <u>θεά</u>

Πηληϊάδεω Ἀχιλῆος , (2) οὐλομένην]

[ἣ μυρί' Ἀχαιοῖς ἄλγε' ἔθηκεν] , (3) [<u>πολλὰς δ'</u> ἰφθίμους +

ψυχὰς Ἄϊδι προΐαψεν, (4) ἡρώων] , <u>αὐτοὺς δὲ</u> ᴬ [ἑλώρια, τεῦχε,

κύνεσσιν , (5) οἰωνοῖσί τε

ᴬ πᾶσι] , [<u>Διὸς δ'</u> ἐτελείετο , βουλή] , (6) <u>ἐξ οὗ δὴ</u>

[τὰ πρῶτα , διαστήτην] [ἐρίσαντε , (7) Ἀτρεΐδης τε ᴬ <u>ἄναξ ἀνδρῶν</u>

<u>καὶ δῖος Ἀχιλλεύς.</u>]

(8) [τίς τάρ σφωε , θεῶν ἔριδι ξυνέηκε , μάχεσθαι]

(9) <u>Λητοῦς καὶ Διὸς υἱός</u> (.) <u>ὃ γὰρ</u> ᴬ [βασιλῆϊ , χολωθείς]

(10) [νοῦσον ἀνὰ στρατὸν ὦρσε , κακήν]

[ὀλέκοντο δὲ ᵀ <u>λαοί</u> , (11) <u>οὕνεκα</u> [τὸν Χρύσην ἠτίμασεν

ἀρητῆρα , (12) <u>Ἀτρεΐδης</u>]

<u>ὃ γὰρ</u> ᵀ [ἦλθε , θοὰς ἐπὶ νῆας Ἀχαιῶν +

(13) λυσόμενός τε ᴬ θύγατρα , φέρων τ' ἀπερείσι'

ἄποινα, (14) στέμματ' ἔχων ἐν χερσὶν ἑκηβόλου

Ἀπόλλωνος , (15) χρυσέῳ ἀνὰ σκήπτρῳ]

<u>καὶ</u> [λίσσετο , πάντας Ἀχαιούς] (16) Ἀτρεΐδα δὲ ᴬ <u>μάλιστα , δύω</u>

<u>κοσμήτορε , λαῶν</u>

(17) «<u>Ἀτρεῖδαι τε</u> ᴬ <u>καὶ ἄλλοι ἐϋκνήμιδες Ἀχαιοί</u> , (18) <u>ὑμῖν μὲν</u> ᴬ

[θεοὶ , δοῖεν Ὀλύμπια , δώματ' ἔχοντες , (19) ἐκπέρσαι +

Πριάμοιο , πόλιν]

[<u>εὖ δ'</u> οἴκαδ' ἱκέσθαι] , (20) [<u>παῖδα δ'</u> ἐμοὶ +

λύσαιτε , φίλην]

[<u>τὰ δ'</u> ἄποινα , δέχεσθαι , (21) ἀζόμενοι

Διὸς υἱὸν <u>ἑκηβόλον Ἀπόλλωνα»</u>] , (22) <u>ἔνθ' ἄλλοι μὲν</u> ᵀ [πάντες

ἐπευφήμησαν Ἀχαιοί , (23) αἰδεῖσθαί θ' ἱερῆα , <u>καὶ</u> ἀγλαὰ ,

δέχθαι ἄποινα] , (24) [<u>ἀλλ'</u> οὐκ Ἀτρεΐδη Ἀγαμέμνονι ,

ἥνδανε , θυμῷ] , (25) <u>ἀλλὰ</u> [κακῶς ἀφίει]

[κρατερὸν δ' ἐπὶ μῦθον ἔτελλεν] , (26) [«μή σε <u>γέρον</u> κοίλησιν ἐγὼ

+

παρὰ νηυσὶ , κιχείω , (27) ἢ νῦν δηθύνοντ' ἠ' ὕστερον αὖτις

ἰόντα] , (28) <u>μή νύ τοι</u> [οὐ χραίσμη +

σκῆπτρον καὶ στέμμα , θεοῖο] , (29) [<u>τὴν δ'</u> ἐγὼ οὐ λύσω]

[<u>πρίν μιν</u> ᵀ καὶ γῆρας ἔπεισιν , (30) ἡμετέρῳ ἐνὶ οἴκῳ ἐν Ἄργεϊ ,

τηλόθι πάτρης (31) ἱστὸν ἐποιχομένην]

<u>καὶ</u> [ἐμὸν λέχος ἀντιόωσαν] , (32) [<u>ἀλλ'</u> ἴθι] , [<u>μή μ'</u> ἐρέθιζε] ,

[<u>σαώτερος ὥς</u> κε νέηαι»] , (33) [<u>ὣς ἔφατ'</u>] [<u>ἔδδεισεν δ'</u> ὁ

γέρων]

<u>καὶ</u> [ἐπείθετο , μύθῳ]

(34) [<u>βῆ δ’</u> ἀκέων +

παρὰ θῖνα , πολυφλοίσβοιο , θαλάσσης]

(35) [<u>πολλὰ δ’ ἔπειτ’</u> ἀπάνευθε κιὼν ἠρᾶθ’ ὁ
       γεραιός , (36) Ἀπόλλωνι , ἄνακτι] , [τὸν ἤϋκομος τέκε ,
       Λητώ]

(37) [«κλῦθί μοι] , <u>Ἀργυρότοξ’</u> [ὃς Χρύσην
       ἀμφιβέβηκας , (38) Κίλλάν τε ᴬ ζαθέην]

[Τενέδοιό τε ᵀ ἶφι , ἀνάσσεις]

(39) <u>Σμινθεῦ</u> , <u>εἴ ποτέ τοι</u>

[χαρίεντ’ ἐπὶ νηὸν ἔρεψα] , (40) <u>ἠ’ εἰ δή ποτέ τοι</u>

[κατὰ πίονα , μηρί’ ἔκηα , (41) ταύρων ἠδ’ αἰγῶν,]

[τόδε μοι +

κρήηνον ἐέλδωρ]

(42) [τείσειαν Δαναοὶ

ἐμὰ δάκρυα , σοῖσι βέλεσσιν»] , (43) [ὣς ἔφατ’ εὐχόμενος] [<u>τοῦ δ’</u>
       ἔκλυε , Φοῖβος Ἀπόλλων]

(44) [<u>βῆ δὲ</u> ᴬ κατ’ Οὐλύμποιο , καρήνων

χωόμενος κῆρ

(45) τόξ’ ὤμοισιν ἔχων ἀμφηρεφέα τε ᴬ
       φαρέτρην·] (46) [<u>ἔκλαγξαν δ’ ἄρ’</u> ὀϊστοὶ ἐπ’ ὤμων

χωομένοιο , (47) αὐτοῦ κινηθέντος] [<u>ὃ δ’</u> ἤϊε , νυκτὶ , ἐοικώς]
       , (48) [ἕζετ’ ἔπειτ’ ἀπάνευθε νεῶν]

[<u>μετὰ δ’</u> ἰὸν ἕηκε] , (49) <u>δεινὴ δὲ</u> ᴬ [κλαγγὴ

γένετ’ ἀργυρέοιο , βιοῖο] , (50) <u>οὐρῆας μὲν</u> ᵀ πρῶτον ἐπῴχετο , καὶ
       κύνας ἀργούς] (51) <u>αὐτὰρ ἔπειτ’</u> [αὐτοῖσι , βέλος

ἐχεπευκὲς ἐφιείς

(52) βάλλ’] <u>αἰεὶ δὲ</u> ᴬ [πυραὶ +

νεκύων +

καίοντο , θαμειαί] , (53) <u>ἐννῆμαρ μὲν</u> ᴬ [ἀνὰ στρατὸν ᾤχετο , κῆλα
       , θεοῖο] , (54) [<u>τῇ δεκάτῃ δ’</u> ἀγορήνδε , καλέσσατο , <u>λαὸν</u>
       <u>Ἀχιλλεύς</u>]

(55) <u>τῷ γὰρ</u> ᴬ [ἐπὶ φρεσὶ , θῆκε , θεὰ]

<u>λευκώλενος Ἥρη</u> , (56) [<u>κήδετο γὰρ</u> ᴬ Δαναῶν]

<u>ὅτι ῥα</u> ᴬ [θνήσκοντας ὁρᾶτο] , (57) οἳ δ’ ἐπεὶ οὖν [ἤγερθεν]
       [ὁμηγερέες τ’ ἐγένοντο] , (58) [<u>τοῖσι δ’</u> ἀνιστάμενος]
       [μετέφη

<u>πόδας ὠκὺς Ἀχιλλεύς</u>] (59) «<u>Ἀτρεΐδη</u>

[νῦν ἄμμε , πάλιν πλαγχθέντας ὀΐω , (60) ἂψ ἀπονοστήσειν] <u>εἴ κεν</u>
       [θάνατόν γε ᴬ φύγοιμεν] , (61) <u>εἰ δὴ</u> ᴬ [ὁμοῦ

πόλεμός τε ^Α δαμᾷ]

καὶ [λοιμὸς Ἀχαιούς]   (62)   ἀλλ’ ἄγε δή

[τινα μάντιν ἐρείομεν ἢ’ ἱερῆα,   (63)   ἢ καὶ ὀνειροπόλον] [καὶ γάρ τ’
   ὄναρ ἐκ Διός ἐστιν],   (64)   [ὅς κ’ εἴποι] ὅ τι [τόσσον ἐχώσατο
   Φοῖβος Ἀπόλλων]   (65)   εἴ ταρ ^Α [ὅ γ’ εὐχωλῆς ἐπιμέμφεται
   ἠδ’ ἑκατόμβης]   (66)   αἴ κέν πως [ἀρνῶν +

κνίσης αἰγῶν τε ^Α τελείων +

(67)   βούλητ’ ἀντιάσας ἡμῖν ἀπὸ λοιγὸν ἀμῦναι»],   (68)   ἤτοι [ὅ γ’
   ὣς εἰπὼν

κατ’ ἄρ’ ἕζετο], [τοῖσι δ’ ἀνέστη   (69)   Κάλχας Θεστορίδης
   οἰωνοπόλων ὄχ’ ἄριστος],   (70)   [ὃς εἴδη +

τά τ’ ἐόντα, τά τ’ ἐσσόμενα πρό τ’ ἐόντα],   (71)   καὶ [νήεσσ’ ἡγήσατ’
   Ἀχαιῶν Ἴλιον εἴσω,   (72)   ἣν διὰ μαντοσύνην]

[τήν οἱ πόρε, Φοῖβος Ἀπόλλων],   (73)   ὅ σφιν ἐῢ φρονέων
   ἀγορήσατο], καὶ [μετέειπεν],   (74)   «ὦ Ἀχιλεῦ

[κέλεαί με, διΐφιλε, μυθήσασθαι   (75)   μῆνιν Ἀπόλλωνος
   ἑκατηβελέταο, ἄνακτος],   (76)   τοὶ γὰρ ^Α [ἐγὼν ἐρέω,]

σὺ δὲ ^Τ [σύνθεο], καί [μοι ὄμοσσον,   (77)   ἦ μέν ^Τ μοι πρόφρων
   ἔπεσιν +

καὶ χερσὶν ἀρήξειν]   (78)   ἦ γὰρ ^Α [ὀΐομαι ἄνδρα, χολωσέμεν] [ὃς
   μέγα, πάντων   (79)   Ἀργείων +

κρατέει]

καί [οἱ πείθονται Ἀχαιοί],   (80)   [κρέσσων γὰρ ^Α βασιλεύς] ὅτε
   [χώσεται ἀνδρὶ, χέρηϊ],   (81)   εἴ περ γάρ τε ^Α [χόλον γε ^Α
   καὶ αὐτῆμαρ καταπέψῃ]   (82)   ἀλλά τε ^Α καὶ [μετόπισθεν
   ἔχει +

κότον] ὄφρα [τελέσσῃ   (83)   ἐν στήθεσσιν ἑοῖσι], σὺ δὲ ^Α [φράσαι] εἴ
   [με σαώσεις»]

(84)   [τὸν δ’ ἀπαμειβόμενος] [προσέφη
πόδας ὠκὺς Ἀχιλλεύς]

(85)   [«θαρσήσας
μάλα, εἰπὲ, θεοπρόπιον]

ὅ τι [οἶσθα],   (86)   οὐ μὰ γὰρ ^Τ Ἀπόλλωνα, διΐφιλον ᾧ τε, [σύ,
   Κάλχαν,   (87)   εὐχόμενος Δαναοῖσι, θεοπροπίας +

ἀναφαίνεις]   (88)   [οὔ τις ^Α ἐμέο ζῶντος καὶ ἐπὶ χθονὶ,
   δερκομένοιο,   (89)   σοὶ κοίλης +

παρὰ νηυσί, βαρείας χεῖρας ἐποίσει   (90)   συμπάντων +

Δαναῶν] [οὐδ’ ἢν Ἀγαμέμνονα, εἴπῃς]   (91)   ὃς νῦν ^Τ [πολλὸν
   ἄριστος ἐνὶ στρατῷ εὔχεται εἶναι»]   (92)   καὶ τότε δὴ

[θάρσησε] , καὶ [ηὔδα μάντις ἀμύμων·]   (93)   [«οὔτ' ἄρ ᴬ ὅ γ'
εὐχωλῆς ἐπιμέμφεται οὐδ' ἑκατόμβης]   (94)   [ἀλλ' ἕνεκ'
ἀρητῆρος[[ὃν ἠτίμησ' Ἀγαμέμνων]]   (95)   οὐδ' ἀπέλυσε ,
θύγατρα] , καὶ [οὐκ ἀπεδέξατ' ἄποινα] ,   (96)   [τοὔνεκ' ἄρ' ᵀ
ἄλγε' ἔδωκεν Ἑκηβόλος] [ἠδ' ἔτι δώσει] ,   (97)   [οὐδ' ὅ γε ᵀ
πρὶν
λοιμοῖο , βαρείας χεῖρας ἀφέξει]   (98)   [πρίν γ' ἀπὸ πατρὶ φίλῳ +
δόμεναι ἑλικώπιδα , κούρην   (99)   ἀπριάτην ἀνάποινον] [ἄγειν θ'
ἱερὴν ἑκατόμβην   (100)   ἐς Χρύσην]
[τότε κέν μιν ἱλασσάμενοι]
[πεπίθοιμεν»] ,

Odyssey i 1–100

(1)   [ἄνδρα , μοι ἔννεπε , μοῦσα , πολύτροπον] [ὃς μάλα ,
    πολλὰ ,   (2)   πλάγχθη] ἐπεὶ
[Τροίης ἱερὸν +
πτολίεθρον ἔπερσεν] ,   (3)   [πολλῶν δ' ἀνθρώπων ἴδεν ἄστεα] , καὶ
    [νόον ἔγνω]   (4)   πολλὰ δ' [ὅ γ' ἐν πόντῳ +
πάθεν ἄλγεα , ὃν κατὰ θυμόν ,   (5)   ἀρνύμενος ἥν τε ᴬ ψυχὴν +
καὶ νόστον ἑταίρων]   (6)   [ἀλλ' οὐδ' ὣς ἑτάρους ἐρρύσατο , ἱέμενός
    περ] ,   (7)   αὐτῶν γὰρ ᴬ [σφετέρῃσιν ἀτασθαλίῃσιν
    ὄλοντο] ,   (8)   νήπιοι [οἳ κατὰ βοῦς Ὑπερίονος
    Ἠελίοιο ,   (9)   ἤσθιον] αὐτὰρ [ὁ τοῖσιν ἀφείλετο , νόστιμον
    ἦμαρ]   (10)   τῶν ἁμόθεν γε ᴬ θεά
θύγατερ Διός, [εἰπὲ , καὶ ἡμῖν)   (11)   ἔνθ' ἄλλοι μὲν ᵀ [πάντες [[ὅσοι
    φύγον αἰπὺν ὄλεθρον]] ,   (12)   οἴκοι ἔσαν πόλεμόν τε ᴬ
    πεφευγότες ἠδὲ θάλασσαν]   (13)   [τὸν δ' οἶον νόστου +
κεχρημένον ἠδὲ γυναικός   (14)   νύμφη πότνι' ἔρυκε , Καλυψώ
δῖα θεάων   (15)   ἐν σπέσσι γλαφυροῖσι , λιλαιομένη +
πόσιν εἶναι] ,   (16)   ἀλλ' ὅτε δὴ
[ἔτος ἦλθε , περιπλομένων ἐνιαυτῶν]
(17)   [τῷ οἱ ἐπεκλώσαντο , θεοὶ
οἴκόνδε , νέεσθαι ,   (18)   εἰς Ἰθάκην] [οὐδ' ἔνθα , πεφυγμένος ἦεν
    ἀέθλων +
(19)   καὶ μετὰ οἷσι φίλοισι] , [θεοὶ δ' ἐλέαιρον ἅπαντες   (20)   νόσφι
    Ποσειδάωνος·] [ὁ δ' ἀσπερχὲς μενέαινεν ,   (21)   ἀντιθέῳ
    Ὀδυσῆϊ] , πάρος [ἦν γαῖαν ἱκέσθαι] ,   (22)   ἀλλ' ὁ μὲν ᵀ
    [Αἰθίοπας μετεκίαθε , τηλόθ' ἐόντας ,   (23)   (Αἰθίοπας) [τοὶ

διχθά , δεδαίαται] <u>ἔσχατοι ἀνδρῶν</u>　(24)　<u>οἱ μὲν</u> ^T <u>δυσομένου</u>
　　<u>Ὑπερίονος οἱ δ' ἀνιόντος</u>) ,　(25)　[ἀντιόων +
ταύρων τε ^A καὶ ἀρνειῶν ἑκατόμβης]　(26)　<u>ἔνθ'</u> [<u>ὅ γ'</u> ἐτέρπετο ,
　　δαιτὶ , παρήμενος] <u>οἱ δὲ δὴ</u>
[ἄλλοι　(27)　Ζηνὸς ἐνὶ μεγάροισιν Ὀλυμπίου ἀθρόοι
　　ἦσαν]　(28)　<u>τοῖσι δὲ</u> ^T [μύθων ἦρχε , πατὴρ ἀνδρῶν τε ^A
　　θεῶν τε] ^A　(29)　[<u>μνήσατο γὰρ</u> ^A κατὰ θυμὸν ἀμύμονος
　　Αἰγίσθοιο] ,　(30)　[<u>τόν ῥ'</u> Ἀγαμεμνονίδης +
τηλεκλυτὸς ἔκταν' <u>Ὀρέστης</u>]
(31)　[τοῦ <u>ὅ γ'</u> ἐπιμνησθεὶς ἔπε' ἀθανάτοισι , μετηύδα] ,　(32)　«<u>ὦ</u>
　　<u>πόποι</u> , <u>οἷον δή νυ</u> [θεοὺς +
βροτοὶ αἰτιόωνται] ,　(33)　[<u>ἐξ ἡμέων γὰρ</u> ^T φασι , κάκ' ἔμμεναι]
　　<u>οἱ δὲ</u> ^A <u>καὶ</u> [αὐτοὶ　(34)　σφῆσιν ἀτασθαλίῃσιν ὑπὲρ μόρον
　　ἄλγε' ἔχουσιν] ,　(35)　[<u>ὡς καὶ νῦν</u> Αἴγισθος ὑπὲρ μόρον
　　Ἀτρεΐδαο ,　(36)　γῆμ' ἄλοχον μνηστήν]
[<u>τὸν δ'</u> ἔκτανε , νοστήσαντα ,　(37)　εἰδὼς αἰπὺν ὄλεθρον] <u>ἐπεὶ</u>
[πρό οἱ εἴπομεν <u>ἡμεῖς</u>　(38)　Ἑρμείαν πέμψαντες <u>ἐΰσκοπον</u>
　　<u>ἀργεϊφόντην</u>
(39)　μήτ' αὐτὸν κτείνειν +
μήτε μνάασθαι ἄκοιτιν] ,　(40)　[<u>ἐκ γὰρ</u> ^A Ὀρέσταο
τίσις ἔσσεται Ἀτρεΐδαο] ,　(41)　[<u>ὁππότ' ἂν</u> ἡβήσῃ τε] ^A <u>καὶ</u> [ἧς
　　ἱμείρεται αἴης]　(42)　[ὡς ἔφαθ' Ἑρμείας] <u>ἀλλ'</u> [οὐ φρένας
　　Αἰγίσθοιο ,　(43)　πεῖθ' ἀγαθὰ φρονέων]
[<u>νῦν δ'</u> ἀθρόα , πάντ' ἀπέτισεν»] ,　(44)　[<u>τὸν δ'</u> ἠμείβετ' ἔπειτα , θεά,]
<u>γλαυκῶπις Ἀθήνη</u> ,　(45)　«<u>ὦ πάτερ ἡμέτερε Κρονίδη</u>
<u>ὕπατε κρειόντων</u>
(46)　<u>καὶ λίην</u>
[<u>κεῖνός γε</u> ^A ἐοικότι , κεῖται ὀλέθρῳ]　(47)　[ὡς ἀπόλοιτο , καὶ
　　ἄλλος] [ὅτις τοιαῦτά γε ^T ῥέζοι·] ,　(48)　<u>ἀλλά</u> [μοι ἀμφ'
　　Ὀδυσῆϊ , δαΐφρονι , δαίεται ἦτορ　(49)　δυσμόρῳ] <u>ὃς δὴ δηθὰ</u>
　　^A [φίλων ἄπο ^T πήματα , πάσχει　(50)　νήσῳ ἐν ἀμφιρύτῃ]
　　[<u>ὅθι τ'</u> ὀμφαλός ἐστι , θαλάσσης]
(51)　<u>νῆσος δενδρήεσσα</u> , [<u>θεὰ δ'</u> ἐν δώματα , ναίει] ,　(52)　<u>Ἄτλαντος</u>
　　<u>θυγάτηρ ὀλοόφρονος ὅς τε</u> ^A [θαλάσσης +
(53)　πάσης , βένθεα , οἶδεν] [<u>ἔχει δέ τε</u> ^T κίονας
　　αὐτὸς　(54)　μακράς] , [αἵ γαῖάν τε ^A καὶ οὐρανὸν ἀμφὶς
　　ἔχουσιν] ,　(55)　[τοῦ θυγάτηρ +
δύστηνον ὀδυρόμενον κατερύκει] ,　(56)　<u>αἰεὶ δὲ</u> ^A [μαλακοῖσι , καὶ
　　αἱμυλίοισι , λόγοισιν　(57)　θέλγει <u>ὅπως</u> [Ἰθάκης ἐπιλήσεται]

αὐτὰρ Ὀδυσσεύς (58) [ἱέμενος καὶ καπνὸν ἀποθρήσκοντα ,
νοῆσαι , (59) ἧς γαίης, +
θανέειν ἱμείρεται] [οὐδέ νυ ^Τ σοί περ ^Τ (60) ἐντρέπεται +
φίλον ἦτορ,] Ὀλύμπιε , [οὔ νύ τ᾽ Ὀδυσσεὺς (61) Ἀργείων +
παρὰ νηυσὶ , χαρίζετο , ἱερὰ ῥέζων +
(62) Τροίῃ ἐν εὐρείῃ]
[τί νύ ^Τ οἱ τόσον ὠδύσαο] Ζεῦ» (63) [τὴν δ᾽ ἀπαμειβόμενος]
   [προσέφη]
νεφεληγερέτα Ζεύς
(64) «τέκνον ἐμόν [ποῖόν σε , ἔπος φύγεν ἔρκος ὀδόντων]
(65) [πῶς ἂν ἔπειτ᾽ Ὀδυσῆος ἐγὼ +
θείοιο , λαθοίμην] (66) [ὃς περὶ μὲν ^Λ νόον ἐστὶ ^Λ βροτῶν,]
[περὶ δ᾽ ἱρὰ , θεοῖσιν , (67) ἀθανάτοισιν ἔδωκε] , [τοὶ οὐρανὸν εὐρὺν
   ἔχουσιν] , (68) ἀλλὰ [Ποσειδάων +
γαιήοχος ἀσκελὲς αἰὲν (69) Κύκλωπος κεχόλωται] [ὃν ὀφθαλμοῦ +
ἀλάωσεν] , (70) ἀντίθεον Πολύφημον [ὅου κράτος ἐστὶ ,
   μέγιστον (71) πᾶσιν , Κυκλώπεσσι] , [Θόωσα δέ ^Τ μιν
   τέκε] νύμφη (72) Φόρκυνος θυγάτηρ ἁλὸς ἀτρυγέτοιο,
   μέδοντος , (73) [ἐν σπέσσι γλαφυροῖσι , Ποσειδάωνι ,
   μιγεῖσα] , (74) ἐκ τοῦ δὴ
[Ὀδυσῆα , Ποσειδάων ἐνοσίχθων (75) οὔ τι κατακτείνει]
[πλάζει δ᾽ ἀπὸ πατρίδος αἴης] (76) ἀλλ᾽ ἄγεθ᾽ [ἡμεῖς οἵδε ,
   περιφραζώμεθα , πάντες (77) νόστον] ὅπως [ἔλθῃσι·] ,
   Ποσειδάων δὲ ^Λ [μεθήσει , (78) ὃν χόλον] [οὐ μὲν γὰρ ^Λ
   τι δυνήσεται ἀντία , πάντων (79) ἀθανάτων ἀέκητι , θεῶν
   ἐριδαινέμεν οἷος»] (80) [τὸν δ᾽ ἠμείβετ᾽ ἔπειτα θεά]
γλαυκῶπις Ἀθήνη, (81) «ὦ πάτερ ἡμέτερε Κρονίδη
ὕπατε κρειόντων
(82) εἰ μὲν δὴ [νῦν +
τοῦτο φίλον μακάρεσσι , θεοῖσιν (83) νοστῆσαι Ὀδυσῆα ,
   πολύφρονα , ὅνδε δόμονδε] ^Τ (84) [Ἑρμείαν μὲν ^Λ ἔπειτα ,
   διάκτορον ἀργεϊφόντην
(85) νῆσον ἐς Ὠγυγίην ὀτρύνομεν] ὄφρα [τάχιστα , (86) νύμφῃ
   ἐϋπλοκάμῳ εἴπῃ +
νημερτέα , βουλήν]
(87) νόστον Ὀδυσσῆος [ταλασίφρονος, ὥς κε νέηται] , (88) αὐτὰρ
   ἐγὼν [Ἰθάκην ἐσελεύσομαι] ὄφρα [οἱ υἱὸν (89) μᾶλλον
   ἐποτρύνω]
καί [οἱ μένος ἐν φρεσὶ , θείω , (90) εἰς ἀγορὴν +
καλέσαντα , κάρη +

κομόωντας Ἀχαιοὺς +

(91) πᾶσι μνηστήρεσσιν ἀπειπέμεν] <u>οἵ τέ</u> ᴬ [οἳ αἰεὶ (92) μῆλ' ἀδινὰ
σφάζουσι , <u>καὶ</u> εἰλίποδας ἕλικας βοῦς]

(93) [<u>πέμψω δ'</u> ἐς Σπάρτην τε ᴬ <u>καὶ</u> ἐς Πύλον
ἠμαθόεντα , (94) νόστον πευσόμενον πατρὸς φίλου]
<u>ἤν</u> [που ἀκούσῃ] , (95) <u>ἠδ' ἵνα</u> [μιν κλέος ἐσθλὸν ἐν
ἀνθρώποισιν ἔχῃσιν»] , (96) [ὣς εἰποῦσ' ὑπὸ ποσσὶν
ἐδήσατο , καλὰ πέδιλα] , (97) <u>ἀμβρόσια χρύσεια</u> , [τά μιν
φέρον ἠμὲν ἐφ' ὑγρὴν (98) ἠδ' ἐπ' ἀπείρονα , γαῖαν ἅμα
πνοιῇς ἀνέμοιο] , (99) [<u>εἵλετο δ'</u> ἄλκιμον ἔγχος ἀκαχμένον
ὀξέι , χαλκῷ]

(100) <u>βριθὺ</u> , <u>μέγα στιβαρόν</u> [τῷ δάμνησι στίχας
ἀνδρῶν (101: ἡρώων]

κτλ)

227

Conclusion

This study has argued for the identification of the performative pause in Homer. I have defined performative pause as *a rest of some duration in performance due to the termination of phonation*; performance as a *significant enactment or expression for which the initiator takes responsibility before a critical audience that can judge his skill*. The transmitted text of the *Iliad* and *Odyssey* is considered the reflection of a performed or performable narrative, still showing the remnants of the compositional units as they were applied in the first performance of the epic. From this methodological framework followed an approach to pause in performance as the reconstruction of a phonetic reality by means of phonological analysis. Phonology is understood and studied as surface phonetics: phonology rationalizes the metric surface structure, which in turn maintains its ontological basis, the rhythmic regularity that is a cross-linguistic feature of natural languages. Meter thus accounts for both the possibilities for rests in performance and for the restrictions on rests or silence. Both depend on the maintenance of metrical surface structure: certain metrical positions allow for rest in performance without disrupting rhythmic regularity, others do not. Performative pause thus demands termination of phonation and metrical room for extra duration. I have shown that only a selection of the compositional pauses identified in existing studies on Homeric prosody qualifies as a rest of some duration in performance. As a consequence, I have revalued and rejected various prosodic and poetic effects that are commonly assumed as correlates of pause, notably enjambment.

My treatment of pause in prosody takes the phonetics of rest in performance into account; it focuses on the performative perspectives of pause in addition to pause's compositional perspectives. The compositional perspectives of pause have been sufficiently accounted for in studies that analyze the metrical phrases of Homer's *Iliad* and *Odyssey* and their syntactical structure.

In studies on metrical phrasing, the caesurae and the diereses that frame the metrical phrases of colometry are treated as metrical pauses; a role as rest in performance is readily assumed for the verse end and sometimes for the third-foot caesura. Existing studies are reluctant to allow for a nonprepausal verse end. The metrical pauses of colometry are not only appreciated in the study of prosody, but also in discourse analysis: the concepts of appositional syntax, adding style, and nonconfigurationality imply that Homeric discourse is sensitive to the impulse of colometry on sense and organic word groups. In this approach, metrical boundaries also double as pauses, be them (=metrical boundaries) pauses in syntax. Not all metrical pauses, however, are automatically seen as sense-pauses, as Homeric discourse tends to create coherent syntactical wholes that comprise more than a single metrical colon.

I have argued against the notion of enjambment as a result of the mismatch of various compositional pauses: starting from the assumption that syntactical wholes are originally and preferably confined to the metrical unity of the hexametric verse, enjambment studies consider out-of-line composition that straddles the verse end (a compositional pause in both metrics and syntax) a deliberate aberration from standard practice for poetic purposes. Depending on the grammatical incompleteness at verse end, types of verse-end enjambment have been readily categorized with reference to their alleged strength: the verse-end compositional pause is the determining factor in the level of expectation of the listening audience. Incorrectly linked to the concept of enjambment as a poetic device is the notion of affective prosody, the mismatch of expectations as to what follows the various compositional pauses. Since the phonetic effect of compositional pauses, I have argued, is rather arbitrarily assumed (often in accordance with syntactical phrasing), prosodic affectiveness has previously been identified equally arbitrarily.

I have identified pause as a correlate of termination of phonation. Pause is hence theoretically identifiable as phonetic word end. I have distinguished between two qualities of phonetic word end with regard for the possibilities of the crosslinguistic phenomenon of phonetic word-final lengthening: word end on the thesis, allowing for considerable lengthening without disrupting rhythmic regularity, I have labeled *primary*, whereas the phonetic lengthening of *secondary* word end on the metrical arsis is severely restricted, due to the need to maintain surface and podic metrical structure. My assumption has been that metrical speech is like normal speech, and that its rhythmic regularity (though allowing for less variation on the arsis than in nonmetrical speech) is preserved by surface phonetics: the phonology that maintains metrical syllabification.

As phonetic word end comes in two qualities, so does pause, albeit not with an exact correspondence with the word-end bipartition. Metrical structure elicits two types of pause: a primary pause that allows for taking a breath and a secondary that does not. The application of the two pauses to a sample from the *Iliad* and the *Odyssey* brought out a pattern of phonological phrases that (i) straddles numerous compositional pauses, seemingly at random, and (ii) shows a mismatch of the way phrases and clauses start and terminate.

The decisive factor in the realization of phonetic word end as a performative pause is rates of speech in performance. Very low rates of speech lead to an increase of instances of phonetic word realized as audible pause in performance; higher rates of speech tend to allow for breathing pauses at regular temporal intervals, at the expense of milder, nonbreathing pauses. Two types of word end, as found in the phonology of the Homeric epic, suggest normal rates of speech in performance. Phonetic word end in performed metrical texts is sensitive to the differences in temporal allowance between the thesis and the arsis: whereas phonetic word end on the thesis may be lengthened without regard for the subsequent arsis from which it becomes detached, phonetic lengthening of word end on the arsis is always confined by the rhythmic room and temporal allowance left by the thesis in the same foot. The foot-internal proportion that assigns the thesis rhythmical weight equal to, or more than, the arsis, leaves the arsis less room for phonetic lengthening or silence than the thesis; rhythmic regularity depends on the maintenance of this proportion.

The primary pauses are perceptible as rests in performance; they frame the major phonological phrases that are comprised of one or several minor phrases. Secondary pauses are likely to be perceptible as milder pauses when word end is in an enclitic (due to the strong accentual fall), especially when the enclitic is localized on a metrical thesis. As the major phonological phrase tends to become very long in Homer, it cannot be excluded beforehand that other minor phrase boundaries were exploited as stealthy breathing pauses at regular intervals.

The resulting mosaic-like patterning of phonological phrases whose size is various and variable not only leads to a renewed appreciation of performative pause and prosodic affectiveness, but also draws attention towards what happens between the performative pauses.

Performative pausing turns out to be selective in its realization of the compositional pauses of colometry and syntax as audible phenomena. Some compositional pauses are realized as performative pauses, many are not. The disappearance of the automatic claim that *verse end = performative pause* has consequences for the approach to verse-end enjambment as a poetic device due to strength and expectations and to affective prosody due to metrical localization. Both poetically meaningful enjambment, at verse end and verse-internal, and prosodic affectiveness have to be judged in accordance with the realization of compositional pauses as phonetic disruptions. The result of this renewed appreciation is a concept of prosodic affectiveness that seems to equal the use of performative pauses as clausal dividers.

The mismatch between clauses and phonological phrasing leads to intra-pausal phonological substance that does not contain commonsensical syntactical wholes. Pauses may frame complete clauses, but most often they contain parts of clauses in combination with extra-clausal constituents. The phrases that become audible between pauses in performance thus contribute to the perception of Homeric discourse as a movement, as phrases are regularly comprised of parts of clauses concluded by the start of, or the lead-in to, a subsequent clause.

Textual transmission of Homer's *Iliad* and *Odyssey* may have smoothed over many irregularities and aberrations in the formation of verses. Later Greek hexametric poetry, showing a far more persistent coincidence between the metrical unity of the verse and the syntactical unity of the clause, may have contributed to attempts within the manuscript traditions to restrict the variable and unpredictable clause-formation in the Homeric epic. Still there is a lot of nonstichic clause formation in Homer left, which is likely a residue of what must have been common practice in the earlier phases of the tradition.

Homer's success stemmed from performance. The characteristics of spoken language characterize Homer's work. The phonetics of Homer's spoken language can be gauged from the metrical surface structure: performative features are derived from the compositional ones. At the same time, Homer may have been the last trace of a performance-based, written-down spoken language. As performance for a listening audience fades, the specific features of spoken language, suited for aural reception, lose some of their importance and weight in composition as well. Other restrictions take their place. In the development of hexametric poetry, metrical shape gradually overpowered free phonological phrasing. As a result, syntactical phrasing follows its new guide: it tends to align, more and more, with the repetitive metrical phrases. "Breaking the measure" gradually becomes more noticeable, and hence more suitable for usage to poetic effect. In Homer we witness a stage in the development of grammaticalization, despite—though with the aid of—meter, only to conclude that what we see is actually the final stage of this development. Homer's "rhythm without a beat" may have been the last representative of the essence of epic performance: a story well told, in an appropriate style and language that sounds natural, without the dullness of overstretched repetition.

Glossary

The glossary lists all the terms that have been labeled with * on their first occurrence in the chapters of this study. The list below presents the terms' working definitions as they are being used in this study. Page numbers in parentheses refer to where the term is defined or extensively discussed in the text. References are to works in the Bibliography that define the term, or were used as the basis for the definition presented below. Cross-reference within the glossary is indicated with *.

Affective prosody (pp. 59, 164): Emphasis due to metrical localization (Devine and Stephens 1994), especially localization in verse-initial position (Edwards 2002:14).

Ambisyllabic (p. 166n1): Characteristic of the consonantal sound when its adherence to the preceding or subsequent syllable is indeterminate. Ambisyllabism is a phonetic reality (English 'an aim' / 'a name'; Greek ἔστι Νάξιος / ἔστιν ἄξιος) given that the tempo of speech is relatively slow and that the speaker pronounces in a clear and polished manner, and evidenced by *phonology and orthography (Devine and Stephens 1994:25–31, 224–225).

Anaclasis: Reversal of a light and a heavy syllable within a metrical *foot (Rosenmeyer, Ostwald, and Halporn 1963:121).

Anacrusis *see* **Hypercatalexis**

Anceps (element) (pp. 2, 24): Metrically indifferent and rhythmically indeterminate position (Lidov 2010), indicated as x. Van Raalte 1986:12 describes anceps as an "institutionalized divergence," a divergence from the basic metric profile.

Anticipation (p. 64): Word, word-group, or verse that prepares for continuation of the utterance over the verse end (Clark 1997). The level of anticipation or expectancy for syntactically or grammatically required constituents at verse end determines the type of verse end *enjambment (Parry 1929; Kirk 1966; Higbie 1990). Clark 1997 labels frequently recurring anticipations *hooks.

Apposition: Adding in coherence.

- Clisis, *see* **Clisis: Phonological clisis**
- In syntax (p. 46): Development of the syntactical unit through the addition of autonomous words and word groups (Chantraine 1953).

Appositive (p. 71): *Nonlexical word joined with a *lexical head in the *appositive group (Devine and Stephens 1994). Polysyllabic appositives do not have a stable *thesis in *prosody.

Appositive group: *see* **Phonological phrase**

Arsis (A) (p. 22): Second half of the dactylic *foot. Changeable structural element (West 1982; Lidov 1989).

Audible pause: *see* **Pause**

Brevis in longo (p. 77): Adjustment of *syllable quantity resulting in the light syllable meeting the requirements of a metrical position that expects a heavy syllable (more fully *syllaba brevis in elemento longo*; Rosenmeyer, Ostwald and Halporn 1963:122). *Brevis in longo* is an indication of termination (Van Raalte 1986:17).

Bridge (p. 80): Restriction on *phonetic word end at a specific metrical position (Van Raalte 1986; Ruijgh 1987; Devine and Stephens 1978, 1980, 1983, 1984). The various restrictions on word end in the hexameter and the conditions for disregard of bridges are named after the metrical position or the scholars who first defined them:

- **Naeke's Bridge** (p. 130): Restriction on *spondaic word end (|- -|) following position 8 (Maas 1962).
- **Meyer's Law** (p. 170): Restriction on *phonetic word end following position 3½.
- **Hermann's Bridge**: Restriction on *phonetic word end following position 7½.
- **Hilberg's Law**: Restriction on *spondaic word end (|- -|) following position 4 (Maas 1962). Korzeniewski 1968 speaks of the *Bucolic Bridge*.

— **Porson's Law:** Restriction on *phonetic word end following the third *anceps in the iambic trimeter. Parker 1966 and Ruijgh 1987 extend the restriction to explain the restriction on *spondaic word end (|– –|) in the dactylic hexameter.

— **Split fifth foot spondee:** Restriction on *phonetic word end following position 9.

— **Wernicke's Law** (p. 130): Condition under which *spondaic word end (|– –|) is permitted following position 8 : position 8 must be occupied by a heavy syllable featuring a *natura*-long vowel.

Caesura (p. 26): Frequently recurring *phonetic word end within the metrical *foot (Korzeniewski 1968; Devine and Stephens 1980; West 1982).

— **Main caesura** (p. 26): *Phonetic word end within the hexameter's third *foot. It is labelled masculine following position 5, feminine following position 5½. In Fränkel's three-zone system it is indicated as B.

— **Auxiliary caesura** (p. 27): Frequently recurring foot-internal *phonetic word end within the line outside the third *foot. Auxiliary caesurae follow positions 3, 7, and 9.

— **Trochaic caesura** (p. 26): *Phonetic word end following position 5½ within the hexameter's third *foot.

Catalectic verse: *see* **Catalexis**

Catalexis (p. 25): Syncopation of (a syllable on) the foot's *arsis (West 1982). Catalexis is considered a signal of stanza-end (Korzeniewski 1968:6), e.g., in the anapaestic system (Ruijgh 1989).

Clisis: Hierarchical interdependency of words in a word group. Three types of clisis are identified, in order of decreasing importance for word-group coherence (Devine and Stephens 1994):

— **Accentual clisis** (p. 71): "Leaning" of non-accented words onto the accented word preceding or following it within the accentual domain of the clitic group.

— **Phonological clisis** (*or* **apposition**) (p. 72): Dependency of *non-lexicals (and some *lexicals, notably adjectives) on the *lexical head within the rhythmic domain of the *appositive group. At higher rates of speech, non-lexical appositives may well be accentual clitics (Devine and Stephens 1994:354–355).

— **Syntactical clisis** (p. 28n20): Interdependency of words in a word group based on grammatical structure.

A fourth type of clisis is identified in Devine and Stephens 1994, to account for the coherence of words and word groups within the *major phonological phrase:

— **Sentential clisis** (p. 108): Interdependency of *minor phonological phrases to account for the scope of the *major phonological phrase. Intonation and melodic patterns are assumed to reflect this scope (Goldstein 2014; Bonifazi et al. 2016; Blankenborg 2016).

Coda (p. 20): Consonantal closing in the structure of the syllable (Devine and Stephens 1994).

Colometry: *see* **Inner metrics**

Compositional pause: *see* **Pause**

Correption: *see* **Shortening**

Crasis (pp. 70, 73): Adjustment of vowel coalescence that results in the maintenance of the *mora count of the original syllables before contraction with a maximum vocalic *mora count of 2 (Allen 1973:288; Devine and Stephens 1994).

Dieresis (p. 26): *Phonetic word end coinciding with metron end (Korzeniewski 1968). In the hexameter, the main diereses are the dieresis following position 2, the bucolic dieresis following position 8, and the verse end.

Elision (p. 73): Adjustment of vowel coalescence that results in the reduction of a .CV.-syllable to a .C-onset (Allen 1973:226; Ruijgh 1987; Devine and Stephens 1994). Some scholars do not accept that elision implies loss of the vocalic *nucleus of the elided syllable are (prominently, Korzeniewski 1968:26 and West 1982).

Enjambment (p. 59): Continuation of the utterance over the verse end (Parry 1929; Kirk 1966; Higbie 1990; Bakker 1990; Clark 1997; Edwards 2002; Blankenborg 2016).

Ennehemimeres (p. 27): Name given (in antiquity and reused by, among others, Korzeniewski 1968) to the *caesura following position 9.

Ephelcystic *nu*: *see* **Movable** *nu*

Extrametrical syllable (p. 22n7): Non-elidable syllable outside the repetitive metrical phrase (Devine and Stephens 1994). Extrametrical syllables, common in the spoken passages of drama, do not occur in Homer.

Fillers (p. 56, 171): Context neutral, metrically variable, and interchangeable words or word groups that allow the *nucleus to extend to the nearest metrical boundary (Bakker 2005).

Foot (p. 22): Smallest scale unit of prodosic regularity and repetition (Hardie 1920; Rosenmeyer et al. 1963:124; West 1982; Devine and Stephens 1994).

— **Metrical foot**: Single occurrence of the structural elements *thesis (T) and *arsis (A) in a specific direction (either [TA] or [AT]).

— **Stress foot** (p. 33): Typological label for the single occurence of the energized (T) and less energized element (A) in a specific direction (either [TA] or [AT]).

Foot internal proportion (p. 23): Durational proportion between the foot's structural elements *thesis and *arsis (Korzeniewski 1968; Ruijgh 1987, 1989). Any decision or conclusion on the foot-internal proportion has far-reaching consequences for the *phonetics of hexametric poetry like the *Iliad* and *Odyssey*, since the structural elements of the foot have different roles to play when polysyllabic words are mapped onto a sequence or a combination of feet.

Footing: *see* **Meter**

Gemination (p. 77): Doubling of consonants in orthography for metrical purposes (Chantraine 1961).

Gliding (p. 75): Consonantilization of the diphthong's second element (ι or υ) with maintenance of the diphthong's vocalic *mora count (Allen 1973; Henderson 1973; Sihler 1995:175).

Grammatical clause (*or* **predication**) (p. 249): Predicate-centered unit whose valencies are pragmatically realized as topic and focus (S.C. Dik 1997), with a single illocutionary force (Franck 1980; Lyons 1977; Searle 1969; 1976).

Grammatical (sense-)pause: *see* **Pause**

Heavy syllable prolongation (p. 79): *Submoraic adjustment (phonetic *lengthening) of heavy syllable weight on the *thesis to account for phrase-final additional *lengthening (Ruijgh 1989; Devine and Stephens 1994).

Heavy syllable subordination (p. 136): *Submoraic adjustment (phonetic *shortening) of heavy syllable weight on the *arsis framed by theses. The heavy syllable (that belongs on the *thesis) is refooted and mapped onto *arsis ([T][T][T] → [TA][T] or [T][AT]). Devine and Stephens (1994:131) note that "implicit in the hypothesis of subordination is the assumption that, when a heavy syllable is mapped onto arsis, it is pronounced with less duration than a heavy syllable mapped onto thesis." The terminology subordination belongs to the reconstruction of *stress feet, but is useful to describe the restriction on prepausal mapping of heavy syllables onto *arsis in order to retain the unidirectional podic structure. The *submoraic adjustment results in non-prepausal weight for heavy syllables on the *arsis, and forms the basis of the spondaic bridge, the restriction on *spondaic word end.

Hephthemimeres (p. 27): Name given (in antiquity and reused by, among others, Korzeniewski 1968:31) to the *caesura following position 7.

Hermann's Bridge: *see* **Bridge**

Hiatus (p. 75): Vowel coalescence without *crasis, *elision, or *shortening. Hiatus is considered an indicator for termination (Hardie 1920; Rosenmeyer et al. 1963:124; Korzeniewski 1968; Allen 1973; Henderson 1973; West 1982; Van Raalte 1986; Devine and Stephens 1994).

Hilberg's Law: *see* **Bridge**

Hook (p. 65): Frequently recurring *runover word or *anticipation (Clark 1997).

Hypercatalexis *or* **Anacrusis** (p. 22n7): Forward or backward extension of the verse through addition of non-elidable *arsis syllable(s) (Hardie 1920). Hypercatalexis does not occur in Homer.

Hypermetric verse (p. 22n7): Verse featuring an additional syllable that is elided over the verse end (Hardie 1920; Rosenmeyer et al. 1963:124). Homeric epic does not feature hypermetric verse (there is a tradition though that accepts verse-final Ζῆν as Ζῆν' < Ζῆνα).

Ictus (p. 25n14): Indication of the *foot's invariable element (Hardie 1920; Rosenmeyer et al. 1963:125). Often—mistakenly—taken for a perceptible downbeat in *rhythm (Allen 1973:99).

Inner metrics (*or* **Colometry**) (p. 25): Subdivision of the larger line (notably the dactylic hexameter) into smaller size metrical phrases (Korzeniewski 1968; Clark 2004). West 1982:35 argues for colometry into pre-existing cola. Fränkel 1926 advocated colometry of the hexameter into four cola on the basis of the main *caesura (dividing the hexameter into hemistichs) and two *auxiliary caesurae (further dividing the hemistichs); others (notably Kirk 1966) have argued for the possibility to divide certain hexameters into three cola. Some cola appear as metrical phrases in lyric poetry.

Lengthening: Visible (moraic) or assumed (submoraic) prolongation of sounds and syllables. Visible lengthening is known as:

— **Metrical lengthening** (p. 77): Name given (by Wyatt 1969) to the permission for light syllables to occupy the foot's *thesis. Metrical lengthening is sometimes reflected in orthography by *gemination or vowel *protraction.

Submoraic lengthening appears as:

— **Phonetic lengthening**: *see* **Prolongation**
— **Final lengthening**: *see* **Phrase final lengthening**

Lexical (word) (or **content word**, or **open class word**) (p. 72): Word that is expandable into a phrase that it heads. The category of lexicals contains a vast number of members, and new members can be added by neologism. In *prosody, lexicals are not easily reduced or minimalized (Devine and Stephens 1994).

Light syllable prolongation (p. 80): Adjustment (phonetic *lengthening) of light syllable weight resulting in prepausal, additional *final lengthening of the light syllable on the *thesis (Dvine and Stephens 1994). Light syllable prolongation may be expressed in orthography by the use of spurious diphthongs ου and ει (Sihler 1995:71).

Metarrhythmisis (pp. 36, 38): Reversal in the direction of the *rhythmisis (Koster 1953). Metarrhythmisis in the dactylic hexameter may be on the level of the rhythmical word type as the result of the orphaned and isolated *thesis [T(A)], or on the level of the phrase due to *syncopation of feet (*catalexis) in case of phonetic *spondaic word end [(A) T][T][TA].

Meter: Recurrence of quantifiable aspects in the surface structure of a language (Hardie 1920; Rosenmeyer et al. 1963:124; Korzeniewski 1968; Allen 1973; Henderson 1973; West 1982; Van Raalte 1986; Devine and Stephens 1994).

— **Scansion** (p. 20): Bipartition of syllables into the categories *longum* and *breve*, on the basis of *mora count of the syllable's *rime (Clark 2004).

— **Footing** (p. 22): Assignment of syllables to the structural elements *thesis (T) and *arsis (A) on the basis of syllable structure (Allen 1973). **Outer metrics** establishes the equivalence of the dactyl and the spondee in the hexameter.

— **Colometry**: *see* **Inner metrics**

Metrical pause: *see* **Pause**

Meyer's Law: *see* **Bridge**

Mora: Surface structure unit of measurement for syllable length (p. 21), accentuation (p. 30), and *syllable weight (p. 31). The mora is primarily a rhythmic measurement. Nicanor "the Punctuator" uses the mora as a unit of measurement for the *pause (Devine and Stephens 1994).

Mora count: Computation of:

— **Metrical measurement** (in *scansion) (p. 21): Accounts for the length of short (*breve*), long (*longum*), and *overlong syllables and *pauses: syllables' mora count depends on the *rime; *pauses are distinguished based on the mora count of the silence they represent (Devine and Stephens 1994).

— **Accentual measurement** (p. 30): Accounts for the distinction between short (mora count 1) and long (mora count 2) vocalic nuclei, with regard for their position within the *phonetic word: in the word-final syllable, the distinction is always made; in penultimate syllables, long vocalic nuclei have mora count 2 if they are accentuated on the first mora, with the word-final syllable featuring mora count 1. In syllables other than word final or penultimate, mora count of the (accented or non-accented) vocalic *nucleus is 1 (Chandler 1881; Allen 1973).

— **Rhythmic measurement** (p. 31): Accounts for the distinction between heavy (mora count ≥ 2) and light syllables (mora count < 2) in the metrical surface structure, but obscures phonetic (*submoraic) adjustment (Devine and Stephens 1994).

Movable *nu* (*or* **Ephelcystic** *nu*) (p. 112): *Nu* applied as consonantal *coda for no other reason than:

— **Orthographical**: Application of *nu* avoids *hiatus (of light syllables on the *arsis) and *shortening (of heavy syllables on the *thesis) (West 1982).

— **Prosodical**: Application of *nu* contributes to the phonological representation of rhythmical weight as required by the expectations of the metrical position (especially on positions 5 and 12). On position 12, movable *nu* reflects rhythmical indeterminability (see *Anceps).

Naeke's Bridge: *see* **Bridge**

Nonconfigurationality (p. 47): Set of characteristics of discourse lacking hierarchical phrase structure (Devine and Stephens 2000).

Nonlexical (word) (*or* **function word, or closed class word**) (p. 72): Word that cannot be expanded into a phrase, or function as head of an expanding phrase. Nonlexicals are few in number, and new nonlexicals arise as the result of the semantic bleaching of erstwhile *lexicals. Prosodically, nonlexicals are susceptible to reduction in continuous speech (Devine and Stephens 1994).

Nucleus: Core of the syllable and of the syntactical unity.
  — (p. 20) Central, vocalic element in the structure of the syllable, optionally preceded by *onset or followed by *coda (Henderson 1973).
  — (p. 56) Semantically most important constituent of the grammatical or syntactical unity (Bakker 2005).

Onset (p. 20): Consonantal element preceding the vocalic *nucleus in the structure of the syllable (Henderson 1973).

Oral poetry (p. 99): Poetry (including song) whose medium in composition, *performance, and diffusion does not depend on the aid of writing (Parry 1929; Nagy 1996; Oesterreicher 1997; Lord 2000²; Bakker 2005). Written tradition may, however, infuence the oral tradition (Bird 2010; Ready 2015).

Outer metrics: *see* **Meter: Footing**

Overlong (p. 21): Qualification of a syllable with *mora count ≥ 3 (VC or CVC with a long vocalic *nucleus); a more precise, rhythmic denomination for the overlong syllable is *superheavy (Devine and Stephens 1994).

Pausa: *see* **Pause**

Pause (p. 1): Termination of a metrical, phonological, or syntactic unit (Hardie 1920:268; Rosenmeyer et al. 1963:126; Korzeniewski 1968:9; Allen 1973; Henderson 1973; West 1982; Devine and Stephens 1994). The term is loosely applied as if terminations of metrical, phonological, and syntactical units are comparable and coincide. As they do not, pause as terminology is better replaced by more specific terms distinguishing between compositional and phonetic/performative pauses:

— **Compositional pause** (Nagy 1998):

> **Pausa** (pp. 59, 89): Phonological term for frequently occuring word end (Allen 1973; Daitz 1991).
>
> **Metrical pause** (p. 2): Position of frequent word end (caesura or dieresis).
>
> **Rhetorical** *or* **grammatical (sense-)pause** (p. 45): Grammatical or syntactical division, made visible through printed punctuation (West 1982:36).

— **Phonetic** *or* **audible pause** (p. 67): Termination of phonation due to the phonetically lengthened and sandhi-free phonetic word-final syllable. Phonetic lengthening and silence together represent the duration of the phonetic pause.

— **Performative pause** (p. 13): Rest of some duration in performance due to the termination of phonation (either a drawling of speech ending in termination of phonation or a true silence). Usually applied at regular intervals demarcating *minor (non-breathing pauses) and *major phonological phrases (breathing pauses). Realization of phonetic pauses as performative pauses partly depends on tempo of speech: the higher tempo of speech, the wider the intervals between performative pauses (Allen 1973; Devine and Stephens 1994).

Penthemimeres *or* **penthemimeral** (p. 27): Name given (in antiquity and widely reused) to the *caesura following position 5.

Performance (p. 99): Key element in the triad (composition, performance, diffusion) that constitutes the medium of *oral poetry. (Nagy 1996; Bakker 2005). Performance of the Homeric epic may have been poetry recited (Nagy 1998; Daitz 1991) or song (West 1997; David 2006; Beck 2012). Martin defines performance as a significant enactment or expression for which the initiator takes responsibility before a critical audience that can judge his skill (in Finkelberg 2011).

Performative pause: *see* **Pause**

Phonetic pause: *see* **Pause**

Phonetics (p. 69): Sound act of speech in a language (Clark et al. 2007).

Phonetic word: *see* **Phonological phrase**

Phonological phrase: Word group or combination of word groups whose coherence depends on prosodic contours. In order, from smaller to larger scale:

— **Phonetic word** (p. 30): Accentual unit consisting of the accented word and its accentual clitics (clitic group) (West 1982; Ruijgh 1987).

— **Appositive group** (p. 72): Combination of the host *lexical word and one or more *non-lexicals (Devine and Stephens 1994). In the intonation pattern: the domain of accentual rise and fall (Allen 1973, 1987).

— **Minor phonological phrase** (p. 82): Combination of *appositive groups and clitic groups into a single prosodic unit. Adjacent items are put together in a minor phrase, provided that neither of them belongs more closely to a third item, e.g., due to *clisis or *apposition (Devine and Stephens 1994:303).

— **Major phonological phrase** (p. 85): Any syntactic whole framed by *phonetic pauses (Devine and Stephens 1994:414–416). In this study, the major phrase (like the minor phrase) is primarily considered as a rhythmical and phonological unity: in my definition, the major phrase is a phonological unity framed by primary pauses.

Phonology (p. 69): Study of the sound system of a language (Clark et al. 2007).

Phrase-final lengthening (pp. 78, 90): *Submoraic adjustment of *syllable weight to account for the drawling of natural speech due to the slackening of speech tempo towards termination of the utterance. In ancient Greek metrical text, the distribution of syllable structures (structures tend to become less heavy as the utterance develops) is considered the phonological indicator for final lengthening (Ruijgh 1987, 1989; Devine and Stephens 1994).

Pitch (p. 29): Frequency of tone expressed in Hertz (Hz). In ancient Greek, pitch is not assigned to the syllable as a whole, but to the individual vocalic *mora (Allen 1973; West 1997).

Porson's Law: *see* **Bridge**

Postpositive (p. 72): *Appositive that coheres with the preceding word (Devine and Stephens 1994).

Predication *see* **Grammatical clause**

Prepositive (p. 72): *Appositive that coheres with the subsequent word (Devine and Stephens 1994).

Prodelision (p. 73): Adjustment of vowel coalescence that results in a reduction of the vocalic *nucleus of a .V(C).-syllable to a thoracic arrest (Allen 1973). In orthography the vocalic *nucleus disappears and its *mora count is lost.

Prolongation *or* **Phonetic lengthening**: *see* **Heavy syllable prolongation** and **Light syllable prolongation**

Prosodic neutrality (p. 25): Metrical indifference and/or rhythmical indeterminability found in case of metrical *anceps and *brevis in longo*. Prosodic neutrality is considered an indication of termination (Lejeune 1972; Van Raalte 1986).

Prosody (p. 20): Reference to one of (or to the combination of all) three features of sound on the level of the syllable: duration (length), frequency (pitch), and intensity (*stress) (Devine and Stephens 1994).

Protraction (p. 77): Lengthening of the syllable's vocalic *nucleus, sometimes expressed in orthography through a lengthened vowel or a spurious diphthong (Sihler 1995).

Responsive alternation (p. 24n12): Pattern of metrical regularity and repetition within units larger than the single line, usually within the *stanza or the *strophe (Rosenmeyer et al. 1963:127; Dain 1965:20; Korzeniewski 1968:15; West 1982; Lidov 1989).

Resyllabification *see* **Syllabification**

Rhetorical (sense-)pause: *see* **Pause**

Rhythm (p. 35): Perceived recurrence and regularization of auditory stimuli into a timing mechanism for the production of speech (West 1982; Van Raalte 1986; Devine and Stephens 1994). All natural languages strive towards a rhythmic pattern in utterances. Auditory stimulus in ancient Greek stems from syllable *sonority. The rhythmic minimum of both metrical and non-metrical speech is the non-metronomic recurrence of the *thesis syllable (in non-metrical speech the *thesis in the *stress foot); there is no reason to assume that ancient metrical text was performed to a rhythm by the metronome. Compared to non-metrical speech, metrical speech is more regular in the timing of intervals and more restricted in the realization of the *arsis structural element of the *foot.

— **Metrical rhythm**: Rhythm based on the regularization of auditory stimuli into a metrical pattern. Devine and Stephens 1994:101 note that the *submoraic adjustment of *prima facie* *mora count is much more restricted in poetry than it is in prose. The higher level of regulation in verse is not so much due to the non-metronomic character of syllable durations, but rather to "verse rhythms being much more regular than speech rhythms in the durational patterns of their performance."

— **Rising rhythm**: *Rhythmisis starting on the metrical *arsis element.

— **Descending rhythm**: *Rhythmisis starting on the metrical *thesis element.

— **Blunt rhythm**: *Rhythmisis ending on the metrical *thesis element.

— **Pendant rhythm**: *Rhythmisis ending on the metrical *arsis element.

Rhythmical word type (p. 37): *Phonetic word shaped in *scansion like the single foot of a metrical prototype (iamb ∪ –, trochee – ∪, dactyl – ∪ ∪, anapaest ∪ ∪ –, molossus – – –, ionicus ∪ ∪ – –, cretic – ∪ –, choriamb – ∪ ∪ –; the spondee is not considered a metrical prototype) (O'Neill 1942; Ruijgh 1987, 1989).

Rhythmisis (p. 37): Direction of the *rhythm (rising or descending) (Koster 1953; Devine and Stephens 1994).

Rime (p. 20): Combination of the *nucleus and the *coda in the structure of the syllable (Devine and Stephens 1994).

Rising threefolder (p. 28): Name given (by Kirk 1966) to the tripartite hexameter without a *main caesura. Later, the definition was widened to encompass lines where a *main caesura was unlikely due to syntactical *clisis over the third *foot.

Runover (p. 59): word, word-group, or verse that continues the utterance over the verse end (Clark 1997; Edwards 2002). The level of anticipation or expectancy for syntactically or grammatically required constituents at verse end determines the type of verse end *enjambment (Parry 1929; Kirk 1966; Higbie 1990). Clark 1997 labels frequently recurring runovers *hooks.

Sandhi (p. 71): General term for phonological legato due to vowel coalescence (or συναλοιφή) and/or consonantal liaison (or synaphy, συνάφεια) (Sihler 1995:231–233). Sandhi in Greek metrical text appears in orthography in metrical *syllabification. Itself a phonological feature, sandhi reflects phonetic realization.

Scansion: *see* **Meter**

Secondary rise (p. 31): Accentual rise after the word's high tone and accentual fall. Secondary rise is evidenced by the Delphic hymns and restricted to non-prepausal syllables (Devine and Stephens 1994).

Shortening (*or* **Epic Correption**) (p. 75): Adjustment on the arsis of a .CV.-syllable containing a long vocalic *nucleus so that it meets the requirements of a metrical position that expects a light syllable (Devine and Stephens 1994). Shortening is either the *elision or *gliding of the long vowel's second mora (Allen 1973).

Sonority (p. 34): Perceptual correlate of intrinsic intensity or acoustic energy. In a strict sense, sonority refers to voiced phonation and higher intensity of the syllabic *nucleus. The sound trajectory towards the syllabic nucleus is called peak; the trajectory from it, towards the completion of the syllable, the slope. In more general terms, sonority seems to be a useful term to indicate the combination of some or all of the properties of acoustic prominence, including duration (Devine and Stephens 1994). Theory attributes most sonority to the vocalic *nucleus of the syllable and to the consonantal *coda (slope). The sonority of the *onset is limited (Allen 1973).

Split fifth foot spondee: *see* **Bridge**

Spondaic word end (p. 81): Word end in a spondee, that is, on the *arsis. The restriction on spondaic word end in hexametric poetry (on the second, fourth, and fifth spondee) is known as the spondaic *bridge and formulated under Hilberg's Law for the second *foot, and Naeke's Bridge for the fourth.

Stanza (p. 24n12): Cluster of similar, repetitive verses ending in a variant verse-final structural element (*catalexis or *brevis in longo*) (Faraone 2006).

Stichic verse (p. 24): Poetry featuring repeated lines with verse-internal metrical repetition (West 1982; Van Raalte 1986).

στίχος κέφαλος (p. 77): Dactylic line with a light syllable occupying the first foot *thesis (Leaf 1900–1902; Bakker 1988).

στίχος λαγαρός (p. 127): Dactylic line with a light syllable occupying the first foot *arsis (Leaf 1900–1902; Steinrück 2005).

στίχος μείουρος (p. 77): Dactylic line with a light syllable occupying the sixth foot *thesis (Leaf 1900–1902; Steinrück 2005).

Stress (p. 33): Cross-linguistic typologic reference to syllable intensity in speech *rhythm. In Greek, stress is used to refer to the syllable's intensity due to *syllable weight (*sonority) (Allen 1973; Devine and Stephens 1994).

Strophe (p. 24n12): Cluster of responsive verses (Van Raalte 1986).

Submoraic adjustment (p. 33): Adjustment of categorized *syllable weight to phonetic circumstances. In general, submoraic adjustment accounts for the mismatch of *mora count and metrically required or allowed *syllable weight (Devine and Stephens 1994). Conscious disregard of phonetic adjustment results in a lack of rhythmical periodicity for most meters, except the anapaestic dimeter (Golston and Riad 2000).

Subordination: *see* **Heavy syllable subordination**

Superheavy (p. 21): Rhythmical denomination for the .CVC. syllable with a long vocalic *nucleus. The metrical qualification is *overlong (*mora count ≥ 3) (Devine and Stephens 1994).

Suprasegmental (p. 20n1): Characterictic of sound on a level higher than the vocalic and consonantal segment, usually on the level of the syllable (Lehiste 1970).

Syllabification: Syllable division (Devine and Stephens 1994):
— **Linguistic syllabification** (p. 70): Division of words into lexemes according to the word's morphology: prefix, stem, infix, ending, suffix.
— **Orthographic syllabification** (p. 21): Division of words into units of articulatory prominence according to the principle that as many consonants are clustered into the syllable's *onset as is allowed at the beginning of a word. Orthographical syllables do not signify quantity (Devine and Stephens 1994:24–31, 36–41).
— **Metrical syllabification** (pp. 21, 70): Division of words into phonemes according to the principle that a syllable's *coda consists of

one consonant at most, provided the subsequent syllable's *onset consists of at least one consonant. In metrical syllabification, all syllable and word junctions within the verse are treated as word internal. Devine and Stephens 1994 assume that metrical syllabification corresponds with perceived syllable division in natural unplanned speech.

— **Resyllabification** (p. 71): Shift of consonant from *onset to *coda, or from *coda to *onset, over word boundary (Devine and Stephens 1994:235–248).

Syllable division: *see* **Syllabification**

Syllable duration (p. 31): Intrinsic length of the syllable (Devine and Stephens 1994).

Syllable quantity (p. 31): In metrics, categorized duration of the syllable (*longum* or *breve*) based on syllable structure; in rhythmics, categorized weight of the syllable (*heavy* or *light*) based on syllable structure (Devine and Stephens 1994).

Syllable weight (p. 34): Rhythmical categorization of syllables' intensity based on *sonority (Devine and Stephens 1994).

Synaphy: *see* **Sandhi**

Thesis (T) (p. 22): First half of the dactylic *foot. Invariable structural element (West 1982; Lidov 1989).

Trithemimeres (p. 27): Name given (in antiquity and reused by, among others, Korzeniewski 1968:31) to the *caesura following position 3.

Trochaic caesura: *see* **Caesura**

Wernicke's Law: *see* **Bridge**

Appendix

The Grammatical Clause in Homer

When using the grammatical term "clause" and applying it to the Homeric epic, we must define what exactly is meant by *grammatical clause*. Where does such a clause begin? Where does it end? What clues are there in the *Iliad* and the *Odyssey* to enable the listening audience to perceive any clausal structure in performance? This appendix focuses on grammatical clues and characteristics.

In recent years, functional grammar[1] has provided a model for the description of the grammatical clause and the sentence. The central role in this description is that of the *predicate*, the finite verb, because it is the verb form that dictates the further requirements for a grammatically correct and complete clause. The semantics of the predicate determine the *predicate frame*: the meaning of the finite verb creates, or requires, one or more *valencies* for *arguments* with a specific semantic value in relation to the predicate. In *Iliad* I 1, for example, the verb form ἄειδε has a valency of 2: the subject[2] and a direct object:

(200) μῆνιν ἄειδε θεά Πηληιάδεω Ἀχιλῆος

Iliad I 1

Sing, goddess, of the wrath of Achilles, son of Peleus

In *Odyssey* i 1, the verb form ἔννεπε has a valency of 3: subject, direct object, and indirect object:

---

[1] Cf. Van Emden Boas and Huitink 2010.

[2] Though the subject of an imperative is often included in the verbal form itself, as it is here. The vocative θεά is in apposition to the included subject.

(201) ἄνδρα μοι ἔννεπε Μοῦσα πολύτροπον ὃς μάλα πολλὰ

Odyssey i 1

Tell me, Muse, about the man of many devices, who for a very long
    time

The resulting *predicate frame* is referred to as the *nuclear predication*. In *Iliad* I 1,
the nuclear predication is μῆνιν ἄειδε, "sing of the wrath." In *Odyssey* i 1, it is
ἄνδρα μοι ἔννεπε "tell me about the man." The verbs ἀείδω "sing" and ἐνέπω
"tell" are being used as transitive verbs here, but both may be applied as intransitive[3] with similar ease. In functional grammar, this difference in usage *tran-
sitive-intransitive* is seen as a difference in semantics and described as a difference in predicate frames; a verb can be identified as being used with, or within,
various predicate frames, depending on context.

Both in *Iliad* I 1 and in *Odyssey* i 1, the predication consists of more than
the mere predicate frame. In *Iliad* I 1, we find, beside the nuclear predication,
the word group Πηληϊάδεω Ἀχιλῆος "of Achilles, son of Peleus." In *Odyssey* i 1,
there is the describing adjective πολύτροπον "resourceful." In both *Iliad* I 1 and
Odyssey i 1, there is a vocative. These peripheral constituents of the predication,
as opposed to the nuclear predication, are labelled *satellites*.

In general, there are two types of satellites. On the one hand, we find
the *adjuncts*: satellites that further specify the nuclear predication, with the
semantic role *instrument, beneficiary, purpose, time, place, mode*, and *degree*,[4] and
the pragmatic function[5] *setting*. On the other hand, the *disjuncts*, satellites that
render *meta-communicative expressions*; for example, the point of view or opinion
of either the writer or, as understood by the writer, of the audience. The scope
of disjuncts is the predication as a whole. Examples of disjuncts are the *modal
adverbs, opinion-based adverbative elements, style disjuncts, pseudo-final subordinate
clauses, parenthetic conditionals*, constituents with the pragmatic function *theme*
and *tail*,[6] and in addition, as I have argued in §6.2.2.1, the vocative. In the *Iliad*
and the *Odyssey*, examples of each of the usages mentioned can be found:

- Instrument:
    (202) μειδήσασα δὲ παιδὸς ἐδέξατο <u>χειρὶ</u> κύπελλον

Iliad I 596

    smiling, she took the cup from her son <u>with her hand</u>

---

[3] For the intransitive use of ἀείδω, see *Iliad* I 604, *Iliad* II 598, *Iliad* IV 125, *Odyssey* i 154, *Odyssey* i 155,
    Odyssey i 325, *Odyssey* xix 519, *Odyssey* xxi 411; for ἐνέπω, cf. *Iliad* XI 643, *Odyssey* xxiii 301.
[4] Bartsch 1972; Verkuyl 1972; S. C. Dik 1997:I,191–209.
[5] S. C. Dik 1997:I,313–338, II,401–405.
[6] Greenbaum 1969; Meier-Fohrbeck 1978; Quirk 1972; S. C. Dik 1997:I,132–140.

- Beneficiary:

  (203) <u>μητρὶ φίλῃ</u> ἐν χερσὶ τίθει καί μιν προσέειπεν

  Iliad I 585

  placed it in her hand <u>for his mother</u> and spoke to her

- Purpose:

  (204) ἐμοὶ δέ κε ταῦτα μελήσεται <u>ὄφρα τελέσσω</u>

  εἰ δ' ἄγε τοι κεφαλῇ κατανεύσομαι <u>ὄφρα πεποίθῃς</u>

  Iliad I 523–524

  for me these matters will be under my attention <u>to bring about</u>; | well then, I will nod with my head, <u>that you may feel confident</u>[7]

- Time:

  (205) <u>τῇ δεκάτῃ</u> δ' ἀγορήνδε καλέσσατο λαὸν Ἀχιλλεύς

  Iliad I 54

  <u>on the tenth day</u>, Achilles summoned the army to a gathering

Of course, the expression of "time" can also refer to a specific duration or period.

- Place:

  (206) οὐδ' <u>ἔνθα</u> πεφυγμένος ἦεν ἀέθλων

  Odyssey i 18

  not even <u>there</u> was he completely safe from misfortunes

Apart from the actual location, "place" encompasses the direction, the origin, and the route as well.

- Mode:

  (207) ἀλλὰ Ποσειδάων γαιήοχος <u>ἀσκελὲς</u> αἰὲν

  Κύκλωπος κεχόλωται

  Odyssey i 68–69

  but earth-shaking Poseidon is still always, <u>endlessly</u>, | furious because of the Cyclops

- Degree:

  (208) ἂψ ἴτω ἐς μέγαρον πατρὸς <u>μέγα</u> δυναμένοιο

  Odyssey i 276

  she has to leave straightaway for the palace of her father, <u>greatly</u> empowered

---

[7] *Contra* Chantraine 1953:II,297. I do not believe that there is a fundamental difference between the two final clauses that should lead to identification of ὄφρα τελέσσω as an argument. The correspondence in the prosodic patterns of lines *Iliad* I 523–524 is an additional reason to find unlikely an impersonal use of μελέομαι here.

- Setting as a *pragmatic function* means that the constituent provides the audience with a situation or an event that serves as the starting point for the nuclear predication. In Greek, setting, like the semantic function purpose, is regularly expressed by means of a verb form. Examples are the participle or a word group introduced by a conjunction:

(138) τοῦ ὅ γ᾽ <u>ἐπιμνησθεὶς</u> ἔπε᾽ ἀθανάτοισι μετηύδα

Odyssey i 31

<u>thinking of him</u> he spoke the following words to the immortals

(139) <u>εἰ μὲν δὴ νῦν τοῦτο φίλον μακάρεσσι θεοῖσι</u>
νοστῆσαι Ὀδυσῆα πολύφρονα ὅνδε δόμονδε
Ἑρμείαν μὲν ἔπειτα διάκτορον ἀργειφόντην
νῆσον ἐς Ὠγυγίην ὀτρύνομεν κτλ.

Odyssey i 82–85

<u>if that [is] indeed dear to the blessed gods,</u> | that Odysseus returns to what is his, to his home, | then let us send Hermes, the guide, the slayer of Argus | to the island Ogygia ...

These two examples from the first book of the *Odyssey* show that the pragmatic function setting, as does the semantic function purpose, creates the possibility to describe *embedded predications*. The syntax of the Homeric epic, however, is highly paratactic,[8] and allows for a strong progressive and adding tendency (as line 83 in the example *Odyssey* i 82–85 clearly shows). I think this severely limits the application of *setting*, a pragmatic function that seems to me more convincingly identified in written, periodic style.

- Modal adverb: in Homer, modal adverbs are always disjuncts. They cannot be used as independent utterances, as in, for example, Plato (πάνυ γε). They strengthen, weaken, or negate meaning:

(209) ἦε κεν νοστήσας ἀποτίσεται ἦε καὶ <u>οὐκί</u>

Odyssey i 268

whether he will make them pay after his return, or, as is as likely, <u>not</u>

In addition, modal adverbs express the *illocutive* function of a clause, that is, the pragmatic function of the clause as a whole: what is the aim of the clause as a speech-act? what does the clause want the receiver to do in reaction? An example is the indication of the start of a question:

---

[8] Chantraine 1953:II,351–364; Bakker 1997b.

(210) ἦ φὴς τοῦτο κάκιστον ἐν ἀνθρώποισι τετύχθαι

Odyssey i 391

<u>let me ask you</u>, do you think that this has turned out to be the worst thing among mortals?

The particles κε (κεν) and ἄν also serve as disjuncts.[9]

- Opinion-based adverbative elements (or attitudinal disjuncts):
  (211)   <u>καὶ λίην</u> κεῖνός γε ἐοικότι κεῖται ὀλέθρωι

Odyssey i 46

<u>yes, clearly</u>, that man lies low in a destruction that is his due

In many instances, it is difficult to appreciate the opinion-based value of the adverbative element. Three aspects of this difficulty are worth mentioning:

1. the actual opinion in the clause may be expressed by another word (in the example above ἐοικότι, "that is his due") and is merely strengthened, or at least not weakened, by the adverbative element;

2. often in Greek, this type of disjunct will be expressed by a particle, but the meaning and value of various Greek particles remain in dispute. For an overview, see Denniston 1954 and Ruijgh 1971. Clearly, analysis of, for example δή as a near equivalent of ἤδη turns many instances of the latter into opinion-based adverbative elements;

3. identifying opinions and judgements in ancient Greek texts is the aim of studies of *focalizing* and *focalizers*: if it is clear *through the eyes of whom* situations or actions are being seen, presented, and judged, it will become clearer whether single words or combinations of words might or should be regarded as attitudinal. Fundamental research in this domain is presented in De Jong 1987.

- Style disjuncts:
  (212) ὦ γέρον <u>ἤτοι</u> ἐγὼ θεὸς ἄμβροτος εἰλήλουθα
         Ἑρμείας κτλ.

Iliad XXIV 460–461

old man, <u>to be frank</u>, I, an immortal god, have come to your aid: | Hermes ...[10]

---

[9] Cf. Chantraine 1953:II,345–350.
[10] Cf. the use of, e.g., τοι in *Odyssey* xi 252.

- Pseudo-final subordinate clauses:

(213) ἠ' ἀπόειπ' ἐπεὶ οὔ τοι ἔπι δέος <u>ὄφρ' εὖ εἰδῶ</u>
<u>ὄσσον ἐγὼ μετὰ πᾶσιν ἀτιμοτάτη θεός εἰμι</u>

Iliad I 515–516

or say no, since for you there is no reason to fear, <u>that I may know</u>
<u>for sure | how thoroughly without privilege a goddess I am amidst</u>
<u>all</u>

As in the examples given with setting above, the paratactic character of Homeric discourse makes it difficult to distinguish between clauses proper and clauses within a larger scale unit. If ἐπεὶ οὔ τοι ἔπι δέος is not interpreted as a parenthesis, ὄφρ' εὖ εἰδῶ ὄσσον ἐγὼ μετὰ πᾶσιν ἀτιμοτάτη θεός εἰμι is merely pseudo-final.

- Parenthetic conditionals:

(214) <u>εἰ δ' ἐθέλεις καὶ ταῦτα δαήμεναι</u> ὄφρ' εὖ εἰδῇς
ἡμετέρην γενεήν πολλοὶ δέ μιν ἄνδρες ἴσασιν
ἔστι πόλις Ἐφύρη μυχῷ Ἄργεος ἱπποβότοιο
ἔνθα δὲ Σίσυφος ἔσκεν ὃ κέρδιστος γένετ' ἀνδρῶν

Iliad VI 150–153

<u>if you want to know that as well</u>, that you may understand fully | my
lineage–many men know of it: | there is a city Ephyre in a far region
of horse-breeding Argos; | there Sisyphus resided, who grew to be
craftiest of men

Again, as in the preceding example, it proves difficult to label seemingly subordinate clauses in the Homeric epic with semantic or pragmatic functions in relation to what would be called a main clause in written language.[11]

- Theme- and tail-constituents:

(137) <u>Λητοῦς καὶ Διὸς υἱός</u> ὃ γὰρ βασιλῆι χολωθεὶς
νοῦσον ἀνὰ στρατὸν ὦρσε κακήν ὀλέκοντο δὲ λαοί
οὔνεκα τὸν Χρύσην ἠτίμασεν ἀρητῆρα
<u>Ἀτρείδης</u>

Iliad I 9–12

<u>Leto's and Zeus' son [theme]</u>: for he felt angry towards the king
and | sent a foul plague over the army's camp—the soldiers
perished—| since he had dishonored him, Chryses, the priest, | <u>he,</u>
<u>that is, Agamemnon</u> [tail]

---

[11] Cf. the discussion on sentence-structure in these lines in Kirk 1990:176–178.

The model thus described considers predication as equal to the *sentence*, just as it is understood in written language.[12] With the exception of anacolutha, there is a hierarchical relation between the main finite verb and other verb forms within a complex sentence. The subordinate clause or clauses feature verb forms (and their predicate frame) with semantic or pragmatic functions *vis-à-vis* the main verb form: they are either argument to the main nuclear predication, or satellite within the complex predication as a whole. Their sub-position to the main predicate is reflected in terminology: they constitute *embedded predications*. These embedded predications, in turn, serve as the center of their own nuclear predication and predication frame, possibly adorned with their own satellites and, in case of embedded predications with a finite verb, introduced by a conjunction. Schematic representation of a complex sentence or predication resembles a tree, with branches representing embedded predications. *Iliad* I 57–58 would appear as follows:

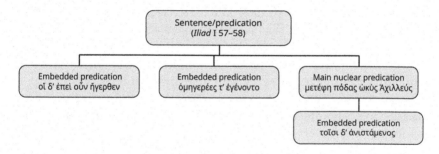

Figure 1. The complex predication

Still, the leap from clause to sentence is a giant one; and the denomination "clause" lies well outside the domain of semantic functions and values. Semantics determine the boundaries of the predications. Functional grammar does not consider an (embedded) predication as equal to a clause, for example (as in this case) to a subordinate clause.

"Clause" is merely useful when dealing with *pragmatic functions*: οἳ δ' ἐπεὶ οὖν ἤγερθεν looks like a complete subordinate clause, but οἳ ought to be labelled extra-clausal. Identification as extra-clausal follows from the identification of pragmatic functions: topic, focus, theme/tail (= left-/right-dislocation) and setting. Pragmatic functions determine whether constituents are part of the clause or not: S. C. Dik[13] labels constituents with function theme/tail and setting

---

[12] Slings 1992.

[13] S. C. Dik 1997:II,381: "[these constituents] are typically set off from the clause proper by breaks or pause-like inflections in the prosodic contour."

as extra-clausal. Strictly "clausal" are the constituents with the function topic and focus, in addition to, of course, the predicate. Since theme, tail, and setting are extra-clausal, their appearance marks the boundaries of the grammatical clause. Anything in between—between the constituents with pragmatic functions inside and outside (especially *following*) the clause—is labelled "extra," but seen as part ("extension") of the clause. This "extra" is not the main problem for now, as it merely extends the nuclear predication into an "extended" clause, nor is the setting, itself clause-like shaped. It is especially the theme/tail-constituent that is left in between: between the *pragmatically confined* clause and the *semantically extended* predication. The same goes for non-clausal appositions: where do they belong in paratactic syntax? What structuring effect do they render? In what respect are they different from "extras"?

The grammatical clause in Homer

In Homer, as in any other text, analysis of the structure and extent of the grammatical clause would start from main verb forms, the finite verbs. All further text elements can be identified in two different ways. First, as single words or word groups, they represent a particular semantic value in relation to a finite verb and its predicate frame. At the same time, as constituents, they serve pragmatic functions within the predication, either within the clause, or as extra-clausals. From these observations, I present the following four working hypotheses for a description of Homeric discourse:

1. Both semantic values *and* pragmatic functions are considered as being confined in their *scope*[14] to the predication.

2. Whereas semantic valuation is derived from the word groups' informational value for the predicate, the pragmatic function of constituents organizes and structures the presentation of information.

3. The denomination "clause" as grammatical terminology signifies the smallest *coherent predicate-centered unit*. As such, the clause can be framed by structuring extra-clausal constituents with pragmatic functions as *theme, tail,* or *setting*. Or, alternatively, by words or word groups with the semantic value *connector* or *coordinator*. The clause itself is free from text elements that are used to structure the complex predication.

4. The clause itself is merely a *grammatically coherent whole*, without any regard for structuring value or effect. As a constituent, the clause

---

[14] Devine and Stephens 2000:72–73.

itself can only serve in the pragmatic functions *discourse topic* and *discourse focus*. Primarily, usage of the denomination "clause" is solely on the level of *illocutionary force*, i.e., on the level of pragmatic functions for predicate frames or predications *as a whole*. Therefore, the clause must be a coherent and, to a large extent, independent and demarcated utterance.

Together, these four working hypotheses lead to a strictly pragmatic definition of "clause" with a specific illocutionary force. As mentioned above, illocutionary force indicates the function of the type of predication,[15] always considered as an independent utterance. In Greek, there are four identifiable illocutionary types of predications: predications are either declarative (*Iliad* I 2 ἣ μυρί᾽ Ἀχαιοῖς ἄλγε᾽ ἔθηκεν, "that bestowed innumerable pains on the Greeks"), interrogative (*Iliad* I 8 τίς τάρ σφωε θεῶν ἔριδι ξυνέηκε μάχεσθαι, "who then of the gods brought these two together in strive?"), imperative (*Iliad* I 1–2 μῆνιν ἄειδε θεά Πηληιάδεω Ἀχιλῆος οὐλομένην, "sing, goddess, of the destructive wrath of Achilles, son of Peleus"), or exclamative (*Odyssey* i 64 ποῖόν σε ἔπος φύγεν ἕρκος ὀδόντων, "what a word has escaped the barrier of your teeth?"). Regularly, the illocutionary force is closely related to the type of predication:[16] declarative predications are assertive, interrogative predications are inquisitive, imperative predications are directive. The illocutionary force can be expressed or strengthened by the use of specific moods of the verb or modal adverbative elements.[17] It is likely that intonation was a determining factor for illocutionary force in ancient Greek as in modern European languages.

Defining the clause as the coherent predicate-centered unit raises questions concerning the position of predicative participles. In a style other than periodic, as is Homer's, labelling a participle word group as "setting" is not necessarily correct or useful. And even if it were, in itself the setting-like participle word group is inevitably predicate-centered, be it in a way different from being centered on a finite verb. Still, the participle is itself a ῥῆμα, a more-or-less finite verb form.[18] Its realization as a minor phrase[19] resembles that of the unit centered on a finite verb. In the appositional syntax of the Homeric epic, the predicative participle may easily be identified as the center of an individual

---

[15] Franck 1980; Lyons 1977; Searle 1969, 1976.

[16] An example of the opposite is the so-called rhetorical question: an interrogative predication with assertive illocutionary force.

[17] Both the usage of specific modes and modal adverbs create the possibility to identify *optative* and *concessive illocutionary force* as well.

[18] Cf. Ruijgh 1987:342n62.

[19] Cf. Devine and Stephens 1994:387–388.

clause, instead of as a *constituent in* a clause.[20] The status of non-finite verb forms is not always different from that of the finite verbs themselves. The use of the predicative participle requires special attention. Its prosodic realization regularly underlines its syntactical application as apposition. When used as an apposition to the subject of a finite verb, its status as a ῥῆμα equals that of the finite verb in an example like *Odyssey* i 156–157:

> (215) αὐτὰρ Τηλέμαχος προσέφη γλαυκῶπιν Ἀθήνην
>   ἄγχι <u>σχὼν</u> κεφαλήν ἵνα μὴ πευθοίαθ' οἱ ἄλλοι
>
> *Odyssey* i 156–157
>
> but Telemachus addressed grey-eyed Athena | <u>and held</u> his head close to hers to prevent the others from noticing

Or even in a well-known formula like *Odyssey* i 63:

> (216) τὴν δ' <u>ἀπαμειβόμενος</u> προσέφη νεφεληγερέτα Ζεύς
>
> *Odyssey* i 63
>
> Zeus the cloud-gatherer <u>gave</u> her <u>an answer</u> and spoke

Easily found are the comparable formulaic verses and expressions in which the non-descriptive "setting" ἀπαμειβόμενος is *not* present. Its presence would neither benefit nor harm the remaining formula.

Both cases of the predicative participle hardly apply as examples of "setting." Chantraine[21] points out that the predicative participle, especially the perfect participle, is frequently being used as predicate in Homer. The second example, *Odyssey* i 63, resembles the usage of two closely related main verbs, itself reminiscent of hendiadys. Numerous are the examples of two conjoining main finite verbs, as in *Odyssey* i 231:

> (217) ἐπεὶ ἄρ δὴ ταῦτά μ' <u>ἀνείρεαι ἠδὲ μεταλλᾷς</u>
>
> *Odyssey* i 231
>
> Since indeed you <u>ask and question</u> me about this

Chantraine assumes that more complex syntactical organization like subordination is in a stage of development in Homer. An indication of the development of verbal hierarchy is found in the usage of modes, other than indicative. I do not subscribe to his point of view. Analysis of the various modes being used in the *Iliad* and the *Odyssey* does not show even a slight trace of "development" of paratactic clauses into verbal hierarchy within a predication. It is noteworthy

---

[20] Chantraine 1953:II,329.
[21] Chantraine 1953:II,321, with examples.

to point out that, apart from the lack of verbal hierarchy, the coordinators and connectors do not suggest a strong sense of hypotaxis:

> Même lorsque les propositions sont liées par des particules de coordination, il se pose des problèmes et il apparaît en particulier que leur disposition n'est pas toujours logique. Le poète énonce en premier lieu le fait qui lui semble le plus important ou que ses yeux aperçoivent d'abord, sans s'astreindre à une succession chronologique ou logique.[22]

The paratactical apposition of verb-centered predications resembles the non-grammatical "flat" apposition of autonomous words. Coordinators and connectors do not "logically" tie predications together. On the contrary: their usage merely underlines the progressive tendency, the movement that characterizes Homeric syntax. Next to the "finite" status of the predicative participle, the lack of syntactical hierarchy between individual verb forms is an indication for the independence of the individual grammatical clause as a syntactical unit.

"Isolating" transition

These two arguments (hierarchical status of the main verb remains unclear; connectives and verb modes do not indicate subordination) support the concept of Homeric discourse as a *series of autonomous verb forms*. The relation of the verb forms to one another is not a hierarchical one. Comparison to the usage, in classical Greek, of certain coordinators may have suggested such verbal hierarchy in the *Iliad* and the *Odyssey*. In Homer, the relation between the verb forms remains a paratactic one. With one important restriction, on my part, on the meaning of "paratactic": the "succession of autonomous finite verbs" is not a description of the internal organization of the complex predication. It is, in fact, a negation of any such internal organization. The progressive movement continues at least[23] up until a shift in discourse type.[24] It is not further, internally, organized towards verbal hierarchy by any predication-structuring devices, such as the use of connectors in written discourse. Connectors play a role as providers of "continuation" due to prosodic isolation. When analyzing the usage of connectors in Homer, the focus should be on a special category of connectors. There is a category of possible "continuations" that is less obvious when judged by the grammatical standards of written discourse. It is, however, understandable as a form of continuation from the point of view of a listening audience.

---

[22] Chantraine 1953:II,351–352.
[23] Cf. Aristotle's remark on the value of written punctuation in *Rhetoric* 1409a29–31.
[24] Possibly even further, if direct speech is considered as embedded predication.

In written discourse, an important continuing, and structuring, device is the combination of μέν in the first member of a grammatically coordinated antithesis, with either ἀλλά, ἀτάρ, εἶτα, ἔπειτα, αὖτε, ἠδέ, οὐδέ, τε, καί, τοίνυν, or δέ in the following limb or limbs. The common answer to μέν is δέ. When combined, μέν is said to raise expectations for an antithesis to be composed of at least two clauses; δέ introduces the second (and subsequent) limb(s). Still, what seems to be the rule knows many exceptions.[25] In fact, the use of δέ as answer to μέν is often not adversative at all. In many instances, δέ is merely continuative.[26] When used as connective, with or without a preparatory particle in the preceding limb, δέ is continuative rather than adversative. In addition, the continuative usage of δέ *without* a preparatory particle in the preceding limb is much more frequent than the usage *with*.

In Homer and Herodotus, the use of connective δέ without a preparatory particle in the preceding limb is predominant. Connective δέ may be used to pile up a considerable number of subsequent limbs. In the opening lines of the *Iliad*, as throughout the Homeric epics, δέ is merely used to mark the introduction of the next step in the narrative:

> (218) μῆνιν ἄειδε θεά Πηληιάδεω Ἀχιλῆος
> οὐλομένην ἣ μυρί᾽ Ἀχαιοῖς ἄλγε᾽ ἔθηκεν
> πολλὰς <u>δ᾽</u> ἰφθίμους ψυχὰς Ἄιδι προίαψεν
> ἡρώων αὐτοὺς <u>δὲ</u> ἑλώρια τεῦχε κύνεσσιν
> οἰωνοῖσί τε πᾶσι Διὸς <u>δ᾽</u> ἐτελείετο βουλή
>
> *Iliad* I 1–5
>
> Sing, Goddess, of the wrath of Achilles, son of Peleus | so destructive, it bestowed innumerable pains on the Greeks; | many excellent souls it sent to the house of Hades | of heroes; their bodies it turned into loot for the dogs | and all birds; the will of Zeus gradually became fulfilled

Regardless of its relation to a preceding protasis, connective δέ redirects the listeners' attention to the next bit of information. In written discourse, there is a limit to the number of δέ-limbs that can be joined to a protasis. The resulting, more balanced alternation of protasis and connective (or adversative) δέ structures written discourse in a way quite unlike the effect of connective δέ in Homer. In written discourse, preparatory μέν and connective (and adversative)

---

[25] Denniston 1954:369.
[26] Denniston 1954:177.

δέ contribute to a division of larger scale units into sentences; in Homer, μέν and δέ do not suggest a sentence-like internal division of discourse.[27]

The Homeric usage of δέ requires new terminology. Apollonius Dyscolus labels it δὲ μεταβατικός; modern scholars, following that lead, speak of δέ *transitive*. In his study on Homeric enjambment, Bakker[28] points out that the transitive usage of δέ may well be compared with the use of "and" when moving to the next step in presenting a narrative in spoken English. Such use of English "and" (as of Greek δέ) is connective, but not so much *coordinative as additive*.[29] The particle keeps the narrative continuing, thus playing various roles as connector. As such, the usage of the particle facilitates the poet's adding style. The position of δέ in the syntax of the Homeric epics corresponds to that in written classical Greek. Occupying the second position in the clause, the localization of δέ (connective or non-connective) serves a purpose in marking transition. In his 1990 article, Bakker postulates that the position of δέ might turn a preceding word group into a *left-dislocated* theme constituent. In subsequent publications[30] he dismisses the terminology, since it suggests an aberration from a standard syntactical realization.

As a continuing, and structuring, device occupying the second position in the clause, the localization of δέ serves a purpose in marking transition. The prosodic character of δέ as a postpositive[31] concludes the phonetic word,[32] the appositive group, but only *after* the initial word of the next syntactical unit has already been introduced. The theme of the subsequent unit has already been introduced in one accentual unit together with δέ. The announcement of this theme is syntactically and phonetically isolated due to the combination of the additive usage and the appositive character of δέ.[33] The location of δέ enables the phonetic word (of which δέ is the closure; for example, αὐτοὺς δὲ in *Iliad* I 4) to fill the metrical colon between two positions of frequent word end. Similar conclusions may be drawn from the usage of γάρ and ἄρα.[34] These two particles are also postpositive; like δέ, γάρ is not only postpositive, but to an extent enclitic as well. The particles δέ, γάρ and ἄρα all isolate an added theme in a

---

27 Bonifazi et al. 2016:2.2.1, 4.2.1.
28 Bakker 1990; cf. 1997a:54–85.
29 Terminology coined by Halliday and Hassan 1976:238.
30 Cf. Bakker 1997a.
31 Koster 1953:51–52; Devine and Stephens 1978. Devine and Stephens (1994:354–355) discuss the possibility of clisis for the particle. Clisis seems to be well possible at higher rates of speech. At lower rates, as evidenced in the musical settings, the grave accent of the non-lexical appositive does not seem to be part of the rising trajectory, as opposed to other word-final grave accents.
32 Goldstein 2014; 2016; cf. Bonifazi et al. 2016:2.1.1, and 4.2.2.
33 "Priming" in Bonifazi et al. 2016:2;2;5; in 4.2 they provide examples of particles δέ, τε, and καί "isolating" subclausal segments.
34 Ruijgh 1990; Devine and Stephens 1994:422–423; Bakker 1993:15–25; 1997b; 2005:92–113.

metrical colon: as postpositives they conclude the phonetic word introducing the new theme before expanding this theme into a new clause. Explicit mention ought to be made here of the use of the pronoun ὁ / ὅς with δέ to indicate a change of subject or a topic shift. The combination of the pronoun with the particle γάρ or δέ can signal either a topic shift or a *semi-relative* continuation. An example of topic shift may be found in *Iliad* I 56–57, of semi-relative continuation in *Iliad* I 46–47:

> (219) κήδετο γὰρ Δαναῶν ὅτι ῥα θνήσκοντας ὁρᾶτο
> οἱ δ' ἐπεὶ οὖν ἤγερθεν ὁμηγερέες τε γένοντο
>
> *Iliad* I 56–57
>
> For she felt for the Greeks as she saw them perish, | as for them, when they had thus gathered and come together

In line 56, the subject is Hera who pities the Greeks, expressed in the accusative case. The combination of pronoun and particle at the start of line 57 indicates the shift: from the start of line 57, the Greeks are the grammatical subject. In *Iliad* I 47 below, the shift is not as radical as in *Iliad* I 57. The person referred to by means of the pronoun (in combination with the particle) was already the "subject" in the preceding participle clause:

> (220) ἔκλαγξαν δ' ἄρ' ὀϊστοὶ ἐπ' ὤμων χωομένοιο
> αὐτοῦ κινηθέντος ὁ δ' ἤϊε νυκτὶ ἐοικώς
>
> *Iliad* I 46–47
>
> The arrows rattled on the shoulder of the enraged | himself as he moved himself into position: he approached like night

In combination with pronouns the particles δέ, γάρ, and ἄρα do not suggest any syntactical hierarchy. The usage of γάρ shows that interpretation of units as subordinate is more often than not highly conjectural. The localization of γάρ resembles epic τε and the Aeolic particle κε. It also resembles their effectiveness as modifiers. The exact modification resulting from γάρ is immediately clear. What is not clear is whether the usage of γάρ results in parataxis or subordination.[35] The formal syncretism of the relative and personal / demonstrative pronoun makes the issue hardly relevant.[36] Still, there are noticeable differences when it comes to the exact localization of the various connectors and of the

---

[35] Cf. the note on *Iliad* I 73 in Denniston 1954:72–73.

[36] That is, for the Homeric epic. In later Greek, the use of a relative pronoun instead of a personal pronoun to start a main clause leads to the identification of the relative pronoun as (part of) a connecting device.

phonetic word groups of which they are part. The phonetic word that fills the metrical colon may well be a chunk itself.[37] The same holds true for the localization of extended "subordinate conjunctions" (like δ' ἐπεὶ οὖν in *Iliad* I 57) in Homer. The continuation, the movement of Homeric discourse, is thus not only visible in the occurrence of discourse markers; it is *audible* in the isolating characterization of discourse markers.

Extra-clausal, intra-clausal, and inter-clausal transition

The progressive movement that defines Homeric syntax or rather replaces a true Homeric "syntax," presents the listening audience with bits and pieces of information. The audience receives grammatical clauses, which do not necessarily have to be interpreted in a periodic relation to what preceded or to what will follow. New, autonomous ideas are being added as grammatical clauses onto what has been told so far. Adding sometimes implies the usage of "transitional"[38] connectors, coordinators, adverbs, or particles, but most often, it does not. Continuation allows the pragmatic positioning of vocatives and "causes" that of theme and tail constituents in a way reminiscent of Clark's semantic "hooks" (§2.4). The presence, however, of such constituents is not a requirement. For Homer's audience, having missed one bit of information need not impede the understanding of subsequent bits. Nor will absorption of every bit of information so far necessarily heighten the level of the audience's understanding with regard to what is about to be told.

On the basis of what I have said so far, we can divide the verses of the *Iliad* and the *Odyssey* into grammatical clauses and extra-clausal constituents. I will present the first sixteen lines of the *Iliad* as an analysis in accordance with this division. At the start of the *Iliad*, the perceptible, translated presentation of bits of information may thus be rewritten in the following way, using subscript for punctuation and all transitional constituents in the translation:

1   μῆνιν ἄειδε θεά Πηληϊάδεω Ἀχιλῆος
      οὐλομένην ἥ μυρί' Ἀχαιοῖς ἄλγε' ἔθηκεν
      πολλὰς δ' ἰφθίμους ψυχὰς Ἄϊδι προΐαψεν
      ἡρώων αὐτοὺς δὲ ἑλώρια τεῦχε κύνεσσιν
5   οἰωνοῖσί τε πᾶσι Διὸς δ' ἐτελείετο βουλή

---

[37] Cf. the remarks on extra-clausal constituents in Hellenistic hexameters in Van Raalte 1986:69–70.

[38] I would argue that connectors and coordinators regularly are best described as *adverbial particles*, cf. Mithun 1988:345: "The lack of a clear distinction between adverbials and clause conjunctions is not unusual among languages."

ἐξ οὗ δὴ τὰ πρῶτα διαστήτην ἐρίσαντε
Ἀτρείδης τε ἄναξ ἀνδρῶν καὶ δῖος Ἀχιλλεύς
τίς τάρ σφωε θεῶν ἔριδι ξυνέηκε μάχεσθαι
Λητοῦς καὶ Διὸς υἱός ὁ γὰρ βασιλῆϊ χολωθεὶς
10   νοῦσον ἀνὰ στρατὸν ὦρσε κακήν ὀλέκοντο δὲ λαοί
οὕνεκα τὸν Χρύσην ἠτίμασεν ἀρητῆρα
Ἀτρείδης ὁ γὰρ ἦλθε θοὰς ἐπὶ νῆας Ἀχαιῶν
λυσόμενός τε θύγατρα φέρων τ' ἀπερείσι' ἄποινα
στέμματ' ἔχων ἐν χερσὶν ἑκηβόλου Ἀπόλλωνος
15   χρυσέωι ἀνὰ σκήπτρωι καὶ λίσσετο πάντας Ἀχαιούς
Ἀτρείδα δὲ μάλιστα δύω κοσμήτορε λαῶν

Iliad I 1–16

Sing of the wrath, _{goddess, (vocative)} of Achilles son of Peleus, _(?) so destructive: _(personal pronoun seemingly used as anaphoric) it bestowed countless pains on the Greeks, _{yes many: (δέ)} excellent souls it sent to the house of Hades of the heroes, _{as for themselves: (δέ)} it made them into loot for the dogs and _(τε) all the birds, _{as for Zeus's: (δέ)} his will gradually became fulfilled, _{from the moment (ἐξ οὗ δή)} the two of them stood up against one another in anger for the first time, _(verse-end) son of Atreus lord of man and (καί) godlike Achilles (shift to another illocutionary force), who then of the gods made the two of them come together to fight in _{strife: (shift to another illocutionary force)} Zeus's and (καί) Leto's son _{(?) for it was him: (γάρ)} out of anger for the king he sent a foul plague over the army's camp, _(δέ) they fell, _{the soldiers, because (οὕνεκα)} he had dishonoured the priest Chryses, _{he, the son of Atreus (verse-end), for it was him: (γάρ)} he came to the fast ships of the Greeks: (τε) to free his daughter _{and (τε)} bringing countless gifts _{and? (τε)} holding in his hand the ribbon(s?) of far-shooting Apollo around the golden priest's staff[39] _{and (καί)} he begged all the Greeks, _{and as for the two sons of Atreus (δέ),} especially those two, the two arrangers of the army: _(discourse shift)

A stop at the end of *Iliad* I 16 is not coincidental: it coincides with a shift in discourse type.

In this representation, the role of δέ, τε, and γάρ to mark the boundaries of the clause is evident. At the same time, it is equally clear that they do not function as organizers in complex predications. The postpositive (and enclitic) character of δέ, τε, and γάρ shows their respective roles in the development of

---

[39] Or rather: "he wanted to free his daughter ... he brought countless gifts ... he held in his hand the ribbon(s) of far-shooting Apollo around the golden priest's staff."

the flow of ideas.[40] This characterization of the particles brings out their usage as "audible punctuation" far better than their semantic contribution to predication-structuring. In verses 3, 4, 5, 10, and 16, δέ is merely used, as throughout the Homeric epics, to mark the introduction of the next step in the narrative. The use of the particle redirects the listeners' attention to the next bit of information. The particle is not meant in any way to structure the predication or restructure the complex predication. Its use does not even suggest a predication limited in size as the result of verbal hierarchy, with every subsequent hierarchical tree as the domain of a new predication. As a means of transition from one clause to the next, δέ itself stands in-between the two clauses but is not part of either. Bakker[41] points out that the transitive usage of δέ may well be compared with the use of *and*[42] when moving[43] to the next step in presenting a narrative in English. The particle links the various bits of information. As such, the usage of the particle facilitates the poet's adding style. Still, the position of δέ as "second constituent" puts both the particle itself (as an appositive) and the preceding constituent in a special light. This special light, however, can only be fully appreciated if the extra-clausal status of the connector retains its pragmatic function as theme-constituent: in other words, as long as its prosodic "isolation" separates the connector from the grammatical clause. As a connector, δέ is part of the developing clause if the particle is *elided*. This observation must result in modification of the analysis of *Iliad* I 1–16: semantically dislocated constituents ending in an elided particle cannot retain their pragmatic function as an *extra*-clausal. Only if the connector is not elided is the preceding word to which δέ is postpositive not a part of the clause that is about to start.[44] Nor is it of the preceding clause, despite the clause's apparent ability to extend by means of "extras": the constituent and its subsequent postpositive are truly "on their own." Together, they constitute the completion of a chunk that is audibly separated from what follows appositive δέ. Depending on speech rates, the position and location of δέ audibly cuts the narrative into pieces that include ones that are not predicate-centered in themselves. Often a verb form appears to be singled out, as in formulaic λῦσε δὲ γυῖα, "and <u>loosened</u> his limbs." Even more often (as is the case in, for example, *Iliad* I 5), the particle is elided. It is then no longer capable of turning the phonetic word into an extra-clausal. The elided phonetic word is drawn into the clause:

---

[40] Bonifazi et al. 2016:4.2.1.

[41] Bakker 1990.

[42] In my view, English progressive "and" may better be compared to Homeric καί, when preceded by an audible pause. In Bakker 1997b, Bakker describes καί as *additive*. See further discussion below.

[43] The preferred term in Bonifazi et al. 2016:2.3.

[44] Devine and Stephens 1994:303: "they are moved into that slot out of the phrasal constituent in which they would have remained had they been nonclitic words."

(221) νίκη <u>δ'</u> ἐπαμείβεται ἄνδρας

Iliad VI 339

Victory randomly finds its way to men

The closure of the appositive group by means of an enclitic particle[45] turns the "transitional" constituent into a separate phonetic word. When elided, the particle and the constituent preceding it are the initial part of a chunk. As appositive group, however, they remain "sentential-prepositive": the appositive group is itself syntactically proclitic to the subsequent grammatical clause that is its scope (indicated as [...]):[46]

(222) [Ἀργεῖοι δὲ → μέγα ἴαχον] [ἐρύσαντο δὲ → νεκρούς]

Iliad XVII 317

The Greeks cheered loudly, and started dragging the corpses away

It depends therefore on the realization of the appositive group as an independent phonetic word, whether it functions as extra-clausal transitional constituent or, in case of elision of the particle, as constituent within a grammatical clause (intra-clausal). The analysis of *Iliad* I 1–16 should hence be modified with respect to line 5: the dislocated constituent in the line is, in fact, intra-clausal.

Like δέ, the connector γάρ is postpositive and tends to occupy a position as sentential "second constituent." Like δέ, and other appositive particles,[47] the occurrence of γάρ actually defines the transitional constituent, and hence the phonetic word. As with δέ, γάρ can turn the preceding constituent, especially when this constituent is a pronoun, into a theme constituent. Notwithstanding that, γάρ has a different semantic value than δέ. While δέ functions as a transitional particle used merely to further the continuation of discourse, γάρ suggests a connection on the level of causality.[48] Scholars have often flagged a lack of logic in the presupposed connection of thoughts:

> Compression of thought is often the source of difficulty, and formal exactitude can then be achieved by supposing an ellipse ... this, though a convenient method of exposition, is psychologically somewhat misleading.[49]

---

[45] Goldstein 2014.
[46] Devine and Stephens 1994:303.
[47] In accordance with Wackernagel's Law; cf. Ruijgh 1990.
[48] Denniston 1954:56–74.
[49] Cf. Denniston 1954:61.

It is, indeed, difficult to see what causal connections underlie *Iliad* XXIV 66–70 (or, alternatively, Herodotus III, 80–82[50]):

(223) οὐ μὲν γὰρ τιμή γε μί' ἔσσεται ἀλλὰ καὶ Ἕκτωρ
      φίλτατος ἔσκε θεοῖσι βροτῶν οἳ ἐν Ἰλίωνι εἰσίν
      ὣς γὰρ ἐμοί γ' ἐπεὶ οὔ τι φίλων ἡμάρτανε δώρων
      οὐ γάρ μοί ποτε βωμὸς ἐδεύετο δαιτὸς ἐΐσης
      λοιβῆς τε κνίσης τε τὸ γὰρ λάχομεν γέρας ἡμεῖς

Iliad XXIV 66–70

For the honor will not be the same, but Hector too | was dearest to the gods of the mortals who are in Troy, | for so he was to me as he did not fail in any way in gifts dear to me, | for never at any time was my altar lacking in the equal banquet, | the drink offering and the savor of burn offering, for that we have received as our privilege

The connective use of the combination γε and ἄρ is far more prominent than the causal value.[51] Rather, the combined use of the postpositive deictic particle γε and resumptive ἄρ highlighting the value of the preceding constituent, together explain the seemingly explanatory character of the subsequent clause. I argue that the particle is better described as "transitional." Hence the ability of γάρ to turn the preceding word or word group into a theme constituent: it resembles a similar ability of δέ. The main difference between the two connectors, as the passages quoted from the *Iliad* show, is that γάρ implies topic continuation, whereas δέ results in topic shift. The topic continuing effect of γάρ stems from two aspects: the extra stress on the preceding constituent rendered by γε, but essentially the resumptive value of ἄρ, turning the preceding constituent into a continuing topic. On the other hand, δέ signals a change of camera-position.

The postpositive character of both γάρ and δέ is functional, in that it creates an audible separation of the phonetic word from what follows, thus emphasizing not the constituent preceding γάρ and δέ, but rather the pragmatic value of γάρ and δέ itself. As "rightbranchers," both conclude the phonetic word before continuing into the informational unit that forms the subsequent clause. The use of the connector τε is not in all instances comparable to that of the connectors γάρ and δέ. The latter two turn the preceding word or word group into an extra-clausal constituent preparing for the subsequent clause. The former

---

[50] Denniston 1954:63 notes that γάρ "refers, not to the immediately preceding sentence, but to something further back. This looseness of structure is characteristic of Homer and Herodotus: the Attic examples are few, and not remarkable."

[51] Cf. τάρ < τε + ἄρ.

is used to play down the disturbance of transition to another addition *within* the grammatical clause.[52] The connector τε is, in other words, an *inter*-clausal transition.

"Subordinating" transition?

Apart from καί, δέ, and τε the first sixteen lines of the *Iliad* contain a few conjunctions that, in classical Greek, are undoubtedly subordinating. In *Iliad* I 6, the combination ἐξ οὗ is taken as the introduction to a subordinate clause.[53] In *Iliad* I 11, οὕνεκα introduces a clause that seems to function as the explanation of the start of the plague and the subsequent suffering of the army as mentioned in *Iliad* I 10. Both conjunctions are built on the pronoun ὁ/ὅς that appears as what can be called in classical Greek, both demonstrative and relative.[54] The problematic identification of the type of pronoun has been dealt with in the description of syntax, especially hypotaxis, by Chantraine. In Homer, the difference between the two denominations of the pronoun is often irrelevant or even non-existant.[55] Nonetheless, the form of the pronoun (οὗ/οὐ(-) versus demonstrative τοῦ/του(-)) suggests usage as relative. Still, even if the conjunctions are analyzed as subordinating, the exact correspondence with a preceding piece of information can remain unclear, as in *Iliad* I 6. When not elided, the subordinating conjunctions resemble καί, δέ, and τε in that the conjunctions are isolating: they *cannot span* the subsequent clause. Conjunctions introduce the subsequent clause and, as such, represent the transition from one clause to the next. Their occurrence signals the beginning of a clause. As a consequence, their

---

[52] For an overview of the usage of τε, with the exception of so-called epic τε, see Denniston 1954:495-520.

[53] Though the dispute continues on whether the subordinate clause is depending on the imperative in line 1 or "Zeus's plan" (according to Aristarchus) in line 5. For recent discussion, see Bakker 1997b and Lacatz 2000 *ad loc.*

[54] In the *Iliad* and the *Odyssey*, the relative use of οὕνεκα seems most easily defensible when applied as correlative as in, e.g., *Iliad* I 111, *Iliad* I 403, *Iliad* XIII 727, *Iliad* XIV 192, and *Odyssey* xiii 332.

[55] Chantraine 1953:II,166 treats the pronoun ὁ as a rudimentary Homeric article, the result of further development of the Mycenaean demonstrative pronoun; as such, he recognizes the ability of the article to retain either demonstrative or relative value: "L'usage homérique appelle diverses observations qui s'expliquent par le caractère originellement démonstratif du pronom. Au nominatif féminin singulier (ἥ) et au nominatif pluriel masculin et féminin (à l'exception de τοί, ταί), il n'est pas possible de distinguer entre le thème de l'article et celui du relatif proprement dit : l'identité de ces formes a pu aider à l'extension du thème d'article à l'emploi de relatif. Les formes atones de l'article (ὁ, ἡ, οἱ, αἱ) sont accentuées lorsqu'elles équivalent au relatif (cf. A 388, etc...). Dans plus d'un exemple, il est malaisé de déterminer si l'article est proprement l'équivalent du relatif ou s'il est démonstratif. A la vérité, la question ne doit pas être tranchée, mais les exemples montrent l'origine de l'emploi « relatif » de l'article. Ces cas ambigus se trouvent surtout dans l'Iliade. ... Ajoutons que la tradition hésite entre ὅ et ὅς."

presence can result in the apparent conclusion of the preceding clause, but they are never being awaited nor expected.[56] In other words, the grammatical clause itself invariably remains open-ended when it comes to its potential length. In *Iliad* I 6, ἐξ οὗ is a fine example. There is no question about which grammatical clause ἐξ οὗ introduces. But the ongoing and persistent call for a correspondence with μῆνιν ἄειδε θεά in *Iliad* I 1 sufficiently shows to what extent the preceding informational unit or "clause" can be expanded in the opinion of various scholars.[57]

Then again, when used in what looks like a periodic utterance, the conjunction does create expectations, at least for a main clause to follow. But syntactical difficulties abound. In an example like *Iliad* I 37–41, the first periodic subordinate clause (line 39) may easily be understood as dependent, if dependent at all,[58] on the imperative κλῦθι in line 37:

> (224) κλῦθί μευ ἀργυρότοξ᾽ ὃς Χρύσην ἀμφιβέβηκας
> Κίλλαν τε ζαθέην Τενέδοιό τε ἶφι ἀνάσσεις
> Σμινθεῦ εἴ ποτέ τοι χαρίεντ᾽ ἐπὶ νηὸν ἔρεψα
> ἢ εἰ δή ποτέ τοι κατὰ πίονα μηρί᾽ ἔκηα
> ταύρων ἠδ᾽ αἰγῶν τόδε μοι κρήηνον ἐέλδωρ
>
> *Iliad* I 37–41

> hear me please, Silverbow, who stand protective over Chryse | and holy Killa and over Tenedus rule with iron fist, | Smitheus, if ever I covered a temple with a roof pleasing to you, | or if ever I gave you full ration when burning the fat shanks | of bulls and goats: fulfil this one hope for me

If it was not dependent on the imperative, alternative expectations are at first frustrated by the addition of another subordinate clause in *Iliad* I 40–41a (ἢ εἰ δή ποτέ τοι κατὰ πίονα μηρί᾽ ἔκηα | ταύρων ἠδ᾽ αἰγῶν). Finally, there is no preparatory effort to create a correlation between the seemingly periodic subordinate clauses in lines 39–41a and the imperative κρήηνον in 41b, unless it were the use of εἰ itself as in, for example, εἰ δ᾽ ἄγετε. Then again, in that case the remaining clauses in lines 39 and 40 should be analyzed as paratactic *main* clauses, as εἰ

---

[56] All correlative adverbs can be used without correspondence.

[57] I agree with Aristarchus (Arn/A) that line 6 gives the starting point of Zeus's plan, on the basis that ἐξ οὗ not only introduces the subsequent clause but concludes a separate grammatical clause ἐτελείετο βουλή as well; in parataxis with a high level of nonconfigurationality it is too farfetched, I think, to suppose a correspondence between grammatical clauses that are not linked by one and the same pragmatic constituent.

[58] Cf. the use of εἰ in combinations like εἰ δ᾽ ἄγε, εἰ δ᾽ ἄγετε, εἰ δέ, reducing εἰ to an introduction of an imperative.

merely prepares for the imperative and not for a subordinate clause. There is not such a huge difference between this passage and passages with an independent[59] protasis. As a result, it seems reasonable to consider the conjunction (in combination with an appositive particle) an extra-clausal constituent with an identifiable pragmatic function.[60]

Following Chantraine,[61] I think it is safe to assume that in Homer the development of particles into subordinating conjunctions is still in its infancy. The Homeric epics present the audience mainly with instances of the original usage of the particles in parataxis.

---

[59] Cf. Chantraine 1953:II,351–352.
[60] Functional grammar does not yet have terminology to cover such a pragmatic function. One might think of "transition-constituent," reorganizing the audience's expectations and hence facilitating the addition of new informational units.
[61] Chantraine 1953:II,232.

Bibliography

Agbayani, B., and C. Golston. 2010. "Phonological Movement in Classical Greek." *Language* 86:133–67.

Allen, T.W., ed. 1917. *Homeri Opera* III. 2nd ed. Oxford.

———, ed. 1919. *Homeri Opera* IV. 2nd ed. Oxford.

———, ed. 1931. *Homeri Ilias*. Oxford.

Allen, W. S. 1973. *Accent and Rhythm: Prosodic Features of Latin and Greek*. Cambridge.

———. 1987. *Vox Graeca*. 3rd ed. Cambridge.

Allerton, D. J. 1982. *Valency and the English Verb*. London.

Aronoff, M., and M.-L. Kean, eds. 1980. *Juncture*. Saratoga.

Arvaniti, A. 1991. *The Phonetics of Greek Rhythm and Its Phonological Implications*. PhD diss., Cambridge University.

———. 2016. "Rhythm, Timing, and the Timing of Rhythm." *Phonetica* 66:46–63.

Aujac, G., and M. Lebel. 1981. *De Compositione Verborum*. Paris.

Bakker, E. J. 1988a. "Long Diphthongs and Hiatus in Early Greek Epic." *Mnemosyne* 41:1–26.

———. 1988b. *Linguistics and Formulas in Homer: Scalarity and the Description of the Particle 'per'*. Amsterdam.

———. 1990. "Homeric Discourse and Enjambment: A Cognitive Approach." *Transactions of the American Philological Association* 120:1–21.

———. 1993. "Discourse and Performance: Involvement, Visualization, and 'Presence' in Homeric Poetry." *Classical Antiquity* 12:1–29.

———. 1997a. *Poetry in Speech*. Ithaca.

———. 1997b. "The Study of Homeric Discourse." In Morris and Powell 1997: 284–304.

———. 1997c. "Storytelling in the Future: Truth, Time, and Tense in Homeric Epic." In Bakker and Kahane 1997:11–36.

———. 1999. "How Oral Is Oral Composition?" In Mackay 1999.

———, ed. 2002. *Grammar as Interpretation: Greek Literature in Its Linguistic Contexts.* Amsterdam.

———. 2005. *Pointing at the Past: From Formula to Performance in Homeric Poetics.* Cambridge, MA.

———, ed. 2010. *A Companion to the Ancient Greek Language.* Oxford.

———. 2013. *The Meaning of Meat and the Structure of the Odyssey.* Cambridge.

Bakker, E. J., and F. Fabricotti. 1991. "Peripheral and Nuclear Semantics in Homeric Diction: The Case of Dative Expressions for Spear." *Mnemosyne* 44:63–84.

Bakker, E. J., and N. Van Der Houten. 1992. "Aspects of Synonymy in Homeric Formulaic Diction: An Investigation of Dative Expressions for Spear." *Classical Philology* 87:1–13.

Bakker, E. J., and A. Kahane, eds. 1997. *Written Voices, Spoken Signs: Tradition, Performance, and the Epic Text.* Cambridge, MA.

Barnes, H. R. 1970. "Enjambement and Oral Composition." *Transactions of the American Philological Association* 109:1–10.

———. 1986. "The Colometric Structure of the Greek Hexameter." *Greek, Roman, and Byzantine Studies* 27:125–150.

———. 1995. "The Structure of the Elegiac Hexameter: A Comparison of the Structure of Elegiac and Stichic Hexameter Verse." In Fantuzzi and Pretagostini 1995:135–161.

Bartsch, R. 1972. *Adverbialsemantik.* Frankfurt.

Basset, L. 1989. "L'augment et la distinction discours/récit dans l'*Iliade* et l'*Odysée*." In *Études homériques: Séminaire de recherché*, ed. M. Casevitz, 9–16. Lyon.

Basset, S. E. 1938. *The Poetry of Homer.* Berkeley.

Beck, D. 2012. "The Presentation of Song in Homer's *Odyssey*." In Minchin 2012: 25–53.

Beekes, R. S. P. 1972. "On the Structure of the Greek Hexameter: O'Neill Interpreted." *Glotta* 50:1–10.

Beekes, R. S. P., and M. Cuypers. 2003. "ΝΕΚΥΣ, ΑΝΤΙΚΡΥ, and Metrical Lengthening in Homer." *Mnemosyne* 56.4:485–491.

Berg, N. 1978. "*Parergon Metricum*: Der Ursprung des griechischen Hexameters." *Münchener Studien zur Sprachwissenschaft* 36:11–36.

Bird, G. D. 2010. *Multitextuality in the Homeric Iliad: The Witness of the Ptolemaic Papyri.* Hellenic Studies Series 43. Washington, DC.

Blankenborg, R. J. J. 2007. Review of *The Dance of the Muses: Choral Theory and Ancient Greek Poetics*, by A. P. David. *Bryn Mawr Classical Review* 2007.04.46.

———. 2008. "Tuning in: Tracing the Rhythmical Phrase in Homer." *Abstracts of the 139th Annual Meeting of the APA.* Chicago.

———. 2016. "Ending in the Middle? Enjambment and Homeric Performance." *Yearbook of Greek Epic* 1:65–105.

———. 2017. "Rhythm for Situational Contexts: The Case of Ancient Greek Epic Performance." *SKENE: Journal of Theatre and Drama Studies* 3.2. www.skenejournal.it/index/php/JTDS/article/view/122.

———. 2018. *Rhythm without Beat.* Washington, DC. http://nrs.harvard.edu/urn-3:hul.ebook:CHS_BlankenborgR.Rhythm_without_Beat.2014.

Bonifazi, A. 2009. "The Pragmatic Meanings of Some Discourse Markers in Homer." In Rieken and Widmer 2009:29–36.

Bonifazi, A., and D. F. Elmer. 2012. "Composing Lines, Performing Acts." In Minchin 2012:89–109.

Bonifazi, A., A. Drummen, and M. De Krey. 2016. *Particles in Ancient Greek Discourse: Five Volumes Exploring Particle Use across Genres.* Hellenic Studies Series 74. Washington, DC.

Brandreth, T. S. 1841. Ὁμήρου ϝιλίας: *Littera digamma restituta ad metri leges redegit et notatione brevi illustravit.* London.

Brooks, C. 2007. *Reading Latin Poetry Aloud.* Cambridge.

Bubeník, V. 1983. *The Phonological Interpretation of Ancient Greek.* Toronto.

Cantilena, M. 1980. *Enjambement e poesia esametrica orale: Ma verifica.* Ferrara.

Cazzato, V., and A. Lardinois, eds. 2016. *The Look of Lyric: Greek Song and the Visual.* Leiden.

Chafe, W. L. 1970. *Meaning and the Structure of Language.* Chicago.

———. 1988. "Linking Intonation Units in Spoken English." In Haiman and Thompson 1988:1–15.

———. 1994. *Discourse, Consciousness, and Time: The Flow and Displacement of Conscious Experience in Speech and Writing.* Chicago.

Chandler, H. 1881. *Greek Accentuation.* Oxford.

Chantraine, P. 1953. *Grammaire Homérique.* 2 vols. Paris.

———. 1961. *Morphologie Historique du Grec.* 3rd ed. Paris.

———. 1968–1980. *Dictionnaire étymologique de la langue grecque.* Paris.

Clark, J., C. Yallop, and J. Fletcher. 2007. *An Introduction to Phonetics and Phonology.* 3rd ed. Oxford.

Clark, M. 1994. "Enjambment and Binding in Homeric Hexameter." *Phoenix* 48:95–114.

———. 1997. *Out of Line: Homeric Composition beyond the Hexameter.* Lanham.

———. 2004. "Formulas, Metre, and Type-scenes." In Fowler 2004:117–138.

Clayman, D. L. 1981. "Sentence Length in Greek Hexameter Poetry." In Grotjahn 1981:107–136.

Clayman, D. L., and T. Nortwick. 1977. "Enjambement in Greek Hexameter Poetry." *Transactions of the American Philological Association* 77:85–92.

Collins, D. 2004. *Master of the Game: Competition and Performance in Greek Poetry.* Cambridge, MA.

Cutler, A., and D. R. Ladd. 1983. *Prosody: Models and Measurements.* Berlin.

Cruttenden, A. 1997. *Intonation.* 2nd ed. Cambridge.

D'Angour, A. 2011. *The Greeks and the New: Novelty in Ancient Greek Imagination and Experience.* Cambridge.

Dain, A. 1965. *Traité de métrique grecque.* Paris.

Daitz, S. G. 1991. "On Reading Homer Aloud: To Pause or Not to Pause." *American Journal of Philology* 112:149–160.

Dale, A. M. 1968. *The Lyric Metres of Greek Drama.* 2nd ed. Cambridge.

David, A. P. 2006. *The Dance of the Muses: Choral Theory and Ancient Greek Poetics.* Oxford.

Dee, J. H. 2004. *A Repertory of the Hexameter Patterns in the Iliad and the Odyssey.* Hildesheim.

De Jong, I. J. F. 1987. *Narrators and Focalizers: the Presentation of the Story in the Iliad.* Amsterdam.

———. 2001. *A Narratological Commentary on the Odyssey.* Cambridge.

Denniston, J. D. 1954. *The Greek Particles.* 2nd ed. Oxford.

Devine, A. M., and I. D. Stephens. 1975. "Anceps." *Greek, Roman, and Byzantine Studies* 16:197–215.

———. 1976. "The Homeric Hexameter and a Basic Principle of Metrical Theory." *Classical Philology* 71:141–163.

———. 1978. "The Greek Appositives: Towards a Linguistically Adequate Definition of Caesura and Bridge." *Classical Philology* 73:314–328.

———. 1980. "On the Phonological Definition of Boundaries." In Aronoff and Kean 1980:57–78.

———. 1984. *Language and Meter: Resolution, Porson's Bridge, and Their Prosodic Basis.* California.

———. 1993. "Evidence from Experimental Psychology for the Rhythm and Meter of Greek Verse." *Transactions of the American Philological Association* 123:379–403.

———. 1994. *The Prosody of Greek Speech.* Oxford.

———. 2000. *Discontinuous Syntax.* Oxford.

Dik, H. 1995. *Word Order in Ancient Greek: A Pragmatic Account of Word Order Variations in Herodotus.* Amsterdam.

———. 2007. *Word Order in Greek Tragic Dialogue.* Oxford.

Dik, S. C. 1997. *The Theory of Functional Grammar.* 2nd ed. Berlin.

Dodds, E. R. 1951. *The Greeks and the Irrational.* Berkeley.

Dover, K. 1997. *The Evolution of Greek Prose Style*. Oxford.

Duhoux, Y. 2000. *Le verbe grec ancien: Éléments de morphologie et de syntaxe historiques*. 2nd ed. Louvain-la-neuve.

Edmunds, L., and R. W. Wallace, eds. 1997. *Poet, Public, and Performance in Ancient Greece*. Baltimore.

Edwards, M., ed. 1991. *The Iliad: A Commentary*. Vol. 5, *Books 17–20*. Cambridge.

———. 2002. *Sound, Sense and Rhythm*. Princeton.

Eichner, H., and H. Rix, eds. 1990. *Sprachwissenschaft und philology: Jacob Wackernagel und die Indogermanistiek heute*. Wiesbaden.

Erbse, H. 1969. *Scholia Graeca in Homeri Iliadem*. Berlin.

Fabb, N., and M. Halle. 2008. *Meter in Poetry: A New Theory*. Cambridge.

Fantuzzi, M., and R. Pretagostini, eds. 1995. *Struttura e storia dell'esametro Greco*. Vol. 1. Rome.

Faraone, C. A. 2006. "Stanzaic Structure and Responsion in the Elegiac Poetry of Tyrtaeus." *Mnemosyne* 59:19–52.

Finkelberg, M. 2011. *The Homer Encyclopedia*. Oxford.

Foley, J. M. 2002. *How to Read an Oral Poem*. Chicago.

Fowler, R. L. 1982. "Aristotle on the Period (*Rhet.* 3.9)." *Classical Quarterly* 32:89–99.

———, ed. 2004. *The Cambridge Companion to Homer*. Cambridge.

Frame, D. 2009. *Hippota Nestor*. Hellenic Studies Series 37. Washington, DC.

Franck, D. 1980. *Grammatik und Konversation*. Tübingen.

Fränkel, H. 1926. "Der kallimachische und der homerische Hexameter." *Nachrichten der Gesellschaft der Wissenschaften zu Göttingen* 1926:197–229.

———. 1968. *Wege und Formen frühgriechischen Denkens*. 3rd ed. Munich.

Friedländer, P. 1948. *Epigrammata: Greek Inscriptions in Verse*. London.

Friedrich, R. 1988. "Is θεῶν ἔριδι (*Il.*1.8 and 20.66) a Formula?" *Hermes* 116:476–477.

Geddes, A. G. 1998. "Homer in Translation." In McAuslan and Walcot 1998:186–198.

Giannakis, G. K., ed. 2014. *Encyclopedia of Ancient Greek Language and Linguistics*. 3 vols. Leiden.

Givón, T. 1984. *Syntax: Functional-Typological Introduction*. Amsterdam.

Goldstein, D. 2014. "Intonational Phrase." In Giannakis 2014.2:253–256.

———. 2016. *Classical Greek Syntax: Wackernagel's Law in Herodotus*. Leiden.

Golston, C., and T. Riad. 2000. "The Phonology of Classical Greek Meter." *Linguistics* 38:99–167.

González, J. M. 2013. *The Epic Rhapsode and His Craft: Homeric Performance in a Diachronic Perspective*. Cambridge, MA.

Goodell, Th. D. 1901. *Chapters on Greek Metric*. New Haven.

Greenbaum, S. 1969. *Studies in English Adverbial Usage*. London.

Grotjahn, R., ed. 1981. *Hexameter Studies*. Bochum.

Gussenhoven, C. 2004. *The Phonology of Tone and Intonation*. Cambridge.

Gussenhoven, C., and H. Jacobs. 2011. *Understanding Phonology.* 3rd ed. London.

Hackstein, O. 1997–1998. "Sprachgeschichte und Kunstsprache: der Perfekttyp bebareotes im frühgriechischen Hexameter (und bei den späteren Daktylikern)." *Glotta* 74:21–53.

Hagel, S. 1994–1995. "Zu den Konstituenten des griechischen Hexameters." *Wiener Studien* 107:77–108.

———. 2002. "Homeric Singing—An Approach to the Original Performance." http://www.oeaw.ac.at/kal/sh/.

———. 2004a. "Caesura and Melody." In Spaltenstein and Bianchi 2004:11–22.

———. 2004b. "Tables beyond O'Neill." In Spaltenstein and Bianchi 2004:135–215.

Haiman, J., and S. A. Thompson, eds. 1988. *Clause Combining in Grammar and Discourse.* Amsterdam.

Hainsworth, B., ed. 1993. *The Iliad: A Commentary.* Vol. 3, *Books 9–12.* Cambridge.

Halliday, M. A. K., and R. Hassan. 1976. *Cohesion in English.* London.

Hardie, W. R. 1920. *Res metrica.* Oxford.

Harrison, S. J. 1991. "Discordia Taetra: The History of a Hexameter-Ending." *Classical Quarterly* 41:139–149.

Haug, D., and E. Welo. 2001. "The Proto-Hexameter Hypothesis: Perspectives for Further Research." *Symbolae Osloenses: Norewegian Journal of Greek and Latin Studies* 76:130–136.

Helbig, G., ed. 1971. *Beiträge zur Valenstheorie.* The Hague.

Heubeck, A., S. West, and J. B. Hainsworth. 1988. *A Commentary on Homer's Odyssey.* Vol. 1. Oxford.

Heubeck, A., and A. Hoekstra. 1989. *A Commentary on Homer's Odyssey.* Vol. 2. Oxford.

Higbie, C. 1990. *Measure and Music: Enjambment and Sentence Structure in the* Iliad. Oxford.

———. 1995. "Archaic Hexameter: The *Iliad, Theogony,* and *Erga.*" In Fantuzzi and Pretagostini 1995:69–119.

Hoekstra, A. 1965. *Homeric Modifications of Formulaic Prototypes.* Amsterdam.

———. 1981. *Epic Verse Before Homer.* Amsterdam.

Horrocks, G. C. 1981. *Space and Time in Homer: Prepositional and Adverbial Particles in the Greek Epic.* New York.

Ingalls, W. B. 1970. "The Structure of the Homeric Hexameter: A Review." *Phoenix* 24:1–12.

———. 1972. "Another Dimension of the Homeric Formula." *Phoenix* 26:111–122.

Janse, M. 1998. "Homerische Metriek. Orale Poëzie in de Praktijk." *Didactica Classica Gandensia* 38:125–151.

———. 2003. "The Metrical Schemes of the Hexameter." *Mnemosyne* 56:343–348.

———. 2012. *Inleiding tot de Homerische Taal en Metriek.* Gent.

Janko, R., ed. 1992. *The Iliad: A Commentary.* Vol. 4, *Books 13-16.* Cambridge.

Jones, A., and R. F. Churchhouse, eds. 1976. *The Computer in Literary and Linguistic Studies.* Cardiff.

Kahane, A. 1994. *The Interpretation of Order: A Study in the Poetics of Homeric Repetition.* Oxford.

———. 1997. "Hexameter Progression and the Homeric Hero's Solitary State." In Bakker and Kahane 1997:110–137.

Kelly, S. T. 1990. *Homeric Correption and the Metrical Distinctions between Speeches and Narrative.* New York.

Kirk, G. S. 1966. "Studies in Some Technical Aspects of Homeric Style." *Yale Classical Studies* 20:75–152.

———. 1976. *Homer and the Oral Tradition.* Cambridge.

———, ed. 1985. *The Iliad: A Commentary.* Vol. 1, *Books 1-4.* Cambridge.

———, ed. 1990. *The Iliad: A Commentary.* Vol. 2, *Books 5-8.* Cambridge.

Korhonen, J. 1977. *Studien zu Dependenz, Valenz and Satzmodell.* Bern.

Korzeniewski, D. 1968. *Griechische Metrik.* Darmstadt.

Koster, W. J. W. 1953. *Traité de métrique grecque.* 2nd ed. Leiden.

Kühner, R., and B. Gerth. 1963. *Ausführliche Grammatik der griechischen Sprache.* 3rd ed. Darmstadt.

Lardinois, A. 1997. "Modern Paroemiology and the Use of Gnomai in Homer's *Iliad.*" *Classical Philology* 92:213–234.

———. 2001. "The Wisdom and Wit of Many: The Orality of Greek Proverbial Expressions." In Watson 2001:93–107.

Latacz, J., ed. 2000–. *Homers Ilias: Gesamtkommentar.* Munich.

Laurand, L. 1926. *Études sur le style des discours de Cicéron.* 2nd ed. Paris.

Leaf, W. 1900–1902. *The Iliad.* 2nd ed. London.

Lehiste, I. 1970. *Suprasegmentals.* Cambridge, MA.

———. 1990. "Phonetic Investigation of Metrical Structure in Orally Produced Poetry." *Journal of Phonetics* 18:123.

Lejeune, M. 1955. *Traité de phonétique grecque.* 2nd ed. Paris.

———. 1972. *Phonétique historique du mycénien et du grec ancien.* Paris

Leumann, M. 1950. *Homerische Wörter.* Basel.

Liddell, H. G., and R. Scott. 1953. *A Greek-English Lexicon.* 9th ed. Oxford.

Lidov, J. B. 1989. "Alternating Rhythm in Archaic Greek Poetry." *Transactions of the American Philological Association* 119:63–85.

———. 1996. "Pindar's 'Hymn to Cybele' (fr. 80 SM): Meter, Form, and Syncretism." *Greek, Roman, and Byzantine Studies* 37.2:129–144.

——— 2010. "Meter, Colon, and Rhythm: Simonides (*PMG* 542) and Pindar Between Archaic and Classical." *Classical Philology* 105:25–53.

———. 2012. "Review of *Metre and Rhythm in Greek Verse,* by J. Silva Barris." *Bryn Mawr Classical Review* 2012.12.18.

Loomis, J. 1972. "Studies in Catullan Verse: An Analysis of Word Types and Patterns in the Polymetra." *Mnemosyne supplement* 24. Leiden.

Lord, A. B. 2000. *The Singer of Tales.* 2nd ed. Cambridge, MA.

Luppe, W. 1992. "Hellenistische Hexameter." *Zeitschrift für Papyrologie und Epigraphik* 93:157.

Luraghi, S. 2003. *On the Meaning of Prepositions and Cases: The Expression of Semantic Roles in Ancient Greek.* Amsterdam.

Lyons, J. 1977. *Semantics.* Cambridge.

Maas, P. 1962. *Greek Metre.* Oxford.

Mackay, A., ed. 1999. *Signs of Orality.* Leiden.

———, ed. 2008. *Orality, Literacy, Memory in the Ancient Greek and Roman World.* Leiden.

Mackie, C. J., ed. 2004. *Oral Performance and Its Context.* Leiden.

Martin, R. P. 1989. *The Language of Heroes: Speech and Performance in the Iliad.* Ithaca.

Matthews, P. H. 1981. *Syntax.* Cambridge.

McAuslan, I., and P. Walcot, eds. 1998. *Homer.* Oxford.

McLennan, G. R. 1978. "The *Longum* and Biceps of the Greek Hexameter." *Mnemosyne* 31:68–70.

Macleod, C. W., ed. 1982. *Iliad Book XXIV.* Cambridge.

Meier-Fohrbeck, Th. 1978. *Kommentierende Adverbien. Ihre semantische und pragmatische Aspekte.* Hamburg.

Minchin, E., ed. 2012. *Orality, Literacy and Performance in the Ancient World.* Leiden.

Mithun, M. 1988. "The Grammaticization of Coordination." In Haiman and Thompson 1988:333–359.

Mojena, A. 1992. "The Behaviour of Prepositives in Theocritus' Hexameter." *Glotta* 70:55–60.

Monro, D. B. 1891. *A Grammar of the Homeric Dialect.* Oxford.

Monro, D. B., and T. W. Allen, eds. 1920a. *Homeri Opera* I. Oxford.

———, eds. 1920b. *Homeri Opera* II. Oxford.

Moorhouse, A. C. 1959. *Studies in the Greek Negative.* Cardiff.

Morpurgo Davies, A., and Y. Duhoux, eds. 1985. *Linear B: A 1984 Survey.* Louvain-la-Neuve.

Morris, I., and B. Powell, eds. 1997. *A New Companion to Homer.* Leiden.

Murray, A. T. 1995. *Homer: Odyssey.* Rev. ed. G. E. Dimock. Cambridge, MA.

———. 1999. *Homer: Iliad.* Rev. ed. W. F. Wyatt. Cambridge, MA.

Nagy, G. 1979. "On the Origin of the Greek Hexameter: Synchronic and Diachronic Perspectives." In *Studies in Diachronic, Synchronic, and Typological Linguistics*, ed. B. Brogyanyi, 611–631.

———. 1990. *Greek Mythology and Poetics*. Ithaca.

———. 1996a. *Homeric Questions*. Austin.

———. 1996b. *Poetry as Performance: Homer and Beyond*. Cambridge.

———. 1998. *The Best of the Achaeans: Concepts of the Hero in Archaic Greek Poetry*. 2nd ed. Baltimore.

———. 2000. "Reading Poetry Aloud: Evidence from the Bacchylides Papyri." *Quaderni Urbinati di Cultura Classica* 46:7–28.

———. 2010. "Language and Meter." In Bakker 2010:370–386.

———. 2013. *The Ancient Greek Hero in 24 Hours*. Cambridge, MA.

Nasta, M. 1994. "Principes d'analyse d'une versification orale (I). Les facteurs specifiques de l'hexametre grec." *Les Etudes classiques* 62:101–129.

Nespor, M., and I. Vogel. 1986. *Prosodic Phonology*. Dordrecht.

Nolan, F. 2014. *Intonation*. http://www.ling.cam.ac.uk/francis/fn_inton_prepub.pdf.

Notopoulos, J. A. 1949. "Parataxis in Homer: A New Approach to Homeric Literary Criticism." *Transactions of the American Philological Association* 80:1–23.

Oesterreicher, W. 1997. "Types of Orality in Texts." In Bakker and Kahane 1997:190–214.

O'Neill Jr., E. G. 1939. "The Importance of Final Syllables in Greek Verse." *Transactions of the American Philological Association* 70:256–294.

———. 1942. "The Localization of Metrical Word-Types in the Greek Hexameter." *Yale Classical Studies* 8:105–178.

Packard, D. W. 1976. "Metrical and Grammatical Patterns in the Greek Hexameter." In Jones and Churchhouse 1976:85–91.

Parker, L. P. E. 1966. "Porson's Law Extended." *Classical Quarterly* 16:1–26.

Parry, A., ed. 1971. *The Making of Homeric Verse: The Collected Papers of Milman Parry*. Oxford.

Parry, M. 1929. "The Distinctive Character of Enjambment in Homeric Verse." In A. Parry 1971:251–265.

Peabody, B. 1975. *The Winged Word*. Albany.

Pierrehumbert, J. 1980. *The Phonology and Phonetics of English Intonation*. PhD diss., Massachusetts Institute of Technology.

Pinkster, H. 1990. *Latin Syntax and Semantics*. London.

Porter, H. N. 1951. "The Early Greek Hexameter." *Yale Classical Studies* 12:3–63.

Quirk, R. 1972. *A Grammar of Contemporary English*. London.

Rathcke, T. V., and R. H. Smith. 2015. "Speech Timing and Linguistic Rhythm: On the Acoustic Bases of Rhythm Typologies." *Journal of the Acoustical Society of America* 137:28–34.

Ready, J. 2015. "The Textualization of Homeric Epic by Means of Dictation." *Transactions of the American Philological Association* 145.1:1–75.

Richardson, N., ed. 1993. *The Iliad: A Commentary.* Vol. 6, *Books 21–24.* Cambridge.

Rieken, E., and P. Widmer, eds. 2009. *Pragmatische Kategorien: Form, Funktion und Diachronie. Akten der Arbeitstagung der Indogermanischen Gesellschaft* von 24. bis 26. Wiesbaden.

Roberts, W. R. 1910. *Dionysus of Halicarnassus on Literary Composition.* London.

Rosenmeyer, T. G., M. Ostwald, and J. W. Halporn. 1963. *The Meters of Greek and Latin Poetry.* London.

Rossbach, A., and R. Westphal. 1854. *Griechische Rhythmik.* Leipzig.

Rossi, L. E. 1963. *Metrica e critica stilistica.* Rome.

———. 1965. "Estensione e valore del 'colon' nell'esametro omerico." *Studi Urbinati* 39:239–273.

———. 1978. "I poemi omerici come testimonianza di poesi orale." *Storia e civiltà dei Greci* 73–147.

Rubin, H. J. 1995. *Memory and Oral Traditions: The Cognitive Psychology of Epic, Ballads, and Counting-Out Rhymes.* New York.

Ruijgh, C. J. 1971. *Autour de τε épique.* Amsterdam.

———. 1985a. "Problèmes de philologie mycénienne." *Minos* 19:119–126.

———. 1985b. "Le mycénien et Homère." In Morpurgo, Davies, and Duhoux 1985:143–190.

———. 1987. "Μακρὰ τελεία et μακρὰ ἄλογος. Le prolongement de la durée d'une syllable finale dans le rhythme du mot grec." *Mnemosyne* 40:313–352.

———. 1989. "Les anapests de marche dans la versification grecque et le rythme du mot grec." *Mnemosyne* 42:308–330.

———. 1990. "La place des enclitiques dans l'ordre des mots chez Homère d'après la loi de Wackernagel." In Eichner and Rix 1990:213–233.

Russo, J., M. Fernandez-Galiano, and A. Heubeck, eds. 1992. *A Commentary on Homer's Odyssey.* Vol. 3. Oxford.

Russo, J. 1966. "The Structural Formula in Homeric Verse." *Yale Classical Studies* 20:219–240.

———. 1976. "Is Oral or Aural Composition the Cause of Homer's Formulaic Style?" In Stolz and Shannon 1976:31–54.

———. 1997. "Prose Genres for the Performance of Traditional Wisdom in Ancient Greece: Proverb, Maxim, Apothegm." In Edmunds and Wallace 1997:49–64.

Scheppers, F. 2011. *The Colon Hypothesis: Word Order, Discourse Segmentation and Discourse Coherence in Ancient Greek*. Brussels.

Schiffrin, D. 1987. *Discourse Markers*. Cambridge.

Schwyzer, E. 1939. *Griechische Grammatik*. Vol. 1. München.

Scodel, R. 2002. *Listening to Homer: Tradition, Narrative, and Audience*. Ann Arbor.

Searle, J. 1969. *Speech Acts*. Cambridge.

———. 1976. "A Classification of Illocutionary Acts." *Language and Society* 5:1–23.

Sicking, C. M. J. 1993. *Griechische Verslehre*. Munich.

Sicking, C. M. J., and M. Van Raalte. 1981. "Word-End after Long Anceps." *Mnemosyne* 34:225–250.

Sihler, A. L. 1995. *New Comparative Grammar of Latin and Greek*. New York.

Silva Barris, J. 2011. *Metre and Rhythm in Greek Verse*. Wiener Studien Beiheft 35. Vienna.

Slings, S. R. 1992. "Written and Spoken Language: An Exercise in the Pragmatics of the Greek Sentence." *Classical Philology* 87:95–109.

Smith, P. L. 1982. "Enclitic Rhythms in the Vergilian Hexameter." *Phoenix* 36:124.

Snell, B. 1982. *Griechische Metrik*. 4th ed. Göttingen.

Sommerstein, A. H. 1973. *The Sound Pattern of Ancient Greek*. Oxford.

Spaltenstein, F., and O. Bianchi, eds. 2004. *Autour de la césure*. Bern.

Spanoudakis, K. 1999. "Hellenistic (?) Hexameters Revisited." *Zeitschrift für Papyrologie und Epigraphik* 127:59–62.

Stanford, W. B. 1950. *The Odyssey of Homer*. London.

Steinrück, M. 1995. "Sprechpause und Wortende: zum Rhythmus des Hexameters." *Quaderni Urbinati di Cultura Classica* 49:135–140.

———. 2004. "La césure hexamétrique: description et rythmes dans l'*Odyssée*." In Spaltenstein and Bianchi 2004:81–94.

———. 2005. "Lagaroi: Le temps de la re-rythmisation de l'hexametre." *Mnemosyne* 58:481–498.

Stolz, B., and R. Shannon, eds. 1976. *Oral Literature and the Formula*. Ann Arbor.

Sturtevant, E. H. 1921. "Word Ends and Pauses in the Hexameter." *American Journal of Philology* 42:289–308.

———. 1924. "The Doctrine of Caesura, a Philological Ghost." *American Journal of Philology* 45:329–350.

Taplin, O. 1992. *Homeric Soundings: The Shaping of the Iliad*. Oxford.

Tesnière, L. 1959. *Éléments de Syntaxe Structurale*. Paris.

Thalmann, W. G. 1984. *Conventions of Form and Thought in Early Greek Poetry*. Baltimore.

Tichy, E. 1981. "Hom. ἀνδροτῆια und die Vorgeschichte des dactylischen Hexameters." *Glotta* 59:28–67.

Usener, H. 1887. *Altgriechischer Versbau*. Osnabrück.

———. 1933. *Dionysius Halicarnaseus Opuscula*. 3rd ed. Leipzig.

Vaissière, J. 1983. "Language-Independent Prosodic Features." In Cutler and Ladd 1983:53–66.

Van Emde Boas, E., and L. Huitink. 2010. "Syntax." In Bakker 2010:134-150.

Van Thiel, H. 1991. *Homeri Odyssea*. Hildesheim.

Van Raalte, M. 1986. *Rhythm and Metre*. PhD diss., Leiden University.

Vendryes, J. 1945. *Traité d'accentuation grecque*. Paris.

Verkuyl, H. L. 1972. *On the Compositional Nature of Aspect*. Dordrecht.

Visser, E. 1987. "Formulae or Single Words? Towards a New Theory on Homeric Verse-making." *Würzburger Jahrbücher für die Altertumswissenschaft* 14:21–37.

Watson, J., ed. 2001. *Speaking Volumes: Orality and Literacy in the Greek and Roman World*. Leiden.

Wefelmeier, C. 1994. "Anmerkungen zum Rhythmus des homerischen Verses." *Hermes* 122:1–12.

———. 2001. "Addenda zum Rhythmus des epischen Verses." *Hermes* 129:542–547.

Werner, R. 1966. *H und ει vor Vokal bei Homer*. Fribourg

West, M. L., ed. 1966. *Hesiod Theogony*. Oxford.

———. 1970. "A New Approach to Greek Prosody." *Glotta* XLVIII:185–194.

———. 1982. *Greek Metre*. Oxford.

———. 1993. *Greek Music*. Oxford.

———. 1997. "Homer's Meter." In Morris and Powell 1997:218–237.

———. 1998/2000. *Homeri Ilias*. Stuttgart.

———. 2011. *The Making of the Iliad*. Oxford.

Wifstrand, A. 1933. *Von Kallimachos zu Nonnos*. Lund.

Wyatt, W. 1969. *Metrical Lengthening in Homer*. Rome.

Zehetmeier, J. 1930. "Die Periodenlehre des Aristoteles." *Philologus* 85:192–208, 255–284, 414–436.

General Index

Index of Passages